VISIONS OF HISTORY

VISIONS
of
HISTORY
INTERVIEWS WITH

E. P. THOMPSON ■ ERIC HOBSBAWM

SHEILA ROWBOTHAM ■ LINDA GORDON

NATALIE ZEMON DAVIS ■ WILLIAM APPLEMAN WILLIAMS

STAUGHTON LYND ■ DAVID MONTGOMERY

HERBERT GUTMAN ■ VINCENT HARDING

JOHN WOMACK ■ C. L. R. JAMES

MOSHE LEWIN

BY MARHO
THE RADICAL HISTORIANS ORGANIZATION

Edited by
Henry Abelove, Betsy Blackmar, Peter Dimock, and Jonathan Schneer
Drawings by Josh Brown

PANTHEON BOOKS, NEW YORK

Interviews with Edward P. Thompson, Eric Hobsbawm, Natalie Zemon
Davis, William Appleman Williams, Staughton Lynd, David
Montgomery, Herbert Gutman, and a portion of the interview with
C. L. R. James first appeared, in somewhat different form, in *Radical
History Review*.

Library of Congress Cataloging in Publication Data

Main entry under title:
Visions of history.

"Interviews with E. P. Thompson, Eric Hobsbawm, Sheila Rowbotham,
Linda Gordon, Natalie Zemon Davis, William Appleman Williams,
Staughton Lynd, David Montgomery, Herbert Gutman, Vincent
Harding, John Womack, C. L. R. James, and Moshe Lewin."
Bibliography: p.
Includes index.
1. Historiography—Addresses, essays, lectures.
2. Historians—Interviews. I. Abalove, Henry.
II. Thompson, E. P. (Edward Palmer), 1924–
III. Mid-Atlantic Radical Historians' Organization.
D13.V57 1984   907'.2   83-47743
ISBN 0-394-53046-2
ISBN 0-394-72200-0 (pbk.)

Book design by Carl Lehmann-Haupt

Manufactured in the United States of America

First Edition

CONTENTS

ACKNOWLEDGMENTS

This book has been a collective project long in the making. In 1976, Jay Faciolo first proposed that the *Radical History Review* interview left-wing historians. Over the last seven years, members of the Boston, New Haven, and New York MARHO collectives have cheerfully volunteered their labor to transcribe, type, and edit interviews for the *Radical History Review*. The New Haven collective, and especially Jean-Christophe Agnew, Eric Arneson, Susan Besse, Judy Coffin, Willy Forbath, Toni Gilpin, Julie Green, Dan Letwin, Priscilla Murolo, David Scobey, Marta Wagner, and Sharon White, took on additional responsibilities in assembling the book. We thank all the collective members for their material and moral support.

We appreciate the assistance of the Connecticut Oral History Center in recovering a seemingly untranscribable tape, and of Lorraine Estra, Madeline Colon, Katrin van der Vaart, and Mary Whitney, who did additional typing under great time pressure. We thank Eleanor Brown and Steve Brier for steering the book through legal and commercial channels, Josh Brown for capturing the essence of our interviews in his drawings, our publisher, André Schiffrin, for making the interviews available to a wider audience, and our editor, Nan Graham, for bringing our collective labors to fruition.

Finally, we thank the interviewers and the historians for their generous contribution to the *Radical History Review* and to history.

Henry Abelove
Betsy Blackmar
Peter Dimock
Jonathan Schneer

INTRODUCTION

WE LIVE IN A SOCIETY WHOSE past is given to us in images that assert the inevitability of the way things are. In more or less subtle ways, politicians and the media invoke history to show that the contemporary distribution of wealth and power is at once freely chosen and preordained. By the same token, past efforts to contest prevailing social and political arrangements disappear from dominant versions of our history—when they are not simply labeled as foreign or dismissed as utopian. Yet there is a tradition of radical history writing that has worked to overcome this kind of historical amnesia. It has sought to rescue from oblivion the experiences and visions of past movements against social and political domination, and to analyze historically the structures and dynamics of domination today. This collection of interviews with radical historians emerges from that tradition.

The collection began in 1976 when the editors of *Radical History Review* decided to interview first Edward Thompson and then a number of other prominent historians on the left. The *RHR*—its editors and MARHO, the organization that publishes the journal—was the offspring of the New Left. The historians whom we interviewed in the first instance belonged mainly to an older generation of radical intellectuals that had come to maturity in the 1940s and 1950s. Through the interviews we hoped to recover a sense of the continuities between their work and experiences and our own. We hoped to initiate a critical dialogue between generations of historians on the Left and to explore together the connections between radical politics and the practice of history. The interview format allowed for exchange and argument about matters shortchanged in conventional scholarly discourse—about theory and political strategy and the history these men and women have lived as well as the history they teach and write. Encouraged by the candor and thoughtfulness of the early interviews, we decided to interview more widely and to include some of our own contemporaries.

Some questions could be put only to the older generation. One was: how did the political repression of the cold war era affect you and your work? The answers are varied and moving. They are a miniature chronicle of the history of radicalism in the 1950s. Natalie Davis, a historian of early modern France, had her passport confiscated by the State Department; her husband was fired from his teaching post at the University of Michigan and later imprisoned for refusing to testify before a congressional committee. When her passport was gone and she could no longer travel to France to read in the archives, Davis turned to rare book libraries here in the U.S., and so managed to continue her research. The English historian Edward Thompson found work teaching in an extension-studies program at the University of Leeds and in Workers' Education Association courses. By teaching working-class people he learned much about them and their trades, and this knowledge turned out to be essential to the book he would ultimately write entitled *The Making of the English Working Class*. American working-class historian David Montgomery's first calling was that of a machinist and labor organizer. In his interview, Montgomery recounts the ways he and other shop floor militants contended with McCarthyism. Blacklisted and driven out of the factories for his politics, Montgomery was forced toward the academy just as other leftists were being forced out of it. Finally, there is William Appleman Williams's sardonic account of his battles with the House Un-American Activities Committee and the petty harassments by which it tried, unsuccessfully, to wear him down.

Another question frequently posed was: what is your assessment of the New Left? Again, the answers vary widely. Some are interestingly ambivalent. David Montgomery criticizes what he takes to be the New Left's condescension to workers, but admires its fervor and commitment to fighting in the here and now. Similarly, Edward Thompson reproaches the New Left for what he takes to be its self-indulgent posturing, but praises its firm belief in democracy. Both historians emphasize the importance of the New Left as an intellectual movement that enriched their own work and the general development of Marxist theory. Younger historians such as Linda Gordon and Vincent Harding offer a different assessment: Gordon describes the interplay between her involvement in the women's movement and her intellectual formation as a historian. Harding underscores the potential he saw in the movements of the sixties for radically transforming American life.

All of those interviewed explore the ways in which their politics inform their practice as historians. Many emphasize that the subject of their study is the oppressed—plebeians, workers, Afro-Americans, women. They go on to say that they see the oppressed not only as victims, but also as actors in their own right, individuals and groups who resisted oppression courageously and creatively and, in so doing, created cultures of their own. Many of these historians also reflect upon the historical and political context from which their own work emerged; they discuss how their experience and the political struggles or issues that engaged them shaped the historical questions they asked. All have had to contend with the difficulties that arise from the narrow boundaries of academic history; all believe that historical knowledge is far too important to be restricted to the university.

There are historians absent from this collection who undoubtedly should be present—for instance, the pioneers in radical lesbian and gay history. Nonetheless, the interviews gathered here attest to the diversity of radical history. Indeed, they carry on the arguments within it that have strengthened and animated its practitioners. They affirm as well the links between personal experience and "history" that underlie the production of all historical knowledge. And, finally, they reveal the basic unity of purpose that all radical historians share. The point, as Marx observed, is not only to interpret the world, but to change it. These men and women have much to teach us about the past and its bearing on the work of liberating the present.

—THE EDITORS

VISIONS OF HISTORY

E. P. THOMPSON

AFTER E. BURNE-JONES

E. P. THOMPSON

E. P. THOMPSON LIVES in Worcester, England. He was interviewed in March 1976 in New York City, where he was living while serving as visiting professor of history at Rutgers University in New Brunswick, New Jersey. At the time of the interview, Thompson was best known as the author of *The Making of the English Working Class* (1963), a history of the English laboring poor between 1790 and 1832 that changed the way social history, and particularly working-class history, was written. Previously, he had written a long study of the career of William Morris, which has since been reissued, bereft of what Thompson calls its "Stalinist pieties," as *William Morris: From Romantic to Revolutionary* (1977). Just prior to the interview, Thompson's study of the origins of the judicial terror in eighteenth-century Britain, *Whigs and Hunters*, appeared, as did a volume of related studies on crime and society, *Albion's Fatal Tree* (1975). Both were done in collaboration with several students and colleagues.

Since the interview, Thompson's career has taken a few unanticipated turns. He has become well known across Europe as a leader of the European Nuclear Disarmament movement, or END. In response to *Protect and Survive*, a British government pamphlet on civil defense measures in the event of a nuclear war, Thompson wrote *Protest and Survive* (1980), which was read by tens if not hundreds of thousands of Britons and others. It later became the centerpiece of and gave its name to a volume, edited by Thompson and Dan Smith, of articles by peace activists on the arms race and the need for disarmament, which has been issued in both Britain and America. The *New Left Review* has recently issued a collection of articles entitled *Exterminism and the Cold War*, which includes Thompson's important essay on "exterminism" and several responses to it. Finally, another volume of writings on nuclear disarmament, entitled *Beyond the Cold War* (1982), has just been published in the United States by Pantheon.

Thompson's role in the movement is not restricted to writing. He has crisscrossed Great Britain and Europe in behalf of END, speaking at its massive rallies and organizing its extensive international network. He has become, while doing so, a figure of considerable notoriety. He was named in a TV poll as one of the four most respected or best-known figures in British public life, along with the Queen Mother, Queen Elizabeth II, and Margaret Thatcher!

For most historians, the transition from the archives to the speaker's platform would not be easily accomplished. But Thompson has always been as much an activist as an archivist, as he tells us briefly in the interview included here. He has also always been an accomplished, if sometimes unheeded, polemicist, and since this interview has published two volumes of political writing. The first was a collection of previously published essays, including "The Peculiarities of the English" and "The Open Letter to Leszek Kolakowski"—which are discussed below—together with a long, previously unpublished polemic against the Althusserian influence in Marxist studies, which gave the whole collection its title, *The Poverty of Theory*.[1]

The second volume, *Writing by Candlelight*, contains an extraordinary series of articles written by Thompson during the seventies, mostly for *New Society* magazine. The subject of these articles centers on the attack by the British authorities on Britain's democratic traditions and institutions. There can be no better demonstration of the importance of an informed political sensibility for the historical imagination than Thompson's work.[2]

This interview was conducted by Mike Merrill, coordinator of the Institute for Labor Education in New York City.

Q. Was *The Making of the English Working Class* [*MEWC*] written with immediate political goals or intentions in mind, as an intervention, somewhat veiled, in the current political scene, or did it come from other preoccupations of yours?

THOMPSON The mediations between any intellectual or artistic work and one's experience and participation in society are never one-to-one; they are never direct. I mean, no painter can paint his political experience like *that*, and if he tries to do so he paints a poster, which has perhaps a good value *as* a poster.

MEWC undoubtedly arose from a two-sided theoretical polemic. On the one hand, it could not have been written without the extremely firm, intellectually very well-based discipline of economic history that has (with notable exceptions) been a continuous tradition from Adam Smith and the orthodox political economists through to the present day. It is a tradition largely contaminated with capitalist ideology. Hence, in one sense, to write the social history of the people in this period demands conducting a polemic against that tradition. On the other hand, it was in a sense a polemic against abbreviated economistic notations of Marxism, which had become very clearly disclosed in the arguments around, inside, and outside of the Communist movement from 1956 onward to the creation of the New Left. In this tradition the very simplified notion of the creation of the working class was that of a determined process: steam power plus the factory system equals the working class. Some kind of raw material, like peasants "flocking to factories," was then processed into so many yards of class-conscious proletarians. I was polemicizing against this notion in order to show the existing plebeian consciousness refracted by new experiences in social being, which experiences were handled in cultural ways by the people, thus giving rise to a transformed consciousness. In this sense the questions being proposed and some of the theoretical equipment being brought to answer them arose out of that distinct ideological moment.

It was not a book written for the academic public. My own work for many years had been as a tutor in adult education, teaching evening classes of working people, trade unionists, white-collar people, teachers, and so on. That audience was there, and the audience of the Left also, of the labor movement and the New Left. I was thinking of that kind of reader when I wrote the book, as is pretty evident in my rather irreverent attitudes to the academic proprieties. I've become a bit more inhibited since, simply because, although the book has been received very generously in some academic quarters, it has also been subjected to very sharp attacks, especially in Britain. In order to meet these I have had to sharpen my own scholarly equipment. When you suddenly realize that you are being watched by this largely conservative profession you have to be very sure that your statements are as accurate, as precise, and as well documented as possible. That can be a slight inhibition.

Q. The care-taking you speak of is evident in *Whigs and Hunters*. But the irreverence in *MEWC* was probably the most attractive thing about the book to many academics.

THOMPSON   Yes, but about *Whigs and Hunters*. It is not quite so formal and reverent a book as it may appear. In the first half, yes, it appears to be academic and almost antiquarian, partly because of the nature of the material out of which a lost set of social relations is reconstructed. This had to be done with minute brush strokes. But it is still an irreverent book. The dominant tradition of eighteenth-century historiography is deeply entrenched and has been almost unchallenged in its main outlines for many years. It is a navy that can't be scattered by one shot of musket fire from a canoe. I had to meet it on its own home waters, and to "Namierize"[3]—by which I mean to examine in minute detail—the interests of foresters and yeomen instead of peers and gentry. Whether the book succeeded or not is for the readers to decide. But it is partly written within an English historiographical argument that may not be wholly apparent to the American reader.

Q. I was thinking of two things when I asked the question earlier. On the one hand, you describe William Morris's poetry, and his utopian and historical fantasies, as things that he wrote for his own pleasure. On the other hand, history has an importance that goes beyond its enjoyment value. Which of these two attitudes toward culture is predominant in your thinking about your historical writing?

THOMPSON   Of course, that doesn't need to be asked, does it? The only thing one has to say is that such questions are sometimes asked by quite different people from you, [people] who have this pompous and pretentious notion that they are *true* historians because they haven't got any commitments. If you then say, "Of course," you are supposedly exposed as something other than a historian—a propagandist. On the contrary, I think that an immense amount of existing historiography, certainly in Britain, has seen society within the expectations, the self-image, the apologetics, of a ruling class: "the propaganda of the victors." Hence, to recover an alternative history often involves a polemic against an established ideology.

The second thing is that, again, someone else may ask this question, wanting to trip you up into saying, "Okay, *all* history is ideology, whether of the Left or of the Right." I don't agree with this at all. One is attempting to approach very complex and objective problems in the historical process (this is what Marx was doing also). This involves a precise discipline that entails distancing and objectifying—becoming aware of one's own predispositions, becoming aware of the questions one is asking—and for a great part of one's work as a historian, one is attempting either to make apparent the intrusion of one's attitudes and values, if they are intruding, or to hold them at a distance and prevent this intrusion from taking place. Otherwise, one assumes that historical process presents no problems that one's already existing attitudes can't provide an answer to. And this is not true. One is in fact approaching a process that discloses under historical examination its own character and its own problems. Only in that sense does one learn from it. This doesn't mean that at a certain stage it is not possible then to make a judgment *upon* that process, but that is a second kind of activity. I'm not in any sense apologetic for making such judgments. But I hope it is clear that when I am looking at a question like work discipline, or like popular ritual in the eighteenth century, I am not bringing to it a whole set of ready-made attitudes. I am holding it at a distance and attempting to examine it in its own terms and within its own set of relations. But having done that, then, if one wishes, one may make a comment. Because one may wish to evaluate the meaning *to us* of that process. The meaning isn't there, in the process; the meaning is in what we make of the process.

Q.   Did it work? Has it made a difference? At the end of *Whigs and Hunters* you intrude yourself rather shockingly, almost, where you wonder whether or not what you do makes you an anachronism. Is this a sign of your feeling that, regardless of all your efforts, *MEWC* fell on deaf ears, that your hopes for historiographical literature have become less defensible?

THOMPSON   No, no. I must have expressed myself unclearly. The question I was raising there is that, quite properly, there is a diminished perspective in which the achievements of that particular moment of Western culture can be regarded. Clearly, in the nineteenth century, and still in my youth, the history schools of Britain or America were staffed by people who had never doubted that their history was the most significant history in the world. But if you are now living on a post-imperial island, which in the conventional terms of capitalist economy is fading rapidly, and if you are aware of the future, in which the emergent nations are going to demand not only a greater presence in the world but also a greater presence in historical consciousness, [then you] are going to turn around and ask what does this peculiar culture of Anglo-Saxon eighteenth-century constitutionalism mean? Wasn't it in fact more important that England was engaged deeply in the slave trade? That the East India Company was amassing its fortune and extending its territory in India? Aren't these the important things for the world to know about England, not whether the English had particular constitutional rituals? That's one of the questions I'm asking.

The other question is in response to, perhaps, a certain view of the *Annales*[4] school as it is sometimes confiscated and interpreted by conservative historians, who talk about the *"longue durée"* and who then say that, really, the only serious thing to concern the historian is the long-term demographic, material, almost geological formations of history. Hence, to become involved in one particular moment—1723—is a very trivial entry into serious historical process. It was in response to those two questions that I asked this of myself, and I justified my local preoccupations by arguing that the English seventeenth-century revolution, despite being defeated in so many of its aspirations, had in the end given rise to a certain set of legal inhibitions upon power, which, however they were manipulated, were a significant cultural achievement. I then argue that the law, which can too easily be dismissed, because it is manipulated in class ways, as being purely a mask for class power, ought not to be seen in that way. Everything we have witnessed in this century suggests that no serious socialist thinker can suppose that a rule of some kind of law —albeit, socialist law and not capitalist law—is not a profound human good. Attempts by socialist theorists to duck this question are failing to come to terms with two things: one, the historical evidence of this century of the appalling powers a socialist state, or a so-called socialist state, can acquire. And, second, the fact that the working people of the advanced countries, and probably of most areas, are profoundly aware of the danger to themselves that exists in the state. So, I say that the history of law does matter and is a very subtle and complex question.

Q. I picked up in others of your later writings, however, a sense of isolation, and I associated the passage we have been discussing in *Whigs and Hunters* with these others. In the "Open Letter to Leszek Kolakowski," for instance, you talk of your political silence for eight years, and you worry that after this you will fall silent again.

What relation does this attitude have to the very evident success of *The*

Making of the English Working Class and the continued importance of the traditions, in the many senses of that word, that your book embodies and of which you are a leading representative? The response to the book would seem to indicate you were much less isolated than you seemed to feel you were.

THOMPSON I apologize. There is some self-dramatization in the letter to Kolakowski. But that the letter was written at all was a coming out of isolation rather than the reverse. It has nothing at all to do with *MEWC* and its generous reception, particularly over here. It has more to do with a side of my writing that is less known in the United States, which is a very distinctly political engagement. I hope to republish some of this writing shortly. I don't now feel as isolated as I did at the height of the sixties. What happened was the creation of a New Left that I and my colleagues in England were very active in, at the time of Wright Mills,[5] who was one of our closest colleagues here in the States. And then the transition to a second New Left. At the same time certain intellectual transitions occurred that to my mind were unfortunate. Expressive activity was raised above more rational and open political activity, and simultaneously a highly sophisticated set of Marxisms developed, particularly in Western Europe, which increasingly, it seemed to me, became theological in character—however sophisticated—and therefore broke with the Marxist tradition with which I had been associated. This was followed by a peculiarly tormented period in the late sixties when an intellectual leftist movement existed that was divorced from larger popular movements and that, in some sense, made a virtue of this isolation and did not take measures to communicate with the labor movement and other, larger, popular movements. On the one hand—and surely I don't have to remind you of this in the States—this New Left had elements within it that could be seen at once by a historian as the revolting bourgeoisie doing its own revolting thing—that is, the expressive and irrationalist, self-exalting gestures of style that do not belong to a serious and deeply rooted, rational revolutionary tradition. On the other hand, there was a sense that enough of the causes that this movement was associated with remained causes of the Left, particularly the struggle against the Vietnam War, and, in general, the struggle to democratize the institutions of education. One could certainly not attack or criticize this movement publicly, except within the movement itself—and even this was difficult. So my sense of isolation resulted from the movement's going in a direction that I in many ways deplored and at the same time was, perforce, silent about. I couldn't join the outcry, or the flight from Columbia, or whatever was going on on the Right or in the comfortable social-democratic "middle."

But now that phase has come to an end and I apologize for the self-dramatization of the Kolakowski letter. I feel in affirmative ways that we are at the beginning of a new period that will integrate much of the good from that period.

Q. How did you decide to become a historian? I know that you went to Cambridge after the war.

THOMPSON   I was at Cambridge during and after the war. This, of course, was a very important formative moment. It is one that is very difficult to translate to people of a different generation. I don't think the effort should be made too much of because people's eyes glaze over very quickly and that is it. However, I am still unrepentantly of the view that no matter what happened at Potsdam, no matter what happened at Yalta, no matter what Stalin was up to, and no matter what British and American imperialism were up to, the Second World War was a very critical moment in human civilization. If the Fascist powers had won we would very possibly be still living in that era. In fact, there wouldn't be a MARHO, and there wouldn't be a history of the New Left, and Kolakowski would have been killed long ago, so we wouldn't be able to argue with him. It would be that sort of future we would still be living in. And hence, one had this extraordinary formative moment in which it was possible to be deeply committed even to the point of life itself in support of a particular political struggle that was at the same time a popular struggle; that is, one didn't feel a sense of being isolated in any way from the peoples of Europe or the peoples of Britain. I suppose this does affect the way one was formed.

I was, of course, very active in the Communist party and remained so until 1956. This didn't mean that one didn't have many inner doubts and also wasn't guilty of many casuistries explaining away what one should have repudiated in the character of Stalinism. But also I am not prepared to accept a Trotskyist interpretation of a whole past that dismisses an entire phase of historical development and all the multiform popular initiatives and authentic areas of self-activity and heroism simply as "Stalinist." The popular dimensions of Communist activity, then and in many cases still today, are such as to prevent this kind of intellectualization.

Q.   I have read through the memoir you and your mother did about your brother, which contains a brief history of his growing up [E. P. Thompson, ed., *There Is a Spirit in Europe: A Memoir of Frank Thompson*]. Your brother had joined the Communist party in 1939, had been an officer in the war, and volunteered to serve with the Bulgarian partisans. While you were growing up, leaders of the Indian liberation movement frequented your parents' house. Were your parents and your brother's earlier decision significant features of your commitment?

THOMPSON   My father—both my parents, but my father in particular—was a very tough liberal. He was a continuous critic of British imperialism, a friend of Nehru's and of other national leaders. So I grew up expecting governments to be mendacious and imperialist and expecting that one's stance ought to be hostile to government. But certainly to join the Communist party was, for my older brother, a cause of conflict in the family. He broke open the way, and when I did the same there was less conflict. This is another example of the ambiguity of that moment of the anti-Fascist war, particularly from 1942 to 1946. My brother's surviving letters are totally at odds with the cardboard ideological picture of what Stalinism was. His commitment was to people and above all to the astonishing heroism of the partisan movements of southern Europe.[6] In a sense that insurgent, popular-front–type political moment reached its peak between '43 and '46. It was destroyed by both British and American reaction and inwardly destroyed by Stalinism. One of the things that makes me feel excited is that, in a curious kind of way, I think Europe is beginning cautiously to resume a kind of advance that was interrupted by the cold war. [Now, in 1976.] The categories of the cold war are beginning to dissolve. Spain, France, Italy, Greece, even perhaps Britain—that sense of opening to the future, independent of the old cold war structures, is beginning to reappear.

Q. Was your own experience in Yugoslavia after the war an extensive one [E. P. Thompson, ed., *The Railway*]? Witnessing the popular movement of peasants, workers, soldiers, and students for the construction of a socialist society in Yugoslavia, one could imagine, could give one a crucial kick when it came to trying to recover and imagine hidden processes and popular movements in the past—something that you do, of course, quite well, perhaps better than anyone.

THOMPSON Yes, yes; but remember, there were workers and soldiers and students in Britain, too. There was a very considerable affirmative movement forward there also. Struggles on housing estates, or strikes, or the sense of euphoria when the mines were nationalized and when the health service was introduced—all these affirmative things were part of one's own experience. So it wasn't just going and seeing it all happen over there. One felt that the Yugoslav partisans were a supreme example of this kind of self-activity, an amazing example, but it wasn't totally different. In 1946, I was a volunteer on the youth brigade constructing a railway in Yugoslavia. There were contingents from most of the countries of Europe—except, very significantly, the Soviet Union. This was a good experience. I also went that year to Bulgaria and met partisans who had survived the extraordinary march my brother had been on. I went across the ground with them and visited the villages. One couldn't for a moment see the situation in terms of the imposition of Russian rule upon Bulgaria. I worked on a youth project building a railway in Bulgaria as well, for a very short time, and I was convinced of the authenticity of the popular front *then*. It was very soon broken, and it was broken by the orthodox, Russian-trained Communists and by Russian pressure. But at that stage there were Communist, socialist, agrarian, and other groups forming an alliance and talking quite freely about their differences. There was a sense of openness. But all that closed down in the cold war. It closed down for both sides. It was a mutual, reciprocal process, immensely damaging, immensely destructive, and probably most destructive at the two extremes: in Russia itself and in America. In America, destroying any continuity of that movement's roots, and in Russia, destroying every opposition, every authentic sort of movement.

Q. And in the midst of the movement that you have been describing, you seem somehow to have decided to become a historian.

THOMPSON Good heavens, no! I never "took a decision" to be a historian. I don't remember taking any decisions of that kind.

I had a year in the war and I went back and finished my first degree. I never did any research or graduate work. I went into adult education because it seemed to me to be an area in which I would learn something about industrial England, and teach people who would teach me. Which they did. And I was very active in political work. I was primarily responsible in my political work for work in the peace movement, above all against the Korean War. We developed a very good movement in West Yorkshire. It was a genuine alliance of Labour party people, who often were expelled from the Labour party, traditional Left pacifists, and Communists and trade unionists. I ran a journal. I was on the Yorkshire district committee of the Communist party. This probably occupied half my time and professional teaching the other half. In both areas one was learning from people all the time.

Q. You delivered a lecture or wrote a little article about William Morris in 1951, and then made a decision at some point in those years to write a study of Morris.

THOMPSON You keep on talking about making decisions. I was preparing my first classes. I was teaching as much literature as history. I thought, how do I, first of all, raise with an adult class, many of them in the labor movement —discuss with them the significance of literature to their lives? And I started reading Morris. I was seized by Morris. I thought, why is this man thought to be an old fuddy-duddy? He is right in with us still. And then I read one or two books *so* dreadful and so ideological about Morris that I thought I *must* answer these. So I wrote an article attacking them, and the editor of the review said, "Thank you very much, but could you write a rather longer article?" Then I wrote an article too long to be published, and they wrote back and said perhaps you would like to make a book of it. So it ended up being an 800-page book. Morris seized me. I took no decision. Morris took the decision that I would have to present him. In the course of doing this I became much more serious about being a historian.

I think it is like being a painter or poet. A poet loves words, a painter loves paint. I found a fascination in getting to the bottom of everything, in the sources themselves. I got this fascination with the archives. I suppose this plus the critical, comradely help of one or two people in particular, especially Dona Torr,[7] and participation in the Communist Party Historians' Group, in which we had theoretical discussions all the time—this made me into a historian. The formal and informal exchange with fellow socialists helped me more than anything I had found in Cambridge University. This is not to say that one can't, fortunately, sometimes find something in a university, but it is to emphasize that socialist intellectuals ought to help each other. We should never be wholly dependent upon institutions, however benevolent, but should maintain groups in which theory is discussed and history is discussed and in which people criticize each other. This principle of being able to give and to receive sharp criticism is very important.

Q. You had your own stint at the University of Warwick, where you established, or helped establish, a Center for the Study of Social History. I don't think most people over here know the full story behind your association with Warwick or the reasons why you left it. Was there some basic conflict between doing history and training historians, and doing it in a university setting?

THOMPSON   I may have found such a conflict but I wouldn't generalize from my own case at all. That's temperamental. I make no virtue of this at all. It is just that a certain degree of personal unhappiness builds up if I find that I cannot get forward in my work. The Center was successful. I think it was good—intellectually good—and stimulating and a surprisingly comradely place. And it remains good today. We all criticized each other very well. But I had reached a total commitment to it and felt the need to complete some of my own work. It was an egotistical decision, but it has no general validity. It is partly the temperament thing: I am more of a writer than a teacher. And it is partly that in Britain, probably more than the States, you get a certain seniority in the profession and you can't opt for a lower place on the status ladder, and perhaps a bit less work. You've got to be a professor or something and take on a lot of administrative duties. Hence, as you get older you are almost forced to cease to be a practicing historian.

Q. How would you pass on the "mysteries of the craft" now? What should one do, in your opinion, to learn to be a proper historian?

THOMPSON   I would appall you if I told you the truth. I agreed to write *MEWC* because I was hard up, and a publisher wanted a textbook on the British labor movement, 1832 to 1945. I suggested it might be 1790 to 1945, and *MEWC* is the first chapter. It is just the same story again as with the Morris. The material took hold of me. I did not at first plan it that way. This is not to say that there was not, as it was written, a great deal of conscious planning. But the fact is, again, that the material took command of me, far more than I ever expected. If you want a generalization I would have to say that the historian has got to be listening all the time. He should not set up a book or a research project with a totally clear sense of exactly what he is going to be able to do. The material itself has got to speak to him. If he listens, then the material itself will begin to speak through him. And I think this happens.

Q. Why did you next turn your attention to the eighteenth century rather than to what could have been the second or the third chapter of a history of the British labor movement to 1945?

THOMPSON   Well, partly because the exciting and challenging study of Chartism is something that my wife has been working on for years. So, I didn't want to move forward into that. Also, a lot of unfinished problems remained in my mind from the beginning of the book. There were certain aspects of plebeian consciousness that I tried to write about in Part One of *The Making* that I felt were still not fully disclosed. These remained as a challenge. And here comes the good part of university teaching, too; that in constructing courses in a very good history school like the University of Warwick, one was trying to present materials in new ways. The two things combined to lead me back into the eighteenth century and to commence the analysis that I have been involved in for ten years now. Probably much more consciously now than in the previous episodes; I am now a more conscious historian. I know why I am going to certain problems and what I hope to get out of them.

Q. There would seem, though, to be some very pressing questions about the later period raised by your work. In particular, what happened to this tradition of radicalism that you discussed for the pre-Chartist period? Does the culture industry of advanced capitalism succeed in breaking the culture of resistance and revolt down?

THOMPSON I have always written about this, but I have written about it mainly at the level of theory. I have presented myself to you as a more muddled and Anglo-Saxon character than is quite true. People in the States very often ask me about methodological problems. I sometimes think that methodology is being used in the place of theory. There is such a thing as methodology, which is the intermediate level at which a theory is broken down into the appropriate methods you are going to use—quantitative or literary, whatever they may be—to test that theory, and equally at which empirical findings are brought up to modify the theory. There is such an intermediate level. But sometimes people talk as if you can have a methodology without a theory or as if you can keep the theory inside a locked drawer in the desk. This is particularly so in what I have described as the ideological Right. I mean, "modernization theory" [the theory that all societies follow the same path from "primitive" to "modern" conditions as Western Europe and North America have] is not a theory at all—or it's a theory wearing the mask of methodology. The theory is locked in the drawer and is, in this case, pure positivistic, capitalist ideology. But modernizers refuse to admit to this. What they pretend is their "theory" is a whole set of positivistic, quantitative, and similar techniques.

When I have suggested that, in writing history in this or that way, I have not made any clear decisions, I do not mean that I have not been engaged all the time in a theoretical argument about the historical process. As far as what happened in the nineteenth and twentieth centuries goes, I have several times attempted to deal with that history at a theoretical level. In "The Peculiarities of the English" there is a kind of sketch map, and in certain writings that were in *New Left Review* back in the early sixties I attempted this approach. This is at a level of argument and of theorizing about the process, but not of testing it. It might well be that if I, or other historians, come with such presuppositions to deal with, for example, the appalling, deep, and complex problem of imperialism—British imperialism—and its effect upon the British working class, when we are immersed in the complexity of the material we will find that this theory is quite inadequate. Gareth Stedman Jones, in a brilliant article in *The Journal of Social History* recently, does very significantly modify some of the received wisdom that most of us offered as theory ten years or more ago.[8] This is the importance of the *real* history: it not only tests theory, it reconstructs theory.

But I don't myself feel inclined to move forward in my historical work, because I have problems I am so deeply committed to that lie both in literature and social history in the eighteenth century. I also have theoretical and political writing that I want to accomplish. This looks as if it is going to keep me busy for a good five years. When it comes to the twentieth century I am almost sure that younger historians must do the work because of my too-great involvement in some episodes. I don't think I can write about these as a historian. I can write political theory, but I can't write as a historian about 1945 because I am too much in there myself. There is a necessary distance to make possible an objective analysis.

Q. That raises a question that has figured in your polemical exchanges with Perry Anderson, in 1965, and most recently with Leszek Kolakowski. Is a historical sensibility disabling for a political analysis, as Anderson, at least, seems to suggest at one point?[9] Can the historian and the polemicist, the propagandist—neither of these terms meant disparagingly—be the same persons? Kolakowski says that there is something flawed about looking at the present as a historian would.

THOMPSON   I don't think that historical consciousness is disabling at all; it is very helpful. In one or two areas it may be disabling in understanding contemporary political situations. The historian may tend to be a bit too generous because a historian has to learn to attend and listen to very disparate groups of people and try and understand their value system and their consciousness. Obviously, in a very committed situation, you can't always afford that kind of generosity. But if you afford it too little then you are impelled into the kind of sectarian position in which you are repeatedly making errors of judgment in your relations with other people. We have seen a lot of that recently. Historical consciousness ought to assist one to understand the possibilities of transformation and the possibilities within people. But that is a very general statement. I think Anderson was suggesting that I have a sentimental populist attitude. What was of substance in what he was saying was that my particular tradition of work, associated to some degree with the literary critical tradition of Raymond Williams and others, has placed great emphasis upon the culture, and Anderson was placing a reemphasis upon power. I think that reemphasis was necessary, although I think it has gone with a certain blindness toward culture. That, I think, is the nub of the question. I don't think it is really about history, but about different kinds of derived historical consciousness. If you look at his own historical work, Anderson is much concerned with power and structures, very little concerned with culture and the inwardness of experience.

Q. Anderson, in his two recent volumes on the transition from slavery to feudalism and on the absolutist state, writes in a very different idiom from yours. Is there something about the way in which things are *said* by "structural Marxists" that produces a blindness or an abstractness that has a pernicious influence on one's historical and perhaps political judgment?

THOMPSON I'm by no means a wholesale critic of structural Marxism. No Marxist can*not* be a structuralist, in a certain sense. One is talking about a society, all of whose parts can only be understood in terms of the whole. In fact, if you look at my chapter "Exploitation" in *MEWC* you can see that what is being offered—although I didn't *know* it because we weren't using that term at the time—is exactly a structuralist statement. So the question of structuralism should not be confused with my theoretical repudiation of Althusser and of the Althusserian mode.

I don't want to become involved in America in argument against Perry Anderson, whom I regard as a comrade and a very able, intelligent, constructive thinker, and whom I do not regard as an Althusserian. He has adopted certain Althusserian concepts and modes but, in my view, is not within the same intellectual system as Althusser.

Q. You include not only Althusser, however, but also, at times, Sartre and the whole Parisian Marxist tradition with its universalist idiom. Of course, you grant that a close relation exists between the French and English traditions. "They propose and we object," you say at one point, so you do not dismiss wholesale what goes on there. . . .

THOMPSON There are two quite distinct questions here; one is part of a polemic, written with a dry grin on my face. I am talking about the extraordinary way in which what one would have thought was prehistory, a Cartesian and a Baconian intellectual and educational tradition, still exists and works its way into even Marxism. This is partly a jesting form of polemic, and it is partly serious. We have had thinkers, in England, who would be unrecognizable as thinkers in any Continental discipline. I think particularly of William Hazlitt and, in his own way, William Morris. But Hazlitt, most particularly, is a writer who is both metaphoric and allusive and whose theoretical intelligence, which is high, is so much masked by an empirical idiom that it is very difficult to make it available to a more lucid, staircase kind of rational style that one associates particularly with a certain French tradition. This, then, is partly a joke. But it is also a serious joke in the sense that this capacity for conceptualization at a high level, and sometimes for the divorce of concepts from empirical testing and empirical engagement, is rather characteristic of a majority tradition in Paris. This sort of dialogue across the channel is a very fruitful one.

But this is a quite distinct question from Althusser's writing, which I see as a mutation or as a fully exposed development of idealism that uses certain Marxist concepts but that is attempting to wall up, totally, the empirical dialogue and the empirical criticism of those concepts. It ranks as a theology, and as between a theology and what I regard as the major tradition of Marx there can be very little common ground. Then, what is at issue is reason itself: whether Marxism is a rational theory available to dialogue with evidence and open rational criticism. If it ceases to be such, then it is disreputable. It is not only disreputable, it is actively injurious, theoretically or practically. It will mislead all the time. Hence, it is a question of principle to oppose this.

Q. There are those, however, who say that what is most illegitimate about what Althusser and others in the tradition of twentieth-century Western Marxism do is that they interrogate Marxism from the standpoint of some non-Marxist discipline of thought. Thus, Althusser is an idealist because he attempts to criticize the Marxist tradition from the standpoint of French thinkers such as Gaston Bachelard and Jacques Lacan. This objection seems to be exactly the opposite of yours, which is, if I understand it, that Althusser does not interrogate Marxism and, therefore, closes off its potential.

THOMPSON   That is really not at odds with what I am saying. You are talking about what the theory is. In formal terms, one of the things that has happened has been the encapsulation—for example, of Husserl and phenomenology—into Althusserian thought. He wouldn't admit that it has happened. But it has happened. So in terms of form, the way Althusser has constructed his particular intellectual system is in terms of those borrowings you mentioned. But I am saying that from these materials Althusser has actually produced an epistemology that excludes the basic dialogue between concept and empirical evidence. He has a total epistemological theory that discards the possibility of putting theory to any empirical critique. Any such critique is dismissed as "empiricism" or "historicism." I think I can show this. This is a very dangerous and irrational moment for the Marxist tradition.

Q. You mentioned that you have made theoretical decisions and have theoretical points of view. Which thinkers are your chief theoretical forebears or inspirations?

THOMPSON   Vico, Marx, Blake, Morris—the last two showing how English I am.

I read Vico at Cambridge. Some Vico. His importance is that he is one of these extraordinarily fertile and contradictory thinkers who—like Rousseau, in a way—contains within him a whole number of possibilities of alternative intellectual development. Arguments in contemporary anthropology, sociology, history, economics, and Marxism can all be traced back to a common theoretical center in Vico. Vico contained all these possibilities, the most important of which were then realized by Marx.[10]

But I don't think I look for finished theory, in that sense, so much. It seems to me that all theory is provisional. The notion of having one consistent, all-embracing theory is itself a heresy. I think—although this may be part of the Baconian tradition—I think of theory as critique, theory as polemic. I believe very much in heightening theoretical awareness of problems, but I think this is very often best done through the method of critique. This is also so in Marx and Engels. I don't think these are the greatest texts in the Marxist tradition, but if you take *Feuerbach*, or *Anti-Duhring*, they are precisely theory being developed as critique. And Marx and Engels in their own correspondence develop theory as critique. We should do this more. Nothing discouraged me more in the sixties than that a whole generation of the Left, and of Marxists, was arising whose arrows were all going straight past the ear of the opposition because they were talking a different vocabulary, and in another place. They very rarely exposed the intellectual or ideological products of the dominant intellectual society to very close polemical, critical examination of a kind that had to be answered. Hence, we have this ridiculous situation in which the established powers regard themselves as being "objective" academics and the Left as being ideologists, when in fact very often the position can clearly be seen to be the reverse.

It is very arduous work. It sounds as if developing theory is very difficult and as if theoretical critique is easy. It isn't.

Q. What about more contemporary figures? Who were the most important influences on you from amongst your own peers or the immediately previous generation?

THOMPSON The two people who were influencing me at school were Christopher Hill, who had just done his first sketch of the English civil war and who is a much more formidable theoretical practitioner than most people realize. Hill has restructured whole areas of historical consciousness in England. He now seems to have been there all the time. But he wasn't. And Christopher Caudwell,[11] whose work I have been rereading in the last year or two. I now can see that almost ninety percent of his work has to be thrown out, but ten percent is marvelous, ten percent extraordinary. He anticipates ways of thinking about linguistics and ideology that are possibly in advance of where we are now. His literary criticism is terrible. But in and out of this there is a kind of cultural criticism, an understanding of the logic of ideological process that influenced me very deeply.

Q. What about Marx himself? In *The Making of the English Working Class* what appears again and again is not "capitalism as system," which appeared and very effectively in the Kolakowski essay, but rather the "factory system" or "industrialism." There is an advantage of concreteness to the notion of factory, as opposed to capital, that is gained, but how do you see the two notions being related? Are they replaceable one with another?

THOMPSON I haven't noticed these supposed contradictions or differences of emphasis. I haven't been aware of them. Perhaps someone should show me. I think the place where this is more clearly written out in *The Making* is the chapter called "Exploitation," which is, in fact, as I have said, a structural argument and a polemic against orthodox economic history, which fragments the whole social process and then puts it together again as a set of interlocking inevitabilities, and also attempts to present exploitation as a category in the mind of a biased historian and not as something that actually occurred. Once you've managed to do that, you can move back into something like modernization theory in which you see not a conflict-process, not a dialectic of class struggle, but simply an exfoliation and differentiation in a continuous process of industrialization, modernization, rationalization, and so on.

The critical concepts, which are being used all the time in *MEWC*, are those of class and of class struggle. I would give primacy to these over a derivative —an economic derivative—from the notion of surplus value on which is then built a whole picture of capital from building block one, which is surplus value. This building-block method, the building up of a model of capitalism as a static structure, is alien to what I got from Marx and continue to get from Marx. But I probably read Marx in a slightly different way from today's readers. The *Grundrisse* was not available to us, for example. A lot of what we got from Marx came from the Marx-Engels correspondence, observing them working upon history in the workshop of their correspondence. This gives one a sense of process. I think the proliferation of *Capital* study groups is very good now. But I think it does sometimes lead to this sense that there is a Theory with a capital *T* with basic building blocks that can all then be put together in a static structure. And yet, above all, Marx's epistemology is historical. It is possible *even* for Marxists not to realize that concepts like class, ideology, and capitalism itself are historical concepts; that is, they are not derived from a static structural analysis but from an examination of repeated patterns emerging over time.

Q. Looking back over your work to date, what would you say is its connecting thread? How did the author of a biography of William Morris come to write about the ecology of Windsor Forest in *Whigs and Hunters?*

THOMPSON   This arises from a preoccupation that runs through all my work, even before I saw its significance fully. It's there in the Morris, although in a muffled way, because I was then still prisoner of some Stalinist pieties. This preoccupation is with what I regard as a real silence in Marx, which lies in the area that anthropologists would call value systems. It is not that Marx said anything incompatible with that silence being filled in, but there is a silence as to cultural and moral mediations; as to the ways in which the human being is imbricated in particular, determined productive relations; the way these material experiences are handled by them culturally; the way in which there are certain value systems that are consonant with certain modes of production, and certain modes of production and productive relations that are inconceivable without consonant value systems. There is not one that is dependent upon the other. There is not a moral ideology that belongs to a "superstructure"; there are these two things that are different sides of the same coin.

This became a major theoretical problem for me. When some of my comrades were reexamining the entire history of communism and of Stalinism in search of theoretical, strategic, or even tactical clues to its degeneration, I remained transfixed by the problem of the degeneration of the theoretical vocabulary of mainstream orthodox Marxism—the impoverishment of its sensibility, the primacy of categories that denied the effective existence (in history or in the present) of the moral consciousness, the extrusion (if you like) of that whole area of imaginative passion that informs the later writings of William Morris. And yet, William Morris was himself a historical materialist, very deeply influenced by Marx; he was, in a sense, the first major English-speaking Marxist. So that everything came together. To defend the tradition of Morris (as I still do) entailed unqualified resistance to Stalinism. But it did *not* entail opposition to Marxism; rather, it entailed rehabilitating lost categories and a lost vocabulary in the Marxist tradition. But this "vocabulary," in Marx, was partly a silence—unarticulated assumptions and unrealized mediations. In *MEWC* I tried to give that silence a voice, and—I hope with increasing theoretical consciousness—this remains a central preoccupation of my historical and political writing.

In the case of *Whigs and Hunters* and *Albion's Fatal Tree*, I am not only concerned with recovering forgotten evidence of class struggle; I am also much concerned with the structure of dominance, the ritual of capital punishment, the symbolic hegemony of the law. In *Customs in Common*, my unfinished book of studies in eighteenth-century social history—on paternalism, riot, enclosure, and common right, and on several popular ritual forms—I am much concerned with noneconomic sanctions and the invisible rules that govern behavior quite as powerfully as military force, the terror of the gallows, or economic domination. In a sense I am still examining "morality" and value systems, as in the "moral economy" of the food-rioting crowd or as in the ritual of *charivari*, but not in the supposedly classic "liberal" way—as areas of "free choice" divorced from economics—nor yet in one classic sociological or anthropological way, in which societies and economics are seen as dependent upon value systems. I am examining the dialectic of interaction, the dialectic between "economics" and "values." This preoccupation has run through all my work, historical and political.

In a very interesting way in Western capitalist ideology, also, a vocabulary of agency and moral choice got completely lost. Parsons and Smelser[12] are perfect examples. But one can find many contemporary examples in which there is a notion of the maximization of productive growth as being the inner motor of a machine that people trail along behind. That area has always been central to my work and I suppose that, if any addition to the sum of understanding is made by my work, this may be the area of my own contribution. This is why I am now particularly interested in anthropological concepts that may be brought to the examination of norms of a noneconomic kind.

The injury that advanced industrial capitalism did, and that the market society did, was to define human relations as being primarily economic. Marx engaged in orthodox political economy and proposed revolutionary-economic man as the answer to exploited-economic man. But it is also implicit, particularly in the early Marx, that the injury is in defining man as "economic" at all. This kind of critique of industrial capitalism is found in Blake and Wordsworth very explicitly and is still present in Morris, and it is wholly complementary and not in any sense at odds with the Marxist tradition. That again is where I am now working. In fact, I may perhaps finish my work on Blake and Wordsworth next, because I think this total critique of bourgeois utilitarianism just at the moment of its full flowering in the Industrial Revolution remains a fertile one and one that I want to recover. This is where my main teaching has been in the States. The Blake is nearly finished—a brief study of the antinomian tradition. *Customs in Common* is very far advanced as well.

There is just one more thing about your feeling a certain kind of silence in my writing about the harder economic analysis. This is partly the consequence of forming one's own sense of what one's own contribution may be while still feeling oneself to be part of a collective. You see? I have comrades and associates, like John Saville and Eric Hobsbawm and many others, who are very sound economic historians. They are better at it than I am, and so I tend to assume that my work falls into place within a wider discourse. In my political writings exactly the same problem arises. If one is part of a collective, in which someone is writing about the welfare service, someone is writing about education, someone is writing about imperialism, one tends to assume this work goes on alongside one's own, and one concentrates on what one can do best. And yet, when the part is taken out of the whole, then it may look as if one is curiously divorced, when one has never felt divorced, from the other arguments.

Q. We're not listening to the entire conversation.

THOMPSON   Exactly. What we want to do is get back to a collective converse again. We need our radical history journals and everything, but we also need mainstream journals in which historians, philosophers, economists, and political activists are all contributing and arguing with each other, and learning from each other. I think we can do it. After all, we have got enough people around. What socialists must never do is allow themselves to become wholly dependent upon established institutions—publishing houses, commercial media, universities, foundations. I don't mean that these institutions are all repressive—certainly, much that is affirmative can be done within them. But socialist intellectuals must occupy some territory that is, without qualification, their own: their own journals, their own theoretical and practical centers— places where no one works for grades or for tenure but for the transformation of society; places where criticism and self-criticism are fierce, but also mutual help and the exchange of theoretical and practical knowledge; places that prefigure in some ways the society of the future.

Notes

1. Perry Anderson's response to the first of these essays appeared in the *New Left Review*, no. 35 (January–February 1966), and Kolakowski's response to the second appeared in the *Socialist Register 1974*. Perry Anderson has written a fuller analysis of Thompson's place in the Marxist tradition entitled *Arguments Within English Marxism* (London: New Left Books, 1980), which also contains interesting material on the early history of the *New Left Review*.

2. The role of his political experiences in shaping Thompson's historical research and writing is discussed by Bryan D. Palmer in his recent book *The Making of E. P. Thompson: Marxism, Humanism, and History* (Toronto: New Hogtown Press, 1981), and by Henry Abelove, in a review of *The Poverty of Theory* that appeared in *History and Theory* 21, no. 1 (1982):132–42.

3. A reference to Sir Lewis Namier (1888–1960). A historian who worked especially on parliamentary politics in eighteenth-century Great Britain, Namier favored a microcosmic approach emphasizing the role of personal influence and connections in the formation of policy.

4. *Annales: Économies, Sociétés, Civilisations* is a French journal that was founded in the 1920s by Mark Bloch and Lucien Febvre. Historians of the contemporary *Annales* school, whose leading figures are Fernand Braudel and Emmanuel Le Roy Ladurie, advocate ecological and demographic explanations of long-term social, economic, and political trends.

5. C. Wright Mills (1916–62) was an American commentator and social critic whose works reflect the influence of Marxist theory. These works include *The Sociological Imagination* (New York: Oxford, 1959) and *The Power Elite* (New York: Oxford, 1956).

6. Frank Thompson served with conspicuous gallantry as a British liaison and adviser to Bulgarian partisans during World War II. He was finally captured and executed. See Freeman Dyson, *Disturbing the Universe* (New York: Harper & Row, 1979), pp. 33–44.

7. Dona Torr (1883–1956) translated into English a selection of the correspondence of Marx and Engels. Long active in the Historians' Group of the British Communist party, she also wrote the first of a projected two-volume biography of the great British labor leader, Tom Mann.

8. Gareth Stedman Jones, "Working-class Culture and Working-class Politics in London, 1870–1900: Notes on the Remaking of a Working Class," *Journal of Social History* 7, no. 4 (Summer 1974):460–508.

9. Perry Anderson, editor of the *New Left Review*, is a prominant English Marxist who has been influenced by the structuralist theories of Louis Althusser. Thompson and

Anderson have disagreed sharply and publicly over the merits of structuralism. Anderson's major works include *Arguments within English Marxism* (London: New Left Books, 1980); *Considerations on Western Marxism* (London: NLB, 1976); *Lineages of the Absolutist State* (London: NLB, 1974); *Passages from Antiquity to Feudalism* (London: NLB, 1974); and *Towards Socialism* (ed.) (Ithaca, N.Y.: Cornell U. Press, 1966).

10. Giambattista Vico (1668–1744), the eighteenth-century Italian philosopher and author of *The New Science*, argued that it was easier to understand society (made by men) than the universe (made by God) and thus was a forerunner of materialist thinkers such as Marx.

11. Thompson's fuller reflections on the work of Christopher Caudwell can be found in "Caudwell," Ralph Miliband and John Saville, eds., *The Socialist Register 1977* (London: Merlin Press, 1977), and available in the United States from Monthly Review Press.

12. Talcott Parsons (1902–79) and Neil Smelser (1930–) are American sociologists who helped to develop and refine modernization theory.

SELECT BIBLIOGRAPHY

Books
Beyond the Cold War. New York: Pantheon Books, 1982
The Making of the English Working Class. New York: Vintage Books, 1963; London: Penguin, 1968.
The Poverty of Theory and Other Essays. New York: Monthly Review Press, 1978.
Protest and Survive, coedited with Dan Smith. Hammondsworth, Eng.: Penguin, 1980.
Protest and Survive, coedited with Dan Smith. New York: Monthly Review Press, 1981.
The Railway. London: British-Yugoslav Assn., 1948.
There Is a Spirit in Europe: A Memoir of Frank Thompson. London: V. Gollancz, 1948.
William Morris—Romantic to Revolutionary. London: Lawrence & Wishart, 1955; revised, New York: Pantheon Books, 1977.
Whigs and Hunters. New York: Pantheon Books, 1975.
Writing by Candlelight. London: Merlin Press, 1980; New York, Monthly Review Press, 1981.

Political Essays
"Caudwell." *The Socialist Register 1977.*
"Introduction." *Review of Security and the State 1978.*
"The Long Revolution." *New Left Review*, nos. 9, 10, 11 (May-June, July-August, September-October 1961).
"Notes of Exterminism, the Last Stage of Civilisation." *New Left Review*, no. 121 (May-June 1980).

"An Open Letter to Leszek Kolakowski." *The Socialist Register 1973.*
"A Psessay in Ephology." *The New Reasoner,* no. 10 (Autumn 1959).
"Revolution." *New Left Review,* no. 3 (May-June 1960).
"Revolution Again." *New Left Review,* no. 6 (November-December 1960).

Historical Essays
"Disenchantment or Default? A Lay Sermon." In *Power and Consciousness,* edited by Conor Cruise O'Brien and William Dean Vanich. New York: N.Y.U. Press, 1969.
"Eighteenth-Century English Society: Class Struggle without Class?" *Social History* 3, no. 2 (May 1978).
"Folklore, Anthropology and Social History." *Indian Historical Review* 3, no. 2 (January 1978).
"The Grid of Inheritance." *Family and Inheritance—Rural Society in Western Europe.* Cambridge: Cambridge University Press, 1976.
"Homage to Tom Maguire." In *Essays in Labour History,* edited by Asa Briggs and John Saville. London: Macmillan, 1960.
"The Moral Economy of the English Crowd in the 18th Century." *Past and Present,* no. 50 (1971).
"Patrician Society, Plebeian Culture." *Journal of Social History,* Summer 1974.
"The Peculiarities of the English." *The Socialist Register 1965.*
"Rough Music: Le Charivari Anglais." *Annales: Économies, Sociétés, Civilisations,* March-April 1972.
"Time, Work-Discipline and Industrial Capitalism." *Past and Present,* no. 38 (1967).

Interviews
"Recovering the Libertarian Tradition." *The Leveller,* no. 22 (January 1979).

ERIC HOBSBAWM

B
AFTER C.A.P. BELLAY

ERIC HOBSBAWM

ERIC HOBSBAWM, WHO teaches at the University of London, is one of the leading living practitioners of Marxist history. He has produced seminal essays on the general European crisis of the seventeenth century, on the British standard of living during the eighteenth and nineteenth centuries, and on British labor and social history from the eighteenth through the twentieth centuries. Many of the latter have been collected in the valuable *Labouring Men* (1964). In *Primitive Rebels* (1959), *Captain Swing* (1968, coauthored with George Rudé), and *Bandits* (1969), he has explored the persistence of preindustrial modes of protest and political behavior in the modern world. Over the past two decades, his major works have been synthetic in character and written for a popular audience. *Industry and Empire* (1968) is an economic history of England since 1750. *The Age of Revolution* (1962) presents the transformation of European life between 1789 and 1848 as a "dual revolution," that is, the bourgeois revolution in its political (French) and industrial (British) forms. His most recent volume, *The Age of Capital* (1975), focuses on the definitive triumph of capitalism as a social system between 1848 and 1875, its worldwide impact, and the consolidation of bourgeois culture. Hobsbawm is also one of the few Marxist historians of the post–World War II era to retain a connection with the British Communist party.

Presently at work on a fourth synthetic volume, this one dealing with Europe during 1875–1914, Hobsbawm continues to produce articles for scholarly journals and pamphlets for the British socialist movement. Of the latter "The Forward March of Labour Halted?," a pessimistic assessment of socialist options in contemporary, crisis-ridden Britain, has served to focus debate on the Left, and has been reprinted as the lead article in a collection of essays by socialist activists and scholars.[1] He is also a noted jazz critic whose essays and reviews are published under the pseudonym Francis Newton.

This interview was conducted during the summer of 1978 by Pat Thane, who teaches British social history at Goldsmiths College, University of London, and Elizabeth Lunbeck, who is a graduate student in history at Harvard University.

Q. It is thirty years since you started publishing. How did you come to "do" history?

HOBSBAWM   Because I discovered when I got to an English secondary school that I was good at it. Before I came to England, I couldn't discover this because most of the history I was taught was by an old gentleman who concentrated on getting the dates of medieval German emperors into our heads and made us memorize them. And we all memorized them, and I've totally forgotten them. I don't blame him, because, as I've since found out, he was an eminent classical scholar, who was probably as bored by medieval history as we were. Still, I didn't develop a great interest in academic history. But when I came to England I did, and I turned out to be good at it because I was a Marxist, or tried to be, and therefore answered questions in examinations in an unexpected way. That's how I got to win a scholarship. I wasn't completely committed to doing history, but by the time I got to university there weren't many other things I could have done—English literature, foreign languages, something like that. It seemed to me that most of these things weren't very original, whereas the kind of history that was being taught at university was quite different from the kind of history that we had been learning at school, and therefore it seemed to be worth going on studying it. The university establishment was generally hostile to Marxism in those days. Nevertheless, we were all Marxists as students in Cambridge and to some extent in Oxford, and, in fact, at university I would have thought most of us learned a good deal more talking to each other than we learned from all except one or two professors. And there were, in fact, attempts to coordinate the discussions of Marxist historians before the war, though I wasn't involved in them. So it was perfectly logical to go on with this after the war, and indeed in 1946–1947 when we came out [of the army] the atmosphere was not yet anti-Marxist. It turned sharply anti-Marxist in '48. After that, we were isolated. This was not without its advantages. The disadvantage, of course, is obvious. The advantage was that we couldn't get away with bullshit. We didn't have a homemade public that expected to read and approve of anything that called itself Marxist. On the contrary, we had to fight our way and be accepted by people who started off with enormous prejudice against anything describing itself as Marxist history. And I think as a matter of intellectual discipline this wasn't all bad.

I began writing about the working class almost by accident. I had originally not intended to work specifically in labor history, though of course as Marxists and Communists we were all interested in labor history. I had originally intended to work on the agrarian problem in North Africa.

We were all very much into imperialism as students, and some of us were closely connected with what in those days were called colonial students, mostly Indians, and I got a travel grant as an undergraduate to go to North Africa and do a brief study, and I thought it was a very interesting problem. I still regret not having carried on with it, but I was called up by the army. And while I was hanging around in the war and trying to think of what to do when I got out, I decided to change for two reasons. One reason was that there was no way of doing any preliminary reading about this, so to speak, "third-world problem" while I was in the army. And the second was that eventually I got married, and my wife was working and I didn't particularly fancy leaving her for a couple of years and going to Algeria. And so I decided, as it turned out not particularly satisfactorily, to work on the Fabian Society, chiefly because you could read a fair amount about that in a preliminary way even before getting out of the army.[2] And it's through that that I got into late–nineteenth-century labor history as a special field.

The Fabian thesis, which I eventually got a Ph.D. on, proved to be very interesting. The subject wasn't interesting, there were a lot of people working on it, and the Fabians didn't seem to me to be all that important, nowhere near as important as they made out. On the other hand, a lot of things that had happened at that time did seem to be very interesting, notably the New Unionism, and I got into trade union and working-class history in that way.[3] And, in fact, one thing that helped me to it was precisely that first book that I was asked to write, or edit, *Labor's Turning Point*, which really forced me to take a much broader perspective on labor history.

But I must confess that I had a rather strong prejudice, and I still have, against institutional labor history, history of labor seen exclusively as a history of the parties, leaders, and others of labor, because it seems to me quite inadequate—necessary but inadequate. It tends to replace the actual history of the movement by the history of the people who *said* they spoke for the movement. It tends to replace the class by the organized sector of the class, and the organized sector of the class by the leaders of the organized sector of the class. And, it leaves the door wide open, partly for the creation of mythologies and for the sort of diplomatic difficulties that have made it extremely hard to write official histories of trade unions, political parties, and other organizations.

Q.   You have written for two audiences, a specialized one and a wider audience of nonspecialists. Is this something we should be committed to?

HOBSBAWM   Yes, I think so. It seems to me that it is very important to write history for people other than pure academics. The tendency in my lifetime has been for intellectual activity to be increasingly concentrated in universities and to be increasingly esoteric, so that it consists of professors talking for other professors and being overheard by students who have to reproduce their ideas or similar ideas in order to pass exams set by professors. This distinctly narrows the intellectual discipline. Particularly in the social sciences that are to be of some political and public use, it is essential to at least try to communicate with ordinary citizens. There is a considerable historical precedent for this. After all, even in economics people like Adam Smith, Karl Marx, and [John Maynard] Keynes were not trying to write exclusively for professors, and in history the same is true. There are some very good historians who expect to be read by the broad public. To some extent this is a bit of an illusion, because one isn't really writing for the average reader of the daily paper or the average television viewer. One does write for people who have a certain basic education. There is an enormous difference between trying to write for people where you can assume a basic elementary culture and education and for people where you can't assume this. I, from time to time, try to do things for mass circulation, and I don't think I'm very good at it. Obviously, the feedback one gets is very occasional. The only systematic feedback one gets is from students. But I'd like to add that the tradition of writing so that you can be understood is quite strong in English history, not only on the Left, although I'm happy to say that on the Left it is very strong, if you look at Edward Thompson and others. The kind of people one aims at are, I hope, a fairly large section of the population—students, trade unionists, plain ordinary citizens who are not professionally committed to passing examinations but do want to know how the past turned into the present and what help it is in looking forward to the future.

Of course, I try and behave like an academic historian because you've got to—I mean, you've got to make it stick. This is the chief lesson that we learned the hard way in the cold war years, when Marxists were a small isolated group. What you said, you had to be able to back, and if you stuck your neck out you had to make your case look plausible. One's got to be academic because there *are* people who will be watching you and trying to catch you out. Sometimes they do. But there are also occasions where one deliberately writes for a specialist audience. Still, I would hope that most of the things that I do are things that could be read by people who are not specialists.

Q. After you published on British labor history, you started writing, in *Primitive Rebels* and elsewhere, about activities of a different nature entirely. Why the new direction?

HOBSBAWM   Well, I wrote about British labor history because these things were largely by-products of my Fabian research and then my research for a fellowship thesis on the New Unionism. I tend to work by putting out sprouts sideways rather than by systematically developing. *Primitive Rebels* was different. It had two origins. I was traveling a good deal at that time, in the fifties, in various Mediterranean countries and got very interested in things that I saw, that my attention was drawn to—particularly in Italy where I made contact with leading Communist intellectuals who had a very substantial knowledge of what was going on in places like south Italy.[4] I was also reading Gramsci, who is extremely good at analyzing this type of nonpolitical protest movement.[5] The other thing was my contact with the social anthropologists in Cambridge, Meyer Fortes and Max Gluckman in Manchester. They were interested in the Mau-Mau [up]risings[6] and wanted to find out from some historians whether there was any European precedent for this type of movement. They asked me to do a paper on that and then they invited me to give the lectures out of which *Primitive Rebels* grew. So it was a combination of those two things. There's a third element that intervened before *Primitive Rebels* actually came out and that was the Twentieth Congress in '56 and de-Stalinization.[7] It's pretty clear that at the time I wrote *Primitive Rebels* I was also trying to rethink the bases of revolutionary activity, rather than to accept uncritically what a lot of militant Communists had accepted in the past. You can read *Primitive Rebels* as an attempt to see whether we were right in believing in a strongly organized party. The answer is *yes*. Were we right in believing that there was only one way, that there was one railroad that alone led forward and everything else could be neglected? The answer is *no*. There were all sorts of other things happening that we should have taken note of. These were all themes that came into *Primitive Rebels*.

Q.   What *was* the effect of the events of 1956?

HOBSBAWM   The effect of '56 on us—and I'm talking about the Marxist historians in Britain—was chiefly to set us free to do more history, because before '56 we'd spent an enormous amount of our time on political activity. If you look at somebody like Christopher Hill and compare what he published between 1940 and 1956 with what he's published since, you can see the difference that can make.[8] Otherwise I don't think it made that much difference because most of the people I knew from about 1946 to 1956 had been meeting regularly in the Communist Party Historians' Group, discussing things and developing them—luckily for us in an atmosphere of comparative freedom. And, above all, we had been encouraged to, and had ourselves taken the initiative in, establishing dialogue with non-Marxists. We were always (at least I was, and several other people, I'm sure, also were) instinctively "popular fronters." We believed that Marxist history was not an isolated truth to be defined by how different it was from everything else, but the spearhead of a broad progressive history that we saw as being represented by all manner of radical and labor traditions in British historiography. We saw ourselves not as trying, say, to distinguish ourselves from Tawney, but to push forward that tradition, to make it more explicit, to see Marxism as what these people *ought* to have been working toward.[9] In the time of the cold war, we were particularly pressed by the tendency to isolate us and establish strongly anti-Marxist orthodoxies in history—Namierism, for instance, as then practiced.[10] And so I think '56 didn't make that much difference, except that those of us who were old CP people had more elbowroom. It was a good deal easier to be Marxist without constantly feeling that you had to toe the line because, by this stage, it wasn't quite clear what the line was.

Before '56, we were obviously very constrained about twentieth-century history, and most of us didn't tackle it. I'll tell you honestly that one reason

I'm primarily a nineteenth-century historian and have been very careful not to push even my labor history much beyond 1914 is that when I became a labor historian you couldn't really be an orthodox Communist and write publicly about, say, the period when the Communist party was active because there was an orthodox belief that everything had changed in 1920 with the founding of the CP. Well, I didn't believe it had, but it would have been impolite, as well as probably unwise, to say so in public. As for the rest, I don't think the constraints were all that big, though there were probably some moral constraints, internal rather than external. I personally, I think, never suffered notably from them because my personal taste had never been to redo what Marx had already done, or Lenin had already done, but to deal with subjects they hadn't dealt with. It seemed a more interesting way of using Marxism. Consequently, there weren't all that many texts that you had to get around or, alternatively, that you could use to support yourself.

Q. Edward Thompson has talked of feeling intellectually and politically very isolated in the early 1960s. Did you experience the same thing?

HOBSBAWM   Yes and no. Isolated yes, because I was, and increasingly felt myself to be, a bit of a freak in the British movement. Somebody with my background—who came from a central European background, who first got politicized as a schoolboy in Berlin before Hitler came to power, who first got organized in a secondary schoolboys' Communist organization in Berlin in 1932, and who then came to England as a teenager (an English teenager, incidentally, because we were resident aliens on the Continent), clearly was a bit different from most of the other people who turned Left in the 1930s. Perhaps in the German, East German, or Austrian Communist party I would have felt less isolated. In another respect, however, I was *not* isolated because, luckily I suppose, people—particularly students and others—did read the stuff I wrote. I've never had the feeling of being cut off. I've sometimes a feeling of being disagreed with but not necessarily of being completely cut off and talking into the void. And certainly in the late sixties the New Left, or the various new lefts, were people with whom on the whole I felt myself engaged in a dialogue, often a critical dialogue but nevertheless on the same side, and vaguely connected with them. So to that extent I can't say I felt this sense of isolation Edward talks about.

In Britain, anybody lucky enough to get into the university before the early summer of 1948, when the curtain went down, on the whole stayed. They didn't get promotion for ten years or eleven years, but they weren't thrown out. There were one or two cases of people who did get thrown out, but on the whole most of us who were lucky enough to get in stayed in. We had to sit it out. But it's equally clear that nobody who wasn't in by, I suppose, May/June 1948—the time of the Berlin airlift—got a job for ten or eleven years.

Of course, conditions varied enormously depending on the university, on the personal relations that people had, and on personal behavior. I don't think *we* were pushed into a corner. I must say I didn't feel my colleagues felt as totally isolated as, say, Paul Baran, who is one of the very, very few Marxists who managed to stay in a university in the United States throughout the fifties. It was a bad period but it was nowhere near as bad in England as it was in the United States.

Q. Is prejudice against Left academics in Britain still a problem?

HOBSBAWM   Well, things have improved enormously since the fifties for obvious reasons. Things are probably beginning to regress a bit in the last year or two simply because the conservative forces are mobilizing more and are expressing themselves more. I think they are not new conservative forces, but the old conservative forces, the same sort of people who were already active in the fifties but who in the sixties fell silent or found themselves rather pushed into a corner. Now they are coming out again and are getting a great deal more exposure in the media, including specialized or general periodicals, as well as in general papers such as the London *Times*. You can see this in the attack on historians who have been associated with the Left and the Marxist Left. I am thinking, for instance, of the fairly persistent campaign against Christopher Hill in the *Times Literary Supplement* and elsewhere, which really is striking. Nonetheless, people like Christopher Hill and myself, or a number of other people of our generation, are for practical purposes no longer vulnerable, partly because, as in Christopher Hill's case, they are on the verge of retiring. But even if they were not, nobody would dream of doing anything about them, or could. The people in real danger are the young students, graduate students, and the young radical historians. It's not easy to see exactly how great that danger is. For one thing, the danger is to some extent obscured by the generally difficult job situation. When people aren't hired they can always say, "Well, we're not hiring a lot of people anyway, and you are just one of the unlucky ones; it isn't because we've got anything against you politically."

So far, I must say, in history in England, I don't think there's been a tremendous problem. The problem, I think, is much more urgent in other fields, in particular sociology and political science. On the whole, the reception the Gould report got, including the reception from the moderate liberals, was pretty negative, and I think there is, at the moment, at least in this country, a sufficiently big bulwark against straight reactionary campaigns in the universities.[11] I may be too optimistic about this but I've noticed that even in West Germany, where this problem is much more urgent, the Right has overdone it to such an extent that middle-of-the-road liberals have been mobilized against them in defense of toleration for the Left. The young radicals have even managed to mount quite a large counterattack, such as on that Nazi prime minister of Baden-Württemberg, who is now being pushed out of politics on the grounds of his record during the war.[12] I am credibly informed that one reason why that campaign has been so big is because he was one of the biggest witch-hunters in his part of Germany. So people have been mobilizing against him in defense of toleration. On the other hand, there is no denying that the anti-Marxists are once again taking the initiative. They argue that they are not attacking Marxism in history or elsewhere. But, in fact, their argument is quite wrong because they are attacking not merely the "lunatic-fringe" Left or those on the Left who are politically unusually active. They are attacking any kind of Marxism because they identify Marxism with whatever they dislike most. The attack is a general attack, although to some extent a shamefaced attack.

It's a delayed response to the radicalization of a large number of people in the universities in the late sixties and early seventies. The universities have always been thought of as being, and I think are to a growing extent, the main recruiting grounds for the cadres of the modern technological, bureaucratized, and even business society. If these universities become, as they did in the late sixties and early seventies, breeding grounds for people who are basically critical of society as it is, that creates problems. The conservative counterattack is, in some ways, a response to this. It's a delayed response because they've only come out of their holes at a time when radicalization in the universities is, at least temporarily, on the decline. Perhaps this very fact has encouraged them to come out and attack the people who were prominent.

Q. Getting back to your more recent work, how did you become interested in Latin America?

HOBSBAWM   When I wrote *Primitive Rebels* it was quite clear that this type of phenomenon was much more important in the Third World than it was in Europe, where it was rather marginal. At the same time, this is the kind of subject that cannot be effectively written about or investigated without knowing languages, without being able not only to read but to talk to people. Well, the only part of the Third World where I thought this might be practical was Latin America because I could manage Spanish. So, sooner or later I thought I'd better try and extend it. And I managed to get myself a travel grant to Latin America and, once there, I did develop a specific interest in some of the things that happened there—but primarily to illustrate the general problem of primitive rebellion, if I may use the phrase—and I've continued to maintain an interest in it since. I would have much preferred to be able to take a different part of the world. For instance, it seems to me quite clear that Southeast Asia and East Asia are absolutely crucial from that point of view. But for linguistic reasons I've just not been able to do it. And there I just have to rely on secondary or tertiary sources.

So far as I can see China is probably the one part of the world that has the longest and most active tradition of what you might call popular politics before the invention of modern politics. They have a tradition of politics in which peasant uprisings, urban movements, secret societies and brotherhoods, and so on are almost institutionalized as part of the mechanism of social change, are accepted not as marginal phenomena, as things for the police-court reporters, but as potentially important factors in the overthrow of dynasties and in revolutions. So clearly it looks to the outsider as though this kind of subject could be studied much better there than elsewhere. But to do that, you'd have to know much more than I know or now have time to start to learn.

Q. What are the main lines of your work on these movements?

HOBSBAWM I look at two problems linked by a common thread. One is the development of capitalism. Even the studies of popular movements depend on that. The whole question of primitive rebellion is one that arises because of the transition from precapitalist or preindustrial societies to capitalist societies, and the basic problem of how capitalist society developed out of feudalism has been central to my own preoccupations, as indeed it must be to those of any Marxist. The other one is the nature of popular movements or mass movements, of which the labor movement is one. I don't know whether I can see more of a common thread in that than, let's say, an approach, a preference, if you like, for looking at the movement in terms of its social bases, its social function, its role in a particular historical conjuncture rather than the study of policies, organizations, and leaderships, which doesn't imply any devaluation of these things. I don't know whether I can say more because most of my historical work has not, in fact, been planned. You can't say that here is a historian who decided at the outset of his career to do certain things, to specialize in certain fields, and carried it out the way Gibbon sat down and decided to write the *Decline and Fall of the Roman Empire* or E. H. Carr decided, at one stage, he was going to write the history of the Bolshevik revolution. A good deal of the stuff I've done, concretely, has been a response to particular situations, either situations in my life or the fact that people asked me to write books or to give lectures. And I then decided whether they fitted in with a sort of broad, general interest. If they did, well, I gave the lecture or wrote the book. So really, I'm in some ways a fairly kind of passive or, if you like, intuitive historian, not one who plans it. I've never really been tempted to be a medieval historian, though I find medieval history terribly interesting. And in spite of everything, I haven't much been tempted to be a sixteenth- or seventeenth-century historian.

Q. Do you think that recent interest in the work of Althusser and Gramsci has led to fruitful advances in Marxist history?

HOBSBAWM The short answer is no. I think Althusser is a very interesting man who has practically nothing to say to historians, but only to people who are interested in what you can and cannot say about history in general. Now there are interesting problems about methodology of history and epistemology, but I'm a sufficiently British type of historian to wish to concentrate on brass tacks, namely, what happened and why. Not to mention that I think Althusser and Althusserians have an actual bias against history. They've clearly had some important functions. Some very good Marxist historians, younger Marxist historians, have got something out of Althusser that I personally have never done, but I cannot think of any important bit of Marxist historical work that can be called Althusserian.

As for Gramsci, I don't know that the Gramscian influence on Marxist history is particularly new. I don't think myself that Gramsci has much of a specific approach to history other than Marx's own approach. He's got a lot of extremely brilliant things to say about Italian history. He's got an enormous amount of very beautiful things to say about the history of the subaltern classes, as he calls it, that I've certainly benefited greatly from. And, of course, if one chooses to be methodological about it, his stress on the importance of what traditional Marxists call superstructure, rather than the economic base, is very useful for those people who are tempted into a simple mechanical economic determinism. But otherwise, I don't think that, as far as writing history is concerned, there is a particularly strong Gramscian influence. Some people, like Gene Genovese in America, have made a great deal of such concepts as hegemony.[13] But frankly, if Gramsci had not invented this particular term, or adapted this term, we would have written much the same, except we would have called it something else.

Recent trends in Marxist historiography seem to me to be rather different. I would say the main trend is toward the revival of a discussion that goes back an awful long time—the discussion of the broad nature of social and economic formations in general and the transition from feudalism to capitalism in particular. And this is a discussion that, to go no further back than the end of the war, came very much into the center of Marxist attention with Maurice Dobb's *Studies in the Development of Capitalism* and shortly afterward with the well-known Dobb-Sweezy controversy, which, as you know, with additions, has been republished quite recently.[14] And the most interesting Marxist development in the past few years has been in people like Perry Anderson and Immanuel Wallerstein who, in different though I think potentially convergent ways, have taken up this sort of theme again. Bob Brenner in the United States has contributed to it and other people have, too. And I hope that it can extend beyond the Marxists into academic history, which increasingly is rediscovering that the "transition question" deserves concentrated study. Otherwise, it's difficult to generalize because there are now so many Marxists, particularly in the United States, and consequently they deal with a great many subjects. I would like to note, however, another new development that I think is less useful. Part of the development of a New Left Marxism from the late sixties on seemed to me to have been a narrowing of focus toward the nineteenth and twentieth centuries and the labor movement, and often the labor movement conceived of in a rather institutional and organizational form. I believe this is a very bad thing because it leaves most of the rest of history to people who aren't Marxists. When we, twenty-five years ago, had our Marxist historians' group we obviously had people who dealt with labor history, myself included. But we had people who dealt with everything— classical antiquity, medieval feudalism, the English revolution. The history of the textbooks of the seventeenth century in this country simply would not have been the same if Marxists had not decided to put this apparently nonrelevant subject of many centuries ago back into the center of our preoccupations. There is a danger in the present phase of Marxist history that it becomes a sort of synonym for radical labor history, and I think this danger should be pointed out.

It may seem paradoxical, but we never really were very much attracted to economic history in the technical sense. We found ourselves economic historians because it was the only slot into which we then could fit within academic history. And for the same reason, nowadays, most people find themselves social historians. But really, the basic interest of Marxist historians was always very much more in the relation between base and superstructure than in the economic laws of the development of the base. Looking back on it, I think it is a weakness. But it must be admitted that this is what most of us were really interested in.

Q. What about the dialogue between Marxists and anti-Marxists?

HOBSBAWM What is important is that there should be such a dialogue. Marxism has become so central that a great many of the non-Marxists accept far more of the Marxist problematic than they ever did. It is impossible for them to get away without considering either Marx or a good many of the subjects raised by Marxists. Take the debate on the transition from feudalism to capitalism; virtually everybody who's engaged in it has either engaged in a dialogue between Marxists and non-Marxists or has been a Marxist at one time or is still a Marxist. Mind you, when we talk about dialogues we're not talking about that kind of pseudodialogue of putting up straw men on the other side that you then shoot down. Marxists used to do this a great deal; they do it a bit less now. Anti-Marxists still do it quite habitually. What they are actually criticizing is some version of vulgar Marxism that nowadays is by no means common among Marxist historians. That isn't dialogue at all. As for the dialogue among the Marxists, that also has developed because Marxism is no longer a single interpretation, it's, you might say, a school. Once people believed that there were single answers and that you ought to get at agreed single answers; it is now quite evident that, even as Marxists, there are various ways in which you can approach the answer to particular problems. Whether they all have equal value is another matter. I personally, as I've already said, believe the Althusserian approach is of no particular interest to the Marxist historian, and I think there are some other approaches of which this can be said.

But I am not sure whether the dialogue is best carried on in Marxist and radical journals. It is a difficult question. There is a scope, obviously, for committed militant journals such as *History Workshop* and the *Radical History Review.* My own instinct, on the basis of my own experience, has always been to avoid isolating Marxist historians from other historians. My own instinct has always been to say that the place for Marxist historians to publish is right where the people that are not Marxists can read them. Nevertheless, it is evident that there are times and places when it is useful and even positive to have special organs—for instance, for the discussion of things that can't be published anywhere else or can't be developed anywhere else. But I still believe that, ideally, Marxists should not isolate themselves unless they are forced to, and they should try to break into the common universe of discourse, largely because the creation in the last ten years of a fairly large Marxist public seems to me to have been a bad thing for Marxism. If there is a public that expects to be talked at in Marxist jargon and expects to be convinced by Marxist arguments, this tends to encourage the writing of jargon and uncritical stuff. You can get away with murder if you write for a captive audience that is prepared to believe that you are telling them the truth, and only great self-criticism prevents you from giving in to this temptation. It's much better to expose yourself to the criticism of the other side.

In this regard, historians seem to have been less at fault than, say, the philosophers, possibly even the economists. The historians on the whole have not concentrated on the kind of esoteric Marxist metaphysics some other disciplines have gone for. There have been, I think, two dangers. One has been the concentration of a number of people, who probably would have made extremely good Marxist historians, on general theoretical questions that take them away from history along Althusserian and other lines, such as the discussion of what exactly, in principle, modes of production are, rather than on the discussion of how capitalism developed out of feudalism. Other Marxists, including some who are not historians and who through these questions have come into history, have raised these questions in a historical way. The Wallerstein-Anderson-Bob Brenner kind of discussion seems to me to be typical of this positive way of handling it. The other narrowing effect isn't so much due to Marxism as to the general radicalization of students, and it has led a number of young radical historians to concentrate—I won't say excessively, but very largely—on recent labor history and often, in a rather rationalist mold, history of organizations, parties, and so on. I would add that I think both these criticisms tend to affect American Marxists or radical historians less than British ones. On the whole, I would say, the situation in America is much more positive than it is in England. In England, we do find ourselves suffering very much from this concentration, and some of us have constantly tried to remind people that (a) there are other classes, and (b) you can't even understand the working class without knowing something about the other classes. It is true that at the moment we know rather more about the nineteenth-century working classes than about the nineteenth-century bourgeoisie.

Q. What do you think are the most fruitful areas that Marxist historians have undertaken or should undertake?

HOBSBAWM   One of the areas in which Marxism has proved to be most fruitful is in the study of class and class relations. There's the whole slavery discussion, in the U.S.A., that has been heavily influenced by the Marxist problematic and in which Marxists like Gene Genovese are still extremely prominent. There is the working-class discussion where, clearly, Edward Thompson's work has been quite fundamental. I think the same is true, to some extent, of the discussion of the peasantry, peasant economics, and so on, where once again, it seems to me, the work that is done by radical and Marxist historians is crucial. And there are even signs, possibly in connection with the peasant discussion, of a revival of an interest in feudalism itself, rather than as something that merely precedes capitalism and has to be superceded by it. The work, for instance, of Guy Bois entitled *La Crise du feudalisme,* is a very bright piece of work indeed, and fortunately it's going to be translated. We need somebody who will reinforce the sort of lonely fight that Rodney Hilton[15] has been fighting for a long time. So here is a huge subject where Marxism has been important.

Secondly, there has been a contribution of Marxism to the history of culture, both in the broad sense, in which anthropologists use it, and in the narrow sense, like art and literature. Here again, I think, the British tradition with people like Edward Thompson and Raymond Williams has been important. And also, here again in Britain more than elsewhere, there has been the revival of what used to be a very flourishing Marxist art history by people like Tim Clark. Remember, we've got a very good tradition of Marxist art history in this country, largely, admittedly, going back to temporary immigrants or permanent immigrants like Klingender and Antal and other people in the thirties. This, I think, is extremely important, and in some ways it's the biggest and most difficult problem for Marxist history, precisely because there's a relationship between the base of society, the economic base, the social relations of production and the ideological and theoretical superstructure. The history of class relations and the history of culture are two broad fields in which there is now quite good work.

I've already mentioned the bigger discussion on the long-term developments from feudalism to capitalism, and even longer-term development of humanity through various socioeconomic formations. I think that's enough to go with. This is offset, however, by the tendency among some of the younger Marxist historians that I've already mentioned both to narrow their scope and, by the tendency of others, to become too much involved in historical methodology or the philosophy of history, rather than actually writing some history. I say this as a historian. No doubt, if I were a philosopher I would take a different point of view.

And there is the history of women. I think one has got to admit there has been far too little of it in the past. Not necessarily because there has been enormous prejudice, but simply because women, just like a number of other oppressed classes, are simply less documented. And a great deal of what women do doesn't come under the heading of orthodox history, which is the great actions, the great public actions, you know, battles, treaties, cabinets, and so on—and in the nature of things that leaves out a great deal about women. And this applies also to traditional economic history, so there has certainly been this gap. I think it has been very important for the women's movement to draw attention to this gap because a lot of historians who didn't really believe that they themselves had fallen into the error of underestimating the part that half the human race plays in its activities have, in fact, done so. That's good. On the other hand, I think there has never been any shortage of good women historians, and I think this should be said. There have been women historians of absolutely top-class quality before anybody thought of the women's movement. I don't think the women's movement has so far made the slightest difference to the number of high-class women working in the field. It has, I think, reoriented in some ways the work of existing historians and, we hope, the younger historians to consider women's history.

I think there are major problems that arise chiefly due to the fact that it seems to be impossible, except within very narrow limits, to write the history of a particular sex separately from the other, just as it's really impossible to write the history of a particular class separately from the other. Consequently, the more positive developments in bringing women into history seem to me to have been those that have set the role of women in what is basically a society of two sexes rather than the ones that have concentrated on a single sex. There are one or two works that have specifically set out recently to discuss the role of women in society. Louise Tilly and Joan Scott's book on women, work, and family[16] seems to me to be the right way of handling this kind of thing. Including the work of historians, male or female, who do not specialize in women's history, a great deal of improvement has really been the broadening of the horizon into writing what one might call, if you will excuse me, bisexual rather than monosexual history. The progress in that field is, therefore, much harder to measure than simply by counting the number of books on the history of menstruation or something of that description, let alone on militants in the women's movement in the past or in the present.

Q. What sort of work are you doing yourself?

HOBSBAWM Well, I'm hoping to finish off those two volumes on the nineteenth century with a third volume that goes up to 1914, if not to get the nineteenth century out of my system then to try to get a synthesis of it. That's one of the hardest things to do, but in some ways the most interesting. And then I hope to carry on the kind of studies I began with _Primitive Rebels_ and carried on with things like _Bandits_ and to generalize a bit, and to try and inquire into the structure of popular politics, as you might say. In other words, to try and not pick out particular themes, particular examples, but see whether you cannot situate all these as different forms of the mode of common people struggling for a just, or indeed free, society in the very long historical period that precedes capitalism or the transition to capitalism. And, of course, this implies a good deal of reading, a lot of which I haven't done yet, and it may take a few years to carry on with that.

I am increasingly coming back to the old-fashioned opinion that it is useful in politics to have historical perspective if you want to know what is new in a situation. You've got to know how it's different from what's gone on before. It seems to me that there is an enormous amount of pseudohistory at the superficial level of political or electoral folklore. People are simply looking for precedents. It does seem to me, particularly at present, that you've got to recognize what's new in a situation and what is, therefore, unprecedented and to what extent old ways of handling it are adequate or not. For instance, the traditional labor movement in the late nineteenth and early twentieth century, including the Marxists, started off with the assumption that the general tendency of capitalist development would multiply an industrial, manual working class until it became the great majority of the population. All other classes would disappear and there would be a polarization between a large mass of toilers on the one hand and a very small number of bourgeois on the other. Well, if people still think this is the basis of the future of labor movements, they are clearly wrong. If you want to understand the present social structure and tendencies among the working population you don't simply take over the older analysis, even though you think in some sense or another it might still be true. You've got to see what is different. What has been happening since the early 1950s has been, in some ways, much more revolutionary than what happened in the early stages of industrialization to the extent that the penetration of capitalism is both more global, goes much more deep, and has transformed the preexisting social structure much more than it was capable of doing a hundred years ago. Consequently, to say that it is still capitalism—therefore, what was said a hundred years ago is still just as true—just won't do. A society like ours in which the peasantry *is,* in fact, disappearing is quite different from a society of a hundred years ago in which the peasantry was not disappearing but to a surprising extent maintaining itself while being integrated into capitalism. Now, all these things require historical perspective that is essentially the capacity to see how society changes and when things are different and when things are the same. This is one big reason, one practical reason, why one should be Marxist. That's the way to ask those types of questions.

Notes

1. Martin Jacques and Francis Mulhern, eds., *The Forward March of Labour Halted?* (London: New Left Books, 1981).
2. The Fabian Society is a British, non-Marxist socialist organization founded in 1883–84 that helped to organize the Labour party in 1906 and still has strong links to it.
3. The New Unionism (1888–93) was a militant movement of previously unorganized British workers; most of its leaders were socialists.

4. Hobsbawm is referring here to the land occupations and organizing drives carried out by southern Italian farmworkers during the late 1940s and to the light they cast upon the origins of the Communist movement.

5. Antonio Gramsci (1891–1937) was a Marxist theorist and activist. He helped to found the Italian Communist party.

6. The Mau-Mau uprisings were carried out during the 1950s by members of the Kikun tribe in central Kenya, who demanded land and political rights. Over the decade, approximately one hundred European settlers were killed. The British put down the "rebellion" at the cost of more than 13,000 African lives.

7. The Twentieth Congress of the Russian Communist Party took place in 1956. It was chiefly notable for Khrushchev's denunciation of Stalin.

8. Christopher Hill, a historian of seventeenth-century England, was master of Balliol College at Oxford University. Before 1956, when he left the Communist party, he had written one major work: *Economic Problems of the Church from Archbishop Whitgift to the Long Parliament* (Oxford: Clarendon, 1956); since then he has written nearly a dozen, including *Puritanism and Revolution* (London: Secker & Warburg, 1958); *The Century of Revolution 1603–1714* (Edinburgh: T. Nelson, 1961); *Society and Puritanism in Pre-Revolutionary England* (New York: Schocken, 1964); *The World Turned Upside Down* (New York: Viking, 1972); *Milton and the English Revolution* (New York: Viking, 1977).

9. Richard Tawney (1880–1962) was a Fabian socialist and scholar who wrote two classic works, *Religion and the Rise of Capitalism* (New York: Harcourt Brace, 1952) and *The Acquisitive Society* (New York: Harcourt Brace, 1948).

10. Sir Lewis Namier (1888–1960) was a historian of eighteenth-century Britain who held that the structure of politics during that century promoted the interests of the majority.

11. The Gould Report complained of Marxist "infiltration" of British universities.

12. Hans Karl Filbinger, of the Christian Democratic Union party, resigned in August 1978 as prime minister of Baden-Württemberg when it was revealed that, despite his repeated denials, he had issued death sentences as a martial law judge for the Nazis during World War II.

13. Eugene Genovese is a leading American Marxist historian who studies the American South. In *Roll, Jordan, Roll: The World the Slaves Made* (New York: Pantheon Books, 1974), he uses the concept of hegemony to explain the process in which slaves adapted their masters' "paternalist" ideology to resist slavery and to "make" their world.

14. The Dobb-Sweezy debate concerns the manner in which European capitalism emerged from feudalism. Maurice Dobb, an economist who taught at Cambridge University, stressed the internal crisis of feudalism as a mode of production. Paul Sweezy, an economist and editor of the American journal, *Monthly Review,* argued that the dynamic features of the market, and especially urban commercialism, dissolved feudal ties. The debate is contained in Rodney Hilton, ed., *The Transition from Feudalism to Capitalism* (London: New Left Books, 1976).

15. Rodney Hilton is one of a small number of Marxist historians to concentrate on

medieval England. His works include *The English Rising of 1381*, with H. Fagan (London: Lawrence & Wishart, 1950), *The Decline of Serfdom in Medieval England* (New York: St. Martins, 1969), *Bond Men Made Free* (London: Temple, Smith, 1973), and *Peasants, Knights and Heretics* (Cambridge: Cambridge University Press, 1976).

16. Joan Scott and Louise Tilley, *Women, Work and Family* (New York: Holt, Rinehart and Winston, 1978).

SELECT BIBLIOGRAPHY

Books (We do not list books edited by Professor Hobsbawm)
The Art of Capital, 1848–1875. London: Weidenfeld & Nicolson, 1975; New York: Scribner, 1975.
The Age of Revolution, 1789–1848. London: Weidenfeld & Nicolson, 1962; New York: New American Library, 1963.
Bandits. London: Weidenfeld & Nicolson, 1969; rev. ed., New York: Pantheon Books, 1981.
Captain Swing, coauthored with George Rudé. London: Lawrence & Wishart, 1969; New York: Norton, 1975.
Industry and Empire. New York: Pantheon Books, 1968.
The Italian Road to Socialism (Interview with Georgio Napolitano). New York: L. Hill, 1977.
Labouring Men. London: Weidenfeld & Nicolson, 1964.
Primitive Rebels. Manchester, Eng.: University Press, 1959; New York: Norton; 1965.
Revolutionaries. New York: Pantheon Books, 1973.
(Note: Professor Hobsbawm has also written extensively on jazz under the pseudonym Francis Newton.)

Articles (We do not list articles reprinted in *Revolutionaries* or *Labouring Men*)
"The British Communist Party." *Political Quarterly* 25 (1954):30–43.
"A Case of Neo-Feudalism: La Convención, Peru." *Journal of Latin American Studies* 1 (1969):31–56.
"Confronting Defeat: The German Communist Party." *New Left Review*, no. 61 (1970):83–92.
"The Contribution of History to Social Science." *International Social Science Journal* 33, no. 4 (1981):624–40.
"The Crisis of the Seventeenth Century, Part 1." *Past and Present*, no. 5 (1954):33–53.
"The Crisis of the Seventeenth Century, Part 2." *Past and Present*, no. 6 (1954):44–65.
"The Economics of the Gangster." *The Quarterly Review*, no. 604 (1955):243–56.
"Eric Hobsbawm Interviews Tony Benu." *Marxism Today* 24, no. 10 (1980):5–13.
"The Forward March of Labour Halted?" *Marxism Today* 22, no. 9 (1978):279–86.
"From Social History to the History of Society." *Daedalus*, 100 (1971):20–45.
"Gramsci and Political Theory." *Marxism Today* 21, no. 7 (1977):205–13.
"Guerillas in Latin America." *The Socialist Register 1970*, 51–61.

"The Historians' Group of the Communist Party." In *Rebels and Their Causes, Essays in Honour of A. J. Morton*, edited by Maurice Cornforth, 21–47. Atlantic Highlands, N.J.: Humanities, 1978.

"Karl Marx's Contribution to Historiography." *Diogenes*, no. 64 (1968):37–56.

"Labour History and Ideology." *Journal of Social History* 7 (1974):371–81.

"Looking Forward: History and the Future." *New Left Review*, no. 125 (1981):3–19.

"Man and Woman in Socialist Iconography." *History Workshop*, no. 6 (1978):121–38.

"Peasant Movements in Colombia." *International Journal of Economic and Social History* 8 (1976):166–86.

"Peasants and Politics." *Past and Present*, no. 62 (1974):120–52.

"The Political Theory of Auschwitz." *The Cambridge Journal* 5 (1952):455–67.

"Religion and the Rise of Socialism." *Marxist Perspectives* 1, no. 1 (1978):14–33.

"The Seventeenth Century in the Development of Capitalism." *Science and Society* 24, no. 2 (1960):97–112.

"The Social Function of the Past: Some Questions." *Past and Present*, no. 55 (1972): 3–17.

"Socialism and the Avant Garde in the Period of the Second International." *Le Mouvement Social*, no. 111 (1980):189–99.

"Some Reflections on 'The Break-Up of Britain.' " *New Left Review*, no. 105 (1977): 3–23.

"The Taming of Parliamentary Democracy in Britain." *The Modern Quarterly* 6 (1951):319–39.

"Twentieth Century British Politics." *Past and Present*, no. 11 (1957):100–108.

"Where Are British Historians Going?" *The Marxist Quarterly* 2, no. 1 (1955):14–26.

SHEILA ROWBOTHAM

AFTER E. PANKHURST

SHEILA ROWBOTHAM

SHEILA ROWBOTHAM'S HIS-
torical work is the product of political activism. Not surprisingly, much of
it first appeared in pamphlet form or in socialist and feminist newspapers. She
has also written a historical drama, *The Friends of Alice Wheeldon.* Her goal
has been to make history accessible to the larger public and to illuminate
through historical example the possibility of combining socialist and feminist
aspirations.

Rowbotham, who was born in 1943, studied at St. Hilda's College, Oxford,
in the early 1960s. At that time the New Left's political critique of Stalinism
was becoming influential while the moral fervor that had animated the Campaign for Nuclear Disarmament was beginning to wane. Rowbotham par-
tially identified with both of these somewhat divergent strands within the
British Left. She was active in the Labour Party Young Socialists, in the
Vietnam Solidarity Campaign, and in the Trotskyist International Socialists.
Above all, she was drawn to the emerging women's movement because it
linked personal and familial issues to more traditional political ones.

Her historical work reflects her concerns. In *Women, Resistance and Revolution* (1972), she examined the attitudes of past revolutionary and radical groups
to women's liberation. *Women's Consciousness, Man's World* (1973), which
immediately followed, broached similar issues but in a more personal manner.
Hidden from History (1973), which grew out of a pamphlet, traced women's
roles and positions in British history from the seventeenth to the twentieth
century. Two works published in 1977, *Socialism and the New Life: The Personal and Sexual Politics of Edward Carpenter and Havelock Ellis* (coauthored
with Jeffrey Weeks) and *A New World for Women: Stella Browne, Socialist
Feminist,* focused upon three extraordinary individuals' struggles to fuse the
diverse aspects of their quests for political, economic, and personal liberation.
Dutiful Daughters (1977), which she coedited with Jean McCrindle, is a collec-

tion of interviews with working women. Her most recent work, *Beyond the Fragments,* which was coauthored with Lynne Segal and Hilary Wainwright and attempts to apply lessons learned from the women's movement to the struggle for socialism, demonstrates Rowbotham's continuing commitment to building a socialist feminist movement in Britain.

———— ————

This interview was conducted in two sessions during the summer of 1981 by Dina Copelman, a graduate student at Princeton University.

————————

Q. Can you say something about your own background and education?

ROWBOTHAM   I was a very late child. My father was a self-made businessman. He was an engineering salesman who sold pit motors. He had been brought up on a farm and educated at night in Sheffield. My grandfather on my mother's side owned a gun workshop in Sheffield where my mother used to work in the office, but she'd never been formally educated. They both went out to India in the 1920s, where my father was a mining engineer, and were there during the nationalist period. They had quite different responses to that. My mother was quite sympathetic and respectful on the basis that she'd met some educated Indians who had talked to her a bit about Indian culture. My father was very imperialistic and hostile—very Tory and right wing. But he did have some rebellious aspects to his politics, too, because he was very anti-bureaucratic, anti-central state, and believed in places like Yorkshire basically ruling themselves. He believed in money as a means of freedom; he wasn't really a conformist. My mother was very personally anarchic and individualistic and disliked anybody laying down the law and telling anybody else what to do.

Nobody stressed education. They wished that I would be quiet, peaceful, and happy, and come to watch television instead of reading books and things. I shouldn't worry and take all of the cares of the world on my shoulders. Yet, I was always reading and writing things. Partly I was encouraged by a girl who was seven years older than me. She used to play with me a lot and encouraged me to write; then I just kept on writing. I decided to go to university because it was the only way to get away from home. I didn't want to live at home and do a secretarial course, which was the main thing that people from my background did, and then get married to a Leeds business-man. From the time I was about fourteen I just knew I wasn't going to do that.

I was quite stupid in the early days at school. I could only do very limited things—I was bad at math and so on. But I was good at English, history, and Scripture. I got my best O-level—that's our first level of exams—in Scripture. I really liked the Bible because it was a kind of ancient history as well as philosophy and theology, and I was interested in those aspects of it since we didn't get taught anything like philosophy.

I went to a Methodist boarding school. Not for educational reasons but because I had very bad catarrh and it was by the sea. But I had a very good history teacher there. It was a toss-up between studying English and history, but I chose history. I got into St. Hilda's, one of the women's colleges at Oxford. To even come from a middle-class, noneducated, northern background was still quite peculiar in the early 1960s. I had a northern accent and felt very out of place. I met a man from a working-class background who was also from the North, from Halifax, so that helped. We were familiar to one another. I felt very uncomfortable at things like sherry parties. The end of my first year I began to meet people who were involved in the socialist movement —this was the old New Left, what remained of it, and the CND [Committee for Nuclear Disarmament]. This was in 1962. I was nineteen when I first got involved in politics through a man I fell in love with. Before that I thought socialists just wanted power for themselves. I was a beatnik.

Q. Were you introduced to feminism as well at this time?

ROWBOTHAM   I was never very interested in the history of the suffrage movement as I knew it when I was a student in the early sixties. But I did get interested in Emma Goldman. I read a book about her, Richard Drinnon's *Rebel in Paradise,* and I instinctively liked the way she combined her politics, her anarchism, with struggle in personal and sexual relationships. I was interested in that because I experienced the double attitudes and confusion in the early sixties, among students, about sexuality. It was a turning point and people were no longer expected to remain virgins in quite the way that our mothers' generation was brought up to. But there was also a kind of ambiguity because, at the same time, people looked down on you if you were interested in sex. I liked Emma Goldman because she discussed those kinds of things, and I hadn't encountered that much in socialist politics. I was searching, I suppose, for a new kind of sexual morality. When I was in school I read Shaw's prefaces and had very iconoclastic views about how you shouldn't be a virgin.[1] But I found it was a bit difficult in practice because (a) I didn't know anything at all about contraception, I mean nothing at all, until I met those socialists when I was nineteen, and then (b) people's attitudes weren't quite so rational as mine were from reading Shaw. For example, my father was totally anti-sex because he had been absolutely notorious for going after women even after he was with my mother—in fact, they weren't married because he was married to someone else, which I learned after he died. He was typical of those men who, when it was his daughter, was terribly possessive. He was obsessed with the dangers of me getting off with somebody. Fortunately, he never thought most of the boys that I brought home were proper men. They didn't look like his ideal of Yorkshire men; he didn't think any of them would be capable of actually doing anything, so he never bothered much about me.

My mother was scornful of hypocrisy. She believed in freedom and passion. She was hazy about contraception and unenthusiastic about sex. I had very advanced theories without any practical experience until I was about eighteen and I was terrified of getting pregnant. But the first person I had a long relationship with knew a woman doctor whose mother had been a suffragette, and she gave diaphragms to girls who weren't married or even engaged. At that time it was such a relief to meet people who had frank and open attitudes to even heterosexual sex. Lesbianism hardly ever came up when I was at university. I don't remember any socialist discussion about sexuality. People talked about those things personally, and were against hypocrisy, but they didn't write about it. The only exception was an article about women by a socialist friend, Judith Okeley, about women in a student paper. At that time we weren't allowed to be members of the Oxford Union. She fought a campaign to get us in, and we also won the right to get married—at St. Hilda's!

Q. Were you taking the same courses as the men at Oxford?

ROWBOTHAM Yes, though there were some differences in the assumptions. The men, who wanted to get good degrees, would be willing to take risks and they were pushed to be original and daring. In the women's colleges I think they aimed to get as many good seconds as they could and not to risk too much. It was actually much harder for a woman than a man to get into Oxford —it was something like one woman to every seven men—but at the same time I don't think we did as well in final exams. We didn't do very badly and we didn't do very well.

There was a feeling that you had to prove yourself still. For instance, one woman student had very bad period pains, and this was really frowned on by the dons because she shouldn't expose this kind of weakness—it could be used against women. I connected this kind of severity, which I disliked, with feminism.

Q. What were university-educated women supposed to do with their futures?

ROWBOTHAM There was still an attitude around then that you were meant to get married to some bloke who was a university teacher. They didn't want you to be secretaries. It was a class thing: the principal of St. Hilda's asked me did I want to give orders or take orders? I decided that I wanted to teach liberal studies in a technical college because I had met some people who were beginning to do that. This was considered very strange. I went to the woman who was the jobs-advice person. She finally came up with a job for me at one of the most exclusive English girls' schools. I told her I was a socialist, but she couldn't see any contradiction.

Instead, I got a research thing in a college of advanced technology at Chelsea (this subsequently became a college of London University). My thesis was on an adult-education movement, University Extension, and working-class men. I wasn't very interested in middle-class women's education, though I was a middle-class woman myself. I thought, "Oh, these are very boring Leeds ladies." I did some liberal-studies teaching at Chelsea, with science students, and at an East London Further Education College. That was for day-release students, engineering apprentices, people who worked on the underground—the subway, as you say in America—and girls doing some kind of clerical work.

Q. What was the political atmosphere at the time, what was your milieu?

ROWBOTHAM   I didn't want to just float around in an intellectual setup. When I came to Hackney in 1964 I joined the Young Socialists in the Labour party. That was still quite large. We were reacting against the CND and that kind of moral protest in politics and very much stressed class issues. We were arguing against incomes policy[2] and supporting the seamen's strike against the Labour government. When Labour got in in 1964 our attitude was "perhaps they can be pushed to the Left." But first the seamen's strike, then the whole Vietnam War, and them having such shitty attitudes meant that we got more and more disillusioned with Labour and were drifting out of the Labour party. A whole generation of left wing people left the Labour party and are only now going back.

Q. How were you supporting yourself at this time?

ROWBOTHAM   Now it's such a major concern in my life. But at the time you could live on quite little money. I did part-time teaching, and after I was sacked from one place I taught in another and started to do some WEA [Workers' Education Association] teaching.[3] I also worked as a doctor's receptionist for six months in 1970. I was earning twelve pounds a week and two pounds was taken off for insurance and tax, and I had ten pounds a week. That was quite hard to live on in 1970, you just survived on it. But it wasn't too bad, and I even managed to go on holidays to other countries. Extraordinary. Things seem to have got harder and harder. It was easier then in Britain than in America to live off part-time work and a lot of us didn't really want careers and jobs.

From the mid-1960s the main thing we were doing then was organizing around Vietnam. We were influenced by the American New Left and by the Black movement in the States. In '68 there was all the upheaval in France and a period of very frantic politics. I got involved with a paper called *Black Dwarf,* a socialist paper. I also got involved in starting a thing called Agit-Prop with some other people. The idea was that we would try to bring together people on the Left who were doing various cultural things, posters, acting, and graphics. There was a lot going on in the student movement. This also involved people in the art schools. Quite a lot of creative people were coming into the Left—musicians, poets, designers, actors, filmmakers—and because of the influence of the May '68 events we emphasized the potential creativity of everyone. There was, for instance, a tenants' movement in London in the late 1960s and tenants got involved in designing their own posters. There was also a Ford strike and we did a play and posters for them. They did the designs.

The History Workshop started off as a quite small meeting in the late sixties and then it became more and more popular as it became a meeting ground for people not just doing work in universities, but wider than that, more political and more personal.[4] It was worker-students doing talks as well as people who studied particular subjects in universities. Right from the beginning it had that combination.

Q. How were women involved in all these activities?

ROWBOTHAM   I don't have any sense of a specific women's involvement until '68, when various things were beginning to happen, like the Ford sewing machinists going on strike in the summer of '68, which was quite important to women on the Left because it was legitimate in the eyes of the men. They could dismiss anything we said, but when it was Ford women, everybody had to support that. Also, the whole way that the press dealt with them—like petticoat pickets—brought out certain issues. Early in 1968, Lil Bilocca, the wife of a fisherman in Hull, got involved in a protest when a trawler sank because it was unsafe. The trawler owners were scornful of her and the men themselves were hostile to women campaigning, but she persisted.

We heard about what was going on in America, the beginnings of the women's movement and about women in the student movement in Germany attacking the authoritarian approach of the men to theory. Very violent sexual pictures of women began to appear in underground papers and that brought out into the open male attitudes that had been concealed in chivalry. We were forced to challenge the contempt by asserting a new way of being women.

A lot of women were coming into the student movement, more women than those of us a bit older who had been around on the Left before. The student movement in Britain, like in America, had quite informal meetings, but that actually made it more difficult for women to speak. For instance, when I'd been in the Young Socialists my friend Mary and I had been duly appointed chairman and vice-chairman—we'd been put on the committee. We were given a space, even though it was a slightly contained space. But in the student movement there was no space at all because only the people with very loud voices were able to get into it. Some women had small children and the men were always at meetings. Influenced by the American New Left, by France and Germany, we began to talk about all these things in our own lives and experience.

The first reaction we got was, "Oh, that's bourgeois feminism; working-class women aren't interested because class is the most important thing." Because I am a historian, I always try and see, when somebody says something, is that really true, has that always been the case? So I read Edith Thomas's *Women Incendiaries*. I found it in a secondhand shop in about 1969 —and that was about women in the commune. I became interested in the history of women in revolutionary movements. This was the source for *Women, Resistance and Revolution*. I was focusing on the history of women and socialism rather than the history of feminism. I found out, for instance, that in the early socialist movements—such as the Owenites—there had been much more emphasis on women's issues. I kept finding new things to read: Edith Thomas had written a book about women in 1848, and I found *La Voix des Femmes,* a socialist feminist newspaper. The fact that there had been people who called themselves socialist feminists in 1848 was a revelation to me.

It was important to find out that a lot of ways in which we were being put down were the same things that people had experienced before. I read Reich's *Sexual Revolution* and discovered Alexandra Kollontai.[5] From reading her, I found a new dimension of Russian history that people never talked about when talking of political revolution. It seemed that all I'd heard about was the points at which the revolution went wrong according to Trotsky or whoever, but it made much more sense to think in terms of the material problems of all those peasant women, of the attempts to change everyday life, of the difficulties of finding a new sexual morality.

Originally, I had thought of *Women, Resistance and Revolution* as part of a more general book that included *Women's Consciousness, Man's World.* I was trying to see the problems that women had faced in revolutionary movements and why certain conditions in capitalism made it rather different this time around and what potentialities that had for women. That was an enormous task, though typical of the times because it felt as though nobody had written anything, so you had to do everything all at once. It was exhilarating to be able to ask big questions. But it also wiped out a great deal by focusing on the high peaks of revolutionary consciousness still.

Q. In your early work you were looking at women in revolutions. Then you shifted the focus to struggle in day-to-day life. More recently you have attempted to develop an analysis of sexuality and personal life, and the political implications of that—still keeping socialism, feminism, and activism together. How do you see this development in your work?

ROWBOTHAM Well, *Hidden from History* came next. And that was a sort of realization—I think I'd sobered up a bit—that I had missed some quite important things by concentrating only on revolution, although I've never been as interested in everyday life as some British feminist historians—Anna Davin and Sally Alexander, for instance. I'm interested in consciousness, and consciousness going in some kind of political direction, but because of the influence of feminism, I don't see politics as being only about public power.

Dorothy and Edward Thompson were very critical of just talking about revolutionary situations. They said things such as, "What about British groups like the Independent Labour party[6] and organizations like the Women's Cooperative Guild?"[7] and I became more interested in thinking about these organizations, which have been terribly important because they've managed to involve large numbers of women for long periods of time. Something like the Women's Coop Guild was a way of organizing that could encompass areas of social life that were very important to working-class women. When it was raining it provided a place for children to play as well as a place for women to meet, and the hall was a kind of social center and actually helped people in everyday life, given that they were very pressed, not only emotionally but sometimes practically.

I have remained more interested in the interconnection between socialism and feminism and the labor movement and the organization of working-class women than in the feminist movement in isolation.

I have become more and more convinced that a wider reassessment of the socialist past is involved. I followed a few clues in the work I did on Stella Browne, a socialist feminist who campaigned for birth control and abortion in Britain between the wars and on Edward Carpenter, a socialist, who wrote on homosexuality and women's liberation in the late nineteenth and early twentieth centuries. Some of the interviews in the book I did with Jean McCrindle, *Dutiful Daughters,* also indicate interconnections between feminism and socialism that have been passed over. They suggest that the socialist movement was rather different from conceptions that came through the Labour party or the Communist party or the official suffrage records.

As historians we're used to looking at things that leave records, so often you start by looking at parties. But through the practice of the women's movement we've become aware that action and association can go on without formal organizations. Things get buried by the stronger weight of papers that come out of formal organizations, and so only certain memories get validated and perpetuated. For example, I think that in British history the relationship between anarchism and syndicalist politics, the Independent Labour party, socialist feminism, and pacificism in the period just before, during, and immediately after the First World War is something that is rarely discussed because the people involved weren't part of either the official suffragette hierarchy or other groups. These connections appear at first as incidental as they surface by finding particular people and then tracing and relating what they say. Jean and I found these connections in Glasgow by talking to people when we worked on *Dutiful Daughters.* They have been confirmed by people doing work in quite different places. Jill Liddington and Jill Norris's study of Lancashire, *One Hand Tied Behind Us* (Virago Books), shows a working-class suffrage movement closely linked to feminism and socialism.

I wrote a play, *Friends of Alice Wheeldon,* about a socialist feminist in Derby called Alice Wheeldon. She was a suffragette and in the Independent Labour party and her daughter Hetty Wheeldon, also a suffragette, joined the Socialist Labour party[8] and was engaged and then married to Arthur McManus.[9] McManus was active in the shop stewards' movement in Glasgow. He also had links to Connolly[10] and Irish nationalism and connections with the American Wobbly movement.[11] Alice Wheeldon would have remained in obscurity except for the accusation of a police spy that she was in a plot to assassinate Lloyd George. She was framed and imprisoned.

Q. Was this direction in your work a result of ways you were rethinking your politics?

ROWBOTHAM Rethinking is a continuous process. It has meant shifts in emphasis. I think there are recognizable sources, returns, approaches from different angles. But you rethink your own past differently at various times. When

I became a socialist in 1962 the main thing was the anti-nuclear movement and the Committee of 100, which stressed direct action.[12] Within the movement there were socialism, anarchism, and syndicalism, so I never really considered that Marxism was the summation of all socialist politics, though I decided that Marxism seemed to be the most developed way of understanding historical movements. But when the women's movement began it raised a lot of issues that could not be clearly fitted into Marxism. The first thing we tended to do was try to make feminism a sort of equivalent for Marxism. So that when we looked at housework we wanted to make it equivalent to work for wages— there was an enormous discussion of that in the women's movement. When I started to look at Stella Browne I was excited to find that there was someone who assumed that control over reproduction was as important as workers' control.[13]

But I think as time has gone by, instead of just making things fit, there's been a struggle to challenge more fundamentally both the notions of economics in capitalism and the emphasis on production in Marxist political economy. Similarly, the women's movement and the gay movement have helped to reveal the silence in Marxism about sexual needs and desires.

In the autumn of 1978 I began writing about what some of these historical questions meant in terms of modern politics. This was the origin of *Beyond the Fragments*, which I wrote with Lynne Segal and Hilary Wainwright. I believe our assumptions on the Left about how to organize need to be completely overhauled. This is daunting but inescapable. I think the failure in the socialist movement to take seriously democracy and the kind of personal democracy that has been a feature of the women's movement—noticing not just resolutions or words but behavior—has contributed to failure and disillusion. Such a new course is clearly vital for women but also I think vital in terms of trying to create a socialism that doesn't just reproduce the worst problems in capitalism.

In thinking about Edward Carpenter[14] and his socialist friends I was tracking a different sort of socialist consciousness. I was trying to enter a frame of mind that was pre-Leninist. Because of the strength in my political background of Leninism I thought it wasn't enough just to say I was opposed to certain aspects of Leninism, because that was conceding that this was the dominant tradition that you just had to then oppose from a feminist point of view. Instead, I wanted to find other sources of socialism, when people actually hadn't *assumed* things that resulted from the impact of the Russian Revolution. I was interested in searching around for a lost idiom of politics not as "the answer" but in order to recover perspective.

It is a trap to make some rigid, dogmatic alternative "good" tradition. That's one of the problems of anarchism: it opposes Leninist forms of organizing but in a rather frozen way so that there is an absolute principle of good anti-authoritarianism. Whereas the point is to see the kinds of problems that Leninism solved, or appeared to solve but actually solved in ways that created

new problems. This is how I understand Marxism. I believe it is a means of
scrutinizing and re-creating. For instance, now I think it is *crucial* for socialists to find new solutions to the relationship between decentralized organization and democracy and centralized coordination and planning. There are
many problems, too, in how both feminists and socialists approach the relation
between personal experience and political action.

Q. Can you say something about the evolution of the feminist movement in
Britain and your own political involvement?

ROWBOTHAM   There has been an erosion of memory even within a relatively
young movement. I think we need to express more theoretically understandings that developed in an ad hoc way out of practice. Otherwise, they could
be lost. For instance, in the early years there was a very strong socialist
influence in the women's movement—we would go on marches against Cam-
bodia and then later on in solidarity with Portugal after the revolution there.
People now have a very clear idea of the difference between the women's
movement and "the Left," but we didn't really at the time. Both then and now
I would regard myself as part of the Left. This does not mean I'm not a
feminist. We tried to involve trade union members in the movement—for
example, we demonstrated for equal pay against the Industrial Relations bill.[15]
All this is totally forgotten, people don't remember that this happened. I
mean, people who did it remember, but it's not really common knowledge.
Also a great deal of experimenting and struggle about organizing has not been
theorized in any complexity.

   In 1970, at the first feminist conference in Oxford, like traditional socialists
we formed a national coordinating committee. But that dissolved as there
were rows between Maoists and others. We then tried to re-create a structure
that would be more regionally based, with the local groups planning conferences; we had national women's liberation conferences and from 1973 national
Women and Socialism conferences.

   Some disagreements have festered rather than been worked through
theoretically. A small group raised the issues of sexuality and sexual choice
early on and quite a lot of those lesbians were socialist as well, so they were
advocating the right of women to decide their own sexuality but not as the
only political solution. The idea of separatism as a political solution became
stronger from about '76. I think an unresolved conflict emerged between
creating a movement of liberated women and a movement for the liberation
of all women. As time passed we did not find a way to transmit and communicate experience. By '77, it was clear also that there was a mixture of ages in
the movement. A lot of us who had started the movement were in our
mid-thirties by then, and we had become politically active in the 1960s. But
the women's movement in the 1970s attracted many young women. So it
suddenly did seem there was a difference—a very big difference—in what
people remembered. For example, when the women's liberation movement
began a lot of women involved had small children. Although now there's a

second wave having children, for a long time people didn't have kids. Now some women assume that children are very important to feminism, but other women don't at all—whereas when we started we took for granted that our feminism implied women should be able to have children and be able to do other things. In rather deep and complicated ways, feminists do not have the same assumptions about what kind of society we want to create.

By the late 1970s, women's liberation conferences became more and more acrimonious as people divided over whether they saw men as the main enemy or thought that there were conflicts with men but also a need to work with them, which is the socialist feminist attitude. The economic crisis overtook us. It intensified the polarization among women. Some of the socialist feminists got into more general socialist politics again, while some women became "purer" feminists. It remains an uneasy problem.

By 1980 I was terribly depressed about what was going on in the British women's movement. Now I feel less depressed because I think that a lot of women in the labor movement are beginning to be influenced by some of the basic ideas of women's liberation. The ideas have had quite an impact on the Labour party and in the trade union movement. Obviously, there's the danger that in an economic depression women's positions in trade unions and women's issues get pushed aside—equal pay has certainly been pushed aside since the late seventies. But on the other hand, things like abortion and the shorter working week have been taken up by the trade union movement, thus raising such issues as men spending more time with kids and taking more responsibility for housework. Because of the mounting pressure in working-class women's lives, particularly in the north, there really is some kind of change in consciousness—particularly among women who are in contact with the trade union movement. They would not identify with the women's liberation movement but some of the ideas are being taken over and reshaped. It has been a gradual process. It isn't something that has just sprung up. Lots of women from the movement have worked since the early 1970s in the trade union movement, raising questions such as abortion, domestic violence. But also battered women's centers, which reach working-class women outside the labor movement—these were all things that were gradually accepted by women's trade union congresses. But the change goes deeper than resolutions. They are the tip of the iceberg. It is evident in personal life among working-class men and women.

On the other hand, Thatcherite Toryism has mounted a devastating attack on the labor movement and radical attitudes. While people are more open to making contact with one another and important links are being made quickly, the disintegration, fragmentation, and isolation of the Left is even more apparent. Events have moved so rapidly since 1979 that we have lost our bearings.

Q. Do you feel that the feminist movement and feminist scholarship developed their own theories?

ROWBOTHAM   In the period 1973–75, *Red Rag* and *Spare Rib*[16] were very important in trying to express our ideas in fairly simple and clear ways. Those years were very exciting and creative ones for the emergence of socialist feminist ideas in the women's movement. The late 1970s were much harder. Theory developed in a much more intellectual and academic way than before. Some feminists were influenced by Althusser and felt that what he wrote was relevant, particularly his thinking about ideology.[17] I think that there was a kind of crisis in that people felt that you couldn't just change yourself by an act of will, and that some aspects of that kind of structuralist Marxism seemed to provide an alternative because it was very much against the influence of American radical feminism and the libertarian, anti-authoritarian Marxism of the late sixties. Like your New Left kind of Marxism. So I think that is why structuralism became popular, but it was curious because it denied many things that I thought were very important in feminism, such as always listening to people's experience and basing politics on that. The attitude was "experience isn't really valid."

Q.   In the book *People's History and Socialist Theory*, which is a collection of the papers from the 1979 History Workshop, there is an exchange between yourself and Sally Alexander and Barbara Taylor over the usefulness of the concept of patriarchy. Can you say something about that?

ROWBOTHAM   I felt that the concept of patriarchy was one that I really couldn't handle as a historian. I didn't feel that anyone particularly agreed with me in Britain, but I had to write down my disagreements. It seemed to me that the idea of patriarchy inevitably inclines toward separatist feminism. Barbara and Sally felt that I was abandoning a feminist theory, but what I was really trying to say was that a feminist theory about relationships between women and men needs to think in terms of mutual needs and relations, positive reasons for relating, as well as conflict. You need the two together. I'm not saying that you don't need to look at the conflict historically and understand the sources of that. But you also need to see why it is not a relation of total conflict, not a Hobbesian situation, otherwise it would deny the experiences of those of us who have either sexual, work, or political relationships with men. I think this is an unreal aspect of separatism. But I was not denying the conflict or the need for autonomous activity. I just believe we have to keep the openings for communication and links as well. Also, I think it is crucial to understand people in specific historical situations all the time, to see relationships in constant movement. The term "patriarchy" implies that the forms of male domination are unchanging.

Feminism, like socialism, is a political, historical movement with different strands in it, and there are some strands that I'm quite hostile to. I agree with what Linda Gordon wrote about it not being a moral absolute, which is how it's often used, because, particularly in Britain, we've had to fight so hard for feminism and we tend to take socialism and class politics for granted. So in Britain it has been very difficult to say that there are strands of feminism that have conservative implications. In Britain, people don't really discuss these tendencies as long-term historical processes. Ideas come up and people get terribly hot and bothered and don't quite know what to think. It's difficult to sit down and assess it all—perhaps you need an older movement to be able to deal with these issues because a young movement is so beleaguered.

Q. I would think that one thing that the British feminist movement has a clearer sense of is the role of the state because of the actual involvement on a large scale of the state in the provision of day-to-day services.

ROWBOTHAM   That's come up in different ways. In the mid-seventies we saw the state as the enemy. Groups like claimants' unions were really battling the state. The attitude was that the welfare state had been imposed as a kind of con trick on the working class. But then that wasn't adequate because the working class also struggled for it and that had to be acknowledged, the two attitudes somehow had to be merged. And people working in social work talked about the problems of women doing those kinds of jobs, the dilemmas they faced in the nature of their work. Then the welfare state began to be dismantled by the Labour party and then more dramatically by the Right. We found ourselves defending the most basic aspects of welfare that we had been busy criticizing. Books like Cynthia Cockburn's *The Local State* and one written by a group of socialists and socialist feminists called *In and Against the State* began to argue that you had to find ways of working within the state yet at the same time resisting it.[18]

From the mid-seventies people were busy fighting cuts and were preoccupied with unemployment. So now we're in a dilemma where we don't want more of the same, yet have to fight the cuts. The most developed approach has been in the area of health. Ideas from American self-help and anti-imperialist critiques of the ways in which health technologies and drugs have been imposed on people have been developed in the women's movement. This has been combined with a basic recognition of class needs and the inequalities in the National Health Service in various struggles over keeping certain hospitals open. But the question of health or even welfare is just one instance of how many of us who are socialist feminists have felt that we can no longer restrict ourselves to political activity around women's issues. Black women have been making the same point in relation to race.

Q. That raises an important point. Your work is impressive because you haven't just looked at Western women or the experience of women in Britain but have also considered Third World women and the divisions that result from imperialism and racialism.

ROWBOTHAM   I wrote about that very early on. As time went by I felt that it was important that women from those places or women who knew more about the situation should write about it. People began first to write about places like China; then Chile, Latin America; then African movements in places like Mozambique and Guinea Bissau; and because of the whole Irish situation, Ireland; then Iran. It tended to be because of political events—

women actually resisting in those countries, raising issues themselves. Western feminists need to be very careful. I remember when I was doing *Women, Resistance and Revolution,* a friend who influenced me a lot was Hermione Harris, an anthropologist.[19] She and other women anthropologists have stressed the dangers of imposing aspects of Western feminism on other countries. I finally decided to take what women in those movements were themselves protesting against as an indication of what was actually oppressive. But it is difficult because sometimes you decide there are things that are absolutely essential to feminism from our vantage point, such as issues relating to the nuclear family and the sharing of housework, but then all that doesn't make much sense in societies where it's possible for older women in a kinship network to be looking after the kids. Then some of our problems don't seem quite so acute. I think that the most crucial thing feminism, as I understand it, has been saying that is relevant both in Western capitalism and the Third World is that you need to change relationships between people in the very process of fighting for revolutionary change. I don't agree that nationalist movements have first to concentrate on economic changes and after that you change relationships. Nor do I agree with folding everything into imperialism —this denies sex and class relationships.

Q. How do you see the overall situation of the Left in Britain today?

ROWBOTHAM People are feeling extremely pressured from all sides and there's been a move back into more traditional forms of politics, either Labour party or trades councils, yet because of the influence of all of the struggles of the past years in the area of social life, there is a different approach to Left politics. There's an attempt to relate some of the things that have been said in the women's movement to make sure that the notion of democratic control includes social life and everyday life, how we live and act. People are coming together from completely different directions and discussing whether the forms of socialism that we've seen since Leninism are necessarily the only models.

When *Beyond the Fragments* came out, we got such a barrage of criticism it was a good thing there were three of us. It would have been terrible to have written it singly. Trotskyists attacked us because of the criticism of the Trotskyist tradition in politics. Some people in the women's movement criticized us on the grounds that feminism and socialism were about different types of things and necessarily had to be separate struggles. But I think that results from a difference in how you define socialism, whether you see socialism, as I do, as a transformation in relationships, stressing alienation and oppression, rather than just seeing it in terms of changes in ownership.

There was and continues to be more positive responses to *Beyond the Fragments.* The three of us—Hilary, Lynne, and myself—and Jean McCrindle, with whom I worked on *Dutiful Daughters,* and a Newcastle friend of Hilary's, Kenny Bell, who was active in a socialist housing network, contacted people and organized a preliminary meeting on some of the issues raised in the book. Already, local groups of socialist feminists, some socialist forums, branches of the Communist party and this tenants' group in Newcastle had discussed *Beyond the Fragments.* People said they were interested in pursuing the discussion, so each of us asked ten people and we had a planning meeting of forty to fifty people. We met a number of times, people from all over Britain, usually meeting somewhere in the North. Finally, in the autumn of 1980, we organized a conference at Leeds University. We wanted to have a big festival at first, going on for several days, sort of a camping thing with kids. But we had to scale that down, especially since the university was hostile to children and had no facilities that were suitable. There were a lot of problems with the conference, partly because nearly two thousand adults and children arrived—about half without registering. The final plenary was too loose—we'd left it open partly because we couldn't bear to think what was going to happen. We'd planned all the workshops very carefully with a lot of different groups involved—environmentalists, socialist scientists, shop stewards, feminists—but there was this almighty explosion at the plenary. Our idea had been that those of us from the women's movement would learn from other groups, like tenants, how they'd organized. But some groups of feminists were hostile to the organization of the conference and there was criticism as well from some gay people. There was also conflict over a resolution we were trying to write over Poland. The plenary really should have been better planned, to make sure that practical results actually happened.

Still, even amidst the confusion and hostility, a lot of people put down their names to be local organizers. But just setting up local groups, a long-standing British tradition, didn't seem to be what people really wanted. They were already going to a lot of meetings and wanted to feel that they were a part of something larger, so we have kept it going as a loose network through bulletins, and we communicate what is going on where we live. Also some of us helped organize a conference in London about alternative economic strategies—we did a meeting on democracy at the Labour party conference at Brighton in autumn of 1981.

All of this activity has been good because it's provided another focus for people who had joined organizations like the Labour party but felt a bit unhappy and wanted to know others like themselves in their local area. It's also been important for women who had become involved in local socialist politics but still wanted to feel that they had some connection with their past in the women's movement. It's a very loose form of organization, but fairly familiar to people who've been in the women's movement. For others it's strange because it feels as if there's nothing tangible and structured. They do not take into account the kind of personal democracy that has been a feature of the women's movement and is vital in order to create a socialism that doesn't reproduce the worst problems of capitalism. On the other hand, how this would be put into effect on a mass scale nobody knows. But in different contexts socialists are asking similar questions in Poland and Spain, for instance.

Q. Is it hard being caught between trying to reform Marxism on the one hand and at the same time trying to go beyond a separatist feminism?

ROWBOTHAM   I'm not sure that I would say "caught" because I've been a socialist feminist since I could even put the words together. I think it's gotten easier to be a feminist in the socialist movement and harder to be a socialist in the feminist movement. It used to be the other way around.

At first we were optimistic: we assumed that feminist consciousness would automatically lead to seeing connections with other people. Many feminists did see the connections, but it doesn't always happen. That was a pertinent criticism made of *Beyond the Fragments;* a woman said to me, "Well, it's alright saying that you can go to a rape crisis center and then you can see the connections between socialism and feminism, or capitalism and sexism, but it does depend very much on who's there to help you see them." It is not to deny the importance of a rape crisis center to say that consciousness does not change so simply. I think the socialist movement's long resistance to feminism is much to blame for the fact that some people just got pissed off and said, "Why the hell should we keep on struggling?" But even so, people change.

Q. Do you see your teaching and your writing as a way of helping people change? Is history a political resource?

ROWBOTHAM   I am interested in how history relates to people—that keeps it alive. I don't like it when people say, "This is all very well but what's the actual lesson?" but I do think about ideas historically. And also I'm just nosy about people in the past. I like to find out about them. I'm interested in this in terms of what their political consciousness was, but I do just have a very deep desire to understand how people in different times lived and felt. I want to know about the people, even ancient people. I yearn to know about these people.

I've always moved between the past and now, and I can never quite settle down in one or the other. I mean, when I'm doing something to do with now I hanker to be off in the past; but as soon as I get among the kind of people who are professional historians, I think I'm not really a proper historian.

My work has often been influenced by my teaching. *Hidden from History*, for instance, was written for WEA students who were housewives in the suburbs and didn't have much time to read. They needed something that could be read in short sections and had complained that *Women, Resistance and Revolution* was a bit remote, the chapters were too long. So I tried to write a book with very short chapters so that women doing housework, who had short bursts of time, could read it, as women read magazine articles. That way, perhaps they'd read something and then think about it while they were doing other things. I wrote that book for them, but it has also been quite popular with trade unionists, perhaps because with a different working pattern they also have short bursts of time.

Q. Can you say more about the other teaching experiences you've had and how you see the relationship between people doing history in universities and those who are writing and teaching history outside of the academic environment?

ROWBOTHAM One WEA course, which went on for years and years, was a history of socialism. We looked at China, America, and Europe as well as Britain from about 1973 to 1978. The students changed over the years but a few carried on. I learned a great deal from those classes; some of the things that came up in the course went into *Beyond the Fragments.* The first lot of us that got interested in women's history tended to work in the WEA and groups like that—Anna Davin, Sally Alexander, and Barbara Taylor, for instance. There was a very organic connection between our historical work and our political work. Ideas about women's history have developed from many group discussions.

Unfortunately the pay is very low, and recently the economic situation has forced some of us to stop working for the WEA because we cannot earn a living from it. I earn only just enough to live. On the other hand, I have been able to do work that interests me, and I have survived. Yet I am conscious that time and economic security are necessary in order to write history that goes deep. I feel I have written general surveys or sketches. I would like to go beyond these. Also, I enjoyed writing the play. You have to restrain your imagination as a historian. I would like to release fancy and dream by writing fiction.

Q. Have feminism and feminist history had an impact on history in general, how it's being written and taught?

ROWBOTHAM Women's history has gained a limited credibility among publishers and in universities. But its impact on history remains rather "ghettoized." For instance, there's a really good book called *A People and a Proletariat* about Welsh nationalism and the labor movement—it examines with great subtlety the relationship of classes and an oppressed nation.[20] If they had also talked about the sexual division of the Welsh people and the Welsh working class it would have added another dimension, made another connection. Their discussion of class and nation is implicitly relevant to feminism. But this is not drawn out in the way in which the studies of Welsh identity are conceived by those Welsh labor historians.

Sometimes it feels as though you have to keep on saying the same things over and over again. This is rather limiting. The most exciting development is an awakening interest among working-class women in women's history and the labor movement.

Q. What are you working on now?

ROWBOTHAM Auugh! I've been devastated by the economic crisis. I'm still reeling. I wrote *Beyond the Fragments* in one room when my son Will was between the age of eighteen months and two years. The need for space became absolutely desperate, a kind of obsession. It made me understand about crowded housing conditions in a totally different way. My room was quite a large room, but it was my workroom, and my bedroom, and it became the television room for the others in the house. I'm quite sociable and can put up with a lot of people around, but it just became impossible because there would be all the baby mess and I couldn't put that aside and get on with my work—I could never leave my work anywhere because it would be eaten by children. Well, we moved. I now have more space but life has increasingly become a scramble for money. The material basis of my existence is very shaky.

I am writing a general summary of ideas in the women's movement—it starts around 1969 and is about Britain, although other influences, particularly American, will also be discussed. I am looking not only at the books that have appeared, but at articles, local newsletters, and letters to *Spare Rib*. I hope it will interest people who are vaguely curious about the women's movement but haven't really read much as well as people who are very familiar with the movement but haven't ever seen it all written down. A lot will be very obvious, but at the same time it could be very illuminating to see that people have often said totally contradictory things. It should be useful to show that these differences have existed, to make them explicit. For instance, there have been divergent opinions over biology and technology. Because we are involved in a current movement, we keep quite contradictory things in our heads at the same time, live with them.

I'm going to be teaching in Amsterdam for a year as a visiting professor in the women's studies department. I'll be lecturing on themes in the history of feminism. I'll also be coordinating a WEA class in Hackney, London, with two other people, a development of some of the *Beyond the Fragments* things, trying to rethink socialist strategy in the areas of family, work and technology, and economics.

In Britain just now there is a strong sense of urgency. The effort to balance economic survival, intellectual and creative work, and political commitment does not get any easier. Nor does a straightforward future seem likely. I am sometimes unsure that I can develop the necessary fortitude and resilience. I've been a socialist for twenty years now. Time has passed quickly. I'm not sure that I/we have learned fast enough for the next twenty years.

Notes

1. George Bernard Shaw wrote prefaces to his plays that were as scintillating and opinionated, and often as lengthy, as the dramas themselves. A favorite subject was relations between the sexes.
2. Incomes policy is a policy of limiting wage increases, by law or otherwise, to the level the government thinks appropriate.
3. The Workers' Educational Association was founded in 1903 to provide university-

level courses for workers. It aimed to form an educational partnership between trade unions, universities, government educational bodies, and other working-class organizations, such as the cooperative movement. It is still active today, providing both trade union and general adult-education courses. In the 1960s and 1970s it employed many young historians and gave them the opportunity to teach and develop their work outside of the academic establishment and in a more political atmosphere.

4. The History Workshop grew out of Ruskin College, Oxford—a workers' college —in the mid-1960s and was devoted to having people write their own history. Through its conferences and pamphlets it spawned an interest in socialist public history throughout Britain. Since 1976 it has published a journal of the same name.

5. Alexandra Kollontai (1872–1952) was a Russian socialist and feminist active in the European and Russian socialist movement before World War I. After the revolution she was a leading Bolshevik, and, for a while, a supporter of movements to democratize the revolution. She held various posts in the early years and between 1924 and 1945 was the Soviet ambassador to Mexico, Norway, and Sweden. Kollontai wrote extensively on the need for women's liberation—the need for women to be freed from their domestic burdens and to have sexual freedom and control of their own bodies in order to be able to participate equally in political and social life.

6. The Independent Labour party, founded in 1893, was a non-revolutionary socialist party active in the trade union movement and in local community struggles. In its early years it was part of a general socialist movement and many of its members had been active in other socialist organizations, such as the Social Democratic Federation and the Socialist League. It wanted to elect Labour candidates to Parliament and, as part of the Labour Representation Committee, was one of the predecessors of the modern Labour party. Keir Hardie was one of its most well-known leaders.

7. The Women's Cooperative Guild is a working-class women's organization founded in 1883. Its primary role was as a part of the national consumers' cooperative movement, but its local branches served as community centers. They provided educational and cultural activities and brought women together. Affiliated with trade unions and the Labour party, it was an important institution building popular support for socialism.

8. Active mostly in Glasgow, the Socialist Labour party was a small syndicalist group founded in 1903. Inspired by the American Daniel De Leon and the IWW (see note 11) it emphasized "dual unionism," that is, the need for creating new, revolutionary unions to replace the established, reformist unions. In 1920 many of its members joined the Communist party.

9. Arthur McManus (1889–1927) was a Glasgow shop steward who helped men opposed to World War I escape to the United States. He was the first president of the British Communist party.

10. James Connolly (1868–1916) was an Irish socialist and Labour party leader. He helped to organize the Dublin Transport Workers before World War I. In 1916 he led the abortive Irish Revolution. He was executed by British troops.

11. American Wobbly Movement, also known as the Industrial Workers of the World (IWW), was a labor organization founded in 1905 that recruited unskilled, non-

white, and immigrant workers. In 1917 the United States government repressed it.

12. The Committee of 100, a militant offshoot of the Campaign for Nuclear Disarmament (CND) led by Bertrand Russell, advocated Ghandian "direct action" in the interests of Britain's unilateral disarmament.

13. Frances Worsley Stella Browne (1882–1936) was a socialist feminist active, around World War I, in campaigns for birth control and abortion. She argued for the right of women to control their own bodies and for the need to combine the quest for sexual liberation with other movements for social change. She joined, for a short time, the Communist party when it was first founded and, in 1936, was a founder of the Abortion Law Reform Association.

14. Edward Carpenter (1844–1929)—socialist, workers' educator, writer, sex reformer, and open homosexual—advocated the development of a simpler life-style and stressed the need to transform sexual and personal relationships in order to create a truly socialist society.

15. The Industrial Relations Act was passed in 1971 while the Heath government was in office. It created several new sorts of "unfair labor practices" and was strongly opposed by the Left. It was repealed in 1974.

16. *Spare Rib* is a feminist journal started in 1972 in reaction against the sexism of underground newspapers. It tries to bring feminist and countercultural ideas to a larger public by using some of the traditional means of women's magazines. Well produced, it combines fiction, poetry, and news and encourages reader participation as well as providing a forum for already established writers.

17. Louis Althusser, a French Communist and theoretician, emphasizes the importance of structures (such as the mode of production) in history. He denies the separate agency of ideology.

18. *In and Against the State: Discussion Notes for Socialists* (London: London-Edinburgh Weekend Return Group, 1979).

19. Hermione Harris is a socialist feminist anthropologist who serves on the editorial board of the journal *Race and Class.* She has written on black women in Britain and in Nicaragua.

20. David Smith, ed., *A People and a Proletariat* (London: Pluto Press, 1980).

SELECT BIBLIOGRAPHY

Books
Beyond the Fragments, coauthored with Lynne Segal and Hilary Wainwright. London: Merlin Press, 1980; Boston: Alyson Publications, 1981.
Dutiful Daughters: Women Talk About Their Lives, coauthored with Jean McCrindle. Austin: University of Texas Press, 1977.
Hidden from History. New York: Vintage Books, 1976 (c. 1973).
A New World for Women: Stella Browne, Socialist Feminist. London: Pluto Press, 1977.
Socialism and the New Life: The Personal and Sexual Politics of Edward Carpenter and Havelock Ellis, coauthored with Jeffrey Weeks. London: Pluto Press, 1977.

Woman's Consciousness, Man's World. Hammondsworth, Eng.: Penguin, 1973.
Women, Resistance and Revolution. New York: Vintage Books, 1974 (c. 1972).

Articles
"Against the Grain." *New Society,* August 10, 1978, 306–307.
"The Human Face of Socialism." *New Society,* December 24, 1981, 556–57.
"In Search of Carpenter." *History Workshop,* no. 3 (Spring 1977):121–33.
"More than Just Cogs in the Machine." *New Society,* September 11, 1980, 518–19.
"Mother, Child and the State." *New Society,* October 1, 1981, 24–25.
"Okay, So Where's the Glue?" *New Statesman,* August 29, 1980, 10–11.
Review of *Woman's Body, Woman's Right* by Linda Gordon. *History Workshop,* no. 7 (Spring 1979):195–200.
"Theory and Practice of Early American Feminism." *New Society,* February 26, 1981, 382–83.
"Travellers in a strange country: responses of working class students to the University Extension Movement—1873–1910." *History Workshop,* no. 12 (Autumn 1981): 63–95.
"The Trouble with Patriarchy." *New Statesman,* December 28, 1979. Reprinted in the Feminist Anthology Group, *No Turning Back: Writings from the Women's Liberation Movement, 1975–80,* 72–78. London: Women's Press, 1981; Raphael Samuel, ed., *People's History and Socialist Theory* (London: Routledge, Kegan & Paul, 1981).
"Women and Radical Politics in Britain, 1830–1914." *Radical History Review,* no. 19 (Winter 1978–79):149–59.
"Women's Liberation and the New Politics" and "The Beginnings of the Women's Liberation Movement." In *The Body Politic: Writings from the Women's Liberation Movement in Britain, 1969–1972,* edited by Micheline Wandor, 3–30, 91–102. London: Stage 1, 1972.

LINDA GORDON

AFTER K. MARION

LINDA GORDON

L INDA GORDON'S IS A
leading voice among contemporary feminist historians. Her path-breaking
work began to appear in the early 1970s, just as the new women's movement
came of age. Noting critically the invisibility of women in mainstream history
and uncovering forgotten women's protests, her articles were soon followed
by *Woman's Body, Woman's Right: A Social History of Birth Control in America*
(1976). This volume demonstrated new ways of thinking about women's
history, the history of sexuality, and the changing social relations of the sexes.
Gordon also coedited *America's Working Women* (1976), a collection of primary documents illustrating the changing nature of female labor over time
and its historical significance.

Gordon's work is perhaps most notable for integrating Marxism with feminism. Occasionally, other scholars in women's history have addressed similar
topics, but few have written with her commitment to class analysis and
dialectical method or with her understanding of political struggle in everyday
life. Similarly, it remains unusual for Marxist scholars studying class conflict
to display interest in the sophisticated gender analysis that permeates Gordon's work.

Her writings have appeared in scholarly journals as well as in *Radical
America*, a unique popular Left magazine of which she is an editor. Gordon
is presently at work on the history of family violence since 1880 and teaches
at the University of Massachusetts, Boston.

*This interview took place in June 1981. The interviewer was Carol Lasser, who
teaches American history and women's history at Oberlin College.*

Q. How did you come to history in general and to women's history in
particular? Women's history is such a politically powerful subject today, but

73

when you got your B.A. from Swarthmore, in 1961, there was very little political activism on the campus.

GORDON   My parents were leftists, and Jews, and immigrants, and rather poor. My relationship with my parents as I entered college was complicated. In one way I was doing what they wanted—seeking upward mobility and becoming an intellectual. In another way I was in reaction against their politics, which I can now characterize as simultaneously Stalinist and reformist, radical and cautious, finely balanced between principle and practicality. I didn't understand these things then. I was, unconsciously, wanting to become a middle-class liberal but feeling I could never quite make it. I was feeling the stresses of upward class mobility—at Swarthmore I learned that my clothing, manners, conversation, and self-confidence were inadequate. I have many students today who feel these complications about leaving their parents' class backgrounds, and I recognize myself.

Today I recognize that my own world view was largely formed by my parents'. I became a New Leftist, intensely angry at the Stalinist tradition. But at a deeper, emotional level my commitments stem from the high ethics, optimism, patience, and irreverence that characterized their generation of Eastern-European Jewish working-class radicals.

But back to Swarthmore. It was a wonderful education and I loved it. I was excited and happy there. I loved studying, although it took me a while to learn how to do it, and I was a poor student at first, being very poorly prepared for an elite school. Mostly I loved the intense intellectual and emotional talks with friends.

Now I am also somewhat critical of Swarthmore's education. To caricature it, to make a point, I felt they were trying to make me into a liberal, and they almost succeeded. Had it not been for the rise of the New Left, they would have succeeded.

Q.   How did you decide to go on to graduate study in history, and Russian history in particular, after leaving Swarthmore?

GORDON   It was an accident. It had to do with two wonderful professors at Swarthmore, Lawrence Lafore and, particularly, Paul Beik. Beik stirred up a lot of people's intellectual imaginations in those years. I took his Russian history course simply because it had a good reputation. He was a thrilling teacher, the best kind of teacher for a liberal arts college—someone who took his students very seriously and who took big ideas very seriously.

After Swarthmore I first tried a straight academic path. I went directly to graduate school at Yale. But I felt there was not enough critical thinking going on. We were trained to write monographs.

It's also true, although I didn't understand it at the time, that there was sexism. Yale had a very small graduate history class. In the early 1960s there were maybe ten to twenty students in my class. I was one of the very few women, if not the only woman. The sexism was present mainly in the way they left me alone. If I had been a man of equal ability I would have been groomed, encouraged by various professors, helped in the job-finding processes, the dissertation-completion processes; I was just left alone. They didn't put me down in any direct way; in fact, my own adviser was an exception, extremely generous toward me.

Q. How and when did you make the switch from Russian history to women's history and women's studies?

GORDON   Well, first I became very disillusioned with the extreme and vulgar politicization of the field of Russian history, particularly modern Russian history, and the dryness of graduate school. So I dropped out. But I could find no interesting work. I did clerical work for four years and then returned to graduate school and found a less politically difficult path by choosing a dissertation topic on the sixteenth century. In some ways, the research for it was disappointing. I could not get access to any archives in the Soviet Union then and, with my topic, about the Ukrainian cossacks, they probably would not allow a Westerner into any archives even today. [A book based on this dissertation was published by SUNY Press in 1983.] I lived in London for a year working on it, went to Warsaw and Cracow for research, and participated in the anti-war movement in Europe.

I got my first and only job teaching at the University of Massachusetts, Boston, amazingly easily, simply by writing and applying, without even an interview, since I was living in London, just on the basis of my dossier. (The job market was a bit different in 1968!) I returned to Boston for the job in September '68. Those were very activist years, and there was a very rich New Left in the area. I was immediately and very, very suddenly hit by the women's liberation movement. It was an instant transformation. The moment I heard a feminist, I knew everything she was saying was true. I had no resistance. It made my whole previous life more explicable and understandable to me. It was as if I had previously been seeing everything through a distorted glass.

I became part of a small group of women, most of them a bit younger than me, and most of them veterans of SDS (which I was not), who were beginning to discover sexism. We organized the women's liberation collective that later started Bread and Roses.[1] We were ten women who met for—not such a long time as these things go—every week for about two years. And it was, I think, the most important political group of my life.

I had previously worked with Friends of SNCC [Student Nonviolent Coordinating Committee], very uncomfortably, in Washington, D.C. I helped lobby congressmen to try to get people out of jail, keep people from being beaten up, raise money. This was during the famous COFO [Council of Federated Organizations] summer of 1964.[2] I certainly learned an enormous amount, but I wasn't comfortable. Probably the sexual contradictions made me uncomfortable. I was never able to develop close relations with Black women, and I learned very quickly that I didn't want to develop close relations with Black men because of sex, sexism, and sexist contradictions. I was personally isolated. In 1967, in the anti-war movement in Washington, D.C., I did mimeographing.

Anyway, by 1969 it seemed completely natural and logical that as a feminist and a historian just finishing a dissertation, I should do something about women. Also, I was ripe for a switch to American history. I had minored in it at Yale and was encouraged by John Morton Blum—to whom I feel grateful now. I had found the attempts at research in the Soviet Union frustrating, yet loved the process of archival work, the sense of discovery and revelation.

I wanted to be able to do this where I lived; it didn't seem easy for me to organize my life on the basis of trips every summer to distant places.

I was lucky in terms of timing, and in those years, in the early seventies, I worked very hard. When I look back on it I'm shocked at how hard I worked. Partly I was young and didn't have a child so I had a lot of energy, but also I was carried away by the political necessity of the historical research that I and a number of people were doing. I think I looked at every women's history book in the Schlesinger Library (Radcliffe College) and Widener Library (Harvard University). Schlesinger was often deserted then. This period produced my intense relationship with Widener, resentment, anger, and love—resentment because of how difficult it was for me to get access, anger because I felt that I had a *right* to those books, love of the library itself.

There was a very strong sense of collective process. For a number of years we had a kind of ever-changing, free-floating, women's history discussion group here in Boston. It included, in its first life, Mari Jo Buhle, Meredith Tax, Ellen DuBois, Maureen Greenwald, Priscilla Long, Lise Vogel, and myself. From time to time there were also Kathryn Sklar, Nancy Cott, Ros Baxandall. We learned a lot from each other, although it was an inefficient process, because we discovered all over again work that had been done in the 1910s and 1920s. We had no sense of historical continuity. I remember when I discovered Rolla Tryon's book on household manufacturing, and Alice Clark's,[3] and I thought, my God, this is incredible; these two women's history books had been available for half a century and ought to have been absolute staples for any historian—but they were brand-new to me. It's that kind of emotion that fueled my research for the birth control book. It was work I might now describe as rediscovering the obvious, but also discovering how possible and shameful the suppression of knowledge is.

Q.   Yet how obvious *was* that work? As I reread the conclusion to *Woman's Body, Woman's Right*, I was struck by how prescient you were in 1976, when the book was published, to see the way in which the gains made in the birth control movement were, in fact, so fragile. At that time few of us saw the possibility of the kind of onslaught against abortion that we see today. How did you come to your understanding?

GORDON   In part, perhaps, it is a question of method, a method I think I learned from some good training, a method in which there is, after all, a continuity between what I learned at Swarthmore and at Yale, between research about the cossacks and about the modern U.S. It involves, first, reading very closely and taking sources very seriously—that may seem obvious, but it is often not done. What was new, perhaps, in my first article on birth control, "Voluntary Motherhood," was that I listened to what those feminists of the 1870s were saying and tried to put myself in their place. History needs a subjective, imaginative, emulative process of communication. But, second, at the same time one can never and should never completely put oneself in the place of one's historical subjects. This is hindsight—I didn't understand this then—but now I have seen the mistake in other historical work: it is the attempt to ignore the time that has passed between oneself and one's subject, to ignore one's own historical place. Walter Benjamin says that one cannot recognize the past "as it really was," as Ranke asked, but only as its image flits by and becomes visible because it is recognizable in the terms of present concerns. (E. P. Thompson says this too, beautifully.) In other words, there has got to be a tension between historical empathy and rootedness in one's own present, a rigorous defense both against presentism and against the illusion that the historian remains outside history.

Another methodological aspect, very related, is the need to avoid reductionism. In the 1960s what there was of a modern women's history, indeed of much of the history of social movements and groups on the bottom of society, was often reductionist. You can see this, for example, in the put-downs of feminists as malcontents, neurotics, prudes, as if there were something embarrassing and shameful about being driven by personal unhappiness. Feminists were reduced to one or another of their faults, which were usually genuine faults. I felt the need to assume, as a starting place, that the face value of what they had said was what they meant; I did not wish to begin by seeking for hidden motives unless illogic and contradiction in the feminist ideas led me there. It was these nineteenth-century feminists, not my own prescience, that pointed out how contradictory and frightening the issue of reproductive rights for women was. It was their own perception of how radical what they were demanding was, how much it attacked the essence of the organization of society, that led me to think about the contemporary abortion struggle in that way.

Taking them seriously also confirmed my suspicion of determinism as a historical approach or as an interpretation of Marxism. In the determinist model, Marxists and liberals agree that what we have now is what we had to have, what was functional, and that the defeat of the utopian, liberatory vision of the feminists, socialists, and socialist feminists in the birth control movement was inevitable, whatever that means. On the contrary, looking at their political struggles from their point of view, it did not seem at all inevitable that they would be defeated, nor did it seem clear that their opponents had programs in any way superior or more functional. As always, functionalism and other determinisms can actually mask power relations and prevent class and gender analysis. Functional for whom?

Q. As you studied these people, then, did you have a sense of some of your Old Left background creeping in and influencing what you were doing?

GORDON   Very much. When I think about the Old Left influences I think of them in two ways: one strictly intellectual, and the other having to do with ethics.

To take the latter first, there's no question in my mind but that I am the creature of my father and my mother. In terms of their faults I tend toward a certain moralism that I have to be wary of. I need to feel, actually experience, the social usefulness of any intellectual work in order to operate at my highest energy level. This is so basic that I don't even notice it. It was very striking to me, for example, that my parents reacted to feminism with complete, wholehearted, unambiguous support. It never occurred to them that there was anything wrong with it. They responded with total generosity, even toward what I now think of as the excesses of feminist separatism. I think that it also showed in my upbringing as a girl—there were high expectations of me.

Intellectually the story is much more complicated. Like many women I was influenced by a lover, a Brazilian Marxist who was a graduate student at Yale and the first sophisticated Marxist I knew. He was a person with a European education who introduced me to the Frankfurt School and thus taught me a new kind of Marxism that, in turn, allowed me to reclaim my own parents and their community's heritage. I now think with shame of the ways in which I tried to distance myself from their radicalism. Today I think that the differences between me and them are very minor compared to the vast areas of agreement.

I think I should say more about Marxist as opposed to Old Left influences on me. I went through two separate periods of intense study of Marx. One was when I was in graduate school. Then there was a long hiatus in my intellectual life because, in 1963, I dropped out of school intending not to return, and in Washington, D.C., I did not hang out with intellectuals or Marxists. Then in the 1970s I went back again and studied Marx. It wasn't until then that I read *Capital*. I read it very carefully, in a group with three others, two of whom are still among my closest friends.

I think that, despite everything, Marxism remains the single most important intellectual influence on my work. Frankly, I cannot grasp how one can learn to think historically without reading Marx.

A friend of mine recently commented—it was partly a complaint—"Oh, there you go again, you always say, 'No, it's more complicated than that.' " I realized that this is true in my thinking, and that it comes from Marx, in two ways. (Marx didn't invent either of these things, of course.) First, there is the fundamental notion of difference between appearance and reality, and a rejection of empiricism. And then there is also a sense of dialectics and contradiction. I have been told by social theorists that when I call something historical a contradiction, or say something is dialectical, I'm using those terms in a nonrigorous, philosophically incorrect way. I'm quite prepared to admit that. Furthermore, I have serious doubts about the usefulness of dialectics as anything more than a metaphor. But I am committed to a method that sees reality as composed of conflicting needs, pressures, and forces, and all historical situations as driven by conflict. If that is not a method, then I think it's a philosophical stance that comes from Marxism.

Q. When you went back to reading Marx in the 1970s and, at the same time, immersed yourself in the feminist movement, did you feel any of the conflict that feminists have sometimes experienced in reconciling a commitment to Marxism with a commitment to feminism?

GORDON   It has been a big issue politically, but for me it has not been much of an issue intellectually. Intellectually I was never attracted to a dogmatic Marxism. It was never a problem for me to say about Marx, well, he was wrong about this, although I have known a lot of people for whom that seems to represent an enormous difficulty.

On the other hand I have also known and have been sympathetic to a feminist impulse of anger toward the entire Left tradition, including the entire Marxist intellectual tradition, from sexist boys in SDS to the Marxist political and intellectual leaders today who will neither read nor listen to feminist work.

Politically the conflicts can be difficult, for me especially, because I feel committed to making my work politically useful. My history work puts me in arguments with large sections of the feminist community as well as with large sections of the nonfeminist Left. I wish it weren't so. It's going to become a very big problem in the work I'm doing right now about violence against women and children.

I am doing a historical study of sexual and family violence since 1880, using Boston as a case study and using records from several social service agencies in Boston, particularly the Massachusetts Society for the Prevention of Cruelty to Children. I am looking at child abuse, child neglect, wife beating, incest, and other family or household sexual assault. I am interested in what the social service agencies were doing about these problems and how the clients themselves were trying to cope with violence. Virtually all studies of social work in the past have been based on records that show what the social workers wanted to do or wanted us to think they were doing; no one has looked at actual client records that provide evidence about what social workers actually were doing. In terms of finding out about the clients there is, of course, a serious bias in the records, which were written by the social workers. Yet frequently there is the possibility of compensating for that bias—we find letters from the clients themselves, accounts of what the clients were actually doing, stories too complicated and unexpected to be untrue.

The study of family violence has important political implications. It has never been studied historically at all. The mainstream psychologists and sociologists who study this problem treat it ahistorically, outside any context of economic development, family, child raising, gender, or sexual politics.

Most of this new family-violence scholarship, produced by the new wave of concern with the family, scrupulously avoids questions of power that might lead to general social critique. (With my friend Wini Breines, a sociologist, I have written a critical review essay on family-violence literature for *Signs,* Spring 1983.)

When radicals look at the problem, there are two, I'm sorry to say, rather vulgar political positions that are laid out by the Left, to the very minor extent that the Left has given a damn about this. What you might call the Marxist position was staked out by David Gil of Brandeis over ten years ago. He wrote the first recent book about child abuse, and basically he said capitalism causes child abuse.[4] People abuse their children because they have so much stress, poverty, and oppression. I have a lot of respect for David Gil's work, but that position, it seems to me, is wrong. Most poor people don't abuse their children. It is a reductionist position—a removal of subjectivity and conscious-ness, not to mention of the issue of gender in child abuse.

Then, there is the mainstream feminist position. It tends to ignore child abuse. It strikes me as remarkable that there is no feminist analysis of child abuse. Somehow, because it's between parents and children, it's as if a gender analysis were not necessary. On the contrary, a gender analysis is *always* necessary—nothing, no social relations are free of gender.

So the feminist analysis focuses on wife beating and essentially argues that sexism causes wife beating—that men beat up on women because they are men, because of patriarchy—that is a concept I avoid, since it is ahistorical. The problem is, methodologically, that most men, in fact, do not beat women. Many of them do, but it's still not a majority; most women do not get beaten. It's precisely these finer distinctions we can learn from. To say that men beat women because they are socialized to do so tells us nothing that is interesting, as far as I'm concerned. And to say that women get beaten because they are powerless is true, but also tells us nothing that is interesting.

I am arguing that women participate in violent relationships. Their partici-pation does not excuse sexism or deny that women are victimized, but it means that we have to talk about how women have struggled within the parameters of a sexist society.

It also means that, in relation to what might be called the school of external stresses, my disagreement is that explanations for family violence require a psychology. Certainly not sociology, not even Marxism can explain society without a psychology to theorize the emotional construction of human in-dividuals and how they act.

I think, inevitably, I am quite Freudian if for no other reason than because Freud's is the only major investigation to psychology that approaches the necessary complexity. Obviously, there has been excellent feminist critique of Freud, but I think that there is a structure of his understanding of the human personality that still stands. I am still operating, although perhaps more explic-itly now, on what I was doing in the birth control book—that is, trying above all else to avoid reductionism, always beginning by taking what people say at face value and assuming that people *do* have insight into their own motives. One just needs to listen very carefully.

What I'm reading in this study are the case records of social service agencies —usually the social workers' notes, often extending over a period of years and years and years of interviews and visits with various people. I'm overpowered by them as a source material. One of the things I like is that reading it is like reading a detective story, or writing one. People tell falsehoods all the time, out of a survival instinct. You have to lie to a social worker or you're really in trouble, so there's a lot of work trying to find clues that tell you when something is true and when it is not true. You find the inconsistencies in people's stories. I love the process. I am convinced that within that context of constant lying on everybody's behalf, if you listen to people talk, you find them enormously astute—about themselves and about each other.

For example, I just read a case yesterday, one of those cases of alleged incest —I don't know whether it really happened or not. The accusation was that a woman who had separated from her husband was having an incestuous relationship with her father. At one point, the social worker interviewed the woman's aunt, that is, her mother's sister, and this woman gave an astute and implicitly feminist analysis of what was going on. The aunt said, more or less, "Look, she had her choice between a husband who, if she slept with him, would beat her up and not support her, and her father who, if she slept with him, would take care of her, give her money, and assure security for her and her children." She was begging the social worker not to have too moralistic a judgment of this woman. This was a harsh view for me to accept, but I was moved and carried along by the understanding and wisdom people can have about themselves and others. I realize this may be running the risk of a certain kind of romanticism, but when I put it all together I'll become appropriately cynical!

Q. But even if we understand these working-class people in this way, can we do the same thing when we study social workers? Historians have imputed to them very different motives, from Richard Hofstadter's theories of their status anxiety to more recent work by William Leach and Christopher Lasch interpreting them in terms of the control they exerted over working people.[5]

GORDON I think the problem with many such interpretations is that they present history as one-dimensional, without conflict, or ignore many important kinds of conflict. First of all, many of these social workers were, individually, very kind people. Especially in the period when social work was just becoming professionalized, and especially in its bottom ranks, people became social workers with the most altruistic, humanitarian, even loving motives. Limited as they may have been by their own gender or class perspectives, they were trying to help and often rejecting the elite and competitive values of their own background.

Second, it is too easy for historians and sociologists to romanticize the working class and its hardships. The social workers had to go into their homes and see not only the effects of poverty but the other miseries that may have been in part the indirect effects of poverty but were nevertheless painful and ugly—brutality toward children, indifference toward children, depression and anxiety, self-destructive habits such as drinking. Child-welfare workers were faced with no-win choices about whether children could survive at all decently in such environments, or whether to yank them away from their parents to send them to God knows what, likely worse fates—and I find myself deeply, deeply sympathetic to the social workers' predicament.

So one problem with social-control explanations of social work is that they isolate the controlling function, separating it analytically as it cannot be separated in practice, from other "helping" aspects of the work. Not only were helping and controlling interconnected, but so were agitating for social welfare and social change also involved. Furthermore, social control is not in itself bad; its values arise from the class, or gender, or generational powers and interests of the people involved. A general condemnation of social control is ahistorical and treats the clients as objects. The child abuse and child neglect that abound in the case records of the social work agencies I study were not mere labels, applied to a deviance defined exclusively by the professionals; they were problems defined by the clients as well. Even radical social change —indeed, especially democratic social change—may require reducing the level of chaos, disorder, and violence among the oppressed, as many of these oppressed would be the first to insist. The issue is toward what values will this control be directed?

The worst problem with social-control interpretations is that they usually —not always—objectify the clients and depict them as passive. Lasch's social control is a one-dimensional imposition of domination with no resistance— something that never actually occurred. This social-control model is also, incidentally, bad Marxism. Marxist history has to deal with class struggle, not just domination (as, I might add, feminist history must deal with struggle between the sexes, not just male domination). In the case of social work we need to see both sides of the conflict between the poor and the social agencies. One reason someone like Lasch misses this is that he sees women and feminism exclusively on the side of the professionals. Most women were on the other side, they were the clients, and these people's needs and aspirations rendered many of them quite feminist in their eagerness for more power vis-à-vis the men in their lives and the men who controlled their destinies. In any social work situation, both sides are active and clever in their efforts to impose their interpretation of the problem and the solutions, and over time the clients often strongly influenced agency policy. In the majority of cases I read for this study the initial approach to the agencies came from the clients themselves. These clients were not only labeled by professionals; they felt that they were not living up to their *own* standards and aspirations for good child rearing and right family life. Granted, they did not often get what they asked for but instead got what the social workers wanted to, or could, give. There were conflicts, but also sometimes agreement between social workers and clients. Women of immigrant families, for example, seized enthusiastically upon the American norm that they perceived among social workers, that wives need not be beaten; they used the threat of social agencies in their own interest against their husbands and for their children.

Furthermore, the social workers had their own struggles with supervisors, with overall agency policy. The social workers' notes were read and evaluated by their supervisors; they had to write what their supervisors wanted to read, so social workers told lies of another sort. The claimed to have made visits they did not in fact make; they claimed to have done work that they ought to have done but hadn't had time to do or had not given a damn to do, perhaps because the case loads were too high. This is what I mean about a detective story. The social-control model contains truth about how the ruling class operates, but it's a model that has outlived its usefulness because it hasn't been pushed to a more complex understanding.

In addition, not only is the social-control model wrong because it isn't a class-struggle model, but the class-struggle model will also be inadequate because you also need a model of gender struggle. Clients are engaged in a struggle with social workers, but among clients, as well as among the social workers, there are sharp conflicts and struggles that are often built around gender. There is, as well, a generational struggle because kids are trying to escape from the authority of their parents.

Q. You mention here generational struggle, which alludes to another area of debate between Marxists and feminists: the question of how to conceptualize the construction of the family. On the one side is a Marxist-influenced school of thought that sees the family, particularly the working-class family, as a potential unit of resistance and something to be strengthened in opposition to capitalist domination. On the other side is a feminist analysis that sees the family as the locus of women's oppression. How do you negotiate between these two points of view?

GORDON   First, any further study of the family has to talk about conflict *within* the family if we are to learn anything new at all. The problem with most of the so-called New Social History, which studies the family on the basis of external objective indicators, is that it reifies and hypostatizes the unit, as if the family was a thing in itself instead of a set of complicated social relations among people. It's a very deep and binding set of social relations. Despite the fact that kinship may be less important in modern society than it has been, it is still one of the first things children learn about, and a very powerful force.

One of the reasons I became interested in family violence is that it gives me a way to look at conflict within the family. I don't mean to suggest that violence is the essence of family life, but I do think that conflict is part of the essence. My work right now interests me because of the unpredictable ways in which, within the same family, I find not only intense conflict—even betrayal of other family members—but, at the same time, loyalties and commitments, and the assumption that you have to take care of other family members. Similarly, in relation to the larger social relations of society, families in these case records behaved in complex ways. They did support people and give them some separateness from the pressures of the larger society. Yet they also trapped people into a greater vulnerability to those external pressures.

Studying the family, we also face a very complicated problem of nomenclature, especially confronting the New Right and pro-family Moral Majority. There's a split on the Left today on the family issue. There's a sentiment that I think of as social democratic and somewhat economistic saying, "Well, we're pro-family, too. Let's not let these right-wingers claim that they are the ones who stand for the family." And you find people saying, "Well, a family can be anything—two lesbians and a child is a family; three women living together is also a family." I don't agree. The word *family* does have an ideological meaning that cannot be defined away simply by the decision of leftists to make it mean something else. The family does *not* mean two lesbians and a child. Words can't be redefined according to our wishes. I admit that more and more people can use the word *family* as I do, in relation to the people that I live with, to refer to something that is not a formal, legal family; but I don't think that we can try to make politics at this time by redefining the word *family*. No concept of family can become a progressive rallying point except around very limited campaigns. It can remind us of needed defenses, but family loyalties will not help us to build the larger solidarities and visions needed for democratic social change.

I think that—and I felt this about the nineteenth-century feminists, too—to deny that there is a way in which we are anti-family is foolish, because people will know that to be the truth about us in any case. We *are* against the family in its traditional form that is *essentially* (not peripherally) oppressive to women and children, even as it is also often supportive and strengthening. We are rejecting certain very fundamental religious and even nonreligious but traditional presuppositions about the way in which people ought to live, love, have sex, reproduce, and pool labor.

Q. Can you offer some suggestions about how to use these insights in a historical way? How can we see the family in a changing historical context? How do we avoid constructing an ahistorical model in which the same family dynamics are played out in the same way across all time?

GORDON You're right, we can't establish an ahistorical notion of family; yet, on the other hand, I think that as feminists and historians we have to face the fact that male supremacy, while it has certainly changed historically, has had a remarkable tenacity across centuries of historical time. Similarly, kinship has a remarkable tenacity. We don't know of any human societies without something called the family. We need to be clear; the family is not changeless, but it is also not endlessly changing.

I hope my current material will enable me to talk in specifics and in the flesh, not in the abstract, about what families were and how people acted around family relations. I think that the records I'm using can show how people acted on what they felt were their obligations as well as how they acted in defiance of family structures. As one example, I'm finding sibling relationships extremely interesting. I'm struck by how intense these relationships were, particularly among girls, and by the degree to which, in the late nineteenth and early twentieth centuries, older siblings accepted responsibility over long periods of time, even for a lifetime, for other siblings. This has changed markedly; the important role married siblings played in each others' lives in the late–nineteenth-century Boston working class contrasts strikingly with what I think we could observe today, and particularly with the family of the New Right. The Moral Majority's family, and that of Left groups who define themselves as pro-family, is often an impoverished set of relations— instrumental and dishonest—that cannot offer a basis (psychological or other) for resistance to oppression.

Q. I was struck by the way in which your work suggests a tension between the demands of the women's movement and scholarship. In an article you wrote for *Marxist Perspectives* in the fall of 1978 you reflected that, in the early days, "the women's historians with whom I met and talked in Boston imagined ourselves simply propagandists for the women's liberation movement. I myself wrote some polemical pieces that I soon came to reject."[6] You go on to discuss some of the ways in which you have since reconceptualized your model of advocacy scholarship. What are your current thoughts about the tasks facing women historians today?

GORDON I think I should start by saying that, advocacy or nonadvocacy, it *is* the responsibility of historians to tell the truth. Some may think that a needless moralism, but there were strands of our Left tradition, not only Stalinist, that said that it was not always necessary to tell the truth, and that, at times, it was justifiable to stretch the truth, to present the truth in this way or that way or some other way according to what was useful to the tasks at hand. (The Right also has this tradition of falsifying history.) Nor is truth telling simple: in reporting truths there is a necessity to interpret them correctly to the best of one's ability. The facts reported without the correct interpretation may be destructive.

A good example of the wrong kind of advocacy scholarship—which I never did myself, but I supported and now reject—and I trust they won't take this too harshly—is the famous piece by Barbara Ehrenreich and Deirdre English, *Witches, Midwives and Nurses.*[7] Feminists liked witches, whom they saw as cryptofeminist, powerful women trying to help other women. But it isn't true; it is too simple and distorted, and it is not good for people to be taught that. Unfortunately, one of the painful things I now see is that a good advocacy scholarship—or, as I would prefer to call it, a committed scholarship— often means criticizing assumptions that are widespread on the Left.

I once believed that there could be a perfect harmony between activists and scholars: scholars could see the needs of activists for more understanding and fill them. Now I see, and it's saddening, that, to some extent, there is an inevitable tension between activists and scholars. Unfortunately, good scholarship is very time consuming—and that doesn't allow much time for other things. Worse, it is hard, economically and emotionally, to do serious scholarship outside the universities, and inside them the competitiveness and pressure for quantity of production militate against anything but narrow concentration on research and writing. It is much worse for women, who experience internal and external desires and pressure toward devoting time and energy to other activities, family, friendship, children. . . .

Another problem is anti-intellectualism in the American Left, both feminist and nonfeminist. Feminists are not worse about this than any other leftists. Sometimes there is a reason for it, a justifiable criticism of most Left scholars in all fields: people are not making many serious attempts to popularize their work. They fail to do so for a number of reasons. One is job pressures; another is that they are afraid they won't do a good job or that they don't know how to write for a popular audience; and a third is that we all spend so much of our time so exclusively within a community of people in our fields that we don't even notice we are not talking a language other people can understand.

I think it would be good for us if every Left scholar could participate in some kind of outreach or popular writing project. I think it is something one can do without too much time, and I feel that we *do* have an obligation to try to talk to people beyond our fields. I don't think that means sacrificing serious research and hard, critical scholarship, if that's what one likes to do, as I do.

It would be useful if progressive scholars felt an obligation to confront questions that are important politically. I often read articles, papers, and dissertations by people who have feminist and other Left views, and it's hard for me to understand why they chose the topic they did. It seems to me that it is almost always possible to find a topic that will satisfy the academic canons of good scholarship and is also useful to the world, that has got some breadth, that looks at the kinds of questions it is important to look at.

Q. You seem to demonstrate the ability of academic historians to participate in outreach efforts through your ongoing involvement with the publication *Radical America,* a magazine that has a unique position as a nonacademic Left vehicle. Can you explain more about the concrete meaning of the publication and your involvement in it?

GORDON *Radical America* is one of the pleasures of my life. I feel that I get much more than I give to it, first, because it's my chance to participate in a collective that is committed to more popular kinds of work; and second, because, particularly in the earlier years of my involvement, I learned a lot about the alternative currents within Marxism that had been hidden from me —council communism, certain kinds of workerist movements, and other democratic and libertarian tendencies of socialism. A great deal of this political richness in *Radical America* was attributable to its founder, Paul Buhle, although I hardly knew him since he left town very shortly after I joined *RA*. But his influence was there, both in the themes he had staked out and in the remarkable group of people he had drawn in. I joined *Radical America* about 1971. It is an unusual group; it made the transition from an all-male to a sexually equal group. When I joined, another woman, Margery Davies, and I were the token women. At one point, there was a very sharp struggle that essentially involved a purge; we gathered our nerve and said that it was either him or us. I'm a nonconfrontational kind of person. I don't usually do that sort of thing. I was amazed that we were able to do it and at the degree of support from other people in the group—and all the others were men. When it came time to take sides, the other editors saw that the future of the magazine was with us, not with the man who dominated it at that time. We then quickly moved to a requirement of fifty percent women editors. Most of the men on *Radical America* take feminism seriously.

It's a hard struggle keeping *Radical America* alive. We're probably more financially stable than most other Left journals, but that is because we have a very old-fashioned way of proceeding: to maintain low overhead, we do everything ourselves, with virtually no staff. One of the good things about the group is that we have a flexible division of labor in which we don't expect everyone to do the same amount of work; we just accept that some people have more time than others.

People are generous with other people in the *Radical America* group. It's a group that no one ever leaves unless they move away. It's also nice to have a concrete product come out of a political discussion. Slowly and unevenly, *Radical America* is getting better. I am aware of its limitations and our failures; but I do think that in this particular period, merely sustaining it is a service and a victory.

Q. *Radical America*, then, seems a unique way to integrate scholarship and outreach; but is it so easy? I remember hearing you comment, at a forum in 1976 sponsored by the Schlesinger Library, that one could take questions from the movement and answers from the scholarship. Do you still hold up this model?

GORDON Well, that is a bit too simple; sometimes the movement isn't asking the right questions, but I would still stand by that if you interpret it loosely. I don't think that means that everybody has to rush out and write about the New Right or abortion struggles, but I do think that one can at least ask about every piece of work, "In what way could this possibly be useful to somebody?"

Q. Is the question of the significance and utility of historical work one that women's historians face in a particular way, differently from people trying to do work in Black history or labor history? Or are those situations basically similar?

GORDON The situations with Black history and labor history are different because of the degree of activity and militance in the movements, but I don't think women's history is fundamentally different in terms of the choice of questions. Obviously there are differences in the sources; they are much harder to find for women—particularly in the increasingly important area of lesbian and gay history. At the most recent Berkshire women's history conference, it was clear that there is real energy now in lesbian and gay history, as there was in women's history ten years ago, and that brings both strength and weakness. The strength is that the people doing it feel that they have an audience; they are in a relationship with a constituency that needs what they have to say. The disadvantage is the pressure from that audience, the pressure to tell them certain things, to tell them quickly, and not necessarily to be as critical or as analytical as one needs to be.

In labor history today there is a different situation: there is no longer any coherent, active constituency to which one has a relationship. As a result, scholars work mostly alone and are only sometimes, occasionally, able to grasp the interests of, or attend to the needs of, activists concerned with working-class struggles. Furthermore, labor history is often lacking in a critical, political edge.

Q. You seem to be suggesting a creative tension between professionalism and political commitment for academics.

GORDON   Yes, but there is a big difference between women and men scholars. Women academics are today a second wave; there was a professional women's-studies movement in the 1910s and 1920s. Much good scholarship about women was produced then, but most of it was buried and delegitimized soon after. Now we begin again. It is important that we have the opportunity; but it is still incomparably more difficult for women than for men to be professionals. For myself, I don't usually talk about how difficult it is; I only feel safe having this discussion with friends who already know it. I tend to put my head down and plunge ahead, but then I get very grouchy about how hard it all is.

Think about what it's like to operate at the same time in a university and in a family as a woman and mother. Furthermore, one of the characteristics of professional, especially academic, work is its lack of boundaries. There are always piles of things on your desk you are trying to get to. If you are ambitious, either for recognition or to produce or both, and they usually go together, you are competing with men who almost never—even the most anti-sexist of them—carry the domestic or other personal-life burden of work that women have.

In a way, we are middle-class women discovering what so many working-class women have had for decades: the double day.

Unfortunately this is one of those problems that has no solution, so far as I can see, short of the revolutionary. Getting men to help isn't enough. Only a thorough-going melt-down of the sexual division of labor, of gender, only a society in which everyone worked less, and, above all, a society in which people worked *differently* with nonhierarchical and unalienated organization, would answer this problem. In the early twentieth century, women who wanted to be professionals did not usually marry; mainly they were rejecting motherhood, which was inseparable from marriage at that time. It was a solution that had a fit with the more elite status of women professionals at that time—their actual position and sense of themselves as part of the privileged and talented minority. The spread, democratization, of higher education since World War II has changed that and women have been wanting to have it all. That wanting is one of the most hopeful things, but it leads to a lot of high-stress, exhausting, nerve-wracking schedules.

Looking back on it, for example, I might have liked to have had a number of years without working or working part-time when my child was a baby. I couldn't afford this, and being in that situation perhaps gives me a more working-class perspective on domestic work—I see the chance to stay home and not work for money as a luxury, not an oppression, but, of course, when I stay home I'm still an active scholar. (My job provides *no* maternity leave.) The ability to be a mother and a successful professional very often depends on women having plenty of money. Just being a woman college professor is hard, let alone the domestic work. At U. Mass.–Boston, we have a socialist faculty group, including many other women and mothers, and it is supportive; but I still notice that it takes more energy for women to operate within it. It definitely takes much more energy for women to teach in the university. Women work harder at being good teachers, and students demand much more of women, particularly women students. And the energy it takes constantly to wear a mask, as I think women must, is substantial.

What is the mask? At the university I have my guard up at all times. Realistically, I am in a secure position—I have had tenure for quite a while, I dress the way I want to, and I have grown accustomed to exclusion from power. But I can never be exactly who I am in relation to other people in the university. Many colleagues see only a caricature of me—someone doing women's history, which is not really history at all but a kind of complaint, and a Marxist, often known by the code word "dogmatic." Some members of the U. Mass. faculty are afraid of me, believing that I would kill men and destroy the university. Others simply cannot hear what I say because of what they expect I am going to say. It's also particularly a women's problem. One of the privileges of men is being more themselves in public spaces, of relaxing, of feeling that they are going to receive a fair estimate of who they are. Women don't have that privilege, so women are much more emotionally exhausted at the end of a day of work at the university than men are.

This exhaustion also has a lot to do with the highly charged relationship between a feminist and her students. I feel my women students particularly are scrutinizing every gesture, that the things I say are extremely important to them—which doesn't mean that they always agree; sometimes they are in violent rebellion and defiance.

To some extent, the stress of being in the university would have been much less if I myself had grown up with more women as models to make me more relaxed about what it is to be an academic woman. In all of college and graduate school, I had only one woman instructor, my Russian teacher, a wonderful person, Olga Abramovna Lang, a former Bolshevik. I feel the absence of women teachers has marked me permanently. One of the things I would hope is that the younger generation would find it possible to be more relaxed about the variety of ways in which to be a woman, that they would not have to feel so masked.

Q. Do you think that part of this unmasking may occur because women will have other women to work with in academic settings? That women will provide support for each other, and work together, thus helping to create a new, more collective style of work?

GORDON Well, it's true that women work together better than men; while it's not universal it's an important fact with historical implications. But like many such facts it's easily exaggerated and romanticized.

Yet one has to understand that the pressures toward working alone, keeping one's sources close to one's chest, and being very individualistic were not invented by us. They come from a system we're embedded in; on the whole we do pretty well. Collective projects are really hard, but I'd like to do more than I've done. I have found that any time I have written something collectively, it took much longer, was harder work, and the final product was better.

I also think that an ability to work together well involves an ability to deal with conflict, which does not mean having as a goal the absence of conflict. I think women are fearful of overt conflict and that this has held women's history back. Women are more or less instructed not to speak in sharp disagreement with one another, and that is too bad.

Q. Certainly there has been overt conflict in one important area of women's history; I'm referring to the debate in *Feminist Studies* in the spring of 1980 in which we saw an argument between two schools of women's history. On the one side were the advocates of women's political history, who saw women's culture as at times apolitical; and on the other side were historians of women's culture, who criticized the ways in which a rejection of women's culture meant an acceptance of male definitions of women. What was your reaction to this debate?[8]

GORDON To be honest, I thought the symposium was superficial and unenlightening, that it was organized around a false issue and did not reflect the existence of two real sides of disagreement. I don't think the political historians have neglected cultural issues to the same degree that many social and cultural historians have avoided confronting political issues. For example, nothing in Ellen DuBois's work on suffrage implies the unimportance of women's community and culture; while historical descriptions of the family, and of women's networks, have, I think, been misleading in their failure to remind the reader of the societal distribution of power. But these differences in emphasis don't compare, as a real problem, to the increasing depoliticization of women's history on a larger scale, to the damage done in a recessionary economy by pressures to produce narrow, cautious, blindered monographs.

With just a bit of daring, I think women's historians can easily show the fit between the nurturing, sexualized, and intense "female worlds of love and ritual" we have created and our exclusion from power.

I'm also, however, interested in the other side of the equation; we cannot talk only about the world that men made and the way in which it victimizes women. That is talking only of social control without seeing the struggle. I think there is a tendency in cultural analysis to leave out struggle, to leave out complexity, to leave out conflict, and, particularly, to minimize differences among women, conflicts like generational conflicts between mothers and daughters, for example. In my study of family violence, I find women fought with each other, physically, violently. I also think the "female world" model, if too simply employed, exaggerates not only the autonomy of women's culture but also the nurturant quality of women's relationships.

Q. Didn't *Radical America* publish something on quilts as an example of women's culture at one point?

GORDON   We published Patricia Mainardi's article on quilts[9]; she is an art historian. But, you know, ironically, many people who remember the lovely quilt pictures don't remember, perhaps they never really *heard*, what the article actually said, a blocking out of what they didn't expect to hear. She wrote that the quilts were not in fact collective projects, that although women helped each other, they cared a lot about their individual authorship and getting credit for their own designs, and *signed* their quilts. They were competitive about their work. I remember when we discussed publishing this article some *RA* editors didn't like it because it was politically incorrect.

On another level, I think all the new social history has a tendency to be too apolitical, if by "politics" we mean the relations of power. I don't mean you have to study the presidency or the state or the government, indeed a redefinition of how and where power is manipulated is necessary, but I do think you have to look at who holds power and in what ways other people are trying to get some of it.

Some aspects of the study of women's culture have pushed us ahead a lot. Carroll Smith-Rosenberg's article, "The Female World of Love and Ritual," when it first came out in 1975 made people pay attention, in a nonreductionist way, to what women were saying about how they felt about each other, how important they were to each other.[10]

Yet, I think we still have a lot to learn about the mediations by which groups of people, including subordinate groups, create what you might call a culture, something that's deeper than style, but not the same as a fundamental power structure. Perhaps to do this we would look to ethnography and anthropology. Anthropologists have probably contributed more than any other discipline to women's history recently, both on a theoretical level and on a much more nitty-gritty level. I'm thinking here particularly of what was, for me, the high point of the last Berkshire conference. It was a paper by the Buffalo Women's History Project on the history of the Buffalo lesbian community. It was wonderful ethnography, it allowed one to feel and to have insight into the culture of a historically changing group of lesbians and their bars. I think we should do more of this, but, unfortunately, since Carroll Smith-Rosenberg's wonderful article, much that has been written about women's culture, particularly in the more popular feminist press, is abstract, rhetorical, polemical, or without critical analysis. It celebrates sisterhood and cooking and crafts and quilts, but it filters out a great deal of what I think is important about how people actually relate to each other.

I think that we need more research about what seems to many people to be old-fashioned: nineteenth-century feminism and related movements. It's become unfashionable to do research about feminism itself, about social movements, and I think this was one of the things that made Ellen DuBois overstate her position in the *Feminist Studies* debate. She's working very much alone.

There is a lack of clarity about our continuity from the past. Left wing feminists have rejected much of what they like to call "bourgeois feminism" or "liberal feminism."[11] This, I think, has weakened the contemporary feminist movement. I also think it has led some liberal feminists to the delusion that what they are after can be encompassed in a reform program, while, in fact, the bourgeois feminism of the nineteenth century was extremely radical, more radical than people have been willing to admit.

What Marxists have seen as peripheral or superstructural—the gender order of society—is actually fundamental to the entire social, economic, and political order. When you start to talk about altering traditional gender relations, you are getting at part of the material base. Gender is not cultural as opposed to material. It is part of the fundamental economic and social organization of society, and change will produce enormous resistance and backlash. That's why feminism itself needs to be studied—feminist politics, feminist strategies, feminist constituencies, feminist theory.

After I finished the birth control book, I thought at first that I would work on the history of feminist political and social theory, which has hardly been touched by historians. I still experience my giving this up as a failure influenced by my own much greater comfort with social history. I like anecdotes, events, the detail and inexactitude of the odd and unpredictable way things actually happen. I know how to find and read social-history kinds of sources; I know how to exploit them and draw out their meanings, and how to draw conclusions. In the back of my mind I still cherish the idea of returning to a history of feminist thought someday.

Q. Yet, isn't it a particularly difficult time to try to do historical work on feminist theory? The women's movement is in flux. There is no coherent theoretical synthesis at present, and we seem to be in the midst of a period of enormous change in social and economic conditions.

GORDON I think that's right, but I'm not sure when it would be easier. That's not to say that work in the so-called New Social History is not important. It has led to many surprises that can usefully be explored. I think, however, that one should first decide what's important to write about, and then look for the sources, as opposed to happening upon a source and then saying, "Oh, I'll do this." This latter way may be easier, but it doesn't always lead to the most important work.

You may have to reject three or four topics because they are not possible, but then you find one topic that is important *and* possible. People tend to fall into a graduate school pattern in which you first find the source and then you choose the topic because you see that it can be done. Sometimes this results in very good work; particularly in women's history where there is so much undone—you don't have to search very hard for an important topic no one has written about.

My recent experience with computer work, which I have done on the family-violence research, underscores this problem. The main effect of this experience has been to deepen my critique of quantification. Methods are like sources: if you're not careful, you start to design your research to let you exploit a method, rather than to force the method to serve your intellectual purposes and questions.

Q. If these are the tasks before us in terms of writing history, could you perhaps reflect upon some of the challenges we face because of the current political climate?

GORDON First, I would say that I think it's possible right now to get too nervous about the costs of being politically outspoken. The number of political firings is slowly mounting, although we are still far from the academic purges of the McCarthy era. But it has seemed to me that academics associated with the Left who have been quiet about their political commitments have been as vulnerable as those who are activists or publicly outspoken in their writing. Some colleagues of mine think that outspokenness can be a strength, creating a real or imagined connection with a constituency that leads universities to hesitate in firing otherwise competent scholars.

There is greater danger for feminists, for women's historians, or for women in general, and I think that nonfeminist Left historians are partly responsible. A few Marxists or other critical historians have secured prestigious positions, as feminists by and large have not, but these established historians have not generally (and there are some fine exceptions) viewed feminists as part of the community of radical scholars that must be defended and promoted. Just as many radicals do not understand that feminism is central in the modern Left, so many radical historians do not know that women's historians today produce some of the most energetic and creative new work. Most nonfeminist historians (and again there are exceptions) do not read feminist scholarship. (It is, of course, possible that much of women's history is widely read by other historians and knowledgeably disrespected, but I doubt it.) . . . Still, even for women and feminists I am not convinced that quiet and caution are wise or even practical choices. You're just as likely to lose your job without having said or written anything useful.

Q. So the moral of this is, at least say something useful?

GORDON Well, it's small comfort, since I think we're in for a hard time. Teaching in a state university now will be increasingly difficult, with budget cut-backs and new pressures on students. They will have particular effects on women, forcing many of them to reduce their aspirations.

Q. Then you think we may lose many of the gains made by the women's movement in the last twelve years?

GORDON Oh, we're certainly going to lose some gains, there's no question about that. Yet I do cling to the conviction that certain changes in women's consciousness are now irrevocable. The younger women I meet simply do not think as I did when I was their age. They conceive of themselves as having certain options not necessarily based on class privilege. They choose whether they're going to marry or not, whether they're going to have children or not. They aspire to control over their lives; it isn't just destiny. This is really new. It's one of the reasons that it's both harder and much more challenging for me as a teacher to reach the people who come to my courses now. On the other hand, it's very sustaining. I find that, on the whole, being a teacher makes one hopeful, despite the hardships.

Q. So you remain hopeful?

GORDON (Laughter) You offer that as the happy ending?

NOTES

1. Bread and Roses was a feminist organization based in Cambridge, Mass., known for its socialist orientation. It existed from 1969 into the mid-1970s.
2. The Council of Federated Organizations was an umbrella group sponsoring a variety of civil rights activities in the South, particularly Mississippi, in the summer of 1964.
3. Rolla M. Tryon, *Household Manufacturers in the United States, 1640–1860* (Chicago: University of Chicago, 1917); Alice Clark, *The Working Life of Women in the Seventeenth Century* (New York: E. P. Dutton, 1919).
4. David Gil, *Violence Against Children: Physical Child Abuse in the United States* (Cambridge, Mass.: Harvard University Press, 1970).
5. Christopher Lasch, *Haven in a Heartless World* (New York: Basic Books, 1977) and *The Culture of Narcissism* (New York: Norton, 1979); William Leach, *True Love and Perfect Union: The Feminist Reform of Sex and Society* (New York: Basic Books, 1980); Richard Hofstadter, *The Age of Reform* (New York: Knopf, 1955).
6. Linda Gordon, "What Should Women's Historians Do: Politics, Social Theory, and Women's History," *Marxist Perspectives* 3 (Fall 1978): 128–36.

7. Barbara Ehrenreich and Deirdre English, *Witches, Midwives and Nurses: A History of Women Healers* (Old Westbury: Feminist Press, 1973).
8. Ellen DuBois, Mari Jo Buhle, Temma Kaplan, Gerda Lerner, and Carroll Smith-Rosenberg, "Politics and Culture in Women's History: A Symposium," *Feminist Studies* 6 (Spring 1980): 26–64.
9. Patricia Mainardi, "Quilts: The Great American Art," *Radical America* 7 (Jan.–Feb. 1973): 36–42.
10. Carroll Smith-Rosenberg, "The Female World of Love and Ritual: Relations between Women in Nineteenth Century America," *Signs* 1 (Autumn 1975): 1–30.
11. "Bourgeois" or "liberal" feminism are terms denoting feminist movements organized to achieve political rights such as the vote for women, but that fail to define feminism as explicitly and necessarily embodying a fundamental critique of capitalist social relations.

SELECT BIBLIOGRAPHY

Books
America's Working Women: A Documentary History, coauthored with Rosalyn Baxandall and Susan Reverby. New York: Random House/Vintage, 1976.
Cossack Rebellions: Social Turmoil in the Sixteenth-Century Ukraine. Albany: SUNY Press, 1983.
Woman's Body, Woman's Right: A Social History of Birth Control in America. New York: Grossman-Viking, 1976, and Penguin, 1977; London: Penguin, 1977.

Articles
"Are the Interests of Men and Women Identical?" *Signs* 1 (Summer 1976).
"Birth Control and Social Revolution." In *A Heritage of Her Own*, edited by Nancy Cott and Elizabeth Pleck. New York: Simon and Schuster, 1979.
"The Family." In *The Capitalist System*, edited by Richard C. Edwards, Michael Reich, and Thomas E. Weisskopf. Englewood Cliffs, N.J.: Prentice-Hall, 1972; reprinted in *Voices from Women's Liberation*, edited by Leslie B. Tanner (New York: New American Library, 1970).
"Family Violence Scholarship: A Review Essay," coauthored with W. Breines. *Signs* 8, no. 3 (Spring 1983).
"The Fourth Mountain: Women in China." *Working Papers*, Fall 1973. Issued as a pamphlet by New England Free Press, 1974; reprinted in *Liberating Women's History*, edited by Berenice A. Carroll. Urbana: University of Illinois Press, 1976.
"Historical Phalacies: Sexism in American Historical Writing," coauthored with Persis Hunt, Elizabeth Pleck, Rochelle Goldberg Ruthchild, and Marcia Scott. *International Journal of Women's Studies* 1, no. 1 (Winter 1972). Reprinted in *Liberating Women's History*, edited by Berenice A. Carroll. Urbana: University of Illinois Press, 1976.

"Incest as a Form of Family Violence: Historical Evidence." *Journal of Marriage and the Family* (forthcoming).

"The Politics of Birth Control, 1920–40: The Impact of Professionalism." *International Journal of Health Issues* 5, no. 2 (Fall 1975). Reprinted in *The Cultural Crisis of Modern Medicine*, edited by John Ehrenreich. New York: Monthly Review Press, 1978.

"The Politics of Population: Birth Control and the Eugenics Movement." *Radical America* 8, no. 4 (July-August 1974).

"Seeking Ecstasy on a Battlefield: Danger and Pleasure in Feminist Sexual Thought." *Feminist Studies* 9, no. 1 (Spring 1983).

"Social Purity: The Use of Eugenics Ideas by Feminists in the 1890s." *Transactions* of the Conference Group for Social and Administrative History, University of Wisconsin, VI, 1976.

"The Struggle for Reproductive Freedom: Three Stages of Feminism." In *Capitalist Patriarchy and the Case for Socialist Feminism*, edited by Zillah R. Eisenstein. New York: Monthly Review Press, 1978.

"Voluntary Motherhood." *Feminist Studies* 1, nos. 3–4 (Winter-Spring, 1973–74). Reprinted in *Clio's Consciousness Raised*, edited by Lois Banner and Mary S. Hartmann. New York: Harper and Row, 1974.

"What Should Women's Historians Do: Politics, Social Theory, and Women's History." *Marxist Perspectives*, 3 (Fall 1978).

"Why Nineteenth-Century Feminists Didn't Support 'Birth Control' and Twentieth-Century Feminists Do: Feminism, Reproduction, and the Family." In *Rethinking the Family*, edited by Barrie Thorne. New York: Longman, 1982.

"The Women's Liberation Movement." In *Seasons of Rebellion*, edited by Joseph Boskin. New York: Glencoe/Free Press, 1972.

"The Working Class Has Two Sexes," coauthored with Rosalyn Baxandall and Elizabeth Ewen. In *Technology, The Labor Process and the Working Class*. New York: Monthly Review Press, 1977.

"Working Women in U.S. History, An Archive." *Signs* 1, no. 3–4 (Spring-Summer 1976).

NATALIE ZEMON DAVIS

AFTER DELACROIX

NATALIE ZEMON DAVIS

Natalie Zemon Davis's teaching and scholarship has been concentrated on French history in the sixteenth century, especially on cultural and religious life. When she started her doctoral research in the 1950s, the social history of the Reformation had not gotten much beyond the point where Henri Hauser[1] had left it early in this century—a few unverified hypotheses about the connection between religion and social class. Davis's early work took this discussion to a new level of sophistication and inspired many followers. From the beginning one of the durable features of her work has been her focus on the city of Lyon. Yet she has always used local history as an occasion to ask general questions, and she has busily erected bridge after bridge between history and other disciplines, especially literature, history of art, and anthropology. She is widely known and read outside the historical profession.

Natalie Davis's scholarship has especially taken the form of essays oriented around single problems. Many of these, including several classics, are now available in her collection, *Culture and Society in Early Modern France* (1975). Her most recent book, *The Return of Martin Guerre* (1983), is an example of microhistory, the study of imposture in a Languedoc village as a means of reflecting more generally on peasant identity and class relations. Davis worked as a historical consultant on the film *The Return of Martin Guerre*, directed by Daniel Vigne.

Academic appointments have taken her to many places. The longest stints were at the universities of Toronto, California at Berkeley, and Princeton, where she is now the Henry Charles Lea Professor of History. In addition to her scholarship and teaching, Natalie Davis has a long history of active concern for the issues of peace, anti-racism, women's rights, and freedom of speech.

This interview was conducted during the summer of 1981 by Rob Harding, who was then teaching French history at Yale University, and by Judy Coffin, who studies French history at Yale.

Q. How did you come to be a historian?

DAVIS My interest in history started in high school. I went to a school for wealthy Detroit girls whose fathers were in the automobile business or perhaps running the local newspapers. It took in a few Jewish people, maybe two or three per class, and I was one of them. In my last years there I started taking history, and in some sense I found my past in those courses. It wasn't my Jewish past speaking to me, though I did go through a period of going to Sunday school and to synagogue. My grandparents had never communicated anything to me about the old country, and my parents were very present-minded. It wasn't the past of my classmates speaking to me, either. It was the Enlightenment and the French Revolution and the American Revolution. I hadn't known anything about them and I thought they were wonderful; I loved history. I was probably more interested in Europe than in America. I have subsequently thought about that and talked about it with other historians of Jewish background. In some ways it's easier to look into the European past, which is where your ancestors were in the nineteenth century, than into the American past.

Q. You seem to have felt quite different from your classmates. Was that important for your ideas about history and politics?

DAVIS Very important. All the time I was at Kingswood I was always of two minds. I was very eager to be a good student and to be popular and do all the other things you were supposed to do, but I was Jewish. Although I wasn't poor, I was certainly an outsider. This was near the end of the war, and the story of the concentration camps was being told; I had a special connection with those pictures we would see in current events class. Whenever we sang Christian hymns at assembly, I always had my fingers crossed so God wouldn't be angry with me. It wasn't simply that I suffered from being an outsider; I see that as a very creative experience, but one that distanced me from that upper-class world.

The psychological thing that bothered me was competitiveness, wanting to be a good little girl and get all A's, the way bourgeois Jewish families expected. I wanted this, but I also didn't like the way in which competitiveness made me relate to my girl friends at school. That was something I had to struggle with a great deal.

There were literature courses and a religious studies course, which was the one that came closest to talking about the ethical questions that concerned me. I remember reading something that now seems sort of embarrassing to have admired so much: Emerson's "Compensation." It first gave me a different way of looking at the social structure I was a part of. The idea of the essay is that some people have great rewards in money or fame, but people with other skills and talents can still be rewarded in another way, say, by doing whatever they can do well and taking satisfaction in it. The essay could excuse all kinds of social inequality, but I didn't take it in that sense. I saw in it a way around feeling competitive, an alternative to the viewpoint of achievement. You don't have to be at the top. It was very important to me at the time.

The only political thing to say about that phase of my life is that my father subscribed to *P.M.* [2] You seem not to have heard of it; it was a neat newspaper and shouldn't be forgotten. It was a liberal-Left, New York–tabloid format, not associated with any political party. Beginning in grade school I read *P.M.* every day after school. In high school I supported Roosevelt, though almost everyone else was a Republican. In our mock elections senior year I even voted for Norman Thomas, [3] though I can't imagine what I knew about socialism. Also in my senior year I was president of the student council, a perfect example of my mixed minds. On the one hand I was delighted to be president. On the other hand I really did use that office to try to change things, reform things, get the girls active and not just be run by the active, very devoted headmistress that we had.

Q. What about your college and graduate work in the late 1940s and 1950s? How did the climate of the cold war influence your life and career?

DAVIS   I got very active in politics. I really rebelled when I was in college the way that you did in the late forties, which was not like it was in the sixties. In general I continued my high school strategy. I wanted to be a very successful Smith girl. I was called Bunny Zemon then. I wrote songs for Rally Day (some of which are now Smith songs), I was on the Judicial Board, I played tennis, and I went out on dates all the time. As at Kingswood, I also had another life, but here it became more public. I teamed up with a few other left-wingers and read the *Communist Manifesto* for my history class. I never digested a lot of Marx, Engels, and Lenin, although I read all the standard things—*State and Revolution, Socialism, Utopian and Scientific,* and the like. I think that activity had much to do with my friendship with these marvelous women. But also I was moving from my sense of injustice about discrimination and about nazism, my dislike of competition and of the bourgeois world and its materialism, to a much broader sphere. At the time I was poorly informed about the prison camps and political terror in the Soviet Union, and in any case, my utopian yearning for a cooperative society didn't stand or fall by what was happening over there.

So I was head of the Marxist Discussion Group at Smith one year and president of the Young Progressives another. We were all in the AYD, the American Youth for Democracy (this was a left wing group supported by the Communist party). Though I hold no brief for the intolerance or the blindness of some people on the Left, I think our little band did much good political work. We protested the Marshall Plan; we wanted the aid to go through the United Nations and not just be a means to expand American power. We worked to help the Hollywood Ten (little did I know that my husband would later be indicted for the same offense); we worked against the Taft-Hartley Law, which limited collective bargaining; and we worked hard on the Black question. Earlier than many other white people, we tried not to use the wrong language and we raised the question of Negro self-determination, as it was then called. Years before the Montgomery bus boycott, anytime we got onto a bus we always went and sat next to a Black person. Always. And that was good. . . .

This political activity was very important for my work. It gave me a whole new way to look at revolutions and history in general. I had some excellent teachers at Smith, but none seemed to approach the big questions that fascinated me—about class and class conflict, about how the social world related to the intellectual world, about the big motors of historical change, and so on. My little association with Marxism (I never really read all of *Capital*!) was terrific for my development as a historian; there's no other way I could have latched onto those questions. I wasn't writing about the working classes at the time. In fact, my senior thesis was on Pomponazzi, the Renaissance Aristotelian. But I could see him as part of the history of rationalism, of the left wing of philosophical thought, and relate his double-truth theory to his situation and his time. I was also helped by the hours and hours I spent talking about history with friends in the honors program. I probably had a closer discussion group then than I've ever had since.

Q. How did your marriage come into the story?

DAVIS I met Chandler Davis at a meeting of the Young Progressives at the end of my junior year. Chan was at the Harvard Graduate School, and he was also very active on the Left. We worked together for Wallace for President.[4] I eloped with him a few weeks after meeting him, and I'm still married to him today.

Q. Was that considered a defiant thing to do?

DAVIS Eloping with Chandler at nineteen? It was a terrible rebellion. Oh, it was just incredible: (a) I eloped; (b) he wasn't Jewish; (c) though he was from a very distinguished *Mayflower*-type family and his father was a professor, he wasn't rich. It was just absolutely a disaster. I had a big break with my family, which I felt very bad about, though eventually it got patched up. It was illegal to get married at Smith without permission, but since I was an all-A student, I wasn't going to be kicked out. My teachers disapproved of my marriage, but they tried not to express it. It was clear they were worried about combining marriage and a career.

I can't remember whether I knew I was going to go on to graduate school before I was married. I had a plan to make documentary films based on history (it's funny, now I'm fifty-two and I'm finally working on a historical movie). Anyway, Chan was in mathematics, and he was just about to start his dissertation. So when I married him, it was a commitment to a left-winger and a way of life. I was just going to go on and be a professor or, at least, a historian.

It solved a lot of problems that young women have about being a scholar and finding a mate. I just got on with it. I guess we were very lucky, or maybe just stubborn.

We believed in equality of careers, though many things that happened in those early years didn't express perfect equality. I was offered a special teaching assistantship with W. K. Jordan[5] at Harvard after my first year there. But at the same time Chan got his first job at UCLA, and I was going to change to the UCLA graduate school. Well, that was the year of the oath, the anti-Communist oath that all University of California professors had to take. Chan resigned within a few months. He was trying to get something else and he had a choice between Michigan, which would have been a first-rate job in mathematics, and perhaps Tufts. Rather than even wait for Tufts to come through, I simply resigned my assistantship at Harvard and went to Michigan Graduate School. We did that without a moment's thought. I was not talked into it. And I don't regret it, given the wonderful friends I made at Ann Arbor and the interdisciplinary turn my work took. I'm just saying that we believed in equality, and yet when it came to an actual decision, we automatically put the husband's interest first.

Q. Would you backtrack and tell us how you came to be interested in early modern history?

DAVIS My first interest in early modern had to do with the social position of the intellectual rather than the kinds of things I wrote on later. It was a continuation of my high school interest in the emergence of intellectuals with their individualism, their competitiveness, and their desire for fame. Now, I thought, here's where it began. It began with capitalism, with commercial capitalism. When I got to Harvard my work went on two paths. The one path was to look at the connection between the cultural program of the humanists and their struggle for a social position. I did a seminar paper on the sixteenth-century humanist Guillaume Budé and the social context of his humanism. He wanted a revival of French political and religious life, and he thought it would come about through increased prestige and power for men of letters like himself.

The other path was social history and that was with W. K. Jordan. I wanted to do Kett's peasant rebellion in Norfolk, England, and social conflicts in Norwich with a kind of Marxist approach. I plunged into the sources, into the world of the peasants and artisans and merchants and city councils. By that time I had moved away from my concern with intellectual individualism and was more interested in working on larger groups of people, especially lower-class people. My interest in Marxism and the Left was feeding this.

Another nice thing that happened to me at Harvard was having W. K. Jordan for a teacher. Hobsbawm and Thompson might not have needed to talk about this when you interviewed them for the *Radical History Review*, but I do because I'm a woman. I had gone to a girls' high school and no one had said to me that I was dumb because I was a female. Then I went to a women's college where I had been a successful student and where many of my teachers were women. It never occurred to me when I got to Harvard that a woman should have any problem. That's how naive I was. I believed in equality, but I wasn't into the "woman question." I wasn't about to slip into the silent fifties, but I was more interested in the revolution, the transformation of society, the working class, Negroes, and anti-Semitism. It never occurred to me that I wouldn't go on with my work. I didn't have to worry about finding a husband who would respect me, as I already had one. I also had Jordan as a teacher. He was president of Radcliffe and wedded to the notion that women should be able to make it. So I really had a lot of good reinforcement.

Q. So you were not particularly conscious of professional problems related to being a woman?

DAVIS You can see my state of mind by what happened to me at Michigan. I was taking a great seminar on sociological approaches to the Renaissance. Professor Palmer Throop had me do a paper on Christine de Pisan, and I ended up typically doing it on her social position as the first professional literary woman. (I've just used some of that research in a new paper called "Gender and Genre: Women as Historical Writers, 1400–1820.")[6] But at that point I was so interested in the working class that I wouldn't have dreamed of continuing with Christine. I thought, Professor Throop wants me to do this because I'm a woman and I'm not going to do women just because I'm a woman. I didn't want to be put in the category of a woman doing a woman's thing. I was interested in another project on the workers and revolts in Lyon. I had been reading on the Reformation and I stumbled on these revolts, including the grain riot of 1529, in Henri Hauser's writings on workers and printers. What I wanted to do was a study of the Reformation from a Marxist point of view.

Q. What about politics at that time?

DAVIS The year we went to Michigan, 1950, was a bad year. You had to sign oaths to get scientific fellowships, and Chan wouldn't sign them. He wouldn't sign the anti-Communist oath to take the job at UCLA. Things were beginning to close in on us politically. Also the Korean War had broken out, and people who were opposed to it were completely isolated. Things were starting to get really bad. They had already gotten bad for the Hollywood Ten, but now they started to get bad for little politically active students like us.

Before I left for Europe, in 1952, a psychology graduate student friend and I wrote something that I really ought to add to my formal bibliography. It was a pamphlet called *Operation Mind*, published anonymously before the visit of HUAC [House Un-American Activities Committee] to Michigan. We reviewed the history of the committee and showed by excerpts from testimony that it was ideas about peace, trade unions, and equality that were being attacked, not efforts to overthrow the government by force and violence. The pamphlet was published by the Council of the Arts, Sciences and Professions, which was a kind of left wing group of professors and graduate students. It was what we called "progressive."

Then I went to Europe and I began my lifelong love affair with the archives. It was hard to learn how to read the sixteenth-century handwriting, since I had had no guidance, but I finally did it. We met marvelous people, communist Left, Catholic Left, and so on. Franz Fanon was in our gang in Lyon, and others, too, who grew up to be fine lawyers and teachers and moviemakers in France. We participated with them in Bastille Day activities —they had much more revolutionary spirit in 1952 than they seem to have today—and did all kinds of things.

It was also a very critical summer for me. I saw some of the women in our group of friends with their babies on the back of their bikes, and I thought that I had been married four years now and people were wondering when we were going to have babies. Chandler came from a family of five. It was a left wing family, but his mother, although she taught, had more or less sacrificed her own career, as an economist, to the family. Chan first told me he wanted to have five children, which terrified me. It was very helpful to see those Frenchwomen with their babies and realize that someone else was doing it. By the way, it would never have occurred to me not to have a child, never. Nowadays, I am well educated by my daughters and my young feminist friends, and I realize it is important to have a choice. But as for me, I'm very glad I just decided, "This is what I'm here for, in part," and just did it.

So when we came back from Europe, I was pregnant. The first thing that happened was that the State Department arrived at our apartment and took away our passports. It makes me feel bad to have to tell you about this because you know what a passport means to a historian of France. We decided not to protest it even though it was unjust. We didn't think we could have gotten the passports back without swearing a loyalty oath and that we refused to do. So for many years I was without a passport.

Q. How did you combine raising children with doing your dissertation?

DAVIS I took my general exams when I was seven months pregnant. (My department was just able to get through that!) I embarked with no American role models. I was scared, I remember. I wondered, "Can I do this?" "Will they take away my fellowship?" "Can I really manage this?" But I just plunged along and somehow it worked. I did slow down in my production, but not in any way that I regret. It helped me to have children; it humanized me; it made me a better teacher. I liked the contrast between the conscious shaping of my life that went into my historical work and the effortlessness of my pregnancies. Later on it helped me understand the notion of the Virgin Mary as a vessel. I liked the idea of being a vessel for something that was joint between my husband and myself, of not being private property, of sharing my body with my child. Here was a situation where personal achievement was not the goal.

The only thing wrong with that period was that for political reasons that

I'll tell you about, I was very, very isolated for five years. Except for one or two women, Chan, friends who wrote me about the things I published, and people I saw at professional meetings, I was very alone. And that wasn't good. I always tell my students, "You mustn't get yourself isolated." "You must have a collectivity that you know, other women or men who are doing scholarly work." "You've got to go to meetings." I don't regret the things I wrote in those years, but I think my work would have gone to a higher level sooner if I had had somebody to talk to.

Though it's not always easy to take care of children, I look at our child-rearing of that period, as does Chandler, as very happy. We enjoyed the children so much. I got enormous help from him, especially given what happened to his career. He couldn't always do it half and half, but on week-ends he would take full charge of the children so I could go to the library. He believed completely in my career.

After our first child was born, Chandler was summoned by HUAC. It was 1953, a few months after the Rosenbergs were executed. We both decided that in refusing to answer he would take the First rather than the Fifth Amendment, which is what the Hollywood Ten had done. It was a conscious decision to make a test case. He did a very good testimony, arguing that the committee had no right to legislate in the area of free speech or belief. He did it unaccompanied by a lawyer because no lawyer would come with him, though he had had legal advice beforehand. The committee especially questioned him about *Operation Mind.* They didn't know I had written it, but they did know he had signed the printer's bill for the Council of the Arts, Sciences and Professions. Poor Chan . . . well, maybe they would have gotten him anyway.

Then he and the other unfriendly witnesses were put on trial at the University of Michigan. Chan was fired for refusing to be forthcoming with the campus committee. He was not a Communist at the time, but he would not dissociate himself from the Party. Many of us wanted him to, and thought he was being too uncompromising, but he came from such a long line of left-wingers that he wasn't about to break loyalty. He also said that professors should not be required to discuss their political views under duress, which was a good point. He was fired without even severance pay. Some of his friends in the math department raised money to help.

He had some hard years professionally because he was blacklisted; no American university would give him a regular position. So we went to New York, and he got a job, without talking about his case, in advertising. After a while he started teaching at night at the New School and at Columbia's School of General Studies. They knew about his case, but were willing to take him on because it wasn't public and these were temporary posts. A year later I urged him simply to stop working at advertising and patch together a career of part-time teaching, even though it was economically risky. Then, in 1957, a miracle happened and he got a fellowship from the National Science Foundation, which he used at the Institute for Advanced Studies. Though all his friends got their grants extended for a second year, his was not renewed. I interpreted this, rightly or wrongly, as more political persecution.

I always try to look on the positive side of these things if I can, but occasionally I will say that I'm sorry they happened. I could have done without having my passport lifted because I wanted to get back to France and do research; and I could have done without having to move again because now our third child had been born, I was almost finished with my thesis, and I had been offered my first real job at Douglass College. But the mathematics community rallied round Chan somewhat and got him an editorship of *Mathematical Reviews* in Providence, so I told Douglass I couldn't teach there after all. We moved to Rhode Island, and that's where I completed my thesis in 1959.

Personally, I would say there were a few good things that came out of that period. Until then, most of my work had been archival. Because I had no passport and then because I had three children, I started working with rare books. When we lived in New York I spent lots of time at the rare-book rooms at the New York Public Library, Columbia, and other libraries. My work acquired that quality that it has had ever since of combining archival materials with sixteenth-century printed texts. I might have used these texts anyway, but I had to then because I couldn't get to anything else.

My isolation was quite hard on me. But it also kept me out of situations that might have been demoralizing. I did at least follow my own path. I wasn't being looked over by people whom I had to please to get tenure. I was interested in Marx and Weber and the question of the relationship of culture to capitalism. I took time out from my thesis and did an article for the *Journal of the History of Ideas* in which I examined mathematical texts by reckonmasters (that is, by the people who taught businessmen arithmetical techniques, including how to calculate and to compound interest) and looked for what they had to say about the ethics of business.[7] I wanted to see whether they brought into their practice the kinds of reservations about usury that you would find if you were looking at a theological text.

It's funny, because my husband was blacklisted I never had the difficult experience of being a faculty wife with no identity of my own. I started teaching at Brown part-time and then full time. Not on tenure track—I didn't even know about tenure track. I'm almost glad, because I didn't bite my nails worrying about how I was doing. I had no sense of how you make a career. I didn't worry about it because I didn't know enough to worry and also because there were so many more important things to worry about, like Chan's case. This kept me from getting hooked into the American success system. I still wanted to be a very fine historian, but if I had ever needed anything to give me the detachment from competitive success I was already seeking in high school, it was those years.

I would like to introduce a word I should have mentioned before. I think of myself as having a vocation. I hope I'm an intellectual and not just a professional. That is the way I want to be. But I also *had* to be that way because I was not in the ordinary path or mainstream, and Chan certainly wasn't because he was blacklisted.

Chan's case got up to the Supreme Court along with the cases of two friends of ours. They had also taken the First Amendment position before the committee, and all three lost by a close vote and got prison terms. Chan served six months minus time for good behavior, and so you see I am the wife of an ex-con. He was in Danbury, he played the organ at prison services, played jazz, built up his muscles in the weight room, and even wrote mathematical articles. My community at Brown was very supportive, and if you have to go to prison, Rhode Island is not a bad place to be living—they have a tradition of dissenters. But it was also horrible—for him and for me. It's not nice to have your husband in prison, and it was very hard on me in ways that are not professionally important.

When he got out, Chan was offered a professorship at the University of Toronto, and we went to Canada.

Q. Could we pick up another aspect of what you were saying about combining research and raising children? Did you feel there were political implications to what you were doing?

DAVIS Yes, I did. When I arrived in Toronto in 1962 there were no university nursery schools, there was no housing for married students, and scheduling and residence requirements were inflexible. This made it very difficult for married women. With some graduate students I organized a questionnaire to women who were in graduate programs at the university and also raising children. We submitted our results to the administration, who ignored it. But we tried, and later some of these changes were made.

That was a political action. But I also felt that my way of trying to combine scholarship and motherhood had political importance—that is, I was trying to raise children, write articles, and teach at the same time. Maybe I overestimated the importance of my own role. People speak of the danger of collapsing the personal with the political in the feminist movement; I feel I was in danger of doing that myself.

But I find myself dismayed when young people don't feel that they have the option of careers and children together. I'm worried about going back to the Bryn-Mawr model of the 1920s. According to it, you could either teach or marry, and in the twenties and thirties it was very hard for married women to get jobs in universities and harder yet if they had children. Those Bryn-Mawr women were great; I had a wonderful teacher at Smith who was like that. But in my generation some of us tried a new path. I don't want our experiment to go for naught. I don't think you should have to choose between being a successful professional woman and having children. Better to change the criteria for success: what's so marvelous for anybody about being a full professor at age thirty-three? Better to change the way careers are for *both* sexes.

Q. Let's turn back to your scholarly work. The title of your doctoral dissertation was "Protestantism and the Printing Workers of Lyon: A Study in the Problem of Religion and Social Class in the Reformation." Has your attention turned away from class and class conflict as your interest in anthropology has grown?

DAVIS Well, I wouldn't say that it's turned away from class and class conflict if that means ignoring socioeconomic groupings and conflicts of interest among them. I don't want to ignore class, but I have certainly been struck by other ways in which society is organized and divided.

First, I'd say that the findings of the thesis itself made me rethink the significance of social class and of class conflict in religious change. The Reformation, in its formative decades at Lyon, cut across rather than reflected class lines, but it did this for reasons that were completely understandable in socioeconomic terms. There was a socioeconomic context for the Reformation, but this did not mean that all the wage earners in the printing industry went in one direction—say, Protestant—while all the masters and publishers went in another. The whole industry for several decades was primarily Protestant, despite economic conflict within it. In publishers, master printers, and journeymen alike, social and occupational life stimulated certain kinds of consciousness—about priests, about their own ability to do priests' work, about hierarchy, about books, and so on. I was also interested in the geographical mobility of the publishers and printers, not merely because it involved their being uprooted and possibly open to new forms of organizational and liturgical experience, but also because it meant that they were often different from their fathers, and the Reformation is partly a quarrel about paternal authority among adult men. Then I tried to generalize this approach when I found other Protestant trades and elites in Lyon had similar characteristics.

In other words, long before I turned to anthropology, I was reconsidering class as a determinant for all behavior. It seemed to me that social and economic life had an important influence on consciousness, but it didn't move through narrow materialistic channels in which economic issues were simply replicated in religion—or, at least, in a differentiated society like sixteenth-century Lyon, it didn't. You had to deal directly with the appeal of religious ideas in their own terms.

The one other thing that came out earliest in my work was the difference between laity and clergy. You might call these sociopsychological groupings, since the Catholic clergy claimed to have a monopoly over certain emotional and intellectual resources. I began to think you needed a much more complicated and multidimensional view of society than I had had; societies could be organized around very different systems. Then I got interested in male and female, partly because I was a mother and because of the early stages of the new feminist movement. Here was yet another kind of grouping.

Then, in 1968, I began to work on youth groups, *charivaris,* and carnivals. I didn't know what *charivaris* really were when I got started. I had talked about them in my thesis and in a paper on the activity of an early trade union, or *compagnonnage,* in Lyon.[8] I had found documents in which trade-union people revealed all their secret rituals. I had used these materials incidental to writing about labor organizations and the Counter-Reformation, but had never looked at them in their own right. It was in this connection that I had to go to anthropological sources. "What do these activities mean?" I kept asking myself. "What are these organizations?" I couldn't answer these questions with the Marxist or Weberian or sociological concepts that I had before.

Here I had serendipity. I just stumbled onto the right anthropological material in the library. Also Rosalie Colie,[9] an extraordinary literary scholar with historical interests, happened to be in Toronto at the time. She read the first draft of my "Reasons of Misrule" and urged me to add some of the literary material on festivity and folly. She told me about M. M. Bakhtin's *Rabelais*[10] after I had already taken on his way of looking at the world turned upside-down from my own reading and observation.

So now I had yet another way of conceiving social groupings in society. I had age categories plugged in as another kind of division. I had another way of looking at social interactions from this work on festivity and some earlier work on welfare reform.[11] I didn't want to do away with class conflict, but I wanted to redefine it, add to it, and end up with something that would make possible a stronger theory for pulling society together, in particular French society. I think my sense of the importance of conflict kept me from becoming a strict functionalist, as some people do when they get interested in anthropology. They get absorbed in the smooth workings of the system. I always keep looking for resistance to the system and try to keep that conflict dimension in.

Another thing that has happened to my thinking is related to Edward Thompson's notion of the making of the working class. Not only does the consciousness of a group have to be made, but the *way* it's made will be very different depending on the literacy and communications system of the society. What's important is not just what group or class you're in or whether the links to others are close or distant, but how you know and recognize your links. In the nineteenth century, with newspapers and tracts, a worker might read in concrete detail about workers in a different city, or a peasant about peasants in another region; precise histories gave a certain authenticity to their common condition. In the sixteenth century a peasant learned about the estate of the peasant or an artisan of the estate of the artisan from sermons, tales, proverbs, and pictures as well as from experience. You knew the particular details would vary from place to place, but the attributes of your estate were universal. There's a sense of a socioeconomic group in both cases, but in one you have networks of communication and perhaps political organization and in the other you have an assumed cultural code that can be drawn upon by diverse people from time to time. The communicative economy is different in the two periods.

Some historians have used this contrast to say, "Oh, well, there aren't socioeconomic classes before the modern period, there are only vertical orders." That would be a preposterous thing to say to people in the early modern period; it would be like saying there are no poor. They belong to vertical groupings, like the clergy and laity and the third estate, and they also belong to broad horizontal strata of people who have the same kind of work and resources—the peasants, the artisans, the merchants, and the like. There are differences among people in these horizontal strata, but we see many differences among working families or among professional families today and that doesn't prevent us from talking about class. I would say that the way in which the horizontal links are experienced, perceived, understood, and organized is inevitably different in the premodern period because (among other reasons) the communication system is different. This has important implications for the character of social consciousness and, in turn, for the character of political consciousness and conflict.

Yes, my work has broadened out a great deal, and I hope it will continue to do so.

Q. You spoke earlier about your interest in Marxism bringing you to the big questions about class and social conflict. Has anthropology brought you to different kinds of questions?

DAVIS   Yes, it has. For instance, I'm interested now in symbolic behavior and behavior that seems irrational at a glance. In my earlier work, before I turned to misrule, I thought about the ideology of religion, the doctrines of religion, the social and ethical teachings of religion, but not the symbolic or dramatic side. I talked about chumminess, about solidarity in religion; I did a lot with psalm singing. But I didn't consider the kinds of statements you could make about society through symbolism, liturgy, and other forms of religious action.

Now I draw upon a much broader range of material. In my graduate seminar on religion and society we try to interpret liturgy: we study the Catholic mass and Protestant services, confession, and exorcism. We think about metaphor and symbolic meaning. In a new paper entitled "The Sacred and the Body Social in Sixteenth-Century Lyon,"[12] I use things like religious processions in a way I had never dreamed of doing before. I talk about how processions made statements about the city, how they linked different parts together, protected the bridges and the hills and the like. Instead of just looking at what the Catholic and Protestant preachers said about social organization, I examined the images of the body that they used and that were implied by different religious rituals. "The Rites of Violence,"[13] in which I tried to make sense of the cruel and seemingly chaotic actions of religious riots, was an important step for me in this direction.

Reading ethnographic studies has also given me ideas about how I could look at small-scale and informal interactions in sixteenth-century France. I'm just redoing a paper on a single parish in Lyon, where I have very good informants.[14] I've been using godparentage as a way to identify the different networks in the neighborhood, especially the gossip networks among the women. It turns out that this is an important element in artisanal culture, which we ordinarily study through more formally articulated structures like guilds or confraternities.

I am also now very insistent on seeing things relationally. Initially this was an influence from Marxism, but it has been much reinforced by the anthropological stress on system, on finding all parts of an ecological system. Whereas before, when I was examining ideas, I considered the social position of the author and of the author's patrons, now I look for a whole relationship among author, publisher, reader, and the text. In my essay entitled "Printing and the People"[15] I tried to see popular culture as a set of relationships rather than simply describing the ideas that appeared in so-called popular books and hazarding guesses about whether these ideas would be accepted. This was a new approach, at least as applied to the sixteenth century. I've tried to go on with it in other work on proverbs and story telling.

Q. Could you compare the way you use concepts from anthropology with the way some other historians use them? Take Le Roy Ladurie, for instance.[16]

DAVIS   In many cases I think historians draw the wrong lessons from anthropology. They take an idea from anthropology—say, about reciprocity or inversion or sorcery—and they apply it uncritically to the historical case. By uncritically I mean that they assume too readily that the concept is true because it comes from anthropology, and they don't think enough about what is required to establish the case for their historical period or whether historical evidence might not modify the theory. Anthropology offers suggestions not prescriptions, and the most important suggestion is that you look at the period you're studying as a total cultural system. Don't take anything for granted about the categories of thought. I think Peter Brown in his *Making of Late Antiquity* and Carlo Ginzburg in his *Cheese and Worms*[17] have been very successful in creating a historical past as a good anthropologist would, rather than just applying anthropological concepts.

As for Le Roy Ladurie, I did a long review of his *Montaillou*,[18] which in many ways I liked very much. I thought he did a beautiful portrayal of the values of the peasant household, of the nomadic shepherds, and of the relations between men and women. My main reservation had to do with his using social categories and language that didn't fit the categories of the people. For instance, deviant. *Deviant* is a word that comes from a modern social system in which there's considerable consensus. In a society like that of Montaillou in the early 1300s, there's little consensus and not just because there's disagreement between Cathars[19] and Catholics. The peasants and shepherds don't agree about many things, even about the immortality of the soul. There's conflict in the village about who has authority; each of the competing clans thinks it's the center of things. Calling the Cathars mere deviants misleads you about how serious it is when a person does cross the border into really dangerous views; then it becomes heresy and you're in real life or death trouble.

I also had reservations about his sexual categories. I don't think homosexuality is a term that should be used for early–fourteenth-century society—or, if you use it, use it sparingly to introduce your readers to your subject and not as a category for identification and analysis. Not that there wasn't a very fascinating Franciscan in Pamiers involved in erotic relationships with young men, but homosexuality, as Jeffrey Weeks and others have said,[20] is a term that emerges as part of a given sexual economy in the given society of the nineteenth century. It emerges among other reasons when the belief is widespread that persons have a precise sexual orientation. In the late Middle Ages that notion barely exists. You have the sin of concupiscence and you have various kinds of unnatural acts between persons of the same sex and persons of opposite sexes. You don't talk about a homosexual person, you talk about sodomitic acts. And that Franciscan, who inherited other perceptions from the early Middle Ages, didn't even think his acts were so unnatural. The point is sexual economies vary as do political economies.

Q. The comparison between your approach and Le Roy Ladurie's makes me think that there may also be a difference of purpose. You subordinate the theories to other concerns. What you do is almost to create the past and to make people of the past live again by restoring their culture and their subjective life. You treat them very personally and you seem to have a personal empathy with the people you write about. How did you come by this?

DAVIS Well, I think Le Roy Ladurie also tries to create living people of the past, but we may do it for different reasons. I think there's something partly maternal in me with regard to the past. It's wanting to bring people to life again as a mother would want to bear children. It's a sense of those lives that were lived and felt and had their own intent and mustn't be lost or go unmarked. It's a re-creation. I also love stories, and I love to tell stories, so that's part of it, too.

It has to do with a literary sense and a sense of caring about people. Maybe it comes from my having been an outsider myself—that is, from being Jewish, from a group that hasn't been necessarily perceived by history as a winner, and from being a woman.* I care about making heard the voices of people

*This is the attitude of a Jew in the diaspora, of a person committed to the continuing creativity of that role, of the outsider who cleaves to his or her truth against the powers that be, in Rome or New York, in Moscow or Jerusalem. It rests on the belief that Jews have survived all their trials better by the strength of their stiff-necked holding to their identity than by guns and tanks (NZD, September 26, 1982).

who have stood outside. And yet I don't want to re-create only the *menu peuple.* [21] I also teach and write about learned persons, and I hope I extend the same concern to them.

Now I don't think a historian should be or can be a tape recorder. We have a dialogue and sometimes a debate with the past, and part of that dialogue is the scholarly theories and cultural values that we bring. How can I re-create these people without molding them in my own image? I've tried to work this out in three ways. One is a technique of imagining my subjects in a dialogue with me. You know, even if I try to understand why they acted as they did, I didn't always like them or agree with them. I mean I'm of two minds about them. So I try to let my text give them a chance to defend themselves, to answer me back even if I have the last word.

Another technique is the way I write. My husband, who is a science-fiction writer as well as a mathematician, pressed me very early not to be pedantic. I didn't want to be pedantic, but I have scholarly enthusiasms that might have led me to write only for a narrow professional audience. Anyway, I really worked on my writing. I consciously try to make my rhetoric work, every adjective work for my argument. I try to create a structure so that the story is being told on several levels at once.

As for the theories I bring, say, about how the parts of a society fit together or about the sources of change, some of them are inevitably in very great tension with the perceptions of the people of the time. But when I can, I use language that has a resonance for both periods. For example, in my "Body Social" paper, I introduced some ideas from network theory,[22] but as soon as I could I began talking about Catholic arteries and umbilical cords and Protestant nerves and muscles. Also, I guess I am eclectic in the theories I accept. I use the ones that give me the best leverage in a given situation. This means I don't have to worry about stuffing my people into a single scheme.

But there's one point that I hope will be helpful here: it's the most important thing that I can do for the past and the present at the same time. When I was younger, what was important was to show the stages of historical development in the Marxist sense and how society in the next stage was going to be socialist. Now I don't believe in inevitable stages and I don't believe in automatic evolution. These theories end up assigning high marks to some powerful modernizing nation, and they don't give you enough of a critical edge on the present. But I do use the past in another way. I let it speak and I show that things don't have to be the way they are now. I want to show how different the past was. I want to show that even when times were hard, people found ways to cope with what was happening and maybe resist it. I want people today to be able to connect with the past by looking at the tragedies and the sufferings of the past, the cruelties and the hatefulness, the hope of the past, the love the people had, and the beauty that they had. They sought for power over each other, but they helped each other, too. They did things both out of love and fear—that's my message. Especially I want to show that it could be different, that it was different, and that there are alternatives. That's very, very important to me.

Q. Doesn't losing a concern with how subjects make and remake their world lead to nostalgia? Couldn't one see that things could be and were different, but still not understand how change comes about?

DAVIS But I'm very deeply interested in change. After all, I work on the Protestant Reformation and the history of printing and many other novelties. And I'm precisely arguing that people make their own history. There can be a danger of nostalgia when you hold the past up to the present, but I'm not saying it was necessarily better then. To lose five out of eight of one's children is not good. I don't want the past to be a model for the present, but to suggest possibilities to the present.

As for change, I just don't see it as part of a fixed world scheme. I'd like to introduce the notion of a range of typologies, a range of styles of change, alternate paths to the future. I'm not saying there's complete free will. What I'm arguing for is choice within a framework; I try to think about resources —cultural resources, human resources, family resources, social resources, political resources—that allow people to do something within the social and cultural system within which they live. I'm interested in how much give different systems have to them. Even in a complex society with lots of pre-scriptions, there can be give in the way in which human beings manipulate the prescriptions. I'm interested in where the cracks, where the fault lines are in different societies that shake people up to change things. Sometimes the things they try are what you'd expect; other times they are really surprising.

I want to be a historian of hope. That's really what I'm saying.

The other thing I want (and this goes back to the dialogue between the past and the present) is that any subject I take up be important, and not just because it fits into a problem in the field. I love rare books; I can get off on all kinds of little bibliographical problems about who printed a single edition. But that's not really what it's all about. I want my work to make a difference to histori-ans; I do hope the documents I find and the questions I ask will be useful to fellows in my craft. But I also want the questions to be important for political and cultural reasons. This is a residue from the political hopes of my youth.

I worked on sixteenth-century welfare during the 1960s because urban poverty was what we were talking about at the time. I still care about it. I wrote "The Reasons of Misrule" about youth groups and festivals partly because of the Yippies and because of the take-over of the Toronto Adminis-tration Building demanding a day-care center, which was like a ritual of inversion.[23] Ritual festivity and humor were surfacing in what we were doing in politics in the sixties. I wrote "Rites of Violence" not only because of Vietnam, but because I was concerned about the riots I was seeing. I was frightened by some of the things that happened in the demonstrations that I was in in Toronto and Berkeley. I wanted to think about where group violence comes from and how it's shaped and what it means, and the religious riots in sixteenth-century France were a good way to do it. And now I'm working on an exciting new study of gifts because I'm tired of private property.[24] Actually, I was tired of it long ago; what I mean is I'm tired of privatization and price tags. Gifts are problematic and they're no panacea, but the subject is very congenial to me.

That is why I can't write my essays without saying something that goes beyond the professional interest of the historian. Richard Cobb, who wrote a mixed review of my *Society and Culture,* was the only person who made fun of me for this.[25] I think he said I was sermonizing—at any rate, he was impatient with it. But frankly, it isn't possible for me to write without joining the issues in some way. I cannot do it. I am not in this business just to satisfy other historians. So the thing Cobb mocked me for is almost the *sine qua non* for my writing. It's the way I make it more than a professional act.

Q. How would you compare the politics of your history with those of someone like E. P. Thompson? Part of his enterprise, it seems, is to recapture a radical or working-class tradition and to sustain present-day radicalism by anchoring it in that tradition.

DAVIS Well, Thompson does work on a closer period—the eighteenth century is really closer to the twentieth than the sixteenth—and it makes more sense to think of a continuous tradition. I think he's making a very important contribution. But I'm not so sure I'm looking for a single tradition. Let's take as an example my work on women. It can't really feed into a feminist tradition because feminism has taken different forms over time and even in the same period. What I hope my readers will do is not so much learn the precise origins of *the* feminist tradition, but see the varieties of ways of being a woman and the varieties of ideas people have had about why the relations between the sexes were wrong and how they could be changed. I want them to think about the aristocratic Ladies of Llangollen and the republican Mary Wollstonecraft, even though they must have hated each other; of Marie of the Incarnation over in the wilds of Canada in 1639 and of the revolutionary republican women of Paris in 1793. And also I want them to know that the Ladies thought only aristocratic women need be freed from subjection, that Mary built a class bias into her system of coeducation, that Marie lorded it over the Indians, and that the republican women tried to harass the market women of La Halle. So my readers will be able to realize what traditions they have available to them, see what their limitations are, and choose from among them in a way that fits into their own times. Some situations are best corrected or changed in one way, some in another (sometimes assimilation, sometimes separation; sometimes constitutional pluralism, sometimes familistic communitarianism), so it's a good thing you have multiple traditions with dissension and even contradictions among them.

Edward Thompson might think such an approach is wishy-washy, but for me it provides some needed detachment from the past. I don't have to be defensive in writing about the behavior or ideas of people whose hopes I share; I can just savor them in their fullness, I can just let them be. There's no *single* right way to be radical in the past any more than there is today.

Q. Why is it that you haven't picked up on psychology or psychoanalysis the way you have on anthropology?

DAVIS   All historians rest their work on certain assumptions about personality and about human desires and responses, and I'm no different. I do read around eclectically in psychological literature, and it has sometimes informed the things I've written. I even took a seminar once at the San Francisco Psychoanalytic Institute. Whenever I'm focusing on relations between parents and children, I have to think about what's involved in becoming an adult and then I might get suggestions from Freud or Erik Erikson or elsewhere. And did you ever read my piece "Ghosts, Kin and Progeny?"[26] It had a lot on mourning. I wrote it when I was mourning my mother, and I also did some reading in the literature on mourning. Whenever I'm working on the Reformation or on any religious figure, the psychological issues are so central— relations with authority, self-control, trust, guilt—that I have to give them some sustained attention. I like some of Erikson's ideas in *Young Man Luther,*[27] by the way, especially about the overpowering superego of late medieval Catholicism; his work has helped me interpret the different strategies of Luther, Erasmus, and Calvin for fighting despair and keeping active. And I've let insights from psychology lie lightly under the surface here and there; for example, in "Rites of Violence," when I was wondering about the possibility of guilt-free massacre, and in an essay I did on friendship and betrayal between Theodore Beza and the poet Jacques Peletier.[28]

But I would never want to make psychology or psychoanalysis a guiding explanatory principle in my work. That would be reductionist. I'm interested in interpreting social systems and historical change in their own terms, that is, in terms of the cultural values and social dynamics of the period. Calvin's obedience to his father and his youthful passivity are interesting to me insofar as they point to a more general ethical and vocational predicament of men of his time and social position, and insofar as they give clues to how his later theology was experienced. But no more than that. And anyway, many of the teachings of psychoanalysis and its variants seem culture-bound to me. What seems fascinating about Luther is how his obsessive striving—his works-righteousness, as we call it—was not just fixed in childhood, but constantly reinforced by the structures of society as he grew up, especially by the clerical structures. The Freudian literature on women has not especially helped me understand the relations between mothers and daughters and female psychology in the past or present, though I found Clara Thompson's *On Women* interesting and I'm planning to take time out and really digest what Juliet Mitchell in *Psychoanalysis and Feminism* and Nancy Chodorow in *The Reproduction of Mothering* have to say on the subject.[29]

Q. You've done a lot of work in women's history. Do you have any thoughts on the future of the field and the new interpretations and insights it will generate?

DAVIS   Some very good books are appearing, but there's a great deal more to be done in the history of the sexes. First of all, the category of gender has simply got to be as integrated into historical work and teaching as class is now.

You'll notice I'm saying gender. You can't really understand what it is to be a woman, what is distinctive about women's roles, or how the feminine is defined unless you look at the same thing for men. We need to learn much more about the varieties of manliness in a period. We need more books on the creation of male gender, like Philip Greven's *Patterns of Child-Rearing . . . in Early America.*[30]

I don't think our goal should be seeking for universal categories by which to understand male and female, such as culture and nature or public and private. These categories themselves aren't eternal and, anyway, we can think of situations, such as the American frontier, where the female is thought to be closer to civilization and the male closer to nature. What we're after are gender systems in all their variety. We want to understand how gender systems relate to the class system, how the sexual economy relates to the political economy. Already the work in women's history has given us a new understanding of how the modern labor force has been put in place, of the social uses of moral reform movements, of the role of informal networks in social and political life, among other fruits. I tried to elaborate on some of these in " 'Women's History' in Transition."[31]

Q. One motif that emerges from what you've been saying is an opposition to professionalism. You speak of treating scholarship as if it were private property and producing it the way commodities are produced; you advocate generativity as a scholar and as a person. Would you summarize what you feel about what goes on or should go on in academic departments and in the historical profession generally?

DAVIS   Well, I think we need to be fine artisans, masters of our craft. I'm a big one for techniques and paleography and language and knowing how to find the right sources and to interpret texts. We have to be very fond of that. I have no objections to enjoying the game well played. But notice that I said the game, and I say it with a certain irony. What I do object to is thinking that the most important thing in the world is where you get your professorship and that a department has to get the best in the world. There's not any single best. There are different ways to build up a good department. There are many ways to be a historian, and people are doing good history in a variety of settings. Although we do get feedback from our colleagues, and we do write in part for each other (I usually feel I'm part of a little sodality for each subject I take up), I don't think the most important thing about what we've written is the good review. The most important thing is the way your book belongs to the people and it's not yours anymore. It belongs to those readers once you've let it go, and the most important thing is the effect it has on their lives. Maybe you'll never know about it.

Young people need to get jobs. People have to have a place in which to teach. There is a workplace. But as I said to my colleague Carl Schorske when I came to Princeton, "You know, I really think of myself in a calling or vocation." And he said, "So do I." And although the word intellectual is perhaps more appropriate for his generation than for mine, I'm more comfortable thinking of myself as an intellectual. The only trouble with the word is that it doesn't suggest the artisanal side of the historian's work identity. But I'm more comfortable with intellectual than professional and with vocation rather than career. A career has a certain fixed curve that the profession decides—when you get your honors and so on. I don't think those are totally unimportant. There are certain rituals you need in order to know what a field is and where it's going. You need elder statesmen and stateswomen who can stand for something. I'm not trying to do away with all ritual or structure, but I'm saying that you've got to see beyond it. If there's nothing beyond it, it's not worth it to me. Life is really more than our little ponds.

N O T E S

1. Henri Hauser, "The French Reformation and the French People in the 16th Century," *American Historical Review* IV (1899): 217–27; and *Ouvriers du temps passe* (Paris: Alcan, 1899).

2. *P.M.* was a progressive New York City daily in the 1940s edited by Ralph McAllister Ingersoll. Max Lerner was the paper's chief editorialist; other writers associated with *P.M.* included James Wechsler, I. F. Stone, and Ben Hecht.

3. Norman Thomas (1884–1968) joined the Socialist party in 1918 and became the leader of that party after the death of Eugene Debs in 1926. He was the Socialist party candidate for governor of New York in 1924, for mayor of New York in 1925 and 1929, and for president in every election from 1928 to 1948.

4. Henry Wallace served as secretary of agriculture under Roosevelt (1933–41). During his tenure the Agricultural Adjustment Acts regulating agricultural prices and production (and setting up the food stamp program) were put into effect. Wallace was secretary of commerce until 1946 when he resigned in protest over Truman's foreign policy. In 1948 he ran for president as the candidate of the new Progressive party; he polled one million popular but no electoral votes.

5. W. K. Jordan is a historian and the author of *The Development of Religious Toleration in England,* 4 vols. (Cambridge, Mass.: Harvard University Press, 1932–40); *Philanthropy in England 1480–1660: A Study of the Changing Pattern of English Social Aspirations* (London: G. Allen and Unwin, 1959); and other studies of poor relief and charity in early modern England.

6. Printed in Patricia H. Labalme, ed., *Beyond Their Sex: Learned Women of the European Past* (New York: New York University Press, 1980), pp. 153–82.

7. "Sixteenth-Century French Arithmetics on the Business Life," *Journal of the History of Ideas* 21 (1960):18–48.
8. "A Trade Union in Sixteenth-Century France," *Economic History Review* 19 (1966): 48–69. A *charivari* was a festival or demonstration to humiliate a wrongdoer in the community, usually someone who had violated marriage laws.
9. Rosalie Colie (1924–72) was a literary scholar and the author of *Paradoxia Epidemica; the Renaissance Tradition of Paradox* (Princeton: Princeton University Press, 1966) and other studies of sixteenth- and seventeenth-century literature, philosophy, and intellectual history.
10. M. M. Bakhtin, *Rabelais and His World,* translated by Helene Iswolsky (Cambridge, Mass.: M.I.T. Press, 1968).
11. "Poor Relief, Humanism and Heresy: The Case of Lyon," *Studies in Medieval and Renaissance History* (1968):217–75. Reprinted as Chapter 2 of Natalie Zemon Davis's *Society and Culture in Early Modern France* (Stanford, Calif.: Stanford University Press, 1975).
12. *Past and Present* no. 90 (February 1981):40–70. Reprinted in *Humanities in Review* I (Cambridge, England: Cambridge University Press, 1982).
13. "The Rites of Violence: Religious Riot in Sixteenth-Century France," *Past and Present* no. 59 (May 1973):51–91. Reprinted as Chapter 6 of *Society and Culture in Early Modern France.*
14. "The Stones of Sainte-Croix," forthcoming.
15. "Printing and the People" appears as Chapter 7 of *Society and Culture in Early Modern France.* See also Chapter 8, "Proverbial Wisdom and Popular Errors."
16. Emmanuel Le Roy Ladurie, *Montaillou: The Promised Land of Error,* translated by Barbara Bray (New York: G. Braziller, 1978).
17. Peter Brown, *The Making of Late Antiquity* (Cambridge, Mass.: Harvard University Press, 1978); Carlo Ginzburg, *The Cheese and the Worms: The Cosmos of a Sixteenth-Century Miller,* translated by John and Anne Tedeschi (Baltimore: Johns Hopkins University Press, 1980).
18. "Les conteurs de Montaillou," *Annales: Économies, Sociétés, Civilisations* 34 (1979): 61–73.
19. Cathars was a Christian sect widespread in southwestern France in the twelfth and thirteenth centuries. They stressed the absolute contrast between good and evil, spirit and body, and they believed in the transmigration of souls.
20. Jeffrey Weeks, *Coming Out: Homosexual Politics in Britain from the Nineteenth Century to the Present* (London, New York: Quartet Books, 1977). See also Sheila Rowbotham and Jeffrey Weeks, *Socialism and the New Life: The Personal and Sexual Politics of Edward Carpenter and Havelock Ellis* (London: Pluto Press, 1977).
21. *Menu peuple,* the lower orders, is usually a reference to urban artisans or tradespeople.
22. Network theory is an approach to behavior that looks especially at the kinds and densities of links among people. See, for instance, Jeremy Boissevain, *Friends of My Friends: Networks, Manipulators and Coalitions* (New York: Oxford University Press, 1974).

23. On welfare see "Poor Relief, Humanism and Heresy," Chapter 2, *Society and Culture in Early Modern France;* "The Reasons of Misrule: Youth-Groups and Charivaris in Sixteenth-Century France," *Past and Present* no. 50 (February 1971) 41–75, reprinted as Chapter 4 of *Society and Culture in Early Modern France.*

24. This study is concerned with a whole range of giving and receiving in sixteenth-century France, from alms to bribes, from gifts at New Year's to gifts at one's deathbed. It has been presented as the Merle Curti Lectures at the University of Wisconsin, March 1983, and will be published by the University of Wisconsin Press in 1984.

25. Richard Cobb's review appeared in the *Spectator* (October 18, 1975): 506–508.

26. "Ghosts, Kin and Progeny: Some Features of Family Life in Early Modern France," *Daedalus* (Spring 1977): 87–114.

27. Erik Erikson, *Young Man Luther: A Study in Psychoanalysis and History* (New York: Norton, 1958).

28. "Peletier and Beza Part Company," *Studies in the Renaissance* 11 (1964): 188–222.

29. Clara M. Thompson, *On Women* (New York: New American Library, 1971; original edition, 1964); Juliet Mitchell, *Psychoanalysis and Feminism* (New York: Pantheon Books, 1974); Nancy Chodorow, *The Reproduction of Mothering: Psychoanalysis and the Sociology of Gender* (Berkeley: University of California Press, 1978).

30. Philip Greven, *The Protestant Temperament: Patterns of Child-Rearing, Religious Experience, and the Self in Early America* (New York: New American Library, 1979).

31. " 'Women's History' in Transition: The European Case," *Feminist Studies* 3 (Spring–Summer 1976): 83–103.

SELECT BIBLIOGRAPHY

Books

The Return of Martin Guerre: Imposture and Identity in a Sixteenth-Century Village. Cambridge, Mass.: Harvard University Press, 1983.

Society and Culture in Early Modern France. Eight essays by Natalie Zemon Davis. Palo Alto: Stanford University Press, 1975; paperback editions, 1977, 1979, 1982.

Articles

"Anthropology and History in the 1980s: The Possibilities of the Past." *Journal of Interdisciplinary History* 12, no. 2 (Autumn 1981): 267–75.

"From 'Popular Religion' to Religious Cultures." In *Reformation Europe: A Guide to Research,* edited by Steven Ozment. St. Louis: Center for Reformation Research, 1982.

"Gender and Genre: Women as Historical Writers, 1400–1820." In *Beyond Their Sex: Learned Women of the European Past,* edited by Patricia H. Labalme, 153–82. New York: New York University Press, 1980.

"Ghosts, Kin and Progeny: Some Features of Family Life in Early Modern France." *Daedalus,* issue on The Family (Spring 1977):87–114.

"Les conteurs de Montaillou." *Annales: Économies, Sociétés, Civilisations* 34 (1979): 61–73.

"The Sacred and the Body Social in Sixteenth-Century Lyon." *Past and Present,* no. 90 (February 1981):40–70.

"A Trade Union in Sixteenth-Century France." *Economic History Review* 19 (1966): 48–69.

"Women in the Crafts in Sixteenth-Century Lyon." *Feminist Studies* 8 (Spring 1982):46–80.

" 'Women's History' in Transition: The European Case." *Feminist Studies* 3 (Spring-Summer 1976):83–103.

Film
Le Retour de Martin Guerre, historical consultant. Premiered in France, May 1982; Director, Daniel Vigne; Producer, Société Française de Production Cinématographique.

WILLIAM APPLEMAN WILLIAMS

IN TIMES OF PEACE PREPARE FOR WAR. IN TIMES OF PEACE PREPARE FOR WAR. IN TIMES OF PEACE...

JB
AFTER G. HAMILTON

WILLIAM APPLEMAN WILLIAMS

ILLIAM APPLEMAN WIL-
liams was born in Iowa in 1921. He received his undergraduate education at
Kemper Military School in Missouri and the U.S. Naval Academy at Annapo-
lis, Maryland, graduating in 1944. He served as an executive officer in the
Pacific theater during World War II. He left the Navy to study history at the
University of Wisconsin, earning his Ph.D. in 1950.

In his historical writings Williams has mounted a sustained challenge to
orthodox interpretations of American expansionism. Among his most important works are *The Tragedy of American Diplomacy, The Contours of American
History, The Great Evasion: An Essay on the Contemporary Relevance of Karl
Marx, The Roots of Modern American Empire, History as a Way of Learning,*
and *Empire as a Way of Life.* These works helped inspire a school of revisionist
diplomatic historians to further extend and broaden Williams's critique.

Williams, who taught for many years at the University of Wisconsin,
helped to found *Studies on the Left,* a journal that exercised a profound
influence on the American radical movement during the early 1960s. He was
the president of the Organization of American Historians during 1981. He
now teaches at Oregon State University and writes a weekly newspaper
column.

---

*This interview was conducted during March 1980 by Mike Wallace, editorial
secretary of the* Radical History Review.

Q. Could you tell us about the sources of sustenance and support you drew
upon in producing your first historical work, beginning with your educational experiences? How did you come to do your undergraduate work at the
United States Naval Academy?

WILLIAMS   I think you and others overestimate Annapolis and underestimate my earlier years in Atlantic, Iowa. When I say that I'm just a little boy from Iowa, most people dismiss it for their own reasons. And, having learned that, I use it to find out who knows what is going on and who does not know what is going on. All that aside, there are very important matters involved. Such as an extended family on both sides of my family, working on a farm in the summers, suffering a depression in its psychological as well as economic aspects, and being raised by people who had community values at the center of their lives. Beyond that, a first-rate education, including being a very good basketball player. For that matter, because of the depression, I would not have gone to college, at least when I graduated from high school, if I had not been encouraged to be good in school and supported in being a basketball player. Good grades and good basketball got me into college at Kemper. Both my grandmothers were liberated women: painters and singers; so was my mother. When I talk about community I know whereof I speak. I know about the values and the giving as well as the taking.

Kemper Military School pushed people academically and in terms of disciplining themselves to play it straight. No crap. As with my family experience, it was fun to do the best you could and accept the losses, defeats, along with the victories. Even back then, on the other hand, I learned about the business aspect of collegiate sports: I wanted to quit playing basketball because I was so hopped-up about academics and music, but I could not because if I did I would have lost my scholarship. And working as a counselor in a YMCA camp for three summers taught me how to work with other people and, along with my mother's example, gave me a real feel for the excitement of teaching. In that sense my books and other writings have always grown out of my learning experience in the classroom. I think that is a key to understanding why so many academics find my writings upsetting—they do not teach on a regular, on-going basis and so have no feel for the excitement of dealing with ordinary people on a regular basis.

After I graduated from Kemper [a junior college], I went to the naval academy. I was bored to death the first eighteen months at Annapolis. After all, doing chemistry, physics, calculus, et al., for the second time around is a bore. And, of course, being a rat at Kemper was much tougher—or nastier, have it your way—than being a plebe at Annapolis. So I laughed at it all and went off to read novels, economics, history, and, in general, do my other things. Almost flunked out, of course. But Annapolis was then an interesting and challenging place in many ways—and my last eighteen months were exciting academically and otherwise. We had basic politics, literature, and history every week for three years. Beyond that, my classmates were very high-powered people—surely I have never been in daily direct encounters with that many (one thousand) first-rate people in any academic setting. And we learned about power: how we went to war in the Atlantic long before Pearl Harbor, etc., etc. Finally, we were taken very damn seriously; we were being trained to become captains of ships of the line, and that is no small matter. So we were taken seriously and lots was expected of us. Well, that is a good thing and I am unapologetic for saying I am eternally grateful for the education—education in the broadest sense—that I got from Annapolis.

I finished there in 1944 and then volunteered for the amphibious corps. I served as an executive officer in an LSM [Landing Ship Medium] during the last fifteen months of the Pacific war. A ship can be one of two things: a classic class system run on an authoritarian basis, or an honest community. I think I created a community on the ship. At any rate I tried, and learned much about power relationships in the course of all that. I see no point in talking about combat other than to say that in my opinion there is no first-rate novel about the war at sea in the Pacific. We all knew Japan was defeated before the bomb was dropped and saw absolutely no point in the second bomb. Yes, it was an important part of my life, and surely informs my reading of the record as a historian.

In 1945 I was sent to Corpus Christi, Texas, then the site of the nation's largest air naval training base, to become a naval flyer. My father had been a very hot pilot in World War I, and I soon learned that I would never be *that* good. But flying is exciting and demanding and, frankly, very exhilarating. Operational aircraft are unforgiving, and it is a challenge to fly them well.

Corpus Christi was then caught up in a very complicated struggle for power, involving the King Ranch, General Motors, the Catholic hierarchy, and the navy bosses, and the Blacks were in the middle of this. General Motors was involved in a project to pipe gas from the King Ranch down to Mexico to make steel there and barge it up the Mississippi and break the unions. When I walked into Corpus Christi there was a recall election to remove the mayor and put in the right man who would, in fact, diddle this thing around, facilitate the deal.

At the same time, a man named Boyd Hall—a dentist and leader in the local Black community—was working on getting Blacks to vote. He wanted to give some meaning to the 1944 Supreme Court *Smith* v. *Allwright* decision that said that the Democratic party was not a white man's club. The air safety officer at Corpus Christi, a naval academy graduate named Herb Gilmore, was one of a handful of whites who were willing to work actively with Hall through the NAACP on this. A couple of Quakers and an old Tennessee attorney, whose father had defended a Black man and had been driven out of Tennessee, were also seriously committed. I got involved in this and other projects. We worked to keep the buses running so that women employed in people's homes could get a ride home at midnight. We worked to get some white merchants to hire Blacks in their stores. We started a newspaper.

Meanwhile, inside the naval base, Herb wanted to integrate the flight line. If you've never been a navy pilot you wouldn't have any idea what heresy this is. What an outrage! To have Blacks work on the engine of the plane I'm going to fly?

The Communists were involved in this, too, in their own way. It didn't make any sense to me. The Party line in the South in '45 made about as much sense to me as . . . bah, humbug. That's not what these people needed, they were already an isolated community. Still, I knew some of the Communist organizers well and liked them, a couple of them in particular. Nice people. I had enormous respect for them. They'd been down there a lot longer than I had.

Q. Did you get labeled a Communist?

WILLIAMS   Oh, you name it, and we got labeled it.

Q. So you and your friends managed to enrage the navy hierarchy, General Motors, the King Ranch, and segregationist whites simultaneously.

WILLIAMS   And the Catholic church. The naval leadership and the Catholic hierarchy had always been close, not necessarily because the navy hierarchy was Catholic, but because they were two power structures that had things to do with each other. And the Catholic church didn't want the Blacks to become active and militant.

It was nasty and unpleasant. We got threatened. We got thrown out of the apartment at two o'clock in the morning. I was beaten up a couple of times. The FBI was on both Herb and myself. Herb took a lot of flack and ultimately was forced to resign. This kind of stuff. I resigned, too. I submitted a three-page single-spaced letter that was a real polemical exercise. But they refused to accept it. The admiral called me in and said that this simply was unacceptable and wouldn't go any further than his office. He said he only called me in to decide if he should put a letter of reprimand in my file.

Q. One last question on all this. You hadn't been involved in this kind of political work in Iowa or at the academy. How do you account for your Corpus Christi activities?

WILLIAMS   I guess it was just the fact that I cared about this. I got a lot of this early political involvement from my family, the values that I was taught and that I came to accept and internalize. The more I got out in the world, the more I thought they were good values and I was supposed to *do* something. That's certainly the example my grandmother and my mother—two liberated women—set for me: if you're committed to something then you act.

Q. Where did it go from there?

WILLIAMS   I stayed in the navy. Legally you were bound to stay in for a certain period of time. Then they decided to transfer me. They wanted to send me to Bikini, the atom bomb test site. I knew amphibious warfare, and they wanted to see if you could in fact hit a beach after you've bombarded it with nuclear weapons. The transfer was related to the letter of reprimand, obviously. You talk about learning how power works.

But I didn't go. I had this medical problem so I went over and talked to the flight surgeon and he said, "You've got no more business going out there than your wife does. When you get to San Francisco you check into Treasure Island Hospital." I was in bad shape physically. And I had been worked over a couple of times. So the doctor in San Francisco refused to let me go. In fact

I stayed in various naval hospitals for thirteen months; I was in a cast from my neck to my knees for nine weeks. Finally they decided they couldn't do anything more. I could have had a fusion operation but when my roommate at the hospital went in to have one and came back paralyzed, I decided that there were better things I could do.

When I left the navy I had job offers from General Electric and from Lockheed. Naval academy graduates are good troubleshooters. In one sense that's what you're trained to do, run an operation. And I was tempted because I was challenged. General Electric wanted to make me a field supervisor and engineer in heavy electrical equipment. Lockheed wanted me to get into aircraft design, and that was exciting. But I passed them up.

At that point my mother was teaching in Wisconsin. She was a great teacher in the true sense of the term, a great teacher of third grade, which is kind of a crucial point in a kid's education. When I would see her she would always put me in a classroom and walk out. She'd say, "I want you to give children a sense of what it is to be at the naval academy (or whatever), and what a commitment to quality involves." Well, you know, the first time I was petrified, with twenty third-graders at hand. But then I realized I liked it. I liked the give and take and the excitement. So I knew I was interested in education. . . .

Q. Why history?

WILLIAMS   It was history because I really did want to try and make some sense out of what the hell was going on—the bomb and all that. I figured from my education, my reading, that history was the best way to figure out the way the world ticked.

At that point Wisconsin had the best history department in the country. Not in terms of famous names, but there was a very high-powered collection of people, and they were always there. Not like Columbia or Harvard or Yale where the names were in the catalog but they were never there. So I applied, and they admitted me on probation, and I just went for it like a fish to water. It was a terribly exciting experience, intellectually and every other way. I got hooked.

But it wasn't just the history department that made Wisconsin so exciting. There were a lot of high-powered people there: Hans Gerth and Carl Becker in sociology and social psychology. Becker and Gerth were poles apart. Becker was very conservative, orthodox; but Hans was out of the Frankfurt school.[1] There were people like Bob Lampmann in economics, he became presidential economic council adviser; Hube Wilson in political theory; and Frederick Hoffman in literature. Terribly exciting place.

In addition, the GIs were a lot more political than people think they were. They didn't march in the street, but they were political about their education and the structure of the university. Most of the GIs in history had the same hopped-up concern to figure out what the hell had been going on in the war and the way the world was going.

I originally started out to be a historian of Russia. I'll be damned if I know why. I suppose it came out of curiosity rather than politics. Also, I know that it came out of a certain kind of military respect that most of the people I knew at the naval academy felt. I went into the naval academy in June of 1941. By a year or so later you realized that the Russians were winning the war. That's that and it really doesn't have much to do with ideology. And I found it a fascinating society.

But they were training us as historians at Wisconsin so really the issue came down to the fact that if you're going to work in twentieth-century Russian history, you're smack up against the basic source problem. So I decided I'd work on American foreign policy. But I wrote my master's thesis on an aspect of Russian history. I got my master's degree in '48 and then went to Europe for five months.

I went to a seminar the Labour government put on at Leeds University, which was really an education. It was on socialist economics. We read everything. Even more interesting, the whole cabinet of the Labour government came up and gave us tutorials. The guy who ran the thing was A. J. Brown, an economist at Leeds. He was then and for many years thereafter the shrewdest and toughest liberal in the English tradition. I think that I was certainly affected by the kinds of questions he would not let us evade. He said that if you come to power in a failing capitalism you face enormous problems, and he suggested thinking about decentralization as a partial response. That way the problems wouldn't interact at such a structural level that if one thing went wrong everything would probably go wrong. Schumacher was not there, but obviously that idiom was beginning to be raised in the English liberal tradition. Schumacher was head of the coal board, and coal was a classic example of calling the socialists when capitalism had failed.[2] You know, you do the dirty work. Fix the plumbing. I suppose you could argue that that's one of the places that I first thought about decentralization as part of a program for the Left. It appeals to my whole value system and experience.

Q. Once back at Wisconsin how did you settle on your thesis topic?

WILLIAMS   As I remember it—and I think this is correct but I've never kept a diary—at Wisconsin every month some faculty member in the history department would lead an evening discussion for graduate students. Howard K. Beale was talking abut Theodore Roosevelt and he raised the name of Raymond Robins and said that his life was fascinating.[3] I thought, *aha!* I've got a thesis. After great effort I finally got Robins to agree to talk to me. I went down to Florida and I was really hooked. This guy had been in on so damn many things—the mission to Russia, the Bolshevik revolution. He'd been harried by the FBI. We liked each other. We got along famously. He turned over most of his letters and I began to collect stuff. In the course of doing the thesis I got several different kinds of manuscript collections for the Wisconsin Historical Society. When I finished the thesis in the summer of 1950 and got my degree, Fred Harvey Harrington said I shouldn't try to publish it as a study of Raymond Robins. "Go back to the turn of the century," he advised, "and do it as American-Russian relations, and you've got a book." So that's what I did.

Q. Did the McCarthyite hysteria interfere with your writing the book?

WILLIAMS   A great virtue of the naval academy is that they teach you: don't let the bastards grind you down. Forget it, forget it. *Do what you got to do.* Don't sit down and suck your thumb. I mean, how's anybody going to keep me from writing a book I want to write? What's it got to do with me going to the archives and sweating away till two o'clock and three o'clock, morning after morning, to write the book?

Q. Did the choice of topic perhaps flow in part from a desire to contest prevailing cold war attitudes?

WILLIAMS   No. Wisconsin had a great tradition at that point, whether it was William Best Hesseltine or Howard Beale or Merle Curti or Paul Knaplund or Fred Harrington or Merrill Jensen or whomever. Learn how to do the right kind of research, learn the basic rules (if you don't know them already) of how to think straight, and then make sense out of that material in your own way, to your own satisfaction, and let it go at that. The idea of writing a book about American-Russian relations in response to McCarthyism frankly never occurred to me.

But when I finished the manuscript of that book it ended with Lend-Lease's inclusion of the Russians.[4] Rinehart was at that point still an old-fashioned publishing house with good editors who read the manuscripts and looked at them seriously. They asked me to write an epilogue. I did. The epilogue was basically around George Kennan and the containment thing.[5] They, unbeknownst to me, thought it was so good that they sent it off to *Foreign Affairs.* And *Foreign Affairs* kept it, and kept it, and kept it. Finally, they wrote me a very peculiar letter saying, in effect, that this had been circulated and read with great interest and it had stimulated a lot of discussion. But the decision had finally been that it was a bit too sharp personally. Which meant, I supposed, that I used Kennan's name too often or some damn thing. Anyway, in my naiveté, I wrote the editor and said, well, I don't understand this; if you'll tell me in what respects you think it's too personal, I would think that this could be a matter of discussion and probably resolved without a lot of trouble. I never got an answer.

Historians, too, have given me a hard time. But over the years I've come to realize [that] one of the benefits of being trained in the naval academy, and being in the regular navy, was to learn how to avoid personalizing an issue. You can, as the executive officer of a ship, get really chewed out by a captain if you do something that would risk putting that ship in danger. But thirty minutes later he'll play chess with you. There's very little personalization of a basic confrontation. And there was very little personalization in my athletic career. And very little personalization in my family upbringing. There were issues to be confronted and differences to be clarified and consequences to be accepted, but then you went on from there.

And when I came to realize that the academic world was not like that, I said, well, you're not going to make me live that way. If you don't like my book, fine. All I've done is to make sense out of it the best I can. If you don't agree with it, fine, but I'm not going to get involved in this silly-ass stuff with you. I'm just not going to do it.

If Arthur Schlesinger, Jr., wants to take a document and write ten pages about it, then let me sit down and write ten pages about it and put it in the *New York Review of Books;* the readership can decide who makes the most sense out of that central document. Fine. I'll do that with him any day. But as an athlete you learn never to get caught in reacting. Play your game. This business of trying to deal in a limited space with the misuse of a quotation, it's a loser, baby. That's a no-win situation.

Oh, I understand that the attacks on me are political. But it's also true that I infuriate a certain kind of person simply because I won't get into a silly-ass alley fight with them. And that makes them madder and more frustrated. I'm a certain kind of person, and I'll be damned if I'm going to let them turn me into a different kind of person.

Which isn't to say that McCarthyism hasn't touched me. I ran into McCarthyism in Oregon. I taught at the University of Oregon for five years, 1952–57. Various people there tried to make life miserable for me and some other people on the campus. As a matter of fact, they got rid of at least three of us ultimately. You see, I wasn't all that ready to go to Wisconsin in '57. When Harrington called me and asked if I wanted the job, I told him no twice. I'm not ready to come. I've got this essay I'm really excited about and I want to finish it. (That was *The Tragedy of American Diplomacy.*) And I said I'm learning how to teach large numbers of kids in classes. I'm flattered, but give me a couple of years. He finally said that he was going upstairs and the department wanted me. I agreed to go.

Q. Did you have any difficulties publishing *Tragedy* in 1959?

WILLIAMS I had a real thing with *Tragedy.* It was accepted by Braziller and to be a selection of the Book Find Club. You know it starts out with a quotation from James Reston.[6] Braziller went down to Reston at the *New York Times* and asked him if they could put a wrapper with that quotation around the book jacket, and Reston said yes. Then Braziller gave it to Max Ascoli.[7] And Max Ascoli just went through the ceiling. He said, if you publish this book our friendship is terminated, etc. So this guy called me up—this was just after I got to Madison—and said, "I can't publish the book." And I said, "What! You can't publish the book!" And he said, "I can't publish the book." So I said, "Okay, you can't publish the book." He says, "You can keep the money." I says, "You're damn right I'll keep the money." Not that it was all that much. I think it was something like $2,500. At that point I got an agent. I've never regretted it.

Next thing, when World published it, Adolph Berle[8] used the book in the

New York Times to begin to get off the containment bandwagon. I had a great experience with Berle. The word came through, in '59, that he wanted to talk to me seriously about it, so we got him an invitation to come out to Madison and give two public lectures. We had an absolutely magnificent seminar, with the likes of Tom McCormick and Lloyd Gardner and Walter LaFeber—absolutely superb.

And then, this was in 1960 after the election, he tells me that Kennedy has asked him to come back in and deal with Latin American affairs, and he says, "I want you to be my personal first assistant." Of course, that was intriguing. Sure I was tempted. Fred Harrington said sure, take it, see how it looks from the inside for a while. He said, "If nothing else you'll get to read a lot of stuff you wouldn't get to read for thirty years."

But I couldn't do it. I had five kids at the time, and I liked them. I thought, uproot these people and take them to Washington, D.C.? That's a minus. And then the more I thought about it the more I thought, I don't trust the Kennedys. Don't ask me why, I just didn't trust them. So I went back and read all the stuff on the campaign. I read how he'd used Cuba. I talked to a man who'd been approached by the Kennedys to be head of HEW. He said, "I want it bad, I'd like to be secretary of Health, Education and Welfare. But you can't trust the Kennedys." So I didn't do it. Thank God! I would have had to resign before I'd even found an apartment to live in!

And then, of course, *Tragedy* obviously upset a lot of people in Washington. And in 1960–61 the House Un-American Activities Committee subpoenaed me. The University of Wisconsin would not take a position on any given case, holding that it was a matter for the individual to deal with. The university would not suspend anyone; but the university at the same time would not fund the defense. It was an arguable straightforward proposition. Don't misunderstand me, it was debatable, and I could argue it either way.

I was very lucky. I emphasize, I was very lucky to know some people in the law school. One of my friends said he knew people who knew Arnold, Fortas and Porter. He said he would find out if they would consider taking my case. Word came back that Paul Porter would talk to me. So I went in to Washington and spent a day with Paul Porter. Impressive man. Jesus Christ, impressive man. He took me up and down and sideways and backward trying to figure out why they were after me. Because they were after me in a way they never went after anybody else. They subpoenaed the manuscript of *Contours* [*The Contours of American History*]. This is before it had come out. It was either just in or just about to go into first galleys.

After Porter said he would take the case he said, "I want you to know one thing. This is the first time this has ever been tried." He said, "If you level with me, we will not surrender that manuscript until we get a Supreme Court order." And he said, "Just between you and me, they'll never get a Supreme Court order."

Then we talked about my career and mainly about Texas; sustained, militant activity in the South about the Black question. And he knew as well as everybody else did that us northern kids were Johnny-come-latelies, that the people down there had been the CP. So he wanted to know if I had worked with them. And had I ever joined. It's an eerie experience to be asked about things that were just a matter of course to you fifteen years after the fact. You begin wondering, Jeez, *did* I join the Communist party? I mean it sounds strange but it had never been that formal an operation. Well, could anybody construe anything I'd done as proving that I'd joined the Party? Weird experience. You really get a sense of Kafka.

They were also after me because I'd published with *Science & Society, Monthly Review,* the *Nation,* and had been involved, in an advisory capacity mainly, with *Studies on the Left.* That was basically the students' magazine. I felt very strongly that it should be their magazine. I didn't really want any active part in it because I thought the kids who wanted to start it were quite competent in doing it and that they ought to do it.

I also got a small grant from the Rabinowitz Foundation, and HUAC didn't like that at all.[9] But obviously they were after me to stop the book.

Well, the House Un-American Activities Committee played me like a yo-yo. They'd tell you to report next Wednesday. In those days most people took the train from Chicago; nobody had the money to fly. They would wait until they figured out that you had left and were on the train. Then they'd send a telegram saying "Appearance Canceled." That way you couldn't collect any money for it. With five kids, this is bad stuff.

At one point Porter told me that he had a big antitrust piece of legislation coming up that was important. And Francis Walter was both chairman of HUAC and if not chairman then senior member of the committee that handled antitrust legislation. Porter was very candid about it. He said he couldn't go in there and get this piece of legislation, and then go in there the day after and tell him we'll take him to the Supreme Court. So he turned it over to Judge Arnold. Judge Arnold and I had some very interesting conversations about the folklore of capitalism. Anyway, Arnold got them to back down.

Arnold said that in order to get them to back down for the fundamental reason that they know they can never get this manuscript or we'll blow them out of the water, we had to go over there and pay our respects to them. I said, I really don't want to do that. And he said, "I know you don't, young man. But you don't want to spend the next five years of your life and $50,000 forcing them to say 'we were wrong' in public, do you?" Well, I said, "It might be kind of fun, but I sure ain't got the $50,000." So we went over and had a little tête-à-tête—I suppose it took us ten minutes—and they sent me out of the room. Judge Arnold came out and said, "You handled it perfectly." They realized they made a mistake, and that was that.

But, you know, the House Un-American Activities Committee *will* work its way. They sent my name over to the IRS. And the IRS worked me over for the better part of twenty years. The first time they got me on the Rabinowitz grant. They accepted the House Un-American Activities Committee argument that it was a political thing. I took them to tax court. It was funny. One of the young kids who had been in prelaw when I first came to Wisconsin had graduated, was now a lawyer, and was working on my case for the IRS. They sent the big man up from Indianapolis and we sat there from ten o'clock till three in the afternoon. I said the four hundred dollars was not the issue, that it was matter of an important principle. At one point we had a break, and the young lawyer told me I could win if I took this to court. There wasn't a jury in the world that would convict me, but it would take five years and at least $20,000.

I think that annoyed me more than anything else. I really did want to take them to court, but I didn't have $20,000. So I paid the $400.

And then the Wisconsin legislature wanted to come after me. But I really had the university on my side. There was a lot of mutual esteem and trust. Harrington always figured I could take care of myself. If I had really gotten in trouble I'm sure Harrington would have done everything he could, which would have been considerable. So would some other people. But, well, you know, if you don't like the heat, stay out of the kitchen.

Q. It appears to many people that the 1980s are going to be a replay of the late 1940s, that we are heading into period of renewed militarism and belligerent foreign policy *vis-à-vis* the Soviet Union. How do you assess the likelihood of the cold war being revived?

WILLIAMS It seems to me that in late 1947–48, Churchill understood exactly what was happening. He made several very important speeches to the effect that we made a mistake at the end of the war. American leaders should have been proper imperial leaders and sat down with the Russians and reached a clear formal understanding when the U.S. was in a position of unquestioned supremacy and power. As secretary of state, Dean Acheson refused to do that. Then the Russians tested their hydrogen device and the Achesons responded with NSC [National Security Council Document] 68.[10] It's a dynamite seventy-five pages of stuff because it's so explicit about what American leaders want to do. They even say in it that any negotiations are an elaborate tactic.

I don't think we're headed back into that kind of formulation and commitment. I think that there are groups of people—the Committee on the Present Danger, for example—who would like to, who feel that it's necessary.

But they won't succeed because the world has changed along the way. First of all Korea. When they really tried to roll back the Russians, long before John Foster Dulles ever came into power as secretary of state [1953–59], they discovered that they couldn't do it without using the bomb. Then you began to get people realizing for the first time that the empire had limits. Eisenhower said, in effect, that the empire had limits.

But this poses two problems. One is what are you going to do if the empire has limits? The second is how can you in fact do it unless you confront the fact that it *is* an empire so that you can talk about the issue as an issue? I think that's the crucial issue: talk about it as an empire. Despite all the rhetoric about the lessons of Vietnam, nobody has ever come to terms with it—the Left included.

This is an opportunity for the Left to say: this is an empire. And in the short run you can't stabilize the world unless you accept the fact that it's an empire. The short-run problem is to make it a responsible empire, to give up the messianic global formulation of American national security.

I think that Henry Kissinger understood that. I think that Nixon—I don't know how to separate the two men, I don't think you can at this point—understood that. That all this talk about subverting the Soviet Union was no longer conceivable so you might as well accept that fact. Détente is the acceptance of it. I think they understood it much better than the people from the Left who were criticizing them. Maybe the people on the Right understood what they were up to better than the Left did. Some of the criticisms of Kissinger from the Right are extremely revealing—you can't accept the Soviet Union because once you do that our system is in dire trouble.

Here is where the Nixon-Kissinger opening of China comes in. You can look at China in this context and say that the policy makes sense so long as they don't get ambitious again and think of it as a new containment policy designed to subvert the Soviet society, because we all know that Soviet society is a very delicately balanced operation. The Russians know it even better than we do. You put it in the context that you're going to play the China card in the way that Brzezinski talks about it and all hell's liable to break loose.

Q. How do you account for the battles within the Carter administration between those like Vance, who want to hold the frontier, and those like Brzezinski, who want to confront the Soviets, with the attendant twists and turns of policy?

WILLIAMS   I think this is all connected with domestic things like those I wrote about in *Changing* [*Americans in a Changing World*]. It's a real problem. Unless the leadership—the state—levels with its constituents, the citizenry won't accept a lot of things. The leadership faces a tough problem from their point of view. Do they admit that we're an empire so we can deal with the problems in such a way that we might figure out a way to go on? If they do that, they might get a terrific backlash from a culture that does not think of itself anymore as an empire.

I think Johnson tried to square the circle. I think he's legitimately a tragic figure. He tried to make the empire work at home in the sense of creating an equitable, or more equitable, functioning society while at the same time holding the frontier. It can't be done.

So I think the reason these people stewed around since the end of the Korean War is, goddammit, if I was in their position, looking at it from their point of view, I'd be stewing around, too. It's a tough problem. If they can't be candid, the right wing is going to give them hell and the left wing is going to give them hell. I'm not sympathizing with them, but I understand them.

I can see why they back and fill, why there's tension in every administration between the Vance on one hand and the Brzezinski on the other hand, or the Shulman and the Kissinger. It's really there. They're in a jam.

I think you can bring it right down to the debate about oil. Do you keep oil and gas drilling and production technology from the Russians or don't you? If you do it's going to hurt them, there's no question about it. It's a very serious undertaking because what you're going to do is, in effect, say we're going to punish you in the short run and hope in the long run we don't provoke you to go after the Middle-Eastern oil because you can't get yours out of the ground fast enough.

And if you overplay the China card, good-bye world.

So the backing and filling is indigenous to their problem. Looked at from their point of view it's a tough one to handle. Kissinger tried to bring the country to an awareness that there are limits, but he doesn't have the right idiom for American society. Eisenhower did it, but nobody but Eisenhower could have done it his way and he didn't leave a legacy in the sense of a dynamic understanding of it. But he knew there were limits, and he acted in keeping with the fact he knew there were limits. He also acted out of a very intense awareness of what another war would mean. He walked those battlefields. He was determined that it would not happen again. He knew what was happening, but he just wasn't a leader in the sense that the country could happily have used.

Q. It seems to have been a major argument of your work that past efforts to sell the empire have been largely successful.

WILLIAMS Yes, I think they have, in part simply because an empire does provide all kinds of psychic and material rewards. There isn't any question about that.

Q. Then how do you assess the odds of the Left, or anybody else, being able to mobilize public support for rethinking or rejecting the empire?

WILLIAMS Well, I'm cautiously optimistic. All I can do is answer the question in terms of the people I know and talk to. I live in a community that is not an academic community. It's got everything from retired colonels of the air force to longshoremen and jippo fishermen. And my experience in the last two years is that the absence of leadership is a very important factor in the whole thing. I think there's a greater willingness to face reality now than even at the end of the Vietnam War. If someone were to come out and talk hard cold turkey, we might all be dumbfounded at the extent of the positive response. I find that a surprising number of people—if you talk *with* them, not *at* them—are also willing to accept that we *shouldn't* be policemen.

The choice of idioms is maybe not crucial, but it's important. I don't make a business of going around the country, but I do give lectures, and I find that when talking to people in communities the policeman image is useful. Most of the people I get at lectures, and they're not all in academic settings, are willing to accept that proposition.

So I think that's a useful idiom because it's a way to get at the self-image of America. What is a policeman? In current criminology there are three images or concepts of the policeman. They all cut across the idea of the United States as a reformer. The only way a policeman can function as a reformer is if he sticks to his own neighborhood and walks the beat. Then he becomes a part of the community. The image of America as the policeman of the world is the worst image of a policeman that can be put in people's minds because it's wholly negative. It's a policeman acting at the behest of, and in keeping with, an outside definition of the law. He's an instrument. So I find that if a person says to you, yeah, we shouldn't be policemen, it helps you get at the idea of America reforming the world.

Q. But can't the architects of empire draw upon another, more beneficent sense of policing? After World War II wasn't it commonly argued that there had to be some agency that would secure international order by preventing a relapse into new nationalisms—new Germanys—and so prevent a new war? Or block aggression by Soviet or Soviet-controlled "criminals," as in the Korean police action? Wasn't an expansive U.S. imperialism portrayed in part as necessary to guarantee national and global security?

WILLIAMS I understand what you're saying. I'm merely saying that people have come to understand that doing that involves you in being a policeman in the other, more negative sense. They realize that this is going to get you into what you're supposed to be avoiding. Today they see that contradiction much more than they did, say, in Korea. Although, and I do not think that anyone has seriously studied this, there was a lot of opposition to the Korean War. Iowa is an interesting case in point. There was a lot of opposition to the Korean War in Iowa. I'm sure if there was in Iowa, there was in other places.

Q. There are those who agree with your characterization of the U.S. postwar empire as being simply the latest step in a long line of development that had been going on since the 1870s—the insistence on maintaining or extending the open door for U.S. capital. There are those, on the other hand, who suggest that there was a qualitative transformation after World War II, that the U.S. stopped being simply one among many competing national capitals and that, partly because of the bomb and partly because of the commanding position of the U.S. after the war, it became the centerpiece of a highly integrated global economy. What do you think would happen if the U.S. did reject the role of policeman, or guarantor of the world capitalist system? This raises an associated question about the nature of that system: *is* it in fact limitable?

WILLIAMS Well I think you've raised two or three issues there.

I certainly would argue that America came out of World War II running the show, but I don't see how that makes my understanding of how it got to that point irrelevant. It's merely doing what it was working away at doing for the better part of a century beforehand. There was a debate in the twenties about the nature and the limits of the empire; a debate that I've tried in my new book [*Empire as a Way of Life*] to go into a little more, and probably more thoughtfully, than I had before.

What would happen if we said, well, we understand, and it's time we talked about it among ourselves candidly, that we have, in fact, been an empire. And that we are now in a position of needing to confront that and its implications and to have serious talks among ourselves, and ultimately with other people, about where we go from here. Because if we persist in our conception of ourselves as the very visible hand, to use Alfred Chandler's delightful term,[11] in the world economy and in being the world's policeman, then we're undoubtedly going to end up in a nuclear holocaust. There's simply no question about this.

But the Left cannot simply focus on defining the limits of empire. We have got to talk seriously about the quality of life rather than the quantity of life. And that's tough to do because the Left is hooked on the standard of living as bad as anybody. I think we're at the point where it's impossible for the world to function on the American definition of democracy. It's now impossible for the United States to function that way—namely, a surplus of space and a surplus of resources. It's no longer possible. So you've got to face that fact and begin seriously as a culture to redefine democracy. What does it mean if we can no longer start over and over and over in the old classic idiom? Well, I don't know how to do it except do it.

I think that people can only come to changing their way of life by realizing the implications, in a no-nonsense way, of the kind of life they're leading. Kennan did a pretty good job of it on oil recently when he said that if we don't get off being hooked on oil then we're going to have a nuclear war; let's quit kidding ourselves about it.

I'm a little more optimistic about this than I used to be. I think that from my experience, and that's all I've got to go on, people do understand, feel, sense that the crunch is here.

I'm not sure historians understand this. If we accept that the capitalist political economy is inherently imperialist and so confront the nature of the world in which we live, then we obviously have to change the system. Obviously they're not ready to get on with that one.

I'm fascinated—I mean this intellectually though I also think it's politically revealing, maybe even psychologically—by why nobody said, yeah, the revisionists are right, but America as an empire is a defensible proposition. So we'll rewrite our history, too. We will accept the basic argument of the revisionists and show why imperialism is good, and healthy, and consequential, and brought many benefits to the American people. Now *that* would be an interesting dialogue. That would force them to come to terms with the price of the empire *circa* 1980. Then you could really get into the dialogue about what the future cost of this defensible political economy really is. That would force them to come to terms with the ever-increasing risk of a nuclear exchange. Or do you want to settle down and say maybe Herbert Hoover was right, maybe we can make it with the hemisphere. Maybe John Quincy Adams was right and we can make it with the hemisphere.[12] We've never tried. It might be worth a go.

Of course, that would still leave us with an empire. It's a halfway house. I don't think you're going to turn this country around in one fell swoop. The point I was getting at, or trying to get at, is this: since there isn't any candid, responsible liberal center *or* Right, that means that the Left must in truth honor if not indeed rehabilitate the best of our conservative tradition just in order to have a serious dialogue. To oversimplify it: I talk with John Quincy Adams simply because there is not any conservative of his integrity or quality around today to talk with. It is as simple as that. You might say the same thing about Madison and Jefferson, or Lincoln—hell, why bother with contemporary liberals when you can confront those kinds of people? But I think the Left in general fails to realize the self-defeating and soft-headed consequences of arguing with second-raters. So, sure, I'd rather deal with Hoover than Buckley or Schlesinger, Jr. Those people had a true sense of history, of the forces at work, the direction of movement, and the fundamental choices.

Q.   How do you assess the general level of awareness of history in the public at large? Do you think Americans are more divorced from their own past than citizens of other societies?

WILLIAMS   My wife Wendy is an Englishwoman and I certainly think, from being with her family, I'd say, sure, England has a stronger sense of history in a classic sense. I think American society has had one from time to time that's rather impressive. After all, Charles Beard was speaking to the public, and he did so effectively in many, many respects. I think the problem is a complicated one. Partly it's the media revolution.[13] The media fragments things; it puts a tremendous burden on educators trying to develop any kind of historical sense, not in a narrow professional way, but any sense of cause and consequence down the line over a period of time. Newspapers and television fragment time into twenty-four-hour units. Or decades. Every decade you've got to have a special issue of *Time* and all that crap, as if that was significant.

I think the whole social science business in primary and secondary education has been a disaster because it doesn't give people any sense of history. You define things as problems and you've fragmented the culture again. I'm deeply concerned about it. I don't think the battle's lost, but I think a lot of hard work is demanded to get history, in the sense we're talking about history, back in the secondary curriculum. I think that the consciousness of history in the public at large is weaker than it has been in many times.

Q.   How does it feel to have come from the position of the late fifties and early sixties, when you were ignored or attacked by most of the profession, to being the president-elect of the Organization of American Historians?

WILLIAMS   Well, I was certainly very moved by the experience of being elected president of the OAH, and by the tribute to my work in New York in 1978. It meant a great deal to me. I thought that what happened there, with serious people talking seriously about serious issues, was an honest coming to terms with some things.

And I do think that as long as I'm president the OAH should be doing important things. I don't consider it to be what it once obviously was, simply an honor. I've tried to use the year as president-elect to initiate some momentum, to do some things that will in fact improve morale, and hopefully, directly or indirectly, create a significant number of jobs.

I intend to be an active president. I will focus on two problems. One is that the OAH doesn't have the money to do routinely the kinds of things that it should do and also deal with matters like the Freedom of Information Act and related research issues. So the first thing I did was to work up a challenge grant proposal to the National Endowment for the Humanities to create a big capital fund for the OAH so it could in fact hire some more people and institute some programs.

The second thing I want to do is to get off the ground with the idea of a massive oral history of the Vietnamese experience, by which I mean what happened to American culture around the Vietnam War. Not just policy makers or the veterans, but the culture at large. How did people understand and try and come to terms with this? What did they come out of the experience with? I think that we can generate a lot of historical consciousness in the public at large. And, incidentally or not so incidentally, it ought to provide a lot of jobs.

One of the aspects of oral history that's sometimes overlooked is that if you get a lot of people doing it, you're going to get professionals out there talking to ordinary folk, which is a very useful thing to do. It has, incidentally, provoked an enormous response in the short period of time since it was mentioned in the *OAH Newsletter.*

Q. Do you think the OAH should make some organized response to the recent Supreme Court decision in the *Yeshiva* case where they outlawed faculty unions in private universities?[14]

WILLIAMS   I don't think it's an issue that the organization can usefully confront at this point because, from my experience at Oregon State University and Oregon in general, this thing has divided people at the honest-to-God grass-roots level in such a way that if a national organization attempted to come in with a consensus of the professionals, I think it would be counterproductive. I think the OAH has, over the past three or four years, supported specific cases or confrontations that have grown out of this or that academic freedom matter, and it has done so rather effectively. Dick Kirkendall, who is executive secretary of the OAH, is good. I have a lot of respect for him.

My longer-range view of it is that if you get a serious movement under way in the country to organize, to accept unionization, then it seems to me that the OAH and/or other such groups might usefully try to define the terms of contract negotiations. They might seriously raise in the minds of people who are going to go the union route *the things that should never be put on the table.*

That's some of the tough politics in Oregon. If you go the union route are you going to have to put everything on the table? Or are there certain things that are going to be negotiated once and will then thereafter be taken as given? I think maybe the OAH might have a useful dialogue, sponsor these kinds of debates. One of the things I hope to do if we get the capital fund is to have the *Newsletter* come out every month, in which case you could have dialogues in it and reports on experiences.

Also, I think the OAH can and should do more with historians who are not in academic jobs. I think it can try to encourage the people who are working in other things to try to also keep on being historians. I think the profession needs to have a debate about the degree to which you have to be an academic to be a historian.

Beyond that, we have not established any significant, on-going relationship with Blacks and other minorities or even nonacademic white historians. Clearly, the burden is on the OAH. I welcome any thoughts on how to get at that problem in a sustained and creative way.

I think we are doing a bit better or, at any rate, trying to do better in a consequential way with historians who work beyond the campus. There are many, many excellent people out there doing very good work and caring deeply about history. We must come together with them, help them, learn from them, and ask them to help us in return.

I do not want to be misunderstood on this final point, but women have to help us. Women are a long way from being equal in the profession—that is simply a statement of fact. On the other hand, they have put their act together better than other groups and so we can learn from them while responding to them. And they need to teach us how they have done as much as they have.

It isn't easy, but then neither is anything else. I said to Harrington once, about halfway through the Ph.D., "You know, Fred, I did a lot of other things before I became a historian, and I'm not sure that academic life is going to be all that great." He said, "I don't blame you. But the point is, get the training and then if you want to be a newspaperman or something else you can still write good history." And it's true; you can. It's in some ways harder work to do, to maintain the energy.

But there is this to be said about it: if you've got a job you can walk off of at five and you want to be a writing historian, then in certain ways you're better off than if you're stuck in the academic world where you can't walk off the job at five o'clock. Writing books is damn hard work whether you are teaching freshmen or Ph.D.s or laying down insulation in an old attic. No easy way to do it.

There's an honest issue to debate here. One of the problems with American academics is they think they're the only ones who use their minds. That's one of the reasons I left Wisconsin. Got weary of it. I'm into an idiom that is much closer to the real world.

The OAH should try to bridge the gap between professional historians and the real world. The current president of the OAH, Carl Degler, has been trying to do this. The organization has to reach into the secondary schools. It has to say in effect, look, we've been, if not intellectually arrogant, then taking you people for granted. We've been wrong. We're going to come to you and try to establish a relationship so that you can educate us and we can help you. I think Degler has been trying to do that.

I'm concerned very strongly about establishing a Center for the Teaching of American History. It would deal with the politics as well as the intellectual side of reestablishing history at the community as well as the secondary school level. It would obviously involve local politics.

We should make contact with unions and church groups, too. I was into that when I first went back to Wisconsin. I worked with the Masey brothers in the UAW. At least once a month I'd go over there and have all-day workshops with people off the line about American foreign policy.

It was an exciting thing to do. The Masey brothers were very articulate socially as well as historically conscious. I found I didn't have any serious communication problem.

When the OAH has its convention in Detroit we're going to have sessions out in the community, in the plants. Warren Susman is working with the UAW and community centers. We will address historical questions that speak to the different communities or body politics in Detroit: labor, Blacks, the poor in general.

Q. Who's going to do this, the professional historians?

WILLIAMS   Well, this is one of the problems. It's a problem that the profession has. Not to personalize this in a silly sense, but the Oscar Handlins and the Arthur Schlesinger, Jr.s do speak for a deep concern that this might turn out to be very consequential action, and they're not sure they want to get into it. There are a lot of liberals who are what we might call tolerant of me, but if you really started to use the organization in what they consider to be an effort to create a political movement, they might just up and quit.

I want to get the profession reaching out to the public at large, in some instances through secondary schools, in some instances through local history work. Sure. Because otherwise we don't have any constituency. We're talking to ourselves, which is what we've been doing for a while.

Q. Good luck.

WILLIAMS   Good luck is right, I'll need it.

POSTSCRIPT

The editors of this collection very thoughtfully extended me an invitation to write an additional four or five pages. I thank them. In my view that creates an artificial situation. If the interview had taken place this year, it would have developed in different ways around different issues. I see no useful purpose in artificially updating a specific historical document. I said what I had to say at a specific time in answer to the questions that were asked at that time. Let it go at that.

NOTES

1. The Frankfurt Institute for Social Research was founded in the mid-1920s as an association of Left intellectuals dedicated to "critical theory" in the tradition of Marxian critiques of ideology and of critical philosophy. It was comprised of intellectuals from many different fields and included Theodor Adorno, Walter Benjamin, Eric Fromm, Max Horkheimer, and Herbert Marcuse. Several of its members spent time or settled permanently in the U.S. during the 1930s. The institute eventually broke up in the late 1960s.

2. Ernst F. Schumacher (1911–77), author and economist, worked on theories for Britain's welfare state after World War II and served on the National Coal Board as economic adviser from 1950 to 1970. He founded the Intermediate Technology Development Group in London in 1966 and was a strong advocate of small-scale technology and decentralization. He is the author of the best-selling *Small Is Beautiful: Economics as if People Mattered* (New York: Harper and Row, 1973).

3. Howard Beale wrote *Theodore Roosevelt and the Rise of America to World Power* (Baltimore: Johns Hopkins Press, 1956) among other works. Raymond Robins (1873–1954) was a Chicago social reformer and a leader of the Progressive party. In 1917 he headed the American Red Cross mission to Russia, and in 1933 he returned to the Soviet Union to study economic conditions and education.

4. Lend-lease was necessary to get around the law of 1934 that required any nation at war to pay cash for goods purchased in the United States. Passed in 1941, the Lend-Lease Act allowed Roosevelt to supply Britain and any other nation fighting Germany with economic and logistical support. It helped to enlarge presidential power and was the precursor of America's postwar foreign aid policy and programs.

5. George Kennan is considered the chief architect of the shift in postwar American foreign policy from cooperation to confrontation with the Soviet Union. As chargé d'affaires in Moscow 1944–46 and as director of the State Department's policy planning staff in 1947, Kennan argued that Soviet international policy sought to undermine Western capitalism and "advance the official limits of Soviet power" through an "elaborate apparatus for exerting influence in other countries." He advocated the containment of Soviet expansionist tendencies through strong resistance at any point and the threat of American force.

6. In 1958, James Reston wrote, "This is a time for searching criticism, all right, but for criticism of the whole society."

7. From 1949 to 1968, Max Ascoli was publisher and editor of *The Reporter,* a liberal, anti-Communist journal of national and international politics.

8. Adolph Berle, diplomat and member of Roosevelt's brain trust, served as assistant secretary of state for Latin American affairs from 1938 to 1944 and became chief coordinator of Kennedy's Latin American policy in 1961.

9. The Rabinowitz Foundation was established in 1945 to foster international under-standing through supporting research on foreign countries.

10. NSC-68, the major American policy statement of the cold war signed by President Truman in 1950, launched the arms race. In it, Dean Acheson's State Department portrayed the United States and the Soviet Union as irreconcilable superpowers, with the latter bent on world domination. NSC-68 held that the aggressive expansionism of Communist ideology and Soviet military power fundamentally threatened American security and called for American rearmament. Concluding that the only effective negotiation with the Soviet Union was "by act rather than by words," this policy paper set the stage for the Korean War.

11. Alfred D. Chandler, Jr., *The Visible Hand: The Managerial Revolution in American Business* (Cambridge, Mass.: Harvard University Press, 1977).

12. Herbert Hoover's foreign policy was based upon the notion of American economic prosperity and domestic political stability being sustained by access to overseas markets but not entailing direct military intervention abroad. John Quincy Adams was largely responsible for the Monroe Doctrine of 1823 announcing to the world American determination to resist European encroachment anywhere in the hemisphere as a threat to United States hegemony while pledging "not to interfere in the internal concerns" of Europe.

13. Charles Beard (1874–1948) published *An Economic Interpretation of the Constitution of the United States* in 1913, a controversial and seminal foray into the social and economic analysis of American political culture. He resigned from his professorship at Columbia in 1917 in protest over the university's attempt to suppress criticism of American intervention in World War I, although he himself favored it at the time. He remained active in both public affairs and the world of historical scholarship into the 1940s. He strongly opposed United States entry into World War II.

14. In *NLRB* v. *Yeshiva* and *Yeshiva University Faculty Association* v. *Yeshiva University*, decided February 20, 1980, the Supreme Court ruled 5–4 that Yeshiva University was justified in refusing to negotiate with the NLRB-certified Yeshiva Faculty Association because the faculty played a "crucial role" in university decision-making. As "managerial employees," the Court held, faculty at "mature universities" are not entitled to collective bargaining rights.

SELECT BIBLIOGRAPHY

Books
America and the Middle East: Open Door Imperialism or Enlightened Leadership? New York: Rinehart, 1958.
America Confronts a Revolutionary World, 1776–1976. New York: William Morrow & Co., 1976.
American-Russian Relations, 1781–1947. New York: Rinehart, 1952.
Americans in a Changing World: A History of the United States in the Twentieth Century. New York: Harper & Row, 1978.

The Contours of American History. Cleveland, Ohio: World Publishing Co., 1961.

Empire as a Way of Life: An Essay on the Causes and Character of America's Present Predicament, Along with a Few Thoughts About an Alternative. New York: Oxford University Press, 1980.

From Colony to Empire: Essays in the History of American Foreign Relations, editor. New York: John Wiley & Sons, Inc., 1972.

The Great Evasion: An Essay on the Contemporary Relevance of Karl Marx and the Wisdom of Admitting the Heretic into the Dialogue About America's Future. Chicago: Quadrangle Books, 1964.

History as a Way of Learning: Articles, Excerpts, and Essays. New York: New Viewpoints, 1973.

The Roots of the Modern American Empire: A Study of the Growth and Shaping of a Social Consciousness in a Marketplace Society. New York: Random House, 1969.

The Shaping of American Diplomacy: Readings and Documents in American Foreign Relations, 1750–1955. Chicago: Rand McNally, 1956.

The Tragedy of American Diplomacy. Cleveland, Ohio: World Publishing Co., 1959; rev. ed., 1962.

The United States, Cuba and Castro: An Essay on the Dynamics of Revolution and the Dissolution of Empire. New York: Monthly Review Press, 1962.

Articles

"Demystifying Cold War Orthodoxy." *Science and Society* 39 (1975):316–51.

"Notes on the Death of a Ship and the End of a World: The Grounding of the British Bark 'Glenesslin' at Mount Neahkahnie on 1 October 1913." *American Neptune,* 41 (1981):122–38.

"Thoughts on Reading Henry Adams." *Journal of American History,* 68 (1981):7–15.

S T A U G H T O N L Y N D

STAUGHTON LYND

STAUGHTON LYND STANDS out among historians for his remarkable capacity to combine intellectual radicalism and social activism at the grass-roots level.

Born in 1929, the son of sociologists Robert S. and Helen M. Lynd, Staughton Lynd received his B.A. from Harvard College in 1951 and his Ph.D. from Columbia University in 1962. He taught American history at Yale University, Spelman College, and other institutions of higher learning during the 1960s. Simultaneously he was becoming deeply involved in the civil rights and peace movements. He directed the Freedom Schools of the Mississippi Summer Project in 1964. In April 1965 he chaired the first mass march on Washington, D.C., to protest the Vietnam War and a few months later journeyed to Hanoi on a peace mission in defiance of the United States government. Over the next several years he continued to speak out publicly in opposition to the war, and he played a major role in building support for draft resisters. His wide-ranging activities earned him a reputation as a leader of the New Left.

With his academic career at an end as a result of these activities, Lynd became a community organizer in Chicago and returned to school as a law student. In 1976 he began to practice labor law in Youngstown, Ohio. Lynd has recently served as legal representative of Youngstown steelworkers in their fight to halt plant closings and to institute worker or community management in them.

Lynd's scholarship reflects his enduring commitment to the intrinsic value of participatory democracy and his long-standing belief in the historical efficacy of popularly based movements against class, racial, and bureaucratic oppression. His first book, *Anti-Federalism in Dutchess County New York: A Study of Democracy and Class Conflict in the Revolutionary Era*, published in 1962, revived and revitalized the Progressive interpretation of the ratification struggle over the Constitution in an open challenge to the then-dominant consensus approach. This analysis was extended in *Class Conflict, Slavery and the United States Constitution*, a collection of essays that appeared in 1967. During the same period he edited two volumes that brought history to bear on issues raised by the civil rights movement: *Nonviolence in America: A Documentary History* (1966) and *Reconstruction*. With Tom Hayden he coauthored an account of their trip to North Vietnam, entitled *The Other Side* (1966). Two years later he published *Intellectual Origins of American Radicalism*, which concentrates on the era between the American Revolution and Civil War.

Since leaving academia, Lynd has turned his scholarly attention increasingly to the history of American radicalism in the twentieth century. His history of the draft resistance movement, coauthored with Michael Ferber, appeared in 1971 under the simple title *The Resistance*. As editor or author he contributed to three books published in 1973: *American Labor Radicalism: Testimonies and Interpretations; Strategy and Program: Two Essays Toward a New American Socialism;* and *Rank and File: Personal Histories by Working-Class Organizers*.

Lynd's most recent book is *Labor Law for the Rank and Filer.* (2d ed., 1982). Presently at work on a study of the steel plant closings in Youngstown, Lynd continues to contribute frequently to leftist publications such as *Radical America, Radical History Review, In These Times,* and *democracy*.

This interview was conducted in the spring of 1977 by Len Calabrese, a neighborhood activist in Cleveland who teaches at the University of Akron.

John Barbero, mentioned at several points in this interview and one of the giants of the Rank and File *movement, was present throughout the taping. He died in a tragic accident in 1981. This interview is dedicated to his memory.*

Q How did you get involved in the project that led to *Rank and File?*
LYND I found myself more and more frustrated by the fact that a historian is not supposed to attach values to his or her conclusions, a historian is not supposed to say at the end of the book, "Now this means we should all go out and do so and so." And I felt that, as a person with an activist orientation to life, I had trapped myself into a discipline that was inherently schizophrenic for a person such as myself. If you try to infuse your objective work with your values, to comment on it, then, of course, you are "presentist." If, on the other hand, you bend over backward not to do that, you run a danger of losing track of who you are, of disassociating yourself from your own values. I wasn't happy with that dilemma, and I don't believe that radical historians have adequately resolved it. I sense a strong tendency among radical historians to project their own sublimated activism on whatever group they happen to be studying. I remember one radical historian who referred to the lower-class group he was researching as "my boys." And yet, as I say, when you see a

person consciously take himself or herself in hand and surmount that, the result is almost as distressing because you tend to find a person who will then laboriously try to convince you that it is really valuable to try to study some obscure thirteenth-century group for its own sake. Why? Other than as art?

So in any case, I—no doubt because of, as I say, my own penchant for action—struggled with that a lot. I wasn't happy editorializing. It seemed a violation of the limits of the craft and I wanted to be a good craftsman. But I sure wasn't going to do that other thing, which was score brownie points with senior conservative historians for the rest of my life to prove that, even though I was a radical, I could be a good historian, too. In addition, I was very conscious that the student movement had wound up cutting itself off from ordinary working people, that the worker looked at what was going on on the campus and felt, "Who are these crazy kids who are lucky enough to be able to go to college and spend their time tearing it up?" Whatever I was able to come up with methodologically, I wanted it to be in the direction of working-class studies and, specifically, of seeking an answer to the question of whether there was something that history, since that was the thing I was doing, could do to be of help to all the young people who were again trying to take jobs in factories, take teaching jobs in working-class community colleges, and so on. And then, of course, I was in the process of being blacklisted just at this same time. This was not insignificant in that while I was very much discontented at Yale, maybe I wasn't discontented enough to have turned my back on it and looked in new directions unless they pushed me out.

This yeast was bubbling within me, and it's funny, but one of the occasions when I can remember trying to discuss it most systematically was during a sit-in at the University of Chicago. In the first days of the sit-in they attempted to offer an intellectual program for professors who weren't quite prepared simply to "sit in" as such, but nevertheless would show up in the occupied buildings and manifest their solidarity with the students. So Jesse Lemisch and I spent a whole afternoon talking about, on the one hand, history from the bottom up and, on the other hand, what at the time I was calling guerrilla history—that is, a way to break through the methodological impasse of being an observer, a way of ceasing to be an eye and becoming also a hand.[1]

Thereafter, my wife Alice and I began the process that became *Rank and File*, seeking out older union organizers and having a tape-recorded conversation with them in the hope that somehow the material could be made available to younger people who were again trying the same sort of thing. Chronologically, we were located halfway between these folks in their sixties, who very often had just retired or were on the verge of retiring and had been active during the 1930s, and people in their twenties, who were "colonizing" with roughly the same perspective of those older people a generation ago, but often knowing very little in a practical way about what the older people felt they had learned from that experience.

After we had done that a while we got what to me was a very exciting insight. Usually when you do oral history the idea is that you are gathering material for Your Book, in capital letters, and then lots of people will read Your Book and, incidentally, you will become a hot-shot. It occurred to us that the middle link was basically unnecessary—the book part—and that the way the process should be envisioned is the older person directly telling younger people about the older person's experience. If the historian wants to be there with a tape recorder and make the results available to a wider audience, that's fine, but basically the historian is only a catalyst, an organizer, the one who creates the occasion for the older people to share their experiences. If you look at _Rank and File,_ at least 50 percent of the book was a community forum at St. Joseph's College or a presentation at the Gary Writers' Workshop or whatever. They were speeches, not tape-recorded interviews, although they were speeches in which the speakers had been encouraged to feel that their own lives were significant and to talk about their experiences.

There are all kinds of criticisms of _Rank and File,_ of which I think the most important is that the people in the book are not really rank-and-filers at all, but radical organizers. Now the rebuttal is that, by and large, they are people who became radicals in the course of their experience as rank-and-file workers —that is to say, they were not by and large people who became radicals on a college campus or inherited their radicalism from their parents and applied it in a workplace. The good thing about the book is the description of the experience of becoming a radical; people would tell you how they became disillusioned with the church, and so on. But they are not ordinary people. _Rank and File_ as a product is just a tiny beginning, one variant among many others that could be imagined, but I felt that the process of doing that book was serving the people. From time to time, it would encourage me to hear about historians in Cuba or other revolutionary societies who were doing exactly the same thing, that is, who felt that their first task as historians was to gather up the collective wisdom that was already there, the history that already existed but happened to be in people's heads and not to have been set forth in a permanent medium.

I think of the kind of oral history that I am interested in as a subset of history from the bottom up. It's like history from the bottom up carried a step further because it's people at the bottom doing their own history. But all the criticisms of (1) history from the bottom up, and (2) oral history apply: if you look at the situation from only one side, if you believe everything you are told and don't use written sources as well, etc., etc., then your product as history will be imperfect. Sure. But all of that is easy. All of that is just what a good historian would do anyway: look at the situation from the top down as well as from the bottom up, check out all available written sources as well as talk to people. We're talking—or we ought to be talking—about something that you don't do _instead_ of doing all the other things, but that you do _in addition_ to all the other things because, let's face it, all the other things added together very often leave you looking through a telescope from a great distance at what ordinary people were supposed to have been doing in whatever period you are talking about. One of the strong arguments, I think, for oral history as a specialization for radical historians is that it's so difficult to know what's going on with ordinary people unless you ask them. I have very mixed feelings looking at a study of, say, the seventeenth century from the bottom up. Scholars perform Herculean feats: they dig up the records at the municipal court, they figure out that a lot of people were arrested for poaching, or whatever, and they make interesting conclusions on the basis of much more innovative use of evidence, much more assiduous digging than historians who just go to the nearest library and read some great man's manuscript collection. Nevertheless, when you consider the product, how much do you really know about those people, especially what went on inside their heads, how they felt about things? That is why I say that even from the standpoint of knowledge, just knowledge—the historian's traditional standpoint—I question how much about the bottom really can be derived from the fragmentary documentary sources that we're perforce driven to use. Just from the standpoint of knowledge I think that a much more satisfactory, three-dimensional feeling about your product is possible if you are able to use both oral and written sources. Then, when you add to that the dimension of talking to people still alive, you have an opportunity to assist them in making their lives useful to younger comrades, it seems to me the method has very strong claims. I think of the three women in *Union Maids*,[2] what it's meant to each of their lives to have had this opportunity to sum up and share with younger people. And, of course, they do it not only through the film, but by going to places where the film is being shown and adding a new layer of oral history to a film that was originally inspired by oral history, so that it becomes quite a dense process.

So I think there are strong, strong arguments for oral history from the bottom up as a methodology of specific interest to radical historians. But only if they remain radical historians—I mean, only if they remain *historians* in the doing of it, which is to say only if they look at the situation from the viewpoints of all the protagonists, only if they use written as well as oral sources and so on. To whatever extent I failed in that, and I think it is probably true I have failed, that I didn't adequately check out the written sources available for each and every episode mentioned by narrators in *Rank and File*, which was a criticism made of the work, then that's my fault, not the fault of the method. If I was limited, or if I was lazy, or if I was pressed by other things in my life, it doesn't mean that the method is invalidated thereby; it just means I didn't carry it as far as it should have been carried.

Q. So you really saw *Rank and File* as a way out of the methodological impasse, as a contribution to creating or elaborating on a new method more than as the expression of any particular historiographical interest in, say, the thirties or the creation of the CIO?

LYND   Absolutely, the original idea was helping older people to share their experience with younger people, and it wasn't so much that I had a subject matter interest in the thirties; it was because of an interest in helping younger people to benefit from the experience of those who had tried the same thing before so they wouldn't have to go through all the same things again.

Two kinds of younger people: middle class students leaving the campus to colonize, but also a group that Alice and I became more and more aware of, the younger generation in working-class communities, many of whom, we noticed in Gary, were trying very courageously to find ways to live as what they were—people who had been away to college and gotten radical ideas, people who didn't want to spend their whole lives working in a mill in order to buy a home but who nevertheless wanted to live in that community and make a contribution to it. And we felt that maybe they were the most important audience. In the end, of course, even that definition of being a historian wound up not being entirely satisfying, so now I am a lawyer—and yet I am very enamored with what I was trying to do with history.

Q.   Do you feel a strong continuity between being a historian and a lawyer? Or are you embarked on a new career?

LYND   Law is like history with dessert. For instance, I'm working on a case that involves a company moving away from Youngstown after allegedly promising to the union, during collective bargaining negotiations five years ago, that it would stay. Maybe it's called law instead of history, but I'm doing exactly what I used to do as a historian. I'm ferreting out documents. I'm talking to people. I'm trying to understand why the policy changed from one point in time to another. But as a historian when you get to the last chapter, that's it; whereas a lawyer has the chance of going a little further.

I have all the questions that anybody else does about the law and whether it misleads people more than it helps them to hold out a sense that maybe you can accomplish something in the courts. But at least for me there's the satisfaction that after you get done analyzing the situation, you can have a shot at trying to do something about it. I find that very satisfying. And another thing, I noticed in looking at the E. P. Thompson interview his comment on *Whigs and Hunters* where, in the last chapter, he suddenly bursts forth and says, in effect, "You know, the law is not such a bad thing. Marxists have gone overboard with the idea that everything is relative. There's something about the law as a society's encapsulation of its sense of right and wrong that's extremely important." (See page 9.) I suppose it's very obvious that he also spoke for me in saying that.

That certainly is a continuity in my own life. I can remember as a Harvard undergraduate sitting in Cronin's, the local pub, with the rest of the Harvard John Reed Society and they were pounding away at my ridiculous bourgeois notion that there were certain concepts of right and wrong that didn't change from one period of class rule to another, that were more or less the same throughout human history because human beings were human. Sometimes I feel I spend my life having that argument. One year it's with the John Reed Society, the next year it's with Eugene Genovese. But it's the same argument and it helps to explain, I suppose, how someone like myself is a sucker for the law in the sense that I really do have the notion that there's something called Justice with a capital "J," that there's something you can appeal to even in people whose experiences wouldn't ordinarily lead them to understand what you're trying to say. Of course, when I put it that way you can see the connection with notions of nonviolence as well. I'm afraid the continuities become so overwhelming the question is whether there is really any change.

Q. Could you describe how you decided to go into law?

LYND   Alice and I decided together about going into law. In doing *Rank and File* we were increasingly struck by the number of working people whom we met who felt messed over by both the company and the union. Often their problems had a legal aspect. They didn't know where to turn. We put a lot of energy into finding legal help for these friends. It turned out that the available movement lawyers were not into labor law, and the labor lawyers were working either for unions or companies and were unavailable. Finally, Alice and I decided that it would save time for one of us to go to law school.

I felt Alice would very likely make a better lawyer than I because of her draft counseling experience. However, she has a reading problem and dreaded law school, so in the end I became a lawyer and she a paralegal. Alice's experience as a draft counselor remains a model for us as to how professionals can relate as co-workers to those they serve. The idea is that both the professional and the client are experts: the professional in a technique, such as interpreting Selective Service regulations, or law, and the nonprofessional in the problem. This is obvious in labor law where the worker is the expert on the nature of his or her work, the history of the particular workplace, the contract and its interpretation. As Alice and I see it, professionals and nonprofessionals are equals, each contributing expert knowledge.

Q. Do you think the law can be used as a tool for radical change?

LYND   I think of trying to use the law as a shield rather than a sword. For instance, John Barbero[3] and I were involved in a suit to challenge ENA [Experimental Negotiating Agreement] when it was first adopted. I don't think either of us feels bad about that. As a matter of fact, I now find everybody, Ed Sadlowski included, refers to that suit almost as if they had a part in it.[4] At the time, Sadlowski very definitely stood aloof. In any case, the weakness of it was that we were trying to use a lawsuit to do something that only a social movement could have done. I don't believe, by and large, in the Ralph Nader idea of changing society by means of the law. I believe in trying to use the law to protect people as best you can as they try to change society in other ways. Which really has been my own personal experience with the law. I've had five or six fairly serious encounters with the law and I don't think

I've ever paid a lawyer a penny. The ACLU was always there to defend me.

But there's yet another aspect of the law that intrigues me. One of the problems with a radical movement or a socialist movement attempting to speak to American working people is that it's as if we just haven't found the language. I almost feel that it's not essentially a problem of ideas, but somehow the language isn't a natural language. As the son of two professors who grew up on the eighth floor of an apartment house in New York City, I am very unlikely to be able to make much of a contribution to the discovery of that language. But yet and still I'm intrigued by the precision the law can give you in talking about, for example, the idea of being innocent until proven guilty. By the time Sadlowski and Lloyd McBride came down to the wire they were both advocating the concept that if the worker in the shop is disciplined, accused of something, he or she gets full pay until the thing is finally adjudicated.

I had the experience in the anti-war movement that I could get up in front of thousands of people and talk about what I personally was feeling at that moment and people out there would feel I had found the words to express their feelings, too. That was because they were people like me, college students, etc. It's a sadness to me but I don't anticipate that happening before a local union audience or in a strike situation. But that doesn't mean I can't make some contribution toward the discovery of the language that I think needs to be discovered. I do have the basic conviction that there are, as it were, two express trains passing each other in American factories. Here are all the former student radicals of the sixties adopting very heavy Marxist vocabularies in order to communicate with the working class, and here are working people who are increasingly interested in participatory democracy and helping to make the decisions that affect their lives and all the things that the student radicals used to believe in.

Q. You have written important analytic pieces about the 1930s. What issues there presently concern you?

LYND   There is a historiographical debate about the thirties, which, as far as I am concerned, is still completely up for grabs. Where did the initiatives from above come from, who was really responsible for the Wagner Act?[5] It is all very well to say—and I think it is the best we can say for the moment—that there were two kinds of motivations. There was a motivation from below to get a little help from the government in trying to organize. There surely was also a motivation from above to give these crazy workers something so they would get off the streets. Senator Wagner felt that; Heber Blankenhorn, who did Wagner's drafting, felt that; John L. Lewis appears to have felt that. The big question, it seems to me, the big unanswered question, is whether there was any industry input in the genesis of the Wagner Act or whether it was only after the fact that the Thomas Lamonts and the J. P. Morgans decided, as U.S. Steel did decide after the General Motors sit-down, "Hey, let's live with this thing." That, it seems to me, is the unanswered question about where all of that came from. I don't know the answer, but what I do know is that when the ACLU and the Communist party initially opposed the Wagner Act, they weren't as screwy as people have thought for the last forty years. When they said that this could lead to an American fascism they may have been right; look at the way labor is tied hand and foot by legal regulations today. If you set the end product beside what the Communist party and the ACLU predicted forty years ago, they weren't so off base. Now, it took a lot of backtracking by the Supreme Court to get there, but maybe that was part of the prediction, at least in its more sophisticated form: no matter how the law was written, once you had the government that far into controlling the labor movement, given the nature of power in American society, it was going to wind up controlling the labor movement for the sake of business.

Just to add one little historical footnote for the benefit of anyone who wants to work on this problem: there is a very important difference between the Wagner Act as it was introduced in 1934 and as it was passed in 1935, and the difference is that the 1934 draft of the Wagner Act provides for compulsory arbitration. Now, why is that important? Number one, it helps to explain the reaction of groups such as the ACLU and the Communist party. Number two, the reaction of groups such as the ACLU and the Communist party may explain why that feature was dropped in 1935. And it's a riot to read the report of the Senate Committee on Labor in recommending the 1934 version of the Wagner Act—or the United States Supreme Court in the Jones and Laughlin case holding the Act constitutional—because both piously say, "Of course, we're not telling business and labor what to agree to, we're only telling them to sit down together and bargain—that's the American way." In 1934, they wanted to put compulsory arbitration into the law. This is a kind of value-free observation. I don't know if it was good or bad that the bill was changed. Maybe it should have been left in its original form and rejected. Maybe it was a people's victory that it was modified. All I'm saying, as stimulus for some historian who wants to figure all this out, is that it happened. And it is a very important thing that it happened because the whole thrust of labor law under the Wagner Act is a double whammy: "We're not going to tell you what to do, but once you've agreed on what to do, we're going to enforce it." Since the people who do the agreeing are not the rank and file but the union bureaucrats and business, the upshot has tended to be the present legal apparatus enforcing collective bargaining agreements against workers who try to wildcat or whatever. To understand it you have to go all the way back and realize that, originally, at least some of the forces behind the Wagner Act wanted arbitration, they wanted to stop strikes. They didn't want a sophisticated system of free collective bargaining; they wanted to put a hammer on working people and get them to stop all this uproar.

Q. What about the role of the Communist party in the thirties?

LYND I think we've all sort of shot from the hip on that question, and maybe there should be a moratorium on one-sentence summaries until someone has done a little more work. There probably has been a good deal of work in the last year or two that I am not entirely caught up with. But if I had to make a one-sentence summary, I would say you have a feeling of a tragedy that is very different from melodrama. I think both the Third Period and the Popular Front periods were extremely creative, significant episodes. If you compare what the Communist party did between 1929 and 1935—let's call that the Third Period—and what it did between 1935 and the beginning of the war, if you compare what the Popular Front did in those two five-year spans with everything it's done before and since, then the rest is just dust in the balance, the rest is inner-party squabbles and the international Communist banquet circuit. Nothing is really happening in this country as compared with either of those periods. Now the tragedy comes in that I think there was a certain exaggeration in each of those episodes that probably had to do with taking cues from abroad. It's a complicated question. I think Al Richmond is probably right in criticizing me, in saying I underemphasize the degree to which these lines grew out of the experience of the American party.[6] Maybe you have to make a more sophisticated, a more complex statement about the fact of overseas direction, and say that it lent a certain quality of artificiality and exaggeration to each of these initiatives. What is for sure is that the extremely militant, creative, courageous, never-to-be-forgotten Third Period conduct of the Communist party went overboard in the direction of calling socialists "social fascists." No question of that. And not just in the attitudes toward the Socialist party, but in the attitude toward indigenous working-class organizations, toward AF of L locals, toward independent locals where the working class in response to the NRA founded their own unions. The Communist party was, for a period, out in left field in saying that the only important thing was the CP-sponsored Trade Union Unity League. So that there *were* tremendous missed opportunities.

As another element of complexity, I think there was a kind of golden age, maybe occurring at different times in different parts of the country but generally in 1934–35, when the Communist party in practice revised its Third Period orientation. And the word hadn't come down from the Seventh Party Congress yet, so it could be done creatively, and humanly, and with tactical flexibility. That was the period when the socialists and the Communists all over the country initiated local labor parties. That was the period when Norman Thomas and Earl Browder appeared together in Madison Square Garden—a forgotten time, a time that, in a *Radical America* article, I tried to call the period of the "united front from below" intervening between the sectarian Third Period and the sectarian Popular Front.[7]

Even in the Popular Front period, as David Montgomery was reminding me recently, there were tremendous missed opportunities. George Powers, who was in the Communist party in the Monongahela Valley, told me that there was a certain period of time in the late thirties where every single important steel union president in the valley was a Communist. Now it was also the case that in every one of those little towns—Ambridge, Clairton, McKeesport, all those places, venerable places—the local Republican administration was thrown out by the steelworkers, by the CIO, and replaced by Democrats. Now, my question is why? Did it have to be that way? The steelworkers were so strong in every one of those places that they could have done anything they wanted to do. And, in fact, of course—complexities again —even though they called themselves Democrats, I suspect that if one could really dig out the history of each of those little towns you'd find that there were steelworkers elected to office, that they had pretty tough programs in terms of rent control, things of this kind; in other words, they tried—and not for the last time—working within the Democratic party to give it an independent politics, a working-class content. But still, suppose instead of doing that, say from 1935 to 1945, the Communist party had had the insight to say, "We're going to support Roosevelt *nationally*, he's earned it; it is necessary in order to present some kind of united resistance to fascism"—all the things that they did say—but also that *locally* they would try to build independent labor parties. There would have been nothing inconsistent between critical support for Roosevelt and saying after the Memorial Day Massacre in Chicago that Mayor Kelley, who ordered the police to fire, had to go.[8] Whereas the Communists, to the best of my knowledge, supported Mayor Kelley in the election after the Memorial Day Massacre. And I just say that that is asinine. So that, there again, I think the Popular Front impulse was an extremely creative, interesting thing, and even the idea of communism as twentieth-century Americanism—that's not such a bad idea. If it isn't twentieth-century Americanism what is it? Russian subversion? There's nothing wrong with being twentieth-century American, but they overdid it. They did it mechanically; they did it artificially; they did it in such a way as to give up their own independent voice.

For those who do additional primary research on the thirties I would like to say, "Don't go looking for scapegoats." There were giants in that era. We should be so lucky if we should ever in our lives do anything as significant as the Communist party did in the 1930s. But that doesn't mean we can't think about it, learn from it, and discuss it analytically and critically.

Q. You've spoken of rank and file as the fundamental reality, not the crowd and not the Party. Could you encapsulate the essence of that reality, that rank and file?

LYND That's interesting. I've been thinking about that because there is a screwy notion of the rank and file loose in the land, two screwy notions really.

One is that the rank and file is an electoral organization. Most of the so-called rank-and-file groups that people get excited about are nothing but electoral organizations that happen to be electoral organizations for union politics, which greatly resembles Democratic party politics and in which most of the candidates bear a striking resemblance to liberal Democrats. It doesn't mean that it is wicked; it just means that that is what it is, and I would say for instance that the Sadlowski campaign, the Fight Back organization, had no independent reality other than that election and, if it continues, continues for the purpose of the next election. He didn't put out a newspaper in District 31 as he promised to do. To the best of my knowledge Fight Back, as Fight Back, has no autonomous activities other than his electoral campaign. Certainly the organization doesn't exist to criticize the candidate, you can be sure of that. And as a matter of fact, the universal complaint of rank-and-file groups in steel from California to Youngstown to Canada is that Sadlowski didn't approach them, didn't work with them, didn't use them. Why? He figured he had their votes anyway, and he wanted to keep the apparatus tightly under his control.

Another form of rank and file that I would think of as a pseudo form is the little group of former radical students who get together and call themselves —and I've done this—the concerned this or the rank-and-file that and put out their little newspaper. Which is fine and makes a certain contribution; it really does make a contribution. But it is not the self-activity of the working class. It just isn't. And it tends not to become that because it is very difficult for workers with different backgrounds to become a part of such a group. The nucleus of such a group is made up of former students. When an ordinary worker comes into the group he or she is in the minority. The atmosphere of the group is already set. If workers become a part of it, they do it in such a way as to give up their own identity, take on a foreign lingo.

A much more difficult question is: what could a rank and file do? It would have to involve forms of day-to-day activity. It would have to be more than, on the one hand, election campaigns and, on the other hand, passing out radical literature, which are the two main things that rank-and-file groups do these days. And it's understandable that that is all they do because of the tremendous legal restrictions on doing anything else.

But that is just not enough. A rank-and-file group ought to be present, day to day, in working-class communities and workplaces—a group that acts differently, a group that you can turn to when you have a problem, a group that creates change. I don't sense that anywhere. Now, that may be my own limitation, but I just don't sense that kind of a rank-and-file presence in any union or the places where members of a union live. Another missing dimension in most rank-and-file movements is, I think, a cultural dimension, and I'm not even quite sure what I mean by that. But someone was telling me that at the St. Thérèse General Motors plant what became a sit-down had its origins in an insistence of French-speaking workers that their language be respected; that is, the group that formed around that demand became the group that sparked the sit-down. And, of course, in the short-lived Black Revolutionary Union movement in Detroit, one sensed that extra dimension. It was the dimension that the church contributed to the southern civil rights movement. One just took it for granted that freedom meetings were in churches, and there was an entire rhetoric—not just We Shall Overcome but Solidarity Forever, and how many others that were originally hymns—because people shared a common religious background. Somehow, after they had all become atheists, that still continued to matter in the cultural forms that they found to express themselves. I sense the absence of that in movements that call themselves rank and file, and I think it is absolutely critical. We are talking about something that gives people the courage to say, "Hey! I have two kids and I'm going to risk my job for this." That has got to come from somewhere. That has got to have deep roots.

Another thing I sense lacking in most rank-and-file movements is something I sense in the activity of someone like John Barbero. He has a personal relationship with everyone, and oftentimes it may be two candidates for the same office or people on opposite sides of the question, but somehow the way John conducts himself, he's entered into that other person's life, but without surrendering his own identity or integrity. That other person considers him a friend, and John thinks of this other person as a friend. Now that quality —maybe that's just what all human beings should have in the way they live their lives. There's not going to be any rank and file, or any other Left movement in this country, until the people in it have the knack of constantly reaching out beyond the movement to establish contact with those who are not in it.

Q. Do you see rank-and-file organizers, and your work with them as a lawyer, as part of the American tradition of radicalism that you tried to delineate in *Intellectual Origins?*⁹

LYND Yes, I do. My approach to labor law is right out of that book in the sense that the only way to free up rank-and-file people is to take the position that prior to the creation of unions, prior to the initiation of collective bargaining, they have rights, and that the institutional apparatus exists to protect and enhance those rights. But if it betrays those rights, power returns to the rank and file to do as it wishes. The funny thing is that you can argue that point of view much more credibly in the area of labor law than in the area of the creation of government. Because if you are going to talk about the creation of government you are driven to talk about natural rights, and about 95 percent of the Left goes up the wall. However, if you're talking about the labor movement you can make the same argument by saying, "Hey, honest, fellows, I'm not talking about natural rights. These are statutory rights. This is Section 7 of the National Labor Relations Act. This talks about the right to engage in concerted activity. It doesn't say 'after you have a union' or 'so that you can be part of a union.' It's just there. And if, in the course of engaging in concerted activity, you want to create a union, great. And if having created it you want to destroy it, great. You have the right to do that under the NLRA." So that, as I say, for better or worse, I find myself using the same intellectual apparatus that I tried to work out in that book, perhaps more credibly in the area of labor law and rank and file.

POSTSCRIPT

During the five years since Len Calabrese and I had the foregoing conversation, I have been continually involved in a popular movement against the closing of Youngstown's steel mills. In a forthcoming book, *The Fight Against Shutdowns: Youngstown's Steel Mill Closings* (Singlejack Books: San Pedro, Calif.), I try to tell the history of that movement. The experience has enriched my appreciation of the possibilities of "oral history from the bottom up."

I participated as a lawyer in the Youngstown struggle to save the mills. I represented an interdenominational church coalition that sought to reopen the Campbell Works under employee-community ownership; the local union of production and maintenance workers at the Brier Hill Works; and six local unions, unemployed steelworkers, and others, who attempted to stop U.S. Steel from closing its Youngstown Works.

The following struck me when, as a participant-observer, I wrote the story of what happened:

1. It seems more true to me than ever that *unless the experience of working-class participants in popular struggles is recorded promptly, important pieces of history may be lost forever.* For instance, employee-community ownership in Youngstown was first suggested by a local union officer named Gerald Dickey in September 1977. I interviewed Dickey in the spring of 1981. He was at first unable to remember how the idea of employee-community ownership had come to him. Only after he had been talking for half an hour, and started the second side of the tape, did Dickey suddenly exclaim, *"Now* I remember," and proceed to tell the story. I felt that had I interviewed Dickey even a week later it might have been too late.

2. There is a patronizing assumption in the doing of much history, including oral history, that the participant provides the experience and the historian provides the interpretation. I found this not to be true in Youngstown. Rather, *the participants themselves interpreted their own struggle more and more profoundly as the struggle unfolded.*

When the first mill closed there was a general tendency to blame what happened on foreign imports and environmental laws. This view soon gave way to a perception that the Campbell Works had been closed by a conglomerate that used the cash flow generated by its steel facilities for corporate empire-building rather than to modernize the mills. At that stage, Youngstown steelworkers blamed mill closings on the acquisition of steel companies like Youngstown Sheet & Tube and Jones & Laughlin by conglomerates such as Lykes and Ling–Temco–Vought.

But then came the closing of U.S. Steel's Youngstown mills, and this explanation no longer was adequate. A consensus emerged that the problem was not *who* made investment decisions but the *basis* on which they were made. The mills were closed because companies like U.S. Steel insisted not just on making a profit but on making as much profit as possible.

In opposition to the concept of profit maximization, Youngstown steelworkers said that modernization of industries like steel should (in the words of a favorite Youngstown picket sign) put "People First, Profits Second." John Barbero, like Dickey a local union officer, was the first person in the area to popularize the idea that modernization should take place in communities where the industry already existed rather than in new, "greenfield" sites. This "brownfield" strategy for modernization tapped sentiments with deep roots in Youngstown's working-class community. Rather than labor following capital, Barbero and others called for capital investment where workers already lived. They emphasized the value of several generations of a family living near to one another; as Ed Mann, another spokesperson, put it, "We're not gypsies." It came to be felt in Youngstown that when an enterprise has induced a community to depend on its presence, then the enterprise has an obligation to stay in the community as long as it can make *some* profit there.

Gerald Dickey's vision of employee-community ownership and John Barbero's concept of brownfield modernization became the principal ideas both of the Youngstown movement and of my history. Strictly speaking, Dickey and Barbero did not create these ideas. Dickey heard a school board candidate at a mass meeting throw out the notion, "Why don't we buy the damn place?" Barbero read about brownfield modernization in a newspaper account of a speech by Stewart Udall. What these participants did was to recognize the importance of an idea, seize it, and organize their fellow workers around it.

3. A common criticism of oral history is that it tells what happens only from one point of view, that of the inarticulate. In Youngstown, however, *the struggle drove us to probe the reasoning of corporate and government decision makers by unearthing existing documents and to generate data that would not otherwise have existed.*

When the Lykes Corporation closed the Campbell Works I filed a suit, on behalf of the local congressman, requesting Justice Department documents concerning the merger of Lykes and Youngstown Sheet & Tube several years before. Later, when the Department of Commerce denied the loan guarantees necessary to reopen the Campbell Works, another suit under the Freedom of Information Act obtained documents exposing the bias against worker-ownership on the part of the men who made the decision.

U.S. Steel's decision to close its local mills prompted a lawsuit that obtained a twenty-two-day injunction restraining the company from shutting down. In the course of preparation for trial we deposed [questioned under oath] a variety of corporate actors, including the superintendent of the mills, and the two top officers of the corporation and required the company to produce (make available for inspection) their profit data for the Youngstown mills. All this information would not otherwise have been available either to the public at the time or, in good part, to a subsequent historian.

In practice, therefore, chronicling the experience of the inarticulate and probing the experience of the mighty were not mutually exclusive, but parts of the same process.

NOTES

1. Jesse Lemisch is a radical historian who coined the phrase "history from the bottom up" in his essay "American Revolution Seen from the Bottom Up" in *Towards a New Past: Dissenting Essays in American History*, Barton J. Bernstein, ed. (New York: Pantheon Books, 1970).

2. *Union Maids* is a film about three of the women in *Rank and File*. It is distributed by New Day Films, P. O. Box 315, Franklin Lakes, NJ 07417.

3. John Barbero was a rank-and-file steelworker, peace activist, and socialist from Youngstown, Ohio. He died in 1981. Barbero described his personal history in *Rank and File*, pages 264–84.

4. The ENA was an agreement entered into between the major steel companies and the steelworkers union in 1973 that forbade strikes at the expiration of the Basic Steel Contract. Ed Sadlowski is a United Steelworkers union dissident who challenged union leadership and Lloyd McBride for the presidency of the union in 1977. He received 40 percent of the vote. McBride subsequently led a successful move to prohibit outside funding in union elections thereby limiting dissidents' access to financial support for their campaigns. Sadlowski had been director of the union's Chicago-Gary district.

5. The Wagner Act (National Labor Relations Act) was passed by Congress in 1935. It created the National Labor Relations Board (NLRB) with the power to recognize collective bargaining units and define unfair labor practices. Section 7 upheld the right of employees to join labor organizations and bargain collectively through representatives of their own choosing.

6. Al Richmond is the author of *A Long View from the Left: Memoirs of an American Revolutionary* (Boston: Houghton Mifflin, 1973). At pages 238 and 245–46 he comments on Lynd's writing about the thirties.

7. Norman Thomas (1884–1968) became leader of the Socialist party in 1926. He was codirector of the League for Industrial Democracy, the educational arm of the Socialist party from 1922 to 1937. Earl Browder (1891–1973) was general secretary of the Communist party of the United States during the years of its largest membership and greatest influence, 1930–46. He was expelled from the Party in 1946 after acrimonious debate over his leadership. The article referred to in the text is "The United Front in America: A Note," *Radical America* 8 (July–August 1974): 29–37. See also Lynd's "The Possibility of Radicalism in the Early 1930s: The Case of Steel," *Radical America* 6 (November–December 1972): 37–64.

8. On May 30, 1937, Chicago police fired on a group of demonstrators before the gates of Republic Steel in south Chicago leaving ten dead and eighty-four injured. "Little Steel," under the leadership of Republic Steel, refused to recognize the Steelworkers Organizing Committee as the bargaining agent for its employees though SWOC had

secured recognition from U.S. Steel. By 1941 virtually all independent steel companies signed agreements with the CIO. The suggestion in the text that the Left in
the late thirties could have founded independent local labor parties is developed in
Eric Leif Davin and Staughton Lynd, "Picket Line and Ballot Box: The Forgotten
Legacy of the Local Labor Party Movement, 1932–1936," *Radical History Review*, no.
22 (Winter 1979–80): 43–63.

9. Staughton Lynd, *Intellectual Origins of American Radicalism* (New York: Pantheon
Books, 1968).

SELECT BIBLIOGRAPHY

Books
American Labor Radicalism: Testimonies and Interpretations, editor. New York: John
Wiley & Sons, Inc., 1973.
*Anti-Federalism in Dutchess County, NY: A Study of Democracy and Class Conflict in
the Revolutionary Era.* Chicago: Loyola University Press, 1962.
Class Conflict, Slavery, and the United States Constitution. Indianapolis: Bobbs-Mer-
rill, 1967.
Intellectual Origins of American Radicalism. New York: Pantheon Books, 1968.
Labor Law for the Rank and Filer, 2nd ed. San Pedro, Calif.: Singlejack Books, 1982.
Nonviolence in America: A Documentary History. Indianapolis: Bobbs-Merrill, 1966.
The Other Side, coauthored with Tom Hayden. New York: New American Library,
1967.
Rank and File: Personal Histories by Working-Class Organizers, coedited with Alice
Lynd. Boston: Beacon Press, 1973.
Reconstruction. New York: Harper & Row, 1967.
The Resistance, coauthored with Michael Ferber. Boston: Beacon Press, 1971.

Articles
"Archie Bunker, 1776." *Indiana Social Studies Quarterly* 27 (1974–75): 38–43.
"Beyond Beard." In *Towards a New Past: Dissenting Essays in American History,*
edited by Barton J. Bernstein. New York: Pantheon Books, 1968.
"The New Left." *Annals of the American Academy of Political and Social Science,* no.
382 (1969):64–72.
"Picket Line and Ballot Box: The Forgotten Legacy of the Local Labor Party
Movement, 1932–36." *Radical History Review,* no. 22 (1979–80):43–63.
"The Possibility of Radicalism in the Early 1930s: The Case of Steel." *Radical
America* 6 (1972):37–65.
"Rethinking Slavery and Reconstruction." *Journal of Negro History* 50 (1965):198–
209.
"The United Front in America: A Note." *Radical America* 8 (1974):29–37.
"Workers' Control in a Time of Diminished Workers' Rights." *Radical America* 10
(1976):4–19.

DAVID MONTGOMERY

DAVID MONTGOMERY

AMONG THE MARXIST scholars who have reshaped the writing of American history since the 1960s, David Montgomery has played a unique role. At a time when many radical historians have focused on patterns of resistance among preindustrial populations or on ethnic and community-centered sources of working-class resistance, Montgomery has concentrated on class struggles in the electoral arena and at the workplace. His foremost works, *Beyond Equality* and *Workers' Control in America,* are richly detailed studies of how workers influenced crucial developments in American society since the Civil War: the politics of Reconstruction and the social organization of production in the modern factory system.

As the following interview suggests, Montgomery's historical writing reflects his experience as a factory worker, union organizer, and Communist militant in the 1950s. Despite the disarray of the Left during this period and the political repression it suffered, which ultimately cost Montgomery his job as a machinist, his on-the-line experiences convinced him that the working class had not been thoroughly pacified, as most intellectuals insisted, and that its protests would become more articulate as the Left revived. Forced out of the factory, Montgomery turned to scholarship to document and explore lost traditions of working-class self-assertion. Challenging the dominant image of working-class conservatism, his work has helped to shape the perceptions of a generation of New Left scholars. By keeping close ties to labor activists in the communities where he lived, and by contributing articles to Left publications, he encouraged the revival of a spirit of cooperation between workers and radicals in the wake of the Vietnam War. Montgomery is professor of history at Yale University and editor of the journal, *International Labor and Working-Class History.*

This interview was conducted during the spring of 1981 by Mark Naison, who teaches American history at Fordham University, and by Paul Buhle, who is the director of the oral history of the American Left project.

Q. It has been fashionable to write about the American Communist party as intellectually retrograde and thoroughly Stalinized. Yet a sizable number of the creative scholars in American history, particularly people who came of age as scholars in the 1960s, were products of the American Communist party and its surrounding organizations. How do you explain this?

MONTGOMERY   I think there are two important ways in which the Communist party and the political world around it influenced the historical vision of the scholars you have in mind. The first is that it was the main Marxist organization in the country. Through it, more than any other organization of the time, it was possible to link Marxist analysis to effective daily action. This connection to the everyday struggles of Americans and to an international movement for socialism guided us toward styles of social analysis that were rooted in the hard and complex realities of experience and away from phrase-mongering and dogmatic abstractions. The second is the central importance the Party always gave to the struggles of Black America and to creating the basis for united action between Black and white workers.

The negative side of the experience is also important. The real flowering of creative work among the people you are thinking of came after they had left the Party. The official intellectual life of the Party, as found for example in the Jefferson School, was stifling.[1] In spite of the familiar slogan, "Marxism is a guide to action, not a dogma," theory appeared at that level of the movement in the form of explanations of official texts or even *ex post facto* justifications of actions taken, and not as a rigorous method of analyzing and changing social realities. In this sense, both the roots and the breaking away were important.

Later, although I perceived inner turmoil and a sense of weakness in the CP, what I saw of other groups in the political spectrum, especially through the mid-fifties, was virtually no action at all, or the spectacle of them all running to jump on the bandwagon of the cold war. I saw little of the world Joe Starobin describes in his *American Communism in Crisis* because I never held any office or contemplated the world from the underground.[2] Reading the memoirs of ex-leaders has taught me how very different their lives were from those of the rank and file. At my level of activity we continued from day to day doing our thing. If anything, the frequent disappearance of leadership reinforced a sense of self-reliance in the shop sections.

We had to base every analysis and every decision we made on the realities of daily life that we saw around us. If we tried to conjure up some notion out of our heads, above all in a period of retreat, we were going to get smashed. The fact of the matter is that it was still possible, in the early fifties, to play a role of some influence among large numbers of workers. But this could be done only if your discussions and analysis were as thoroughly down to earth as you could possibly make them. It is true that most of the discussion took the form of receiving a general policy decision and then figuring out how to apply it in a realistic and sensible way, rather than vice versa. But on the shop level we had to apply the slogan one of my good friends came up with: "Stick close to the working class even when they are throwing you out the shop window."

The mid-fifties were different from the period at the peak of the Party's influence, in the 1930s, or a situation I have been recently studying in Lawrence, Massachusetts, where in 1919, there was no question but that much of the cultural and intellectual life of the whole community was organized by the various leftists there. This was not the case in the 1950s anyplace I was. The cultural life of most of the workers was quite separate from ours. People in the Party, whether they came from the ranks of the intellectuals or were Party-educated workers, tended to be much more involved in strictly left wing sorts of cultural activities—Peter Seeger concerts, going to the known left wing movie theaters where they saw films from the Soviet Union. But they were also much more involved in what one might call traditional bourgeois high culture—going to an opera, going to the ballet. In a mass-based socialist movement, large numbers of workers would have been involved in a movement-oriented culture. It was not the case in the Party in the mid-fifties.

There were two partial exceptions. One was the union dances. Even then, however, one could perceive the problem that is so evident in so many unions today, that the workers who came to the dances were overwhelmingly Black and Puerto Rican and white leftists. The more conservative rank-and-file whites didn't take much part in the picnic and dance life of the union, unless it was a union where only they came. The other was found in Paul Robeson's concerts. Especially at those concerts that he offered at Black churches. They were an integral part of community life and reached far beyond the committed Left.

Another difference was the kinds of activities we might go to in the evening. The Left movement knows how to keep you busy seven nights a week. There was *always* an emergency. This could make for a real difference from the other workers around you, who spent more time playing cards, playing ball, or bowling. Racing all over the place night after night could make for intense strains inside a family.

Q. Throughout the 1950s the Communist party was distinguished from most groups on the Left by its commitment to interracialism as a political principle and by its ability to attract talented Black members. Was this something that, as some people have suggested, left a mark on everyone who went through the Party?

MONTGOMERY   I think it definitely did leave a mark on everybody. There is no other organization I know of, in the twentieth-century Left in America, that waged the kind of consistent effort both to organize and involve Blacks and Puerto Rican workers wherever they happened to be and to fight consciously against racism in the thinking and action of its members. Now at times the effort would be a failure and every Black who was in the Party had to make the decision "whether I am going to put up with this crap" in the hope that white comrades were going to get better. This was a common scene. There are certainly tales that all can recount of neglect or abuse of Black members, and there were also times when the charge of white chauvinism was used in a very phony political way, as a club to knock down people who were out of line on almost anything. But that shouldn't be taken to say that therefore the whole effort was phony or mistaken. One of the things that I found hardest to get accustomed to in the 1960s was the frequency with which cartoons and jokes showed up in Left literature that I thought were just plain racist. It was impossible to imagine them seeping into the Party literature in the 1950s.

It also meant that everyplace I ever worked there were a number of older Black workers who had never joined the Party, or if they did were only in it a short time, but had considerable respect for it and would, for the most part, think of the Third Period—the very one that most of us think of as the most outrageous—as the one in which these guys proved themselves, in the unemployed movement, in the Scottsboro campaign.[3] This was the period that the generation of older Blacks looked upon with greatest respect.

The Third Period left a lasting mark in terms both of opening up the possibility for joint interracial action and leaving behind a number of people who, when everybody else was being deluged with McCarthyite propaganda, could say to younger Black workers, "Take that with a grain of salt. Let me remind you what happened when I was young."

Q.   When you finally left the Party, how much of the motivation for leaving was disillusionment with the Party's ideology and how much of it was simply that the Party was losing the practical power and role in the working class that initially made it attractive?

MONTGOMERY   It seems to me that the two alternatives you have posed are very closely related to each other. First of all, there was enormous turmoil inside the Party after the invasion of Hungary. The crisis that developed had the effect of pushing a majority at the 1957 convention, and a majority of the political committee, to a commitment to reshaping the ideology and way of work of the whole organization. And yet, at the same time, as one guy who was in the leadership put it to me recently, as he and others started thinking about how to do it, they found themselves generals without troops. The troops like me were just quitting. And quitting in large measure because we believed that the Party had become virtually irrelevant to the workers of

America. Belonging to it gave no added strength to what anybody was trying to do and, indeed, put big barriers between ourselves and other workers. I was in Minnesota at the time, and there was still enough of a labor flavor and enough activity around peace and civil rights in the Democratic Farmer–Labor party that there was another place where I felt at home and could act without breaking stride. But again, if we had felt we still had in the Party something of real power and that it was worth fighting to the very end to change, there would have been the motivation to do battle on the ideological question. Yes, the Party had to be changed, and there might even have been the forces to do it if enough people had thought they could affect American life by doing it.

One final thing, I think it's true in this country as in England that very few of the people who left in the late 1950s went over to the Right (in the style of *The God That Failed*).[4] But there's an enormous difference between the American experience and the English experience. People who were leaving in England stayed together as a group: published journals, had a movement of their own, had a theoretical voice. Each of us in this country went in a different direction as an individual. There never really was any kind of central focus. There was no mass anti-bomb movement, no *Reasoner*, which began inside the British party.[5] In the U.S., people were dropping out one by one, and this was especially true of rank-and-file industrial workers. The last thing an industrial worker is going to do is to issue a political manifesto as to "why I'm leaving." That would identify you to the feds and the boss and send you right out the back. People in leadership largely thought through their positions in isolation from each other and from action—in the underground. We suffered enormously from the lack of communication. Each of us had to find a new political realm in which to work.

Repression made it enormously hard to continue as a non-Party leftist. Anyone who wasn't a prominent leader would opt for silence. In fact, the FBI came down with special vigor on the people who were leaving, hoping to recruit a lot of people to go back in again. Plus, it was still the rule rather than the exception to be fired from your job if you were publicly identified as being on the Left. Only those people who were already prominent could have much of a public voice at this time.

There's another side to it. The very atmosphere of the repression itself helped intensify the siege mentality inside the Party, helped to create much of this ideological rigidity we were talking about earlier. It was them versus us, two camps. Any thinking that strayed from the straight and narrow path was seen as a sign of petty-bourgeois weakness. In England there was an openness of debate, even before the splits, that was simply impossible here.

But there's also the question of why repression had so much more devastating an impact here than it did in other countries. After all, other movements have been much more severely repressed than we were. It was rough, but times certainly have been rougher. And I think here you've got to start thinking about social changes that were eating away at the very roots of the movement at this time, so that it couldn't just spring back. The early 1950s marked the end of a generational experience among American workers that began in the mid-1920s, ran through the organization of the CIO unions, and broke down in the 1940s. The sorts of organizations and forms of struggle that we produced then could never be re-created in exactly the same way. There would still be remarkable revivals of the Left at times. One thinks of when the Left won leadership of Ford Local 600 in 1951 or 1952, at the height of the Korean War, and doing so with such strength that the trustee sent in by Reuther switched over and ran as the candidate of the Left. There could be revivals, but these were exceptions. The movement's breakdown was really the breaking up of the old patterns of working-class life socially and even physically. One of the great centers of the Left in Pittsburgh from the IWW days on had been the town of East Pittsburgh.[6] East Pittsburgh used to be tenements where people were just jammed on top of each other. Today it's nothing but superhighways. The people themselves are gone.

Things were also changing in the plants, but it seems to me that solidarity was kept most alive on the plant floor, in the shop. This was evident in the proliferation of wildcat strikes in the 1950s, then in the revival of all sorts of unofficial struggles among workers in the sixties and seventies. But notice how seldom those movements had a political ideology of any coherence. Militancy was there, fighting the boss on the shop level, but the sense of political direction, which would virtually have always been there in any rebel movement down through the 1930s, was lacking.

Q. For many Americans of the Left, the 1950s marked a stage where they lost faith in the American working class as an agent of historical change. Influential New Left thinkers—Herbert Marcuse, C. Wright Mills—unlike the British New Left, largely wrote off workers as a progressive force. Why did your sense of the working class as a creative historical agent remain strong when almost all other intellectuals on the Left lacked such a perception?

MONTGOMERY   The answer is twofold: one of experience, and one of principle. In terms of experience, simply being in factories around America every single day through the 1950s, involved in struggles along with other workers there, persuaded me that most of what was written in academic literature about the inherent conservatism or passivity of American workers in fighting to change anything was simply untrue. It also made me aware of the peculiarly opaque character of working-class life. American workers are not going to use a totally different sort of language than everybody else, but they give a very different meaning to the language that they pick up from the television, newspapers, and so forth.

But second, it seemed to me when I thought about the question of socialism, and heard people asking whether the working class was an agent for social change, I found it very hard to even relate to the question. If the working class isn't going to change its own life and make a new world, why bother? To change one boss for another is not something I'm going to go out and put myself on the line for.

From the fifties onward American intellectual life was being inundated by a structuralist analysis of society and history that depicted as ludicrous any attempts by individuals or groups to change the world. Either that or you had analyses that perceived all significant change as coming from enlightened leaders of the society—seen as corporate manipulation if you were on the Left, as rational leadership by responsible leaders of society if you were on the Right. The power elite was depicted as almost omnipotent in contrast to the way Marx used to think about it, as tied up on every side by the economic contradictions within which it lives and finding itself face to face with other social classes with whom it must contest for power. Both were left out of the dominant thinking of the 1950s. In economics the Keynesian formula had shown the answer (the elite had gotten smart), and the elite's exercise of power became the center of everybody's attention. This type of thinking was so dominant that inevitably it became a point of departure for most of the New Left that came along in the sixties. And it would take a lot of experience for people to begin thinking in a different way.

As for the people who had been involved in factory work who were disillusioned—there were plenty of defeats. Moreover, many workers had reasons to be disillusioned with us. They *were* throwing us out the window, but I may have been helped by the fact that I enjoyed a couple of little victories. I can't help remembering that in 1955 when the House Un-American Activities Committee came to Newark, workers from my shop were climbing in the windows of the committee's chambers denouncing their investigation of us and, in effect, running them out of town.

Q. Were you discouraged when you left the factory in 1960 to go to graduate school?

MONTGOMERY   I was driven out of the factory; I was blacklisted. Becoming a historian was *not* my first choice. I had to do something, so I took the second-best choice that was around then. But this personal defeat took place in the context of some very important social developments: political campaigns in Minnesota in 1958 where the question of nuclear disarmament became one of widespread discussion, where the labor forces in the Democratic Farmer–Labor party won a congressional primary in the most clear-cut class campaign that I've ever been involved in in my entire life.[7] These are some of my *last* experiences in the Minnesota labor movement. I was beaten but I never felt that they had wiped out the movement. They just had *me* fenced in.

Q. The first historical piece you published, written when you were still a factory worker, appeared in 1958 in a remarkable series of essays on Minnesota life called *The People Together*. Your article, on an American Railway Union strike in Minneapolis, was written under the name Amos Flaherty. Could you tell us a little about this volume?

MONTGOMERY   The book was put together mainly under the leadership of Meridel Le Sueur,[8] who recognized that Minnesota was having its hundredth anniversary and that the Chamber of Commerce had thought of everything *except* a history of the state. Of course, all of us Minnesota chauvinists knew damn well why they had left out a history of our state. It was too damn good!

So we gathered together a collection of old farmers, workers, CP'ers, and Native Americans. There was never the slightest feeling that we were writing something for the working people. We *were* the working people of Minnesota writing about ourselves. And, of course, Meridel had just the knack of keeping that mood alive and editing the work skillfully enough that it turned out well.

I felt at home in Minnesota the second day I was there. All the time that I worked in Minneapolis Honeywell the shift on which I worked had a group of workers—90 percent men, 10 percent women—among whom communication often didn't even require words. The sense that an injury to one was an injury to all ran through the whole department with such effectiveness that, in the end, the only way Minneapolis Honeywell could get rid of us was to close the entire division. These were the Minnesotans that I knew. That doesn't sound much like Daniel Bell.[9]

An articulation of a mood of this kind requires a movement, requires an organization in order to reach the broader society. An articulation that comes from an organization is always somewhat distorted. But without it, there is no way in which the experiences and struggles of one locality can be more than the life of us in the Twenty-ninth Street Plant.

Q.   What continuity do you see in your own development over the last thirty years?

MONTGOMERY   I went through many different ways of thinking about politics in the course of my life. I did not come out of a left wing family or grow up in any sort of left wing environment. In my early twenties I ran from World Federalism to Harry Trumanism to the Socialist party to you name it. I chose to study political science in college when I came out of the army because I thought I might learn some ways this world could be changed. I'd been haunted since childhood by the oldest question: why do those who work the hardest get the least? After I graduated I tried a little bit of graduate school and dropped out, went to work for about ten years, and found myself getting more and more interested in history while I was a machinist. So there is a clear continuity to what I was after.

I think that in one respect the work I have done lately may be a little misleading. Although my specialty is working-class history, the subject I am trying to get at is the history of capitalism. From this vantage point I have as much respect and esteem for the study of the economy or of foreign relations as for that of working people. But the subject I have been looking at, shop-floor relations, does have a special importance because on-the-job workers must define their own world for themselves. To study the ways they have done this, however, takes an all-consuming amount of time and effort.

Beyond Equality went after the Reconstruction period first of all because that epoch offered me a way to get at the impact American workers have on the main currents of American political life. That has continued to be my basic interest ever since. There I worked directly on the political realm for two reasons. One was that I had simply not started into the kind of work on on-the-job social relations that I have gotten into recently, and didn't know enough, but the second and more important reason is that the Civil War and Reconstruction period was the most revolutionary epoch in American history. I wanted to look at this period to understand the dynamics of the changes that were going on and to find out what role the workers had played in these dynamics—to find out if they had tried to push the social changes of the time beyond the limits of the radical bourgeoisie. And when their efforts failed, to find out what effect those efforts had on the subsequent thinking of the workers themselves.

Q. When we read your work on workers' control and shop-floor struggles, we have the sense that they are no longer as central to class struggle as they were in the late nineteenth and early twentieth centuries. How have the dynamics of class struggle changed?

MONTGOMERY   The work of feminist scholars, indeed the whole *corpus* of recent work on women's history, has been of central importance in getting me to think about what else is involved in class beyond the relations of production. How does a work force overlap with a working class? They are two very different things. A class includes men, women, and children of all ages. The relations of production involve people on the job, earning wages over a relatively narrow span of time. That question, how we treat and analyze class as consciousness and as a political dynamic, is one that I find myself thinking more and more about, with tremendous inspiration from the work of other people. History, like shop work, has to be collective.

But in another sense the discoveries about basic changes in class struggles have been just that, discoveries. I would learn, from evidence that I was studying, that the dynamics around which workers' movements developed—especially shop-floor relationships—in the nineteenth century were just fundamentally different than anything I had ever experienced. And the question then emerged of how to understand that epoch so that I could compare it with what I had gone through myself.

There are certainly elements of continuity, but there is no way, for example, that one can learn about shop-floor relations today by studying published union rules. There is none of the open assertion of the position of the skilled workers. In one sense the shift from the nineteenth to the twentieth century in industry involved the coming of unskilled workers into production. Production in many nineteenth-century industries was carried on by skilled workers; the unskilled workers picked things up and brought them to the skilled and carried them away again. In the twentieth century, for the most part, the skilled workers became the workers outside production—the tool makers, the maintenance people, the supervisors who set up the machinery rather than those who operated it. This makes a very fundamental difference in the types of movements that are created and the types of relationships that exist on the shop floor.

Of course, the factory is still fundamental as a meeting place in a society where there are so few other meeting places. It's a central experience of capitalism that we come to a job in large numbers to create profits in return for wages and therefore move into a conflict situation every day as a result of it. The forms of conflict may change, but the conflict is always going to be there. In the end, a socialist world is going to be one in which those relationships on the job are going to be totally transformed.

But what is also important is to examine the ways in which the struggles outside the factory overlap with this. In the 1920s and 1930s much of the organizing activity, even around strikes, started in fraternal organizations. The ethnic communities became the basis of mobilization in working-class life. If all we see is what's going on in the workplace, we are going to miss a great deal.

Q. When you were looking for alternatives to the dominant historical interpretations of the 1950s, whom did you look to as a model?

MONTGOMERY   Without a doubt, *the* most influential scholar was W. E. B. Du Bois. When I think of someone who just towered over everything throughout that period Du Bois comes to mind. That would even be the answer of why I went back to Reconstruction. In the academic world, Du Bois was not being read seriously. But I think it is safe to say that there would be no name that would be pronounced with greater respect throughout the Black working-class community in America than that of Dr. Du Bois. And indeed, the most memorable single experience in all my days in Local 475, even more than being in the first sit-down strike since the 1930s, was our Negro-history-week meeting to which Dr. Du Bois came; workers were hanging from the rafters.[10] This was in Brooklyn. And Du Bois, as you might expect, pulled absolutely no punches, talked down to nobody. You could have heard a pin drop from beginning to end. This was *their* historian, one giant who never gave in to the enemy.

Q. Do current developments in the labor movement make you feel vindicated in your conviction that the working class has not been totally pacified and that perhaps labor and working-class politics will reinvigorate American socialism?

MONTGOMERY   Yes, I certainly do. I do because there have been both continuing developments in shop-floor struggles, rebel movements, etc., and because of the reappearance of what calls itself a socialist segment within the leader-ship, beginning to discuss questions that would have been unthinkable a while ago. But at the same time we have an awfully long way to go to generate a mass socialist movement because what that means is not only parties and institutions and votes, but also a very large number of people thinking they can live their lives in a fundamentally different way and conducting them-selves accordingly. Now that *is* a long way off.

There is one very important respect in which I agree with Jim Weinstein[11] and that is that the political arm of the socialist movement, whatever form it might take, is going to be useful to the shop-floor and trade-union arm of the struggle only in proportion to its strength outside. To think that a socialist movement can be built solely out of union activity would be the greatest folly —as great a folly as an effort to create socialism without workplace struggle.

Q. This gets us back to a critique of the New Left that is important in understanding your work of the last ten years. One thing is your rejection of the New Left's indifference to proletarian prospects. Another is your continuing belief in the necessity of political leadership and, consequently, your exploration of these nineteenth-century work rules as formulating a real and consistent understanding that workers had with each other, whereas the New Left perspective was perhaps hostile to rules.

MONTGOMERY   That particular impulse in the New Left seemed to me more an echo of contemporary consumerist capitalism than an attack on it. When working people replace capitalism with their own society, they will create not a world without rules, but one based on rules they have made themselves for their own welfare. This is precisely why workers' own ethical codes hold so much interest for me.

What has always been important for a revolutionary movement is that it address the working people with understanding and respect, that its tactics and strategies and ways of behaving break down the wall between it and the rest of the working people, rather than just build them up. That must be done simultaneously with what has been crucial to any kind of socialist movement and was the greatest aspect of the New Left—and that is the absolute commit-ment of the people in it to put an end to an exploitative society and live, right here and now, for that purpose and to judge themselves and others accord-ingly. Any criticism of the New Left has to start with the recognition that "thank God it was here."

Q. As you have described it, becoming a historian was a second choice, something you were forced into by the collapse of the political context in which you were working in the shop. Twenty years have passed since then and a lot of things have changed. Do you think that the Communist party as you experienced it in the United States, in the form it took, is a form that has outlived its usefulness?

MONTGOMERY   Very definitely, I think we need new forms of political organization. I think there is an enormous amount we can learn from the experience of the Communist party, especially during what I consider its greatest period, the height of the Popular Front.[12] For all the weaknesses of that time, the Party's presence in the midst of the everyday life of so many people, its sense of total involvement in the struggle and of the necessity of realistic political assessments, means that there is a great deal that can be learned, and it's not just about mistakes to avoid. It's also very difficult to imagine any sort of large-scale popular action in the days to come that doesn't include what's left of the Communist party as well as all the other groups.

Maybe that's the crucial point. In this country, where enormous productive capacity already exists and the talents needed to run a humane society are all around us, what we need is not a single vanguard party but many self-activated centers of popular struggle and a variety of political initiatives. But all those centers of activity need to learn from history and from systematic analysis of the social order against which they are battling as well as from their own immediate experience.

My study of both shop-floor struggles and the Reconstruction period has underscored for me the fact that the working class has always formulated alternatives to bourgeois society in this country, particularly on the job. What I find myself looking for is new forms of political struggle that come out of the everyday lives of working people. But I also think that life involves intellectual exchange; it involves discussion, agitation; it involves collective discussion as to where we are going. This appears more clearly in *Beyond Equality* than it does in the *Workers' Control* essays, except for the piece on the socialists. But that element has to be emphasized in all the work that I've done.

If, as radical historians, we are doing work that has some sort of meaning to politics and to the daily lives of working people, then it's got to be shared with them. And we've got to have their responses, criticisms, and contributions coming back. I think this is both a personal commitment and something crucial in any organized form of activity: that we do not *simply* let our historical work be professional—in the purist sense—for other historians. That is not to say that we can be satisfied just doing a puff job for good causes. Precisely because our historical work is politically important, it must strive for the highest standards of accuracy and rigor.

When you come right down to it, history is the only teacher the workers have. A central task that all of us face today is going back to square one in our own revolutionary experience. Very clearly, as we survey the great struggles that need to be recounted, we must look with a cold eye at all of that experience to find where we went wrong, where there were great lessons to be drawn from positive experience, what the propelling forces of historical change have been, and how to make the dynamics of our own movement public knowledge once again. In all my work I've tried to look at the long course of development, in part to avoid terms of analysis that have been reified by society, or by our movement, at particular times. But also to show how many long familiar struggles keep reappearing in different forms.

Notes

1. The Jefferson School of Social Science in New York City was part of a Communist system of popular, adult, labor-progressive educational institutions during the 1930s. It had its own building and at its height an enrollment of several thousand.
2. Joseph R. Starobin, *American Communism in Crisis, 1943–1957* (Cambridge, Mass.: Harvard University Press, 1972).
3. In the Third Period (1929–35) the Communist party, at the direction of the Comintern, adhered to a strategy of opposing traditional labor unions by creating rival organizations. It also vigorously fought other groups on the Left, including socialists. In 1931 nine Black youths were arrested in Scottsboro, Alabama, and charged with the rape of two white women. Their convictions in three controversial trials were overturned by the Supreme Court in 1935. The Communist party took a leading role in the defense and helped to bring the case to national and international attention.
4. Richard Crossman, ed., *The God That Failed: Six Studies in Communism* by Arthur Koestler and others (New York: Harper and Row, 1950). In this cold war document six prominent writers explained their disillusionment with communism.
5. The *Reasoner* was founded in 1956 by the British historians Edward Thompson and John Saville. In 1960 it merged with *Universities* and *Left Review* to form *The New Left Review.*
6. The Industrial Workers of the World was organized in Chicago in 1905. It sought the organization of all workers into one big union for the overthrow of capitalism.
7. The Farmer-Labor party of Minnesota (1918–44) was made up of a coalition of radical and progressive agrarian and labor organizations. It quickly displaced the Democratic party as one of the two major political forces in the state. In 1944 it merged with the Democratic party forming the Democratic Farmer–Labor party.
8. Born in 1900 in Iowa, Meridel Le Sueur wrote about and reported on the American Midwest during the depression, gaining a national reputation as author and radical activist. She was blacklisted during the McCarthy years. Since the 1970s her work has again found publishers and a large audience. Her most recent book is *Ripening: Selected Work, 1927–1980,* edited and with an introduction by Elaine Hedges (Old Westbury, N.Y.: Feminist Press, 1982).
9. Daniel Bell, *The End of Ideology: On the Exhaustion of Political Ideas in the Fifties* (Glencoe, Ill.: Free Press, 1960).
10. Local 475 of the United Electrical, Radio and Machine Workers of America (UE) was an amalgamated local in Brooklyn to which Montgomery belonged from 1951 to 1956.
11. James Weinstein is a radical historian associated with the journal *Studies on the Left.*

He has written extensively on American radicalism and in 1976 founded the socialist weekly newspaper *In These Times*.

12. During the Popular Front (1935–39) the Communist party followed a policy of alliance with all groups on the Left to combat fascism. This was the period of the Party's greatest strength and popularity.

SELECT BIBLIOGRAPHY

Books
Beyond Equality: Labor and the Radical Republicans, 1862–1872. New York: Alfred A. Knopf, 1967.
Workers' Control in America: Studies in the History of Work, Technology, and Labor Struggles. New York and London: Cambridge University Press, 1979.

Articles
"The Conventional Wisdom." *Labor History,* 13 (Winter 1972):107–36.
"E. P. Thompson: History as Human Agency." Reprinted in *Monthly Review,* 5 (October 1981):42–48.
"Facing Layoffs," coauthored with Ronald Schatz. *Radical America,* 10 (March-April 1976):15–28.
"Goodwyn's Populists." *Marxist Perspectives,* 1 (Spring 1978):166–73. Reprinted in *The Common People of the Postwar South,* edited by Edward Magdol, 337–43. Westport, Conn.: Greenwood Press, 1970.
"Gutman's Nineteenth-Century America." *Labor History,* 19 (Summer 1978):416–29.
"Immigrant Workers and Managerial Reform." In *Immigrants in Industrial America, 1850–1920,* edited by Richard L. Ehrlich. Charlottesville: University of Virginia Press, 1977.
"The Irish and the American Labor Movement." In *America and Ireland, 1776–1976,* edited by David N. Doyle and Owen Dudley Edwards, 205–18. Westport, Conn.: Greenwood Press, 1980.
"Labor in the Industrial Era." In *The U.S. Department of Labor Bicentennial History of the American Worker,* edited by Richard B. Morris. Washington, D.C.: U.S. Government Printing Office, 1976.
"Labor and the Republic in Industrial America: 1860–1920." *Le Mouvement Social* 3 (April-June 1980):201–15.
"The Past and Future of Workers' Control." *Radical America,* 13 (November-December 1979):7–24.
"Radical Republicanism in Pennsylvania, 1866–1873." *Pennsylvania Magazine of History and Biography,* 85 (October 1961):439–57. Reprinted in *Radical Republicans in the North: State Politics During Reconstruction,* edited by James C. Mohr. Baltimore and London: Johns Hopkins University Press, 1976.
"The Shuttle and the Cross: Weavers and Artisans in the Kensington Riots of 1844." *Journal of Social History,* 5 (Summer 1972):411–66. Reprinted in *Workers in the Indus-*

trial Revolution: Recent Studies in the United States and Europe, edited by Peter N. Stearns and Daniel J. Walkowitz (New Brunswick, N.J.: Transaction Books, 1974); *The Private Side of American History,* edited by Gary B. Nash (New York: Harcourt, Brace, Jovanovich, 1975); and *The Many Faceted Jacksonian Era,* edited by Edward Pessen (Westport, Conn.: Greenwood Press, 1978).

"Strikes in Nineteenth-Century America." *Social Science History,* 4 (February 1980): 81–104.

"To Study the People: The American Working Class." *Labor History,* 21 (Fall 1980):485–512.

What's Happening to the American Worker? Madison, Wis.: Radical America Pamphlets, 1969.

"Work." In *Encyclopedia of American Economic History,* edited by Glenn Porter, 974–87. New York: Charles Scribner's Sons, 1980.

"Workers' Control of Machine Production in the Nineteenth Century." *Labor History,* 17 (Fall 1976):485–509.

"The Working Classes of the Pre-Industrial American City, 1780–1830." *Labor History,* 9 (Winter 1968):3–22. Reprinted in *New Perspectives on the American Past,* 2nd ed., edited by S. N. Katz and S. I. Kutler (Boston: Little, Brown & Co., 1972); *The Record of American History: Interpretive Readings,* edited by I. Unger, D. Brody, and P. Goodman (Waltham, Mass.: Xerox College Publishing Co., 1971); and *Urban America in Historical Perspective,* edited by R. A. Mohl and N. Betten (New York: Weybright and Talley, 1970). Also published as Bobbs-Merrill Reprint in American History, No. H-447.

"Violence and the Struggle for Unions in the South, 1880–1930." In *Perspectives on the American South,* edited by Merle Black. New York: Gordon and Breach, 1981.

HERBERT GUTMAN

HERBERT GUTMAN

THIS INTERVIEW WITH HERBert Gutman, distinguished professor of history at the City University of New York Graduate Center, was conducted in August 1982 in New York City. Professor Gutman is best known for his essays on the working-class experience in the United States during the last quarter of the nineteenth century —many of which have been collected and published in *Work, Culture and Society in Industrializing America*—and for his path-breaking study of Afro-American slaves in *The Black Family from Slavery to Freedom.* Other local studies of working-class life and culture mentioned in this interview will be published in the near future. Professor Gutman is now involved in a major new research project on the origins and history of the United States working class that directly challenges some of the central assumptions shared by most historians about the history of U.S. workers and of the country as a whole.

Besides his academic work, Professor Gutman conducted a series of seminars on working-class history in the late 1970s for trade-union activists that has brought him into contact with many of the new generation of trade-union leaders in this country. This led him in 1981, with other younger historians and trade unionists, to fashion the American Working-Class History Project that is currently developing for use in community colleges and union education programs, a general history of American working people, documentary films, and other materials reflecting the discoveries of the new labor history. The project staff aims at nothing less than providing for the next generation of labor historians what John R. Commons and his associates provided for the last three in *The History of Labor in the United States (1918–46)*—a synthetic and complete history of the working class in this country.

Mike Merrill, who conducted this interview, is codirector of the Institute for Labor Education and Research in New York City.

Q. You have made original and influential contributions to both U.S. labor history and Afro-American history, but let's start with your work in labor history, since it was your first research interest. When did you begin to think systematically about the way labor history ought to be done?

GUTMAN   My interest in working-class history flowed first out of my youth and my early politics. My parents were immigrant Jews and belonged to the International Workers Order. They were not Communists, but I grew up very much influenced by that branch of the Jewish Old Left. As an undergraduate I campaigned vigorously for Henry Wallace, flirted briefly but intensely with the Communist movement, read the Marxist classics, and soon grew wary of and then disgusted with vanguard leftist politics. I remained a socialist—an egalitarian and a democrat. I drifted into American working-class history out of this world. My M.A. thesis at Columbia University (1950) was conventional labor history, and I'm sure it bored my supervisor, Richard Hofstadter—and for good reason! Later, in 1952–53, as a graduate student at the University of Wisconsin, I first confronted problems in writing working-class history as the result of one question: what caused the vast amount of disorder and property destruction during the 1877 railway strikes? Nothing in the secondary literature explained this extraordinary, nationwide disrespect for private property and the law. It was as if the strikes had occurred outside American history, as if they did not belong to (or in) America!

Dissatisfied with what had been written, I devised a simple strategy. I divided the country into several regions and read one or two major newspapers from each [for the years] 1873 to 1878 to find out what Americans, and especially working people, were doing and thinking. I did that for three years looking for labor news, reconstructing working-class experiences from the middle-class press.

The strategy worked well. I began to pick up stories. A brief dispatch in a Cincinnati paper reported: "Special to the *Cincinnati Commercial.* Hocking Valley miners strike has entered its fifth month." Or in the *New York Sun,* which had very, very good labor reporting: "The 'long vacation' in Fall River continues. It's now August, and the textile strike started in May." Or in the Philadelphia paper: "To the great surprise of everyone, the Scranton jury freed the miners."

What surfaced everywhere were dozens of events—whole class experiences —over the entire country that had never made their way into the consciousness of historians. The evidence raised important and little-studied questions. How did this evidence conform to the common historical belief that the Robber Barons had it all going for them in Gilded Age America, and that they found it relatively easy to transform their new power into authority?

What first struck me was the length of strikes and lockouts. Conventional labor historians insisted that the Gilded Age trade-union movement ("organized labor") was very weak. What, then, explained the length of these protracted working-class struggles? Given the absence of powerful unions, benefits, and much else assumed to be necessary to maintain long strikes, what made such intense struggles possible? That's where I started.

I answered such questions in an essay entitled "The Workers' Search for Power." Published in a book on the Gilded Age,[1] it distinguished between workers living in small towns and those living in large cities. I had done most of my research on small towns and very little on large cities. So I argued that face-to-face relationships in small towns created more cross-class solidarities than the seeming anonymity of large cities. The argument would work, I later realized, if Chicago and Pittsburgh didn't exist! Chicago, after all, probably had as large a percentage of its ethnic male work force in trade unions as any other city in the world in the early twentieth century. (Such evidence, incidentally, makes hash of so many fashionable arguments that ethnicity and high rates of social mobility militated against American working-class self-organization.) Rightly or wrongly, these essays argued that the class structure in small towns, coming out of residual or older forms of class relations, gave little-noticed strengths to diverse workers.

I had studied several towns to deal with two questions. First, how and from where did mid- and late-nineteenth-century workers without permanent forms of collective organization derive their strengths? I argued that these strengths came primarily from elements within the class structure unsympathetic to the changing needs of the rising manufacturing class. That seemed a radical explanation to some historians in the late 1950s and early 1960s, when the studies began to appear. It attracted notice. Second, if the power of the manufacturing class was not quickly accepted as legitimate, then another interesting process was at work. How does a powerful new class achieve authority? It always takes time, and it took time for American industrial capitalism to be legitimized, for the power that came with the ownership of new factories to be transformed into authority. Here were clues to the prevalence of violence and corruption in Gilded Age America. New property relations had not yet been fully legitimized.

Q. All this work you are discussing is pre-Thompson, isn't it?

GUTMAN Yes, of course. These essays were finished as part of my dissertation in 1959. Some were soon published. *The Making of the English Working Class* appeared in 1963.

Q. You also published an essay on Blacks and the United Mine Workers and one on labor and American Protestantism in the mid-1960s.[2] What was the occasion for writing each of these pieces?

GUTMAN They were published a few years later. I signed a book contract in the Bobbs-Merrill series edited by Alfred Young and Leonard Levy to be called *The Mind of the Worker in the Gilded Age*. It was to be a book of writings by workers from the 1850s to the election of 1896 that would show that more than just a handful of intellectuals wrote critiques of how Gilded Age capitalism was developing. It showed that a wide-ranging critique appeared every week in the diverse labor press and pamphlet literature that addressed bread and butter issues. These critics challenged the lurid assumptions of laissez-faire capitalism and Social Darwinism.

In reading the *United Mine Workers Journal*, which I did as research for that book, I ran into weekly letters by R. W. Davis. It took me about a month to figure out he was a Black. Those letters astonished me. By the time I finished copying them I had a pile about a foot high, and so when Julius Jacobson asked me to write about Black workers for a book to be called *The Negro and the American Labor Movement*, I proposed to publish a few of the letters with a short introduction. That short introduction became a very long essay.

As I studied those letters a whole world came apart and had to be reconstructed. A little arithmetic applied to the bituminous coal industry showed that in the early years of the UMW, Black unionists were proportionately more important than whites. Into what could we incorporate *that* fact and the wonderful, wonderful letters of this fellow, born a slave and victimized by racism on all sides? I could find no place for him or his letters in conventional labor and Afro-American historical writing. He simply didn't fit. Neither did all those other Black coal miners.

Q. In the beginning of the Protestantism essay, you mention two influences on working-class consciousness that historians had neglected. The first was religion, and you go on to deal with that dimension in the essay. My only problem with this discussion is that you did not say more about Catholicism.

GUTMAN That's true. I failed to explore the Catholic dimension. But my concern was with the way workers legitimized their protests. My central focus was legitimacy, not religion as such. I had Catholic material. Some local priests, for example, in the anthracite mining regions supported the men hung in the Molly Maguire executions.[3] The Philadelphia bishop excommunicated the Molly Maguires, but the local priests knew better. Letters from them to New York newspapers in the summer of 1877 declared the Mollies innocent. One was signed by a Father Sheridan.

Q. The second influence historians had neglected, you charged, was the ideology of radical republicanism and the heritage of republican political institutions. Republicanism offers a small-scale, egalitarian vision. It is individualistic, not in the sense of self-interested but in the sense of self-reliant. Unfortunately, you have not had much to say about this influence in print. What do you make of Alan Dawley's recent argument in *Class and Community* that republicanism, for all its importance in the early part of the nineteenth century, was a dead end for the American working class?[4]

GUTMAN Alan's book is a very important and original one. I disagree with the last third of it, but it is a fine work. Alan was grappling with the false consciousness issue when writing *Class and Community*. He sought reasons why a mass socialist movement did not develop and sustain itself. He couldn't find them where Stephan Thernstrom had, so instead he located them in increasingly archaic postbellum republican beliefs.[5]

I would argue differently. If you look at the behavior of workers and the ideological criticisms of capitalism that they developed in the 1870s, 1880s, and early 1890s, social and political republicanism was at the heart of their critique. That was so even though most workers and their spokesmen were foreign-born or the children of immigrants. If you read J. P. McDonnell, who had been the Irish secretary of the First International before coming to this country in the early 1870s and in his early years was an uncompromising socialist critic of developing American capitalism, his rhetoric was bathed in working-class republican ideology. Saturated by it. He believed in America and also believed it was being ruined. He was a typical radical unionist, and if I had written a companion piece to the Protestantism essay it would have dealt with individuals like McDonnell. Developing capitalism tarnished—perhaps destroyed—the republican promise, but organized workers, among others, sought to retain that promise. That is quite a different emphasis from arguing that republicanism blocked a mass socialist movement before 1900.

Basic to Gilded Age working-class republican ideology was the belief in a relative equality of means. Workers experienced the 1870s and 1880s! They saw John D. Rockefeller earning more in a minute than a molder or a barrel maker in his factories earned in a year. And that was only his stated salary, [it did not include] his income from stocks and bonds. They saw that and much else. They weren't socially blinded. What did that mean for America? they asked. And to happen so rapidly? A four-hundred-page manuscript I have written and rewritten on Paterson and its workers deals with those questions. So does a soon-to-be-published book containing three long essays on Gilded Age workers and their America.[6]

And are you familiar with James Holt's fine essay in *Labor History*?[7] He seeks to explain why mass unionism failed to develop in the United States between 1890 and the First World War. It is the most probing recent piece on the subject. By most measures, American ironworkers and steelworkers were better organized and more militant in the 1880s than their British brothers. Yet mass unionism took root more quickly in England than in the U.S. Why? It cannot be explained by the underdevelopment of the American working class in the 1880s. Holt suggests that failure in the U.S. is not adequately explained by factors internal to the class—such as upward mobility, ethnic division, and make-it-yourself ideology. Instead, he argues that political changes in the late 1880s and early 1890s weakened workers' organizations.

The really critical year, I think, was 1892. If you locate events that tell us something about essential changes that shaped and reshaped the consciousness of working-class leaders and radicals, of trade unionists, on a time continuum, then 1892 was a big year. The Homestead lockout, the Buffalo switchmen's strike, the Tennessee coal strikes, the New Orleans general strike, the Idaho mining strikes in Coeur d'Alene. The use of state power in the early 1890s against these workers was staggering! In the late 1880s and early 1890s there was a growing awareness among workers that the state had become more and more inaccessible to them and especially to their political and economic needs and demands.

You see what I am saying? These repressive political developments were responses to the workers' upsurge in the mid-1880s. And, then, the workers' awareness of these developments revealed itself in their new behavior. Eugene V. Debs, for example, moved to the Left and became a socialist, believing that the ultimate solution was political. And Samuel Gompers moved to the Right, making the argument that workers could not engage in independent politics because they were too weak to influence the political parties. Gompers turned inward to build strength. Debs turned outward. Both were authentic working-class responses.

David Montgomery, incidentally, told aspects of this larger story in *Beyond Equality,*[8] which was so original that few conventional historians understood it when it was first published. He demonstrated how workers' movements in northern and western towns and cities in the Civil War and Reconstruction years raised fundamental questions about prevailing middle-class notions of equality and middle-class definitions of the state. He demonstrated how workers' movements profoundly affected ideology in national politics. That was "history from the bottom up." Go back and read the reviews of *Beyond Equality,* and you will see where the historical profession was at in the good old days. "A curious book about textile workers' strikes and ten-hour movements. What can they have to do with Andrew Johnson and the politics of Reconstruction?" Many historians simply could not grasp the connection.

Montgomery wrote about working-class presence prior to 1873. It resurfaced, more powerfully, in the mid-1880s, and we are just now making sense of this intercession by American workers. It was not predominantly socialist in outlook, but it was anti-capitalist. Leon Fink has pieces of this story in his splendid forthcoming book.[9] The rhetoric these movements and their leaders used to legitimize their attack on developing capitalism drew upon premillennial Christianity and republican ideology. The new inequality had no place in a Christian country (as they understood Christianity) and especially no place in a republican country. Workers in large numbers believed that. Even —indeed, especially—immigrant workers. They hadn't come to America to be proletarianized. "What in hell is going on in America? What kind of country is this becoming?" they asked. In the 1880s a deep struggle over the meaning of America took place. In a recent article, Montgomery insists that the struggle was fought again thirty or forty years later.[10] He is probably right. And a similar struggle had been fought in the 1830s by artisans. These struggles have erupted irregularly in our history and are evidence of powerful lower-class responses to changes in the structure of class inequality. In turn, these struggles shape the on-going historical process and the redefinition of democratic institutions. Theodore Roosevelt and Eugene V. Debs knew that. So should late–twentieth-century American historians, especially those who call themselves radicals.

But let me go on for a moment. The full history of subordinate groups—all of them—involves far more than studying these irregular outbursts of collective, democratic protest. A central tension exists within all modern dependent groups between individualist (utilitarian) and collective (mutualist) ways of dealing with and sometimes overcoming historically specific patterns of dependence and inequality. That tension changes over time. It differs from group to group. It reveals itself in very diverse ways, reflecting regional, racial, ethnic, gender, and other differences. It is little understood, but it always is there and awaits thoughtful historical analysis.

Q. What about socialism? If you look at America in 1840, it seems to me that the republicans are still justified in believing their world is possible. But if you look at America in 1880, if you look at Standard Oil and the other trusts being formed, it seems to me socialism was a much more viable and promising response to the capitalist order than republicanism was. Socialism is much more collective than republicanism. It is a large-scale egalitarianism, with the emphasis on people working together, in contrast to republicanism, with its emphasis on people working for themselves. I don't see how one can say, in retrospect, that Americans should still be republicans in the 1880s.

GUTMAN Socialism was only one expression of collective resistance to the dependencies associated with wage-labor and modern capitalism. I would argue this way: in the 1880s—a period of intense debate over the ways in which capitalism had transformed America and threatened democratic practices—workers began to develop sets of working class—or alternate—institutions and beliefs. I shouldn't say "workers" because that is too facile. Working-class movements developed alternative institutions and beliefs. The cooperative, for example, was a very important central institution in that period. There were thousands of working-class cooperatives. Most of them failed, but that is not the point. If you look at the scale of enterprise, the cooperative was an appropriate response to wage-labor dependency. The Knights of Labor, for example, argued that "natural" monopolies such as railroads should be owned by the state. They were too big to be run cooperatively, but everything else should be run on a cooperative basis, everything else should be produced cooperatively. The cooperatives were anti-capitalist but have often been treated as spurious and utopian working-class efforts. That's a mistake. Theirs was an anti-capitalist and a democratic critique, but socialist movements did not thrive between 1873 and 1896. (Socialists, however, were very important leaders of popular class movements.)

Q. Granted there was no powerful socialist movement before 1896. But it is also important to remember that there was no important working-class republican movement *after* 1896; working-class republicanism collapsed. And while

I know this is an argument largely due to hindsight, still it is because of that collapse that I think we can say—as historians—that republicanism was not an appropriate response to capitalism in the 1880s.

But it would also be a mistake to assume that socialism merely took up among workers where republicanism left off. As your work especially has shown, republicanism was a cross-class movement through the 1890s. The workers enunciated an ideology that many classes could accept. But when workers begin to talk socialism in the early 1900s, they break those cross-class links, which are only going to be re-formed much later, if at all, on a different basis.

GUTMAN   That is well put. We also need to make allowances for changes in the class structure and in the composition of the working class. That gets us into the twentieth century, a very different world from the one I studied.

Q.   Let's change the subject a little. What was the occasion for writing the essay "Work, Culture and Industrializing America," published in the *American Historical Review* in 1973?

GUTMAN   The original version of the paper was prepared for the first Anglo-American colloquium on working-class history in 1968, several years before the revised version was published. My intent in writing it was to go to England, sit down with colleagues whose work I admired, and say to them, "Look, you've been doing so much original and important work, and there is much that American working-class historians can learn from this work. But what you have been doing must first be Americanized." What these British colleagues—Thompson, Hobsbawm, Rudé, Pollard, the several Harrisons, among others—had done was far more than simply study the whole worker. They had begun to reexamine the processes by which new subordinate classes are formed, how they develop. They were studying class conflict and social change in new ways. That, after all, is at the heart of Thompson's work. It is an analysis of the ways in which who workers *had been* affected who they *became.* Our task was to Americanize—so to speak—that insight for wage earners and, of course, other dependent classes in this country such as slaves. What, after all, are the distinctive, much less the universal, problematics essential to understanding changing class relations and behavior in the United States?

Q.   Let me lay out a critical reading of the *AHR* article. The focus is almost one century, a long period of disruptive industrial violence. This goes back to your earliest concerns, clearly. The overarching scheme is to try to figure out why the history of American industrial relations had the violent character it had. If we look at Britain during the same century, the violent period seems to have been much shorter. Why? Your response, in this reading, is to say that there is a need to season a new work force in the United States over and over again. The history of American industrial relations is more violent, you seem to say, because of the continual infusion of new masses of workers coming from premodern and preindustrial backgrounds into this increasingly modern industrial society.

I have two questions about this scheme. First, it seems to me to underestimate the role of indigenous American values in opposing capitalism. If a reader didn't know anything else about American labor history, they might walk away with the impression that peasants came to the New World and weren't able to adjust to the factory so they revolted or resisted. Such a reading places an emphasis on external opposition, on opposition to industrialism as being un-American.

Second, there seems to be a deemphasis in the essay on internal contradictions within the industrial order itself, a deemphasis of any idea that the industrial order might produce its own internal opposition. After all, you don't need to be a peasant in order to hate factory work.

GUTMAN   The essay did not emphasize those internal contradictions, and for good reason. The words *premodern* and *preindustrial* bother me now, but I used them—and this may surprise some readers—as a way of dealing with long-term changes in the American class structure, as a way of enlarging our understanding of changing American class relations and working-class behavior, and as a way of reconceptualizing archaic conflict models used to explain diverse working-class responses to changing patterns of inequality. Of course, the use of the term may have been misleading. The concept of preindustrial covers so much that it can really mean very little. It mixes together very different men and women. Pocahontas, Thomas Jefferson, Nat Turner, and Josiah Wedgwood, after all, were all preindustrial. Precapitalist might have been more appropriate, but it has its problems too.

The most important part of the essay, I think, is not the evidence dealing with recalcitrant work habits, but the argument about periodization and changing class relations. What puzzles me is that even the article's most cogent critics—and I include David Montgomery among them because his remains the most thoughtful discussion of the essay[11]—failed to address that issue. The language I used may have been inappropriate and therefore misled some readers. So let me try a different language to summarize its main points. Differences exist between studying the formation of a new subordinate class and the development of that class, and then the behavior of a well-developed subordinate class. E. P. Thompson's *The Making of the English Working Class*, for example, reshaped our understanding of class formation in the early Industrial Revolution, and the recent writings of Alan Dawley, Thomas Dublin, Paul Faler, Bruce Laurie, and Gary Kulik, among others, have Americanized Thompson's methods in examining class formation prior to 1840.[12] (We should keep in mind, however, that in 1840 only 11 percent of America's 17 million inhabitants lived in towns or cities with more than 2,500 residents and that among the gainfully employed 7 out of 10 labored in agriculture.) Other labor historians have dealt with a very different *moment* in class relations and working-class history. David Brody's study of immigrant steelworkers examined changes in a *developed* working class.[13] So, too, did Montgomery's essays on shop-floor struggles over control of the work process.[14] The *AHR* essay emphasized the differences in the class structure over time—its central point—and then examined behavior and conflicts involving workers new to wage labor in distinct periods. The analysis may have been incomplete. But it had nothing whatever to do with modernization theories and certainly was not intended to explain the full range of working-class behavior between 1815 and 1920.

The *AHR* essay called attention to three distinct periods. In the years before 1843 (the exact date hardly matters), wage labor came unevenly to the United States. The profound transformations associated with the coming of wage labor were not experienced nationally, that happened between 1840 and the turn of the century. In these decades the preindustrial class and social structure were transformed. That transformation occurred unevenly. But it was that transformation in those decades that made the United States the world's preeminent industrial capitalist nation. And the widening importance of wage labor in those decades was experienced mostly by foreign-born workers and their children. David Montgomery correctly criticized my essay for failing to emphasize that many new *American* workers in that period had been wage laborers prior to their emigration. That fact gave special character to class relations in those decades and is the reason, incidentally, why it is so difficult —indeed, erroneous—to deal with American working-class history and immigration history as discrete subjects. I dealt with the transatlantic (and transpacific) connections too simply. And the third period? The decades after the 1890s? It was different again. Working-class behavior then occurs in the most developed of all capitalist settings. Important changes in the class structure occurred between 1890 and the First World War, but the basic structural changes associated with the spread of wage labor took place in the so-called middle period.

Periodization remains a little-studied question. Alan Dawley's *Class and Community*, of course, moved us light-years ahead on this subject. He was the first so-called new labor historian to reperiodize working-class history in a detailed study that covered a long time span. No one had done so before Dawley's book on the Lynn shoemakers. Montgomery didn't do it. Brody didn't do it. Neither did I. Dawley rushed through the full process much too hastily, but he nevertheless indicated important linkages between the formation of a new subordinate class (period one), its subsequent development (period two), and the behavior of a well-developed class (period three). My own essay failed to make these important connections.

Q. Is the violence characteristic of U.S. industrial relations necessarily associated with the need to season new workers?

GUTMAN   Not at all. The issue is not violence, but conflict and its changing nature over time. Conflict does not disappear after the first generation. It is redefined and takes new forms. In the period from the 1840s to the 1880s it was not merely that most workers were new to the factory, but also that the structure of American society changed radically and therefore redefined the sources of new conflict.

Q. I still worry that we are left with the sense that opposition to capitalism was external to America.

GUTMAN   What do you mean by external? So few old-stock, white Americans labored in factories and mines after 1870 that it becomes essential to study the remaking of the American working class in transoceanic ways. But the foreignness of the working class after 1870 does not make American opposition to capitalism external. It means that much of American working-class history between 1840 and 1920 has a transoceanic dimension that cannot be neglected. My current research focuses on this question. Ira Berlin and I have completed an essay on the composition of the southern free working class in 1860 that shows the neglected great importance of urban immigrant male workers there and casts new light on the very low status of urban slaves.[15] My own larger research interest now is on the ways in which immigrants and their children were the critical link between working-class formation prior to 1840 and working-class development between 1840 and 1890. Outside the building trades in nearly all parts of the country, white male workers of old stock were relatively unimportant. Immigrants, their children, and Afro-Americans played central roles in the reproduction of the working class and the development of working-class institutions. It could not have been otherwise in places like Leavenworth, Kansas, where Blacks, immigrants, and the children of immigrants comprised about 90 percent of the working class in 1880. And the Leavenworth pattern was typical for the country at large.

Q. You placed great stress on a distinction between "culture" and "society" in the essay we have been discussing. What part does the distinction play in your thinking about working-class history?

GUTMAN   The distinction seems to be especially appropriate for dealing with transitional periods—when there is an active tension between old and new, when new class institutions and class relationships are being created. It is a more difficult distinction to use in periods of relative tranquillity. The distinction draws upon the work of the cultural anthropologists, Eric Wolf and Sidney Mintz, and it makes good sense.[16] Just how that distinction is useful in studying third- or fourth-generation wage earners in a developed capitalist society remains to be worked out. I'm sure it can, but it means studying the rules by which working men and women organize their everyday lives in a well-developed capitalist society. Those rules change over time as do the constraints operating on a developed subordinate class. These are subjects that should concern students of the twentieth-century American working class. Compare Thompson's *Making* with Gareth Stedman Jones's splendid essay on the remaking of the London working class after the mid-nineteenth century.[17] The developed class differs from the one that engaged the formative experience, but it has not been fully integrated into the new social order. It has its own rules and experiences—its own culture—and sometimes challenges its subordination in new class-specific ways.

My *AHR* essay did not deal with third- or fourth-generation American workers. Such a study involves a different emphasis than the examination of first-generation workers. American capitalism was well developed by 1900. The working class was not new *in America* by then. But large numbers of American workers were new *to American capitalism* in 1900, and the culture/society dichotomy remains very useful in studying how they became American workers. The dialectic, however, is far more subtle than I suggested in the 1973 essay.

Q.   I have problems with the usefulness of the culture/society distinction, even for the 1840 to 1880 period in which you are saying it makes the most sense. From what you were saying earlier, you clearly agree that capitalism is still relatively new in this period. Moreover, because it was new, a different history was still possible. The history we got was not inevitable at any point in that period.

GUTMAN   Quite right. It was not foreordained. It was open, of course, and working-class critics of the developed system acted on that belief.

Q.   Well, it seems to me that the distinction you draw between culture and society closes off the possibility of understanding those historical possibilities. Society comes in as already formed, as finished, complete and single-minded. It comes in as Thompson's windscreen against which the bearers of culture are squashed.[18]

GUTMAN   Put that way it is a static formulation. That is right, and a very fine point. Not only that, the trouble with that formulation is that nothing new is formed among the workers, leaving the impression that what is being described is merely a generational phenomenon. Go on.

Q.   That is the society side of my problem. There is also a culture side. The conception of culture in the essay, especially with the emphasis on culture as inherited belief, is also static. I would contrast it to Thompson's more dynamic conception, which focuses on consciousness a great deal more. Tradition and all that is there in Thompson, but the difference between culture in the sense of tradition and culture in the sense of consciousness is that traditions are slow to change. At one point you say as much, describing culture as the things that change slowly, the things that persist or endure. For Thompson, in contrast, culture—as consciousness—is a volatile thing: it is always under pressure of change; it is always making new discoveries; it is always coming up with new things. That is the source of the electricity to *The Making of the English Working Class*. Traditions do not disappear in such a conception, but instead of simply enduring there, they are thought, they are spoken, and ultimately they are lived.

GUTMAN   Yes, that element is inadequately treated. That is a fine criticism.

Q.   If you put these two criticisms together you get a different emphasis—both on society as something that can be changed and on culture as something always being formed—that avoids the problems I have with the culture/society distinction. Instead of a notion of society as being distinct from culture we get an emphasis on culture as a way of life, in Raymond Williams's terms (or as "social being," in Thompson's terms) embedding culture and society together. One then asks how at each point everything is being formed and is changing. Furthermore, one gets an emphasis on consciousness as active thought. The advantage of working with a distinction between culture and consciousness (or social being and social consciousness) in place of a distinction between society and culture is that the former distinction includes more historical experience and has built into it, at both ends, historical openings and possibilities for change. Thompson, for example, is now saying that we can, simply by virtue of alerting the public mind to the dangers of nuclear war, turn around the greatest juggernaut that humankind has ever faced.[19] That is the possibility of consciousness, that is what its volatility makes possible. (Unfortunately, it doesn't make it certain.) Thompson is saying that we can change the way we think about our history, and if we do, we can change that history itself—at least we can if enough of us change the way we think about it.

In your later book on the Black family, by the way, I think consciousness is there. The book is obviously part of an enormous renaissance in Afro-American studies, but it is different from most other contributions in the area —despite all the work on African traditions and slave traditions—because in the book you can watch the people discovering things for themselves, in their own language, and mulling them over. They are meeting challenges—1861, 1863, 1865—things change and the people are thinking about the changes and that is in the book. That is what is good about it, in my opinion.

GUTMAN   Your distinction between culture and consciousness is a splendid one, and your criticism is on target. The essay dealt with a long period of time, but it lacked movement. That may be the reason so little attention has been given to the issues of periodization it raised. My emphasis on culture at the expense of consciousness meant freezing a series of different moments in time and thereby ignoring the crucial connections between historical being and becoming.

Q.   What is the difference between the new labor history and the old labor history?

GUTMAN   There were really two "old" labor histories: that of the Old Left— such as the work of Philip Foner—and that of John R. Commons and his school.[20] At the core of the labor history of the Old Left was a critique of the traditional leadership of the American labor movement. The labor leadership, it was argued, consistently misled well-intentioned workers and thus was responsible for the failure of a sustained socialist movement to emerge in the United States. This "essentialist" critique was made not simply of the craft unions, but of the earlier, so-called utopian unions as well. The Knights of

Labor, according to the Old Left, were as much the bearers of false consciousness as the American Federation of Labor. This explanation of the absence of a socialist movement in the U.S. was inadequate and misleading. But it rested on a certain politics and a deterministic philosophy of history. So, too, the history associated with John Commons and Selig Perlman rested on a certain politics. They sought to defend the liberal view of the trade unions as institutions essential for balancing inequalities in capitalist society without transforming that society. Commons and his associates shared assumptions about the nature of American society and American politics, most centrally that the narrow craft union fitted American conditions.

The new labor history also rests on a certain politics and is inspired by a distinctive philosophy of history. Much of it, in this country and in Western Europe, developed in response to and out of the decomposition of classical Marxism. One thinks of someone like Thompson. His work comes out of the Marxist tradition while it reacts against Stalinist historiography. This new labor history rejects the deterministic models that the labor history of the Old Left rested on. But it does not reject the vision of a more egalitarian and democratic society. Nor does it reject democratic socialism. I suspect that most of the new labor historians who have done significant work are men and women who define themselves, in one or another fashion, as socialists. The kinds of questions they ask—forgetting about how they go about answering them, which is often technical—come out of a politics broadly associated with the redefinition of socialism, freeing up socialist theory and practice from the totalitarian shroud it has lived in through most of this century.

Much of the new labor history—at least the best of it—rejects what is essentially the Old Left's version of the Whig fallacy of history. It refuses to look at a period of history simply as a precursor of the moment that we currently are living in. Freeing ourselves from the present in that way brings to life movements, brings to life a politics in the past, that were submerged by the crude presentism of the older labor history, whether of the Left or the center.

Q. How does the new labor history answer the question: why has there been no mass socialist movement in the United States?

GUTMAN I don't think that is a well-put historical question. We need to put aside notions that workers' movements have developed properly elsewhere and in the U.S. they developed improperly. We need to put aside the English model, the French model, and the Cuban model, and then ask a set of very, very tough questions about what American workers actually thought and did —and why. Once we free ourselves of the notion that it should have happened in one particular way, then we stop looking for the reasons why it didn't happen that way. If we don't, then we end up offering explanations like the high rate of social mobility or that workers had the vote in America or a whole series of other single-factor explanations, as answers to what is a nonhistorical question.

Q. Based on your work for before 1900 and on Montgomery's for the period after 1900, can you make judgments about whether or not workers' movements in these periods were adequate to the historical tasks they faced if they were to achieve their political goals?

GUTMAN   I don't think that way as a historian. What does it mean to talk about historical tasks that workers faced? We are letting in through the back door a notion of fixed and predetermined historical development. We are measuring the American worker (or the French worker or the Polish worker) against an ideal type. That is the Whig fallacy of history once again.

Q. It is not just the Whig fallacy. Some would call it the Marxist fallacy.

GUTMAN   Yes, there is a Marxist variant of the Whig fallacy. It comes from an essentialist view of workers or the working class, one that emphasizes a predetermined pattern of historical development.

Q. But some would argue that such a notion is central to classical Marxism.

GUTMAN   And it contains within it dangerous notions of vanguard leadership and vanguard parties.

Q. Not necessarily. C. L. R. James, for example, rejects the idea of a vanguard party, but still believes in historical progress and a direction to history; he believes in an essentialism of sorts.

GUTMAN   There is direction, and historians study it. And while I am not so sure about the notion of historical progress, I strongly reject the notion of any vanguard party. As I read James, he has a profoundly anti-Leninist position. Rejection of the vanguard party—and of the problematic out of which it emerged—comes out of the politics of this century. It is not simply a philosophical question. It is based on the real historical experience with what vanguard parties meant to the lives of tens of millions of people.

Q. But vanguard parties are not central to the vision of classical Marxism, the Marxism of Marx. What is central is some notion of historical progress and some direction to history. What is left of Marxism, in your view, when you have stripped away this aspect?

GUTMAN   What is left when you clear away the determinist and teleological elements are good questions that direct your attention to critical ways of looking at on-going historical processes. A fundamental contribution of nineteenth- and twentieth-century Marxist thinking is a set of questions having to do with the way in which one examines class relations and how they change, the way in which one examines the institutionalization of power, the way in which one examines popular oppositional movements, the way in which one examines the integration of subordinate or exploited groups into a social system. These are some of the very useful questions.

I can put it more concretely. What is going on in Poland, for example, poses a whole series of questions for historians dealing with Poland in the 1950s, 1960s, and 1970s. A central question historians should be examining is what was it in the experience of the Polish workers in the period since World War II—and maybe even before—that gave rise to the Solidarity movement?

That is a useful historical question. Look at any given set of class relations. Most of the time subordinate populations live with their exploitation. They make adjustments. They create institutions to deal with inequality, to deal with the unequal distribution of scarce resources and wealth. They do so without seeking to transform the conditions that create or sustain that inequality. Then, under certain circumstances—none of them predictable—that acceptance is transformed into opposition: Chicago in the 1880s, St. Petersburg in 1905, Gdansk in the 1970s. One subject of great interest to democratic socialists—given the collapse of deterministic models—is the study of the historical conditions under which popular opposition emerges. Why does oppositionality emerge in a particular way? Why not in another way? What are the circumstances that give rise to such movements? Explain their successes and/or failures?

Q. So, you are saying that while we can't predict a future outbreak of resistance or revolt, historians can study past outbreaks and try to understand why they happened at that particular moment. What is the point?

GUTMAN Opposition movements surface irregularly. They help shape historical process, sometimes radically. A classic, recent example from the U.S. is that of the civil rights movement. If one reads the literature from the 1930s and 1940s on race relations, little in it gives a clue to the movement that would challenge aspects of an oppressive racial and class structure in the 1950s and 1960s.

Once a movement has emerged, its tenaciousness, its successes, its limitations, are all questions for historians of popular movements, especially if we put aside notions of an elite, vanguard leadership. What sustained the movement? How did the rank and file of the civil rights movement, for example, use everyday (nonpolitical) institutional arrangements that they had developed prior to the 1950s to transform oppressive circumstances in their everyday lives? The same kind of analysis can be made about the rise of the CIO. This kind of history teaches us something genuinely important about everyday struggles and historical change, about human agency. What gives the civil rights movement its great historical importance is the way in which Black and white people in the South—but especially Blacks—transformed traditional institutions that were mechanisms of adaptation and survival into instrumentalities meant to alter radically the structure of southern society.

Q. Do you think that a student of popular movements in the past will have something to say about how popular movements should conduct themselves today? Are there lessons to be learned from the past?

GUTMAN Of course, there is a value in studying history. But it surely does not take the form of practical lessons for today. Class and social relations are constantly changing. That is why there is no direct lesson learned out of, say, Homestead.[21] Events illuminate changing structures and processes at work over time. We also study competing traditions (more than two) over time. And we study the history of popular movements: what gave rise to them, why they went in one direction as contrasted to another. But we don't ransack the past for lessons.

Historical study is liberating for other reasons. The central value of historical understanding is that it transforms historical givens into historical contingencies. It enables us to see the structures in which we live and the inequality people experience as only one among many other possible experiences. By doing that, you free people for creative and critical (or radical) thought. I could give you many examples from the teaching I have done with trade-union people in the last few summers. Things that people had assumed were normal in their lives (like smog, or speed-up, or television, or clocks, or racism) are seen to have a beginning, a middle, and sometimes an end. When people come into contact with that perspective, they are better able to think analytically about the structures that impinge upon them.

How ordinary men and women engage those structures—then and now—should concern us. In his argument with Stalinism and determinist Marxism, Jean-Paul Sartre put it very well. He said that the essential question for study —this is a paraphrase—is not what has been done to men and women but what men and women do with what is done to them. That is also a Thompsonian formulation. And this is precisely what the best Black writers have been writing for the past fifty years. W. E. B. Du Bois argued for this approach when he wrote *Black Reconstruction,* and it is what C. L. R. James's historical writings are about.

Once you surrender the fixed older forms of historical explanation and process, the future becomes open. It then becomes even more important to analyze and examine the history of those structures and ideologies that shape our lives.

Q. When you drop what you call essentialism, don't you run the risk of the meaning disappearing from the history? Don't you run the risk of encouraging a history where people are studied without any judgments being made about what they are doing and whether it makes sense?

GUTMAN   No, I don't think so. We need to be asking ourselves in what ways, if any, working-class presence affected the historical process at changing moments in time. These are important and difficult historical questions. George Rawick, for one, has been asking them for years.[22] They are questions for any country, not just the United States. And the answers to them vary over time. There are so many good examples of work of this sort. Alfred Young's magnificent on-going study of late-eighteenth-century artisans and crowds addresses such questions.[23] So did David Brody's book on immigrant steelworkers. And there are so many others among the younger historians whose on-going work continually examines these questions.

The real problem with the new labor history is not a lack of essentialism.

Q. What is the real problem?

GUTMAN   There is a compelling need for a new national synthesis. Work in labor history and other areas of social history—indeed, much of the so-called new history—is often quite narrow. We need to pull it all together and see how it makes our politics, our national experience, look different. The old Progressive synthesis collapsed long ago, and the so-called corporate liberal synthesis certainly won't do. It simply projects a disillusionment with the New Deal and with the Old Left's uncritical relationship to Roosevelt backward to other movements and moments. If the New Deal successfully incorporated the working class—and that is an open question—and brought them back into the system with the cooperation of the Communist party, that is no reason to create a historical tradition that has its roots in the National Civic Federation.[24] The corporate liberal synthesis of twentieth-century American history is an expression of the political pessimism of the 1950s and early 1960s, which is simply being projected backward.

Any adequate new synthesis has to grapple with the problems of periodization and social class. The strength of large synthetic work depends upon appropriate periodization. But that question has hardly been discussed. The new work in labor history—and in women's history and Afro-American history—all pose very subtle problems for those concerned with rewriting the *national* experience. Why haven't those problems been confronted? We need to do so.

This need has become very clear to me in my recent teaching. I continue teaching graduate students. But each summer from 1977 through 1980 I also taught an NEH [National Endowment for the Humanities] history seminar for trade unionists entitled Americans at Work. And in the past three years I also directed an on-going, NEH-sponsored semester-long seminar on recent American social history for community college teachers in the metropolitan New York City region (CUNY and SUNY faculty). These colleagues teach history and history-related subjects. The new historical works that engage so many of us in intense research and writing and sometimes even in sharp controversy have failed to reach these very different audiences. That is evident to me. We write for each other too often. What might interest these and other audiences never gets to them.

Teaching trade unionists and community college colleagues—men and women so different from each other in so many ways—has taught me that there is an audience willing to read American history afresh and, more important, to grapple with historical thinking. We are reaching out to that audience.

A general social history of the American people, incorporating the best recent scholarship, is one way to reach such audiences. And I am involved in such a project—the American Working-Class History Project—and working with a group of historians, filmmakers, and graphic artists: Steve Brier, Bruce Levine, Josh Brown, Kate Pfordresher, Dorothy Fennell, and Dave Brundage. We are funded by the NEH [National Endowment for the Humanities] and the Ford Foundation and are well under way to making the best of the "old" and the "new" history accessible to community college students and to out-of-school adults, especially trade unionists. We are putting separate strands together in a multimedia social history curriculum that includes a two-volume general history of American working people and a series of innovative slide presentations and short documentary films. The first documentary, which we are now producing, sets the nationwide railroad strikes and riots of 1877 in the larger context of America's economic, political, and social transformation after the Civil War.

Q. In *The Black Family in Slavery and Freedom,* it seems to me that you deal most completely with the kinds of questions about the difference between a developed class and a class in formation that we have been discussing. How do you see the book in relation to other contributions to the history of slavery in the U.S.?

GUTMAN   One of the central assumptions—perhaps the most central—about slavery by historians before 1960 was that, unlike other exploited groups, the slaves could do very little for themselves. That assumption, ultimately, rested on a common view of the slave family. What made slaves different from other exploited groups was not simply that they were owned (which was, of course, central to their experience) but that they were incapable, because of the fragmented nature of the family experience, of transmitting a changing culture over time. The fragmented nature of the family was the reason offered to explain why diverse African practices and beliefs disappeared so quickly. It was offered as the reason "Sambo" really existed.

The slaves, in this view, carried little into relationships with their owners. How could they? Tradition and experience, especially in an illiterate population, are transmitted orally. What was missing in the slave experience, as contrasted to the experience of peasants or wage workers, were the passageways through which class and cultural beliefs could travel. That is what *The Black Family* is about. It shows how the slaves could transmit and develop their own experiences and general beliefs across generations and over time. It is not about the family as such. At the heart of the analysis is an argument about the structure of the slave experience. The seemingly endless comparative data on naming practices was a way of demonstrating—proving—that slaves as a developing class could transfer beliefs between generations. It wasn't simply that they knew their grandparents' names, though that is important for some purposes. The significance of slave naming practices is that events that had occurred sixty or a hundred years earlier had remained part of their life experience.

What I uncovered, in other words, were the passageways through which the experiences and beliefs of these people traveled. Some other historians may have assumed that such passageways existed. But the evidence in *The Black Family* demonstrated their existence. Suddenly, therefore, the same kind of historical questions can be asked of slaves that historians ask about any other exploited population. The *very same* questions! On the first page of *The Black Family* I noted that it was a book about a special aspect of working-class history: the methods, the questions, they were the same. That was not mere rhetoric. I meant it, for better or worse. The answers, of course, would be different because the exploitative relationship differed, but the questions were similar because a similar historical interaction had been uncovered. The slaves could affect historical process. It is precisely what Jean-Paul Sartre was writing about, what Ralph Ellison was writing about, what E. P. Thompson was writing about.

Without these passageways the history of slavery lacked a time dimension. It was impossible to describe changing structures and beliefs. As a result, no one could explain what many very good historians (such as W. E. B. Du Bois, Joel Williamson, and Willie Lee Rose) had discerned about the behavior and beliefs of Black people after emancipation.[25] We could not understand that behavior because of the way slavery as a social system had been conceptualized by at least two generations of historians and social scientists.

Let me be more precise. Historians of slavery in the 1950s and early 1960s explained variations in slave behavior by emphasizing variations in their treatment by their owners. In other words, variations in slave behavior were attributed to external factors. Did the slave live on a plantation? Did the slave live on a farm? Did the slave live in a town, a city, or a rural area? Did the slave live in the upper South or the lower South? Did the slave have a decent owner or a harsh owner? All the "variables"—to use that ugly word—that historians used to explain slave behavior were external stimuli. The slave did no more than react to these stimuli. Variations in slave behavior were a function of their treatment. The study of slaves, not surprisingly, became largely the study of their owners. It was "top down" history at its worst. The slaves were acted upon. They could only be acted upon! That flowed from the assumptions most historians made about either the slaves or the structure of slave society.

In *The Black Family* these assumptions were shown to be entirely mistaken by studying slave behavior in areas very different from the usual concerns of labor historians—household arrangements, naming practices, marriage rules, sexual practices, and related matters. Such class behavior was studied among groups of slaves who *experienced their enslavement differently*. That is the essential point. The case studies in the book emphasized diverse types of slave class experiences, a point many critics ignored. There were slaves who lived in the upper South and in the lower South. There were slaves who had decent, paternalistic owners (among the nicest owners one could ever want, I guess), and there were slaves who had cruel owners. There were slaves who worked for men born plantation owners, and slaves who worked for farmers who became plantation owners. There were slaves who suffered relatively little family break-up, and slaves who suffered such break-up regularly. The types of slaves missing from the analysis were rice plantation slaves and urban slaves. Every other kind of nineteenth-century slave setting was in the analysis. Thus, nearly all the variables were studied.

And then, in spite of the differences, there were regularities in familial and sexual behavior. How could we explain that? It could not be explained by the relationship of these slaves to their immediate owners because those relationships were so varied. The explanation had to start with who these slaves had been before they entered into that immediate relationship (or with who their parents and grandparents had been and what they believed), and it had to go on to who they became. Generational (family) linkages, at least for these diverse Afro-American slaves, connected up the era of class formation to that of the more developed slave class. This hard evidence forced me back into the eighteenth century to argue in *The Black Family* that understanding nineteenth-century slave behavior and belief (the developed class) required a reexamination of the process by which Africans first became a social class in North America (the new class). You see, we find ourselves asking the same questions we would ask if we were studying about any other subordinate population.

Kin and quasi-kin connections served at least two functions for the developing slave class early in the Afro-American experience. They served first as passageways into which and through which experiences and ideas flowed (such as Toussaint l'Ouverture, the Declaration of Independence, the colonization and abolition movements, and even the difference between a nice and a bad owner). The existence of these passageways makes it possible to uncover how slave ideas changed over time, not just ideas about the family. Second, kin networks and concepts of kin obligation functioned as the basis of larger communal relationships and beliefs. Who took care of slave children when their parents died? Owners? Not in the records I read. We learn how the real uncle and aunt became generalized uncles and aunts. When teenagers were sold into the Deep South, for example, they were sold into newly developing slave social networks filled with generalized slave notions of quasi-kin obligation. They experienced deep pain but were not sold to a foreign country.

We have redefined the changing structure within which Africans and Afro-Americans experienced slavery. Without such structures the slaves would have been crushed by the experience; Stanley Elkins was probably right about that.[26] But the slaves were neither crippled nor made totally dependent. The reason my book focused on the family was that the *assumptions* historians made about the family affected how they explained slave behavior. The assumptions were wrong. That much is clear. So we have to look at the evidence afresh, starting in the eighteenth century. When that is done, some of the arguments in my book will be put aside and others modified. That's as it should be. But I very much doubt that the essential arguments in *The Black Family*—the ones that restore structure and process to the study of Afro-American slaves—will be seriously undermined. A changing set of class relationships has been shown to exist. All aspects of that master-slave relationship need to be restudied, and restudied over time—that is, historically.

Q. What do you think historians of slavery and the slave experience ought next to be turning their attention to?

GUTMAN   The formation of the North American slave class is perhaps the most important untold story in Afro-American history and in eighteenth-century American history. The only book that seriously addresses the issue is Peter Wood's *Black Majority,* a very good book.[27] How was that new class formed? The suggestion by some reviewers of *The Black Family* that I argued that slaves learned nothing from whites is ridiculous. The argument I made was that the behavior of slaves in the 1830s, 1840s, and 1850s was not determined simply by their immediate relationship with their owners. And then I went on to suggest, on the basis of scattered evidence, that the formative eighteenth-century period involved the creation of a new subordinate class and culture. Ira Berlin and I have studied mid- and late-eighteenth-century plantation records comparable to those used in *The Black Family,* and we can sketch the beginnings of common Afro-American slave familial cultural patterns in diverse South Carolina, North Carolina, Maryland, and Virginia settings prior to the War for Independence. It is possible to talk about a new class (Afro-American slaves) that is reproducing itself and transmitting a distinctive but changing culture. Old African cultures changed in North America, and African slaves and their immediate descendants borrowed heavily from the main-stream white culture. That happened between 1720 and 1770 (ironically, when the largest number of Africans were sold to North America).

That story has yet to be fully told. What did the slaves encounter when they arrived here? Who bought the slaves? What did it mean to an English Mid-lands farmer who had emigrated to North America and bought a slave? And what did it mean to the slave? What religion did he or she come into contact with? (If Rhys Isaac is right—and he is one of our very best historians—the kind of religious experiences slaves came into contact with in the eighteenth century would make a great deal of difference.[28]) We don't have answers to these questions now. But we can answer them, and there is a spectacular story to be worked out.

We also need fresh study of the interregional slave trade and what it did to the *developed* Afro-American culture. We should start by defining the interregional slave trade as the Second Middle Passage, one experienced primarily by the children and grandchildren of Africans who had experienced an earlier Middle Passage of their own. How did the distinctive slave culture, hammered out by the early generations of slaves, prepare people to deal with the terrible experience of the Second Middle Passage? With the pain of separation? A big book needs to be written just on this subject.

When one looks at the behavior of victims of the Second Middle Passage during the Civil War and immediately afterward and then compares it with the behavior of slaves in other parts of the South who were spared that ordeal, the behavior doesn't look very different. I am not talking about family matters, but about serving in the Union army, about fighting to keep one's children from being apprenticed and reenslaved, about refusing to sign unfair labor contracts (or going to military court to get claims on contracts). When we look at ex-slave behavior in East Texas, in Mississippi, and in Louisiana, it doesn't look very different from that in North Carolina and Virginia. Ten years ago I would have argued that it *had* to be different. But it wasn't different. That means that the interregional slave trade following upon the Industrial Revolution facilitated the spread and then the change of late-eighteenth-century and early-nineteenth-century upper South Afro-American culture. That is why it is so important to know *when* that distinctive culture was formed. And if that makes me a "culturalist," so be it.

This is the context, I think, in which we can best understand Eugene Genovese's work. He posed some important questions. My difficulty is with how he went about answering them. A central question raised in *Roll, Jordan, Roll: The World the Slaves Made* is the effect slaves had on their owners.[29] A splendid question. To answer it one needs to know who the slaves were early in time and how the master-slave relationship was formed and developed.

Think of it this way. Suppose one was writing a book on ironworkers and steelworkers in Pittsburgh called *Roll, Monongahela, Roll: The World the Steelworkers Made*. How would that book begin? It is not a book about the steel industry. It is not a book about class relations in the steel industry. It is subtitled *The World the Steelworkers Made*. Would it begin with a 150-page essay quoting from and explicating Andrew Carnegie's *Autobiography* and his letters? If one writes about the world the steelworkers *made*, the book should begin with the men before they were steelworkers and study how they *became* steelworkers. It would begin with them before they experienced Andrew Carnegie and then watch a world being made as they become steelworkers and interact with Andrew and his factories. Obviously this is precisely the innovative and bold structure of *The Making of the English Working Class*. We don't begin with industrial capitalism already imposed and study strands of upper-class ideology. We begin with the world of the artisan. We begin with the world of the handicraft weaver. We begin with the world before modern capitalism. Then the interaction is intense, painful, sometimes violent, and even creative.

The way in which you examine a world people make is to show that world in formation. A major conceptual problem in *Roll, Jordan, Roll* is that it ignores class formation. A static class relationship is probed for several hundred pages, sometimes imaginatively and brilliantly. We are presented with a fully developed slave system. Class relations and ideologies are described only in the late slave period, the decades immediately prior to emancipation.

The problem with such an approach is that when you freeze a moment in time to examine a structural relationship, you cannot neglect the process by which that relationship was formed, how it developed. If you either ignore or misunderstand that process, then you can give almost any meaning you want to the relationship and to its constituent parts. What struck me on rereading *Roll, Jordan, Roll* is that it is so very functionalist. It is as if we are being told, "This is the way that society worked, why there was so little rebellion, and why slaves and their owners made it through the day and night."

This analysis rests upon a central assertion. Genovese insists that the slaves took the prevailing ideology of the plantation class (paternalism) and transformed it into its opposite, a very interesting idea. It is the heart of the analysis. In much the same way, other historians argue that the Lynn, Massachusetts, shoe workers, for example, took eighteenth-century republican ideology and transformed it in ways appropriate to their new condition as dependent Yankee wage earners. There is fine evidence illustrating that transformation in the works of Paul Faler and Alan Dawley. But Genovese's insight is never made concrete. There isn't empirical evidence showing that it happened, showing how it happened, or showing when it happened. In 1730? In 1770? 1800? 1830? The *dates* are important. We don't know. It just happened!

Q. Genovese does present evidence *that* it happened. The problem may be that most of it was indirect.

GUTMAN: What is indirect evidence? And where is it in the book? Given the book's structure, this argument itself cannot be made. You cannot use a static model to explain a transference and transformation of ideology between a superordinate and a subordinate class. It is that simple. The book lacks a time dimension. Ruling-class ideology therefore cannot be transformed. Class relations and ideologies do not develop and change over time.

Q. Aren't your criticisms of the work of Robert Fogel and Stanley Engerman in *Time on the Cross* very similar?[30]

GUTMAN Yes. The argument in *Time on the Cross* hinged on whether Fogel and Engerman could demonstrate the superior efficiency and productivity of the slave economy. Once convinced that they had demonstrated the slave system's efficiency and productivity, they sought an explanation for it. And they argued that the efficiency and productivity of the system resulted from a positive incentive system constructed by the slave owners. The slaves did the best they could in such a system, and in the process a different slave emerged from the one we knew if we had read about slavery in the 1950s and early 1960s. Sambo became a Black Horatio Alger. Fogel and Engerman made the slaves look different but only by first making their owners look different. That's not the way to write the history of a dependent class, any dependent class!

Genovese did the same thing, only differently. Resident ownership and the relatively early need to reproduce the slave labor force, he argued in *The World the Slaveholders Made* (1969), created the material conditions that encouraged the spread of paternalist ideology among nineteenth-century planters. He asserted the prevalence of that new ideology, but he never demonstrated that it was widespread. These are not trivial points, because in *Roll, Jordan, Roll* the central thesis rested on the capacity of the slaves to transform popular paternalist notions of duty and obligation into common slave notions of right. Remaking the owners into paternalists served Genovese in the same way making the owners into profit-maximizing industrial relations specialists had served Fogel and Engerman. Genovese made the slaves look different but only by *first* making their owners look different. The central argument in both books does not rest on evidence so much as on abstract theoretical models, albeit different ones. And that meant either ignoring or minimizing important lived historical experiences that do not fit into those models.

Take the case of the interregional slave trade in North America. The movement of slaves in North America, between 1790 and 1860, from the upper South to the lower South was probably the largest single internal forced migration in the world in the nineteenth century. That's real lived historical experience. How many moved with their owners? How many moved in family groups? The best evidence we have demonstrates that for older slaves living in Mississippi and northern Louisiana perhaps as many as one out of every three or four marriages was forcibly broken by the interregional slave trade. A staggering percentage. No one, to my knowledge, has challenged it.

To someone interested in slave society, or the world the slaves made, a central question is, how did slaves experience so high a rate of marital break-up? These data were available to Genovese and to Fogel and Engerman before their books appeared. They cited its publication in the *Annales* in 1972, but never considered it. The models that each had constructed to explain slave behavior and slave society were not compatible with a high level of slave family break-up.

Such evidence is central in *The Black Family*. The first chapter considered the contradictory nature of important slave social experiences among the *last* generation of slaves. It demonstrated that a slave's experiences with his or her owner was, on the level of family maintenance, profoundly contradictory. If that was so, a second question quickly followed: did their beliefs and practices as slaves prepare them to deal with and understand those contradictions? If so, why? The next two-thirds of the book dealt at length with how slaves developed certain common institutional arrangements and beliefs to mediate the owner's abuse and exploitation. If none had existed, as Elkins shrewdly argued, the slaves would have been crippled by their oppression. There is no question about it. An isolated slave (or family) could not sustain himself (or itself) in such a setting. However difficult, the slaves, especially in the eighteenth century, had to forge new institutions and beliefs to sustain them in their oppression. That happened, and *The Black Family* showed how some— not all, by any means—of those institutions and beliefs were formed and transmuted.

In other words, there had to be connectedness. The important discovery in the book, I think, is not that slaves lived in families that were frequently broken, but that the family could serve the slaves as a way of creating social and class connections far more important than the family. Call these connections what you will! Once you know such connections exist, then you can also find out when, why, and how they came together. We know those connections began well before the invention of the cotton gin. That is very clear. These new connections—occurring so early in time—make the entire Afro-American experience look different. And they make the slaves look different. And, of course, they make the master-slave relationship look different, too. Just how these new slaves dealt with their owners over time is still unstudied. I didn't study that changing relationship. No one has done that yet. And without such study, the last thing I was going to do, in *The Black Family*, was to put what I had uncovered back into the conventional picture. To do that would have been ridiculous. If one essential part of the picture is changed, then the other parts of the picture also change. It becomes a different picture, a very, very different history.

———————

NOTES

1. The essay appears in H. Wayne Morgan, ed., *The Gilded Age: A Reappraisal* (Syracuse, N.Y.: Syracuse University Press, 1963, 1970).

2. "The Negro and the United Mine Workers of America: The Career and Letters of Richard L. Davis and Something of Their Meaning, 1890–1900" originally appeared in Julius Jacobson, ed., *The Negro and the American Labor Movement* (Garden City, N.Y.: Doubleday, 1968). "Protestantism and the American Labor Movement: The Christian Spirit in the Gilded Age" originally appeared in *The American Historical Review*, October 1966. Both have been collected in Gutman's *Work, Culture and Society in Industrializing America: Essays in American Working-Class and Social History* (New York: Knopf, 1976).

3. In a series of trials from 1875 to 1877, a group of militant miners, known in the press as the Molly Maguires, were convicted of murdering coal company officials and of committing other acts of sabotage in the anthracite region of Pennsylvania. Responding to the trials and executions, labor organizations across the country charged that the coal companies, using Pinkerton detectives, had fabricated evidence of a labor terrorist conspiracy in order to intimidate the miners and remove militant labor leaders.

4. Alan Dawley, *Class and Community: The Industrial Revolution in Lynn* (Cambridge, Mass.: Harvard University Press, 1976).

5. The false consciousness issue addresses the question of why workers did not see their objective interests as an exploited class and act in class-conscious ways to oppose capitalism. In *Poverty and Progress, Social Mobility in a Nineteenth Century City* (Cambridge, Mass.: Harvard University Press, 1964), Stephan Thernstrom argues that workers' opportunities for property and social mobility, though limited, nonetheless contributed to political consensus in late-nineteenth-century Newburyport, Massachusetts.

6. Forthcoming from Pantheon Books.

7. James Holt, "Trade Unionism in the British and U.S. Steel Industries, 1885–1912: A Comparative Study," *Labor History* 18, no. 1 (Winter 1977): 5–35.

8. David Montgomery, *Beyond Equality: Labor and the Radical Republicans, 1862–1872* (New York: Random House, 1967).

9. Leon Fink, *Workingmen's Democracy: The Knights of Labor and American Politics* (Urbana, Ill.: University of Illinois Press, 1982).

10. "The 'New Unionism' and the Transformation of Workers' Consciousness in America" originally appeared in the *Journal of Social History* (Summer 1974). It now appears as Chapter 4 in Montgomery's *Workers' Control in America* (London: Cambridge University Press, 1979).

11. David Montgomery, "Gutman's Nineteenth-Century America," *Labor History* 19, no. 3 (Summer 1978): 416–29.

12. See Thomas Dublin, *Women at Work: The Transformation of Work and Community in Lowell, Massachusetts, 1826–1860* (New York: Columbia University Press, 1975); Paul Faler, *Mechanics and Manufacturers in the Early Industrial Revolution: Lynn, Massachusetts, 1780–1860* (Albany, N.Y.: State University of New York Press, 1981); Bruce Laurie, *Working People of Philadelphia, 1800–1850* (Philadelphia: Temple University Press, 1980); Gary Kulik, "Pawtucket Village and the Strike of 1824: The Origins of Class Conflict in Rhode Island," *Radical History Review*, no. 17 (Spring 1978): 5–37.

13. David Brody, *Steelworkers in America: The Nonunion Era* (Cambridge, Mass.: Harvard University Press, 1960).

14. David Montgomery, *Workers' Control in America* (New York and London: Cambridge University Press, 1979).

15. Herbert Gutman and Ira Berlin's essay was read at the Organization of American Historians convention in Detroit, April 1982.

16. See Eric Wolf, *Peasants* (Englewood Cliffs, N.J.: Prentice-Hall, 1966) and *Peasant Wars of the Twentieth Century* (New York: Harper and Row, 1969); Sidney Mintz, *Worker in Cane: A Puerto Rican Life History* (New Haven, Conn.: Yale University Press, 1960); and Sidney Mintz and Richard Price, *An Anthropological Approach to the Afro-American Past: A Caribbean Perspective* (Philadelphia: Institute for the Study of Human Issues, 1976).

17. Gareth Stedman Jones, "Working-class Culture and Working-class Politics in London 1870–1900: Notes on the Remaking of a Working Class," *Journal of Social History* 7, no. 4 (Summer 1974): 460–508. See also Gareth Stedman Jones, *Outcast London: A Study in the Relationship Between Classes in Victorian Society* (Oxford: Clarendon Press, 1971).

18. Thompson links the prevalence of structuralist paradigms of society within contemporary Marxism to the impact of the cold war upon the Left. In a recent essay he wrote, "Voluntarism crashed against the wall of the Cold War. No account can convey the sickening jerk of deceleration between 1945 and 1948. Even in this country [England] the Marxist Left seemed to be moving with 'the flow of the stream' in 1945; in 1948, it was struggling to survive amidst an antagonistic current. In Eastern Europe that same sickening jerk stopped the hearts of Masaryk, Kostov, and of Rajik. In the West our heads were thrown against the windscreen of capitalist

society; and that screen felt like—*a structure.*" *The Poverty of Theory and Other Essays* (London and New York: Monthly Review Press, 1978), p. 73.

19. See E. P. Thompson, *Beyond the Cold War: A New Approach to the Arms Race and Nuclear Annihilation* (New York: Pantheon Books, 1982); E. P. Thompson and Dan Smith, eds., *Protest and Survive* (New York: Monthly Review Press, 1981).

20. Philip Foner, *History of the Labor Movement in the United States* (New York: International Publishers, 1947–80); John R. Commons, *History of Labor in the United States* (New York: Macmillan Publishing Company, 1918–46).

21. Homestead, Pennsylvania, was the company town of the Carnegie Steel Company. During the bloody Homestead strike of 1892, the Amalgamated Association of Iron and Steel Workers controlled the town and succeeded in defeating three hundred Pinkerton guards hired to keep the mills operating with scab labor. The strike was subsequently crushed by the state militia, and the steelworkers' union was broken for nearly forty years.

22. George Rawick, ed., *The American Slave: A Composite Autobiography*, Vol. I., *From Sundown to Sunup: The Making of the Black Community* (Westport, Conn.: Greenwood Publishing Co., 1972).

23. Alfred Young, ed., *The American Revolution: Explorations in the History of American Radicalism* (Dekalb, Ill.: Northern Illinois University Press, 1976). Young's study of late-eighteenth-century crowds and artisans has not yet been published in a single volume. See "The Mechanics and the Jeffersonians in New York, 1789–1801," *Labor History* 5 (1964).

24. Founded in 1900 as an alliance of major industrialists, labor, and the public, the National Civic Federation advocated the reconciliation of capital and labor through the avoidance of strikes, compulsory arbitration, and welfare capitalism. Organized in response to the growing strength of the socialist movement, the NCF appealed to Samuel Gompers and conservative trade unionists in the American Federation of Labor and was rejected by new unionists involved in fighting the open shop movement and in organizing unskilled workers.

25. See W. E. B. Du Bois, *Black Reconstruction: An Essay toward a History of the Part which Black Folk Played in the Attempt to Reconstruct Democracy in America, 1860–1880* (New York: Atheneum, 1973), originally published in 1935; Joel Williamson, *After Slavery: The Negro in South Carolina during Reconstruction, 1861–1877* (Chapel Hill: University of North Carolina Press, 1965); Willie Lee Rose, *Rehearsal for Reconstruction: The Port Royal Experiment* (New York: Oxford University Press, 1964, 1976); and William W. Freehling, ed., *Slavery and Freedom* (New York: Oxford University Press, 1982).

26. Stanley Elkins, *Slavery: A Problem in American Institutional and Intellectual Life* (Chicago: University of Chicago Press, 3rd. ed., rev., 1976).

27. Peter Wood, *Black Majority: Negroes in Colonial South Carolina from 1670 through the Stono Rebellion* (New York: Norton, 1974).

28. Rhys Isaac, *The Transformation of Virginia, 1740–1790* (Chapel Hill: University of North Carolina Press, 1982); "Evangelical Revolt: The Nature of the Baptists' Chal-

lenge to the Traditional Order in Virginia, 1765–1775," *William and Mary Quarterly* 3rd ser., 31 (July 1974): 345–68.

29. Eugene D. Genovese, *Roll, Jordan, Roll: The World the Slaves Made* (New York: Pantheon Books, 1974).

30. Robert Fogel and Stanley Engerman, *Time on the Cross: The Economics of American Negro Slavery* (Boston: Little Brown, 1974); Herbert Gutman, *Slavery and the Numbers Game: A Critique of Time on the Cross* (Urbana, Ill.: University of Illinois Press, 1975). See also Herbert Gutman, Paul David, Peter Temin, Richard Sutch, and Gavin Wright, *Reckoning With Slavery* (New York: Oxford University Press, 1976).

S E L E C T   B I B L I O G R A P H Y

Books
The Black Family in Slavery and Freedom, 1750–1925. New York: Pantheon Books, 1976.
Many Pasts: Readings in American Social History, coedited with Gregory S. Kealey. 2 vols. Englewood Cliffs, N.J.: Prentice-Hall, 1973.
Reckoning with Slavery, coauthored with Paul David, Peter Temin, Richard Sutch, and Gavin Wright. New York: Oxford University Press, 1976.
Slavery and the Numbers Game: A Critique of Time on the Cross. Urbana: University of Illinois Press, 1976.
Work, Culture, and Society in Industrializing America. New York: Alfred A. Knopf, 1976.

Articles (1975–1982)
"Afro-American History as Immigrant Experience." In *The American Experience in Historical Perspective,* edited by Shlomo Slonin. Jerusalem: Hebrew University, 1978.
"American Ladies Shall Not Be Slaves." Review of *Class and Community, The Industrial Revolution in Lynn* by Alan Dawley. *New York Times Book Review,* May 1977.
"Famille et groupes de parente chez les Afro-Americains en escalvage dans les plantations de Good Hope (Caroline du Sud), 1760–1860." In *Esclave-facteur de production: l'economie politique de l'esclavage,* edited by Sidney Mintz, 141–70. Paris: Dunod, 1982.
"Foreword and Introduction." *Working Southerners, Essays from Southern Exposure.* New York: Pantheon Books, 1980.
"Labor and the 'Sartre Question.' " *Humanities* 1 (September-October 1980).
"Mirrors of Hard and Distorted Glass, The Black Family and Public Policy." In *History and Social Policy,* edited by David Rothman and Staunton Wheeler. New York: Academic Press, 1980.
"The Moynihan Report, Black History Seduced and Abandoned." *The Nation* 229 (September 22, 1979):232–36.

"Persistent Myths About the Afro-American Family." *Journal of Interdisciplinary History* 6 (Autumn 1975):181–210.

"Slave Family and Its Legacies." In *Roots and Branches, Current Directions in Slave Studies,* edited by Michael Craton, 183–99. Toronto: Pergamon Press, 1979.

Articles (1959–1971)

"Class, Status, and Community Power in Nineteenth-Century American Industrial Cities." In *The Age of Industrialism in America,* edited by F. C. Jaher, 263–88. New York: Free Press, 1968.

"An Iron Workers' Strike in the Ohio Valley." *Ohio History Quarterly,* 1959, 353–70.

"The Negro and the United Mine Workers of America: The Career and Letters of Richard L. Davis and Something of Their Meaning." In *The Negro and the American Labor Movement,* edited by Julius Jacobson, 49–127. Garden City, N.Y.: Doubleday, 1968.

"Protestantism and the American Labor Movement, The Christian Spirit in the Gilded Age." *American Historical Review,* 1966, 74–101.

"The Reality of the Rags-to-Riches Myth, The Case of the Paterson, New Jersey, Locomotive, Iron, and Machinery Manufacturers." In *Nineteenth-Century Cities,* edited by Richard Sennett and Stephan Thernstrom, 98–124. New Haven: Yale University, 1969, rev. ed., 1970.

"Reconstruction in Ohio, Negroes in the Hocking Valley Mines." *Labor History,* 1962, 243–62.

"Two Lockouts in Pennsylvania, 1873–1874." *Pennsylvania Magazine of History and Biography,* 1959, 302–26.

"The Workers' Search for Power." In *The Gilded Age,* edited by H. Wayne Morgan, 33–67. Syracuse: Syracuse U. Press, 1963.

VINCENT HARDING

AFTER N. JOCELYN

VINCENT HARDING

V INCENT HARDING IS, AT PRES-
ent, professor of religion and social transformation at the Iliff School of
Theology on the University of Denver campus.

Born in Harlem in 1931, Harding was raised in a predominantly West
Indian community in New York City. He is a graduate of CCNY and Columbia University School of Journalism and holds an M.A. and Ph.D. in
history from the University of Chicago.

During the years 1961 to 1964, Vincent Harding and Rosemarie Freeney-
Harding served in the southern Civil Rights movement as full-time activists,
negotiators, and teachers. After returning to Chicago to finish his dissertation,
Harding went back to the South in 1965 as chair of the history and sociology
department at Spelman College in Atlanta, Georgia. In 1968, following the
assassination of Martin Luther King, Jr., he became the director of the Martin
Luther King Memorial Center in Atlanta and chair of the CBS "Black Heritage" television series. Harding was one of the founders and organizers of the
Institute of the Black World (IBW)—originally part of the King center—and
in 1969 became its first director. He is currently chair of the board of the
Institute and has continued, along with Rosemarie, to be active in movements
for peace, freedom, justice, and human transformation.

Vincent Harding has been a prolific writer of essays, articles, and poetry
for books, journals, and newspapers. His most recently published books are
The Other American Revolution and *There Is a River*, the first in a three-volume
history of the Black struggle for freedom in the United States.

In August 1982 we spent a weekend in Boston with Vincent and Rosemarie
and their two children, Rachel Sojourner and Jonathan DuBois Harding,
sharing their history and their current concerns and activities. What follows
is an extremely abbreviated and edited transcript of interviews tape-recorded
during that weekend. We would like to thank Vincent, Rosemarie, Rachel,

and Jonathan for so lovingly and enthusiastically giving of their time and their energy in order to record both the pain and the joy of their involvement and immersion in the river of Black struggle in the U.S. past, present, and future.

Hazel Carby, assistant professor in the English department and center for Afro-American studies, Wesleyan University, has coauthored The Empire Strikes Back: Race and Racism in 70s Britain *(London: C.C.C.S./Hutchinson, 1982).*

Don Edwards is a graduate student at the Yale School of Nursing and a long-term member of the Institute of the Black World.

Q. I'm interested in the ways in which you feel that education should be a bridge to the community. Could you talk about the community that produced you and the ways in which you took that community with you through the stages of your education?

HARDING One of the most important things about the community—my primary community was a Black church—was that it was in New York, first generation, and largely West Indian. At least 75 or 80 percent of the members of that church were West Indian born, and they were, therefore, models of what we have called striving in the Black community. One of the most important things about them was their tremendous respect for education, and that was modeled in the leadership of the church, particularly the pastor of the church, a man by the name of P. J. Bailey, who did not have any academic degrees himself but was a very real model of that West Indian, self-taught intellectual—in this case, religious intellectual. The church was an offshoot of the Black Seventh-Day Adventist denomination, and it was called Victory Tabernacle Seventh-Day Christian Church.

Like many other Adventist-type churches, Victory Tabernacle was very Bible-study oriented. The literature of the King James Version became part of my life there, and the introduction to a kind of nonconformist Christianity was established in that setting. But there was more as well. The church was a kind of culture center, and it seems to me that at least half of the members were taking voice or piano lessons at one time or another. It was just amazing that Victory had this feeling of a nineteenth-century lyceum. As a matter of fact, at least once a month, on Sunday afternoon, we had what were called Lyceum programs. There were vocal and instrumental presentations, sometimes dramatic readings, and I was a dramatic reader in my time. As I said, it was a kind of cultural center, uniting Western and Afro-American music and other art forms unself-consciously.

That was part of where I came from, a little church of maybe eighty members. Everybody in the church expected that most of the young people would forward themselves through education. Because I had developed a leadership role among the young people of the church, there were a lot of expectations focused on me. I grew up knowing that I was going to college, and because my world was not much larger than a New Yorker's experience, I also knew I was going to City College. Because we didn't have any money the only place I could go and get an excellent education, as far as I knew in those days, was City College. (My mother and father had separated when I was very young, and my mother supported the two of us with domestic jobs and child-welfare checks.) The old Negro race-consciousness was also strong in the church. I remember how many times people said, "You've got to be twice as good as a white man in order to do what they're doing." They talked about Marcus Garvey and about Gandhi. At other levels, perhaps deeper levels, there was a strong tradition of spirituality. All of that is very, very much a part of me.

Both my mother and father were born in Barbados. I was born in Harlem, but I don't think I really came full-blown to the life of the North American Black community until I moved to the South Side of Chicago. My fullest integration into that community was due in large part to the fact that I married someone who came out of a southern Black experience. Although she was born in Chicago, Rosemarie's parents and most of her brothers and sisters were born in Georgia. Ultimately, though, it was participation in the southern freedom movement that brought me fully into the flow of the Black experience in the United States of America. So, I feel myself a true Afro-American, and that all of the Black American experiences in a full sense are mine.

Q. You went to the University of Chicago after CCNY. Why did you choose the graduate program in history?

HARDING   The simplest answer is that I had decided during my draftee army experience that I wanted to teach, and some good and bad advice from high school and college teachers led me to believe that college teaching would be best for me. At CCNY I had been a history major—largely by accident—and so it seemed to make sense that I follow that path in my quest for the Ph.D. union card. At the same time there was another level of development at work. When I went to Chicago in '55 that was my first experience away from my natural community for an extended period of time. I'd already begun a search to try to understand who I really was, and what I believed in relation to that church community. When I got to the University of Chicago and went to the history department, I discovered two things: that there was such a discipline as intellectual history and, even more important to me, that there was such a thing as the history of Christianity in America. The latter really became something that I felt should be very important to me, as far as my own search was concerned. So, as I think has been the case with most of my academic experiences, the study of history was integrated into my personal spiritual quest. Much of the experience of the university was, therefore, not simply an academic experience, but one of a real search, particularly trying to find how I had come to be positioned in the midst of this flow that was called the Christian church experience. A joint chair had been developed between church history in the Divinity school and the history department, and Sidney

Mead, who became my major professor, had a joint appointment to both. I think that became a very important dialectical context for me. From the very outset, I was not confined to the history department, but lived my life, literally, between those two places on campus. The other element that was important was that I had an independent life as a lay pastor in a little Seventh-Day Christian Church on the South Side of Chicago. I think those two kinds of integrations have been, as I see it, of great importance to me: one, the integration of my personal quest with the academic environment and, two, the integration of my life beyond the university into the larger community. Never has the work of the university simply been the end-all of my experience.

Q. How did you overcome the contradictions between the personal and the political quest for meaning and the academic training you had to acquire, in history, that tries to separate and dismiss the personal in favor of an academic objectivity?

HARDING   I'm not sure how conscious I was of that separation at the time. My choice of areas of study, one of which was American intellectual history, allowed more leeway for dealing with things that are not easily quantifiable. As I reflect on it now, I feel that, by and large, I was able to be whatever I wanted to be. I always tried—and I remember this particularly in writing my papers and my exams—to bring to bear my love of writing and style to what I was doing, rather than simply the facts and formulations. By and large, that was appreciated by the faculty rather than discouraged. All things considered, that experience was a positive one, except, of course, for the major gap of the study of the Black experience in America. When I was in graduate school none of the "great universities" in America considered serious study of the Black experience to be worth their time. Nevertheless, I certainly appreciate the range of understanding I gained of the flow of white American history. That understanding helped me as I developed my own education in Black history and then began to develop a new vision of the nation's true history.

Q. Do you remember the fifties as the period of the cold war? Were you drafted into the army?

HARDING   Probably one of the most crucial elements for me was the very strong biblical orientation of the church, which, by and large, encouraged a semi-conscientious objector stance. They took the stance that people could go into the service—it was okay—but you took a noncombatant position. You tried to get some noncombatant assignment, preferably medical corps or something like that. Somebody told me—I always had a certain level of naivete and optimism—that one of the best ways to avoid getting into the business of having to go someplace with a rifle and kill or be killed was to get into military intelligence. So there I was, knowing nothing about military intelligence, except that it had something to do with intelligence, the operation of the brain or the mind, and that, obviously, was what I was being prepared for. People told me that I could probably get accepted into military intelligence because I was so intelligent! So, I actually went through the process of applying for that dubious specialty. However, I was refused as a candidate for officer's candidate school, which meant that all my plans for military intelligence fell through. (The old folks like to say: "God works in mysterious ways His wonders to perform.")

But, more important is what did happen in the military. Two things come to mind and I often refer to them because they are very important to me. One was the experience of being down on my stomach on the Fort Dix, New Jersey, rifle firing range early in the morning, as soon as the sun was up, for rifle practice. Because I like sports and athletics, generally, I was enjoying learning how to get someplace close to the bull's-eye. And all of a sudden it occurred to me one morning that the army was not spending money and rounds of ammunition for me to enjoy myself hitting bull's-eyes. What they were doing was training me to kill another human being whose face I hadn't even seen. It was a very, very powerful understanding.

The second experience was bayonet training. There seems always to be a hardened, veteran drill sergeant who goes up there on the platform in front of you. Meanwhile you face the dummy, who is the enemy, and what you are supposed to learn to do, in approaching the enemy, is to bring forth all kinds of animal sounds—growls, yells, shrieks, and everything else—that, according to the theory, I believe, are supposed to throw this enemy off guard. But how I understood it was that we were being encouraged in such sounds so that we would forget that we were human, until we could move to what was the purpose of that drill—learning how to spill out somebody's guts with just one swipe of the bayonet—and forget about all the things that we had been taught in church school about love and shared humanity under God. Those two training experiences really got to me.

It so happened that during that particular draft period the people coming in during the fall of 1953 included a lot of college graduates. I would say in our company probably the majority were college graduates, including people with master's degrees, like myself, and some people in the midst of graduate school. (Among the most interesting companions I had in that basic training company were Peter Berger, the sociologist, and another friend who is now a literary critic at Yale, Geoffrey Hartmann.) I talked with some of my friends and I know, if I'd had the courage, that I would have simply said, "Dammit, I'm not going to go through with this anymore." But I didn't have the necessary courage at that point, so instead I found some ways to insure that I would, at least, not have to be involved any longer in that process of training to be a killer. Those two years in the military—1953 to 1955—were very important to me on many personal levels, but I don't think I had any clear sense of the politics of that period. My friend, Staughton Lynd, for instance, had much more a sense of those politics, coming out of the kind of radical organizational connections that he had.[1] Though we didn't know each other then, we were in the military about the same time. By the time I went to

Chicago—we were in the midst of the cold war period, '55, '56, '57—what I think was striking me more, as I remember it now, were the powerful developments in the Black community. I remember fairly strongly, while in the army, reading about the *Brown* v. *Topeka* decision and I remember, in Chicago, reading about Montgomery, and I think those events entered much more deeply into me than the cold war experiences that were, in many ways, harder to grasp as you were living through them.[2]

Q. What were your perceptions of men like Robeson or Du Bois during that period and of difficulties they were having?[3] Were you aware of them?

HARDING Not in any active sense. I have come into their orbit largely since then. I am really, I think, a personal witness to the way in which engaging in struggle often leads back to history. So that what I have is a vague memory of the possibility that I heard Du Bois in his 1950 campaign for Congress while I was still at City College. I was, of course, aware of Paul [Robeson] because he was a kind of a hero for a lot of people in our church, primarily, I think, because of his great artistry. We were a church full of musicians. But I don't think I ever heard him sing while I was in Harlem. His name was simply one of those hero names. I don't think that I gained a live sense of what people like Du Bois and Robeson meant before I began to actively join in the life of the struggle. As a matter of fact, even though I grew up in Harlem and the South Bronx I did not have the consciousness of what urban Black life was really about until I began to try to minister to people on the south side of Chicago. It was that experience that opened me up to many of the realities of what it was like to be Black and to live in the northern urban community, under all the duress that that involves. I guess this goes for a lot of people in the movement: many of the people who came into the Freedom Movement in the early sixties did not get involved out of a sense of understanding of the history of the Black struggle. They simply were there. When they got there and found out where they were and who they were, and who was with them, then they had questions they could ask of the past. I think that's the same thing that happened with me.

Q. Was there a place in your community—in the church, for instance—where questions of the impact of race and class were raised?

HARDING Well, there must have been. I need to reflect on that. Thanks for asking. Certainly, Marcus Garvey[4] was a reality for many of those West Indian folks in the church, so there was something there. I have a feeling, though, with that community, as with Garvey himself, there were very mixed feelings about empire. People saw the degradation that empire brought, but they also identified with it. I still kid my mother about her enthusiastic West Indian singing of "Britons never, never shall be slaves." There was, on the other hand, that sense of race-consciousness, that sense that Black people have a special kind of responsibility for the uplifting of their race and a humanizing mission to the world. How much of a larger political consciousness did that represent? Probably it didn't go much beyond the kind of thing that Garvey represented in his more popularized versions; that is, some sense of the necessity for a confluence among all Black peoples. But I don't think I remember hearing any analysis of the significance of the relationship between the fading British and rising American empires.

Q. You heard about Montgomery while you were in the first year of graduate school. When you went to Chicago you entered graduate school and also married. How did you become involved in the southern civil rights movement?

HARDING   Well, by 1958 I had left the Seventh-Day Christian church and became a part of the collective leadership of an interracial Mennonite congregation on Chicago's South Side (another nonconformist context). Partly as a result of our Black community context, partly because of the traditional Mennonite Peace church concerns, and partly because of who we were as persons, some of us in the church decided that we wanted to experience the developments in the South as directly as possible. Five of us, three whites and two Blacks, decided to begin at Little Rock, Arkansas, in the fall of 1958 and spend several weeks driving in one car through the South, covenanting with each other not to submit to segregation and to try to learn as much as we could. We learned a lot! But that's another long story in itself. The main point here is that that was my first personal experience with the South and with the developing southern movement.

Now, as I mentioned earlier, when I married Rosemarie in 1960 it was clear that she had a fundamentally southern family tradition and was very much alive to that world. In 1960, during the sit-in movement, Rose and I decided to go and hear some of the young movement folks—I don't remember exactly who they were—who were traveling in the North and reporting what was going on in their struggle. We went to a Black church in Chicago to hear them. It was a very powerful experience to hear their stories and their songs, to catch their spirit. When I met her, Rosemarie had already been a member of a branch of the Mennonite church through some family connections. Both of us, in our various church communities, had been, naturally, trying to raise the issue of the larger church's responsibility to act in a critical way as far as the racial struggle was concerned and to act with concrete assistance and solidarity. At the end of 1960, the beginning of 1961, the service organization in the Mennonite church (comparable to the American Friends Service Committee), the Mennonite Central Committee, asked us if we would be willing to go south as representatives of the North American Mennonite Churches to be a presence there, to learn as much as we could about what was going on, to raise some of the critical issues, and to be of service in the struggle. That was the fundamental position that we were to be in. At the time, Rose was teaching in an elementary school and I was working on my dissertation. We decided that we should leave both tasks and go to the South, sponsored by the Mennonite Central Committee. I think the fundamental decision was to give ourselves to the struggle for as long as seemed right. At the time, I had doubts about whether I would ever finish the dissertation, but this call from outside of the university seemed absolutely compelling, and it was clear to me that the life in the university had to bend. It seemed to be organic to my life that it have a sense of focus and purpose and direction outside the university. From that point on it became more obvious than ever that the university had to come under the guidance and direction of the rest of my life. It was not my primary vocation.

Q. Looking back, how would you encapsulate the period of the 1960s?

HARDING   I'm more convinced than ever that it was one of those really dramatic turning point opportunities in American history, when the issues of what should be the direction of the nation, who should be in the directing force of the nation, and what vision should define its direction were open for radical questioning. All of those issues were being raised, often in very direct ways, and I think part of what happened was that a lot of us realized how fundamental the issues were and how fundamental was the necessary transformation of our own lives in order to press forward. There was in the sixties a confluence of movements and events and developments that opened up the possibility for a real transformation of American life. The Black movement simply was the way, the opening wedge through which these issues came up. So much of what we were being, doing, and responding to was at the root of the nation's life that even the so-called reformist ideas and programs we were putting forward could not be realized in their fullness without radical transformation and redirection in society. For instance, the fundamental racist nature of the U.S. meant we were of necessity striking at the heart of the situation. When Black people were involved, especially in the South, normal political activities, such as voter registration, became essentially and fundamentally radical. I think that whole experience—that we opened—that brought up a surging of so many people toward seeing new possibilities for themselves and for the society, was probably the most important thing about that period of the sixties. Just that, the fact that people saw there might be real change in society, was really important. What I see in the sixties that continues to give me a sense of real human possibility, is that when you live in the midst of a movement like that you see people transformed, people going far beyond their own previously defined limits, possibilities, and feasibilities. You see all that coming out of people who have been labeled as powerless, coming out of people with no political training, no proper study groups and no ideology—nothing, in some cases, but tremendous hope in truth and righteousness and God.

Q. The idea of people being part of the process of history—your role as part of the forces of history—is that what produces transformed history?

HARDING   I think those connections are there, just the whole idea of what is history and who's making history and what is significant in history. To experience a movement like that was to experience a movement from the bottom up and to recognize the amazing quality of the people. It also meant a recognition at the same time of how those people had simply been totally ignored in the traditions of American history. And to see people like that totally ignored was to recognize the necessity for rethinking the whole business of history: what it means, who it means, and what are the forces that mature our perceptions and the idea of being a witness. As you probably know, my use of the term "witness" is not in the legal sense of the word, but in the church sense of the word. As that kind of a witness I must speak to the reality and the power of the experience. Once you allow yourself to adopt that kind of role, then, of course, you're in all kinds of intellectual and academic trouble and difficulty. The whole business of being in the midst of the people who, in many, many cases totally unconsciously, were moving the entire nation, and realizing how unsung they were, certainly, both consciously and unconsciously, taught me something about what is important in history. It encouraged me to ask repeatedly, what is the history that needs to be told, what is the history that needs to be drawn to the surface? Being a witness is being faithful to those questions and to that experience and to those people, not simply because among them you became involved in an experience and experienced something transformative, but because, out of the experience, you realize how fundamentally important *they* are for the future as well as for the real movements of their own time. Nobody ever told them they were central. Living with those who should be called the salt of the earth, who, beyond ideology, had decided that they must do certain things and be certain things in order to live with themselves—that is powerful, humbling living. Those kinds of people, we discovered, are everywhere, in every social movement in every period. These kinds of grass-roots folks who, in a sense, created their own reality were very important to us.

Q. Did the experience in the southern movement radicalize you in the sense of being politically radical as that phrase is usually understood? Did it transform your perception of the American state?

HARDING   I think that all along I was being radicalized simply by the experience of being Black in America, by my choice of a nonconformist church tradition, and then by bringing those things together and entering into the life of the Freedom Movement. The religious foundations of the movement spoke naturally to us, to the whole business of Black people standing in a position of judgment on American society and, by the power of amazing grace, to being able to pay the price for that kind of nonconformist position. I would say that those things and more contributed to what you might call my radicalization, especially if we move beyond traditional left wing definitions of the word. In 1965, for reasons that, I think, are partly connected to my relationship to what people call one of the peace churches and partly connected to my instinctual anti-militarism, I had come to the conclusion that I had a responsibility to deal with the Vietnam War and the developing peace movement. For reasons that I don't fully understand, I had decided that I had to know more about what was going on in Vietnam, had to search out the essential truth of the situation and especially our nation's role. That summer, with the twentieth anniversary of Hiroshima in mind, I just began to read, and it became a kind of obsession. Then I began to see larger issues having to do with the roles of internal and external empire. So I became a central spokesperson for a radical anti-war position within the Freedom Movement. I began writing things, for various periodicals and particularly for a journal called *Christianity and Crisis,* on Vietnam and the morality of Vietnam and what it meant. The Vietnam War and its relationship to our Black struggle was a growing concern to me. It especially got to me in that summer of 1965. I wrote a letter to the SCLC [Southern Christian Leadership Conference] convention, urging Martin Luther King and the SCLC to take a public stand against the war, partly because we had been expecting other nonwhite, anti-colonial peoples to stand with us.[5] It was important to us to have support from the rest of the nonwhite world, it was important for us to give support, to speak publicly on this issue and to be consistent.

The other factor that has to be considered is that I began my formal teaching career during the upsurge of the whole Black Power movement. What I felt, very strongly, as I tried to explore for myself the meaning of that powerful Black symbolism and its political and religious implications, was that I was in accord with many of the basic concerns, and I had to transmit the implications of that set of ideas to my students. So I got associated with Black Power very quickly. There was another radicalizing element: the connectedness through personal relationship and struggle with the folks who were engaged in all the actual conditions of the erupting movements of the sixties. For so many of them, Black Power was a way of looking behind what they understood to be the traps of the mainline civil rights definitions of the struggle. I felt that the issues had to be linked to a sense of positive Black identity and an independent Black critique of American life and American foreign policy, all encouraging the upsurge of a Black cultural renaissance. It seemed to me that this was part of what naturally followed from my commitment to the struggle and my role as a teacher of Black Studies. So, those things are necessary to understand my own deep involvement with the students who were committed to the whole Black identity issue.

Martin [Luther King] knew of my own commitments regarding Vietnam and that led to a crucial development. It was sometime in the fall of 1966. Martin had already started making more and more public statements about the tragedy of Vietnam as a war, and Lyndon Johnson was on his case. One of the things Johnson had decided to do was to ask Martin if he would go and talk to Arthur Goldberg, who was the head of the U.S. mission to the U.N. at the time. So, in preparation for the visit to Goldberg, Andy [Young] asked me if I would put together a memo on my understanding of what was going on in Vietnam. Martin had already decided, for many, many reasons, to speak more directly and openly and politically to the issue. So it wasn't possible for Goldberg to change Martin's mind about what was going on and about what we had been saying concerning the Americans in Vietnam. Not long after that meeting Martin decided to accept an invitation to make a major anti-Vietnam War presentation at Riverside Church, and he asked me to prepare a draft of what he might say.[6] Essentially, the speech he gave on April 4, 1967, was what I drafted. Certain things happened after that, largely because of what I wrote. I have not been able to forget that Martin was assassinated one year to the day after that speech. And I feel very strongly that the speech and his unflinching role in expressing and organizing opposition to the war—and to the foreign and domestic policy it represented—as well as his ineluctable movement toward the call for nonviolent revolution in the U.S., were among the major reasons for his assassination. It has sometimes been very hard for me to deal with that and with my own contribution to his trajectory. But I know that at his best Martin was his own man, and he would not have made the speech if he had not claimed it fully as his own. It was his. I know that. Still, it's sometimes hard to deal with. The road from Riverside to Memphis seems very direct. And I feel, still feel, very present—and yet not present—on that road.

Q. In *Beyond Chaos, Black History and the Search for the New Land,* you make a distinction between Black historiography and Negro historiography. Could you talk about this and the questions you raised there about American historiography and American society?

HARDING   I feel that one of the most important tasks of the historian is to help us see the magnificent largeness of human life and the richness of human experience. I really feel that the Black and white encounter in this country has been one of the most dramatic meetings that I know of. I think it's very important to try to be true to the paradoxical power of that confrontation and coalescence, both in its tragedy and its possibilities and its amazing, often unpredictable kinds of developments over the decades and centuries. It's important somehow to be faithful to the untamed truth of that experience. Whenever we deal with experiences of such magnitude and such power and such tragedy, it's absolutely necessary that we try to move deep, go to the essence of the human response, the feelings, the emotions, as well as to create the structures of analysis that help us to place those things into a larger context. (Of course, I'm not sure that there is a larger context than the human response to a situation.) I think the entire basis for the differing emphases of Black history and Negro history is grounded in what I try to point out in *Beyond Chaos.* In that work, the antithesis between the two histories was probably made sharper than it might be in many individual situations, partly because of the need at the time to try to press for some clarity. I still feel that the emphases that I tried to bring forward were essentially faithful to the materials and the experience. By and large, the tradition of Negro history (a tradition that has nurtured and taught me more than I can say) was seeking to present the case for our belonging within the mainstream of American life and for the story of Black people belonging within the mainstream of the

American story. Thus, as I saw it, the main focus of Negro historiography presented only an indirect challenge to the essential concepts of mainstream American historiography. It sought acceptance. Whereas, it seemed to me, those of us who were trying to create what we consciously chose to call Black history came out of the Black consciousness movement, out of the confrontative Black struggles of the fifties, sixties, and early seventies. In our work, we were seeking to do precisely what the larger Black movement itself had been seeking to do; that is, to present a fundamental challenge to the accepted truth of white American society. I tried to indicate in my work that it was impossible to absorb the full experience of Black people into some overall telling of the American experience without raising totally new sets of questions about the nature of that mainline American experience as it had been interpreted by traditional historians. One of the things that struck me most was the way in which Henry Adams in *The United States in 1800* wrote about the "cancer of slavery," and then, almost in the next breath, described how American society was essentially healthy, except for slavery. That illustration seemed to touch so much of the sense of what we needed to come to grips with. How a society can be healthy, except for cancer, was one of the kinds of issues I thought we needed to bring up and look at. We needed to be asking a thousand questions about healthy, democratic America and its parallel commitment to slavery, segregation, and white supremacy. I thought we needed to get away from the mentality that seemed to say, "See, we have a history, too; here's our story; will you let us try and fit it in to whatever space is available in the larger story without anything being destroyed or fundamentally reconstructed?" I'm not saying that my forefathers and foremothers, in the writing of Negro history—they taught me so much—were not concerned about challenging America. I simply think they came out of a different, a more rigidly confining political setting. We rejoice that they made the history they were able to make. My generation owes much to them. They were our teachers, and in their own way they helped to make us possible. Men and women like John Hope Franklin, Benjamin Quarles, Helen Edmonds, and Rayford Logan created the ground out of which we sprang—in all of our bold and audacious noisiness.[7] Ultimately, though, we were pressed on and shaped into being by the history our people were creating. The modern struggles of our people empowered those of us who developed in the sixties to create new issues and new history because of the nature of that nation-shaking social movement that had produced us and produced a new moment in American society.

The other thing I want to be clear on is how much a person like Ralph Ellison and his *Invisible Man* helped me to think about our history.[8] I have really profited from the novelists, the poets, the musicians, who, without exception, went to the heart of things far more consistently and sensitively than we who are supposed to be historians of the human experience.

Another matter to consider is this: though we often forget it, the fifties and early sixties was a period in which many people involved in mainstream white education were publicly admitting how close to bankruptcy that system was, especially in regard to its loss of a sense of purpose and direction and its culpability for the kind of new imperialistic society that was being created. There was a sense in which the whole Black movement, and then the movements that built on it, made critical contributions toward injecting a new life and vitality into the university itself. Our academic and personal movement onto the campuses forced people to look at the so-called anonymous peoples of, not only America, but of the world, to look at women and Native Americans and all sorts of groups—even white ethnics. Our challenge, linked to the challenge of the anti-war movement, opened a new period on the university campuses.

Still concentrating on what was produced by· this Black history/Afro-American history movement (and it really was a *movement,* not just a new set of intellectual ideas), it's clear to me that what developed—often querulously and certainly sometimes scurrilously, with a great deal of opposition from many of the respectable academic stalwarts (while others responded with creativity and gratitude)—was a new approach to the understanding of our common Black and white experience in America. On the simplest level, the Black history movement helped to achieve the goals of the Negro history movement; that is, it forced people to include Black folks in the story. On a more profound level, the Black history movement also forced some people to raise new questions and to reunderstand the meaning of such a long period of racist history in America. I think it was absolutely necessary for us to challenge some of those terribly misinformed—to say the least—conventional assumptions about Black people and the American past and present. I think all those struggles and debates over Black Studies were important for everybody involved, Black and white. I think they represent some of the most creative, though sometimes painful, sometimes unnecessarily wild, moments of the life of the academic community.

Q. Would you tell us about the significance of the emergence of the Institute of the Black World in the 1960s and its role in the 1980s for providing support for social change?

HARDING Well, the thing I remember most, the *things* I remember most, include, first, the fact that we had decided that the whole study of the Black experience that was being pressed up as a result of the struggles—both the southern struggles and the northern struggles in keeping with the overall Black Power emphasis—ought to be essentially defined by Black people. That was probably the central vision for the Institute when we began in 1969. The second thing was that most of us who came together to try to conceptualize this were people who had come out of the Freedom Movement. We made a commitment to the idea that our academic work, our intellectual work, be carried on in the service of the continuing struggle, that there must be an integration of struggle and scholarship. It was part of the freedom of the Institute to be able to make it possible to do that.

We saw, sometimes very vaguely, sometimes very sharply, things we wanted to do, and they varied. But one thing that was important to us was to encourage the concept of collective scholarship and work—a collectivity of scholarship that was not simply in the hands of traditional scholars, even Black ones. We felt that we should take the intellectual tasks we had to work on into the midst of people who were not only scholars, but also artists, organizers, and activists. The Black experience was so broad and so varied and so moving that only such a wide gathering of experience could help to clarify it. That kind of gathering essentially occurred at the Institute for some five or six years. During that period men and women such as Lerone Bennett, Joyce Ladner, Bill Strickland, Steve Henderson, Robert Hill, and others were based at the Institute. Other colleagues, from younger and older generations such as Walter Rodney, C. L. R. James, Margaret Walker, St. Clair Drake, Horace Cayton, and Edward Braithwaithe, came from various parts of the Black diaspora to study and work with us for various periods of time.[9] After that a lack of funds, a changing of people's sense of direction and priorities, simply the changing of the historical scene around us, changed the character of IBW. It became less and less a center for people, who were in residence there and working and struggling with concepts, and became more of a resource center. We also began more systematically to share with others some of the results of what we had learned together. All together, it was a very rich time. A great deal of my work came from that earlier period and from the commitment to collective work. One of the things I think we should realize about the Institute is that while there was an opportunity to have a career of life and work and struggle together, like almost everything that's in the Black experience, this was being done always in the context of a hard-fought battle just to stay alive and to justify our right to life. That kind of dialectic is a metaphor of the Black situation itself.

I think one of the things IBW has had to do periodically is to ask basic questions about what is our purpose in the light of what is now going on in the Black community, in the nation, in the world. As a result we have always had to keep for ourselves the option and the recognition that institutions are not going to go on forever. There are times and places for many things, and there are times and places when some things may have to be so radically changed that they become, really, something else. So we are trying to struggle with that right now. The Institute still sees its task as centering on the analysis and understanding of Black life and culture in America and its implications for Black and white people and for the world we have to create. We have been working in two major areas over the last couple of years. The clarification of Black Studies, the teaching of Black Studies, the resources for Black Studies —that's one of the things we've been working on. The other thing we've been trying to move forward, with slow painfulness, is a project to develop a television film series based on my book, *The Other American Revolution*, with the very limited resources we have. We are also trying to keep the Institute available to other institutions and people who are trying to make some sense out of our history for the purposes of the present and our future. The conferences, the seminars, the individual lectures continue, and we still gather participants from many places. I'm not sure about all the ways we can, or should, move in the future. Certainly we see a tremendous amount of work that needs to be done in the clarification of the Black experience and its role in reshaping America. We may concentrate ourselves and our work on the post–World War II period and the tremendous changes that have been taking place within Black America and our place in American society.

Q. How have Marxism, and specific Marxist colleagues, influenced your development?

HARDING   Perhaps I should try to get at that monster of a question by breaking my response into two elements. First, it's important for me to say that I have almost never considered Marxism as an abstract ideological or theoretical system. When it has entered most powerfully into my life, it has come through the life and work of comrades and colleagues who took its approaches with utmost seriousness—especially such persons as Walter Rodney, C. L. R. James, Sylvia Wynter, George Lamming, and Gerald McWorter, each in different ways, each struggling with the truth of the Black experience.[10] Thus I was forced to take Marxism seriously to a large degree because I took these persons seriously. As a result, I have learned to appreciate the great contributions of Marxist thought to an adequate understanding of our modern world. At the same time, I continue to be deeply convinced that Marxism, in any of its known varieties, cannot be an adequate guide for the work of revolutionary transformation that we Americans must carry out in this land. In the dialectic between past and future, it should not be surprising, then, that I am also convinced that while a Marxist analysis can help us to understand certain aspects of American history, its tendency to set aside the life of the spirit actually cripples it as a tool for dealing with much of the Black experience.

As a result, I am very much drawn to people like James and Grace Boggs who have emerged from a deep, powerful, and very disciplined grounding in Marxist thought and who insist that we must develop an American revolutionary ideology that will be based far more on our unique national experience of struggle than on anything that has come before us.[11] They are important to me not only for their ideas and their writing, but for their courageous willingness to put those ideas on the line in developing an organization like the National Organization for an American Revolution. I have benefited greatly from Grace and Jimmy and their comrades in NOAR.

So, to sum it up, I have been powerfully influenced and extensively taught by Marxist friends and comrades, but I have always seen that teaching as only one element of the collection of tools and gifts that we need for an adequate understanding of our past and an adequate revolutionary re-creation of our present and future, I am convinced that we must create the new American revolution. It will learn from the great Marxist contributions of the past, but it will move beyond the best of that past. Marxism simply cannot serve as the fundamental grounding for the necessary revolution in the world's major post-industrial welfare/warfare/racist state.

Now, I also want to mention several other people who have been very important to me and were not Black Marxists. One of them is Lerone Bennett.[12] There is no way you can classify the man, but he has been peer, teacher, inspiration, and friend. I think a lot of my earliest exposure to Black history came from him, from *Ebony* magazine, and the many articles he published. Here is somebody, almost totally outside of the academy, who has taught me some very important lessons. Another person is Howard Thurman because he was one of those older Black men who constantly lived ahead of their time.[13] Like Lerone, Howard cannot easily be labeled. He was theologian, mystic, visionary, pastor, and concerned citizen-creator of a new, multiracial American reality. For me, he was mentor and father-in-the-faith, one who knew both how to listen and to speak. His basic understanding of the role of religion in the creation of a new society of peace, justice, and hope was of great importance, but his influence as a loving, caring person who believed in me and who loved me and my family, was even greater, I think. Bob Moses, the magnificent leader of the Student Non-Violent Coordinating Committee forces in Mississippi, who has now entered fully into the path of spiritual transformation, continues that Thurman tradition in my life, as brother, teacher, and source of great inspiration. Two of my earliest comrades at the Institute, Bill Strickland and Stephen Henderson, very different persons in every way, were also important teachers in my life. So, too, was Robert Hill, the preeminent authority on Marcus Garvey, who worked closely with us at the Institute.

Q. Can you talk about the vulnerability that is present because you have been closely involved in the making of the history that you have written about?

HARDING Let me try to speak to the question of vulnerability. That, for me, means living sometimes on the edges, as well as being involved in the ongoing struggle. As you know, vulnerability is one of the primary signs of humanity, and I do not see the vulnerability of personal involvement as a weakness. As a matter of fact, when I consider the people with whom I have been involved, especially those who are really grass-roots leaders and participants, I think that my work as a historian is actually strengthened. These people, who are the descendants of the early strugglers, really help us to see the history of the eighteenth- and nineteenth-century freedom struggles in a new way. For instance, living among the makers of current movement history helped me to see how often people transcended their predicted limitations to become much more than they themselves could have foreseen. To grasp that may be to apprehend the variety of ways in which people who were classified as slaves or totally untutored freedmen constantly moved beyond their imposed limitations and created far more history than they were supposed to.

There is another, related example of the benefits of the vulnerability that came from involvement. In the sixties, when we started trying to take on, in a new way, the whole business of defining and redefining the nature of American slavery, one of our major concerns as younger Black historians, artists, social scientists, sociologists, and others was—for the most part consciously—to give white folks hell. What we were doing was taking the experience of slavery and, without exaggerating in any way, documenting how terrible human beings could be to other human beings and saying, or trying to say, "*See what you did!* Don't play around with it; don't pass it over; don't Sambo on it. *See* what you did." I remember how I came up short, at one point, on what was going on within ourselves, within that issue, and how we had to allow the present history to speak to us about the past. One day I was teaching at Spelman and basically taking that approach with my students. I used to talk, at the time, of how slavery had dehumanized our people. That day something moved me to ask myself: who are these young people before me? These are the great-great-grandchildren of those folks I'm saying were dehumanized. If those folks had truly been dehumanized, then these students wouldn't be here. There wouldn't be anybody out there struggling, washing, scrubbing, stealing, hustling to make sure they were here. There would have been no tradition in the family that said, "You've got to be there." There would have been no encouragement that said, "Get out of bed in the morning; you've got to go to school." There wouldn't have been any of those things if folks had been dehumanized. So the very act of seeing these young people, some of whom had been actively engaged in the struggles of the early sixties themselves, opened to me the overwhelming power of their humanity. I could no longer glibly talk about the dehumanization of their ancestors because, obviously, that had not taken place. And what that meant was that I and others had to be engaged in new thinking about what really had taken place in slavery, asking who were those men and women called slaves, and what had indeed happened to them in that terrible process. So, that is one way in which just living in this present and being a part of this on-going stream was important to help rethink what the earlier folks were about, especially what initiatives they had taken, singly and collectively, to maintain and forward their sense of integrity and humanity.

Of course, there are other elements to that vulnerability of engagement, of actually being in the streets or the back roads, in houses, in churches with all the men and women whose names are unknown. It was in such settings that I came to understand that part of my responsibility is to see that at least some of those names go in print someplace. To work with men and women like this is to understand that what we're talking about is not simply the superficial amplification of the material culture around them, but fundamental elements of the human spirit. And it also became clear to me how important it is to be true to those folks' lives so that you don't in any way sell them short. I was looking at a lot of Black and white testimony before congressional committees in the Ku Klux Klan investigations of the 1860s and 1870s and putting that together with all of the fragmentary evidence we have of conferences and conventions and meetings and constant activities of Black people right after slavery ended. The important thing to me is that you look at these documents and what you really see are people who yesterday were defined as slaves. In the light of conventional wisdom, they were all the things slaves were supposed to be and not be, yet we read today in the testimony they were going to meetings and saying, "This is what we need, this is what ought to be done." How, then, on the one hand, do you put those together in terms of our understanding of what a slave is and, on the other hand, explain folks coming directly out of slavery and talking about freedom, as it were, twenty-four hours later? What comes to mind are very similar experiences in the South in this country in the 1960s. For instance, it is reminiscent of those Black Mississippians who were supposed to be oppressed and demoralized southern Blacks and who suddenly appear marching in the streets saying to the white powers that be in general, and to their landlords specifically, "I'm going to 'redish' [register] whether you like it or not. I'm going to 'redish'!" To see that, to hear that is to realize that what is going on is that people are maintaining their integrity, their humanity, in all kinds of ways we don't fully understand. So, what I'm trying to say is that living on the edges, living in the midst of personal involvement in the on-going history, provides me with what might be called a window of vulnerability—to recoin a phrase—a window that allows me to see something of the ways in which many contemporary persons have dealt with this almost mysterious challenge of maintaining humanity, and not only maintaining humanity, but *promoting* humanity in the midst of some of the hardest situations people can think of. Seeing it and living among them in the twentieth century gives me some insight into the possibilities of understanding how it might have been among their forebears in the nineteenth and eighteenth centuries. That is why I consider my vulnerability a marvelous gift, for I feel that one of my major functions is understanding the ways in which people have operated, and can operate, in spite of the worst things that could be done to them. I have a responsibility today to share that understanding with a generation who sometimes thinks it is in the worst possible situation. The whole business of interrelated movements, of the history of struggle, and the present and future struggles—all of that—presents one of the greatest challenges of living truly, deeply in history. Trying to make sense of it now, trying to make sense of how it might have been in the past, and trying to encourage people to move forward, that's what I'm all about. If that's vulnerability, I try to make the most of it.

Q. You wrote about Vietnam and went to the Paris peace talks. When the southern civil rights movement started, you went. For the current project you are working on about the underground railroad, you went to those places where the slaves crouched down to feel what they felt, to look at what they might have looked at. What is it like to discipline the forces that bring you in such close proximity to history?

HARDING   I'm not sure how to answer that question. Part of the responsibility I bear to those who have made an earlier history is to try to enter as fully into their world as possible. I guess that brings us back to another aspect of the vulnerability because there is no way to enter the world of the freedom struggles of the oppressed without experiencing what one Black historian, George Washington Williams, described more than a century ago when he wrote:

I have tracked my bleeding countrymen through the widely scattered documents of American history; I have listened to their groans, their clanking chains, and melting prayers, until the woes of a race and the agonies of centuries seem to crowd upon my soul as a bitter reality. Many pages of this history have been blistered with my tears; and, although having lived but a little more than a generation, my mind feels as if it were cycles old.[14]

When I first quoted that as a headpiece to *Beyond Chaos,* I too was still in my thirties and felt I knew exactly what he had felt. To allow oneself to feel such things is, I suppose, to be vulnerable. But it is also to enter the great stream of human experience. Recognizing how privileged I am to share such tears, I simply work to avoid drowning in them, to avoid being overcome by the bitterness. Perhaps the only real discipline I can refer to is my commitment to the future, to the work of the coming generations, to the task of creating a set of new possibilities for us all. Perhaps we could call that the discipline of hope. Perhaps it is that that has continued to provide the strength, the grace to allow me and others to take the title of that essay seriously and more deeply into our history and yet continue forward, beyond chaos. Perhaps, as some people suspect, hope is really another word for God—and vice versa.

Q.   So how have you felt about the varied responses to *There Is a River,* volume I, that embodies your best attempt to be faithful to the people who made the history, to carry forward the hope?

HARDING   As the work moved toward publication, I tried to prepare myself for a variety of responses. Still, there were some things that disappointed me, but that's all right. One was the fact that a number of the people whom I expected to engage the work intellectually on the level of some of my basic ideas and questions seemed unable or unwilling to get into that level. For me, some of the most important things I was trying to get at had to do with a rethinking of the central issues of the history and role of our community in the United States. For example, I felt it was important to look at the slave codes and see them not simply as white initiatives against Black people, but also as responses to Black struggle. Another example is the way I tried to focus on the Black fugitive slave experience, not only as a powerful and often underplayed example of self-liberation, but as a crucial force in exacerbating the North/South conflicts in white America, conflicts that led into the Civil War. For me, these kinds of issues were the serious issues as far as historiography and interpretation of the Black and white struggle in and for America was concerned. Most of the published scholarly responses just didn't take those on. So I was disappointed in the fact that people in the mainstream scholarly community didn't take on what seem to me to be some of the fundamental elements I was trying to get at. (I just had a very interesting letter from Eugene Genovese[15] that made clear the fact that he saw some of the key issues I was trying to press forward. In the light of some of our earlier debates, it was very gratifying to receive such a message.) I am not disappointed with folks disagreeing, but with folks not engaging on the level I felt the book was asking them to. At the same time, I need to say I found much understanding of the issues about which I was concerned in the responses that have come from Black folk, both in the academy and in many other settings. Certainly one of the things I hoped, and continue to hope for, is that people of the African diaspora will be able to take hold of the experience presented in the book and find some way of knowing how it enters their experience and how they enter it. Also, one of the things I feel about the book is that from the time when I began working on it until the time I finished writing, there was an entire field in which all of us were being challenged on the critical matter of the understanding of women and their history, and that's one of the areas in which, I feel, a great deal more could have been done with the book. In other words, how do you see this America through a variety of eyes? We are having a great struggle just trying to see it through women's eyes, through Black people's eyes, through poor people's eyes. How do you see it through the eyes of Native Americans and Chicanos and Asian Americans; how do you see it through the eyes of all the immigrants who came and now are coming into this society and who are constantly remaking the society? How shall we see America through all of those eyes? I know these questions will not be answered except through breaking beyond past Western traditional understandings to some new understandings of our identity, our history, and our destiny as human beings.

Q. So, that's how we come to find you at the conference on Dimensions of the Mind and Spirit?[16]

HARDING   I would say that one of the major reasons why I am here is that I have always understood myself to be not first and foremost a historian, but a human being grounded in the Black experience whose commitment is to the human (and humane) struggle for personal and social transformation. To me, that commitment means I am trying to join myself with what some people from some traditions might call the creative forces of the universe, seeking with others to find the wisdom, courage, and energy we need to help us all move in the pathway that will fulfill us and our planet and make it possible for our children and their children to continue to develop their best human potentials. And so history has been for me a kind of a servant in two basic ways. One is that I have seen history as a way of telling the story of how others struggled in other times and places toward this same humanizing end. And that is why my major interest has always been in the history of human struggles for liberation. In a sense, it's my way of engaging myself with the long tradition of the human freedom movement. History is a way of entering into that flow. It's also, I think, one of the most important ways I know of encouraging others to enter into the flow. Remember, before historian, I see myself as teacher, and teacher in the sense of encourager, helping to evoke and nurture the particular humanizing possibilities and gifts and strengths and powers that are in us all. The strength and humility that creates a human with courage didn't stop in 1776 or in 1865 or in 1968. So in the context of such a conference, I see myself naturally entering another part of my own continuing search for that way of becoming most available to the creative forces of life, to help me and help others move forward in the flow. I don't see myself primarily as Vincent Harding who is periodically a historian, but as Vincent Harding the perennial seeker. That's why I'm here at the conference.

Q. Well, it may be that the response you've just given really answers our next and last question, but we'll ask it anyway. In the light of your personal history, in the light of your work as a historian of the Black experience, in the light of your long history of residence east of the Mississippi, what are you now doing based at the Iliff School of Theology in Denver, Colorado?

HARDING I think I do need periodically to be pressed on that issue, especially —as you put it—in the light of my past. In my own mind, there are three or four reasons that usually make sense to me and to our family. Somehow they also seem to be consistent with my conviction that our past is meant to be a source of liberation and not imprisonment.

I guess I should begin by saying that when Iliff invited me to its faculty in 1981 I had already clearly decided that there were serious problems between me and the world of traditional academe. Part of the difficulty rested with me and my constantly expanding understanding of what I wanted to teach, write, and live about, and how difficult it would be to fit that into, let's say, the history department of any conventional academic institution. Essentially what happened was that I had abandoned the boxed-in world of the traditional academic disciplines—even the new discipline of Black Studies. Partly because of my own experiences, partly because of what I sensed was necessary in our struggle to create a new American nation, I felt called upon to work from a more holistic vision of my subject matter. For many of the same reasons I was convinced I needed to be in a setting where I could bring a clearly articulated spiritual/religious dimension into my teaching. I wanted to expand the definition of history, to use it as a source of encouragement toward the future. In keeping with my research, writing, and personal commitments, I wanted to focus on the history of the Black struggle for freedom in the United States, but I was determined to approach that vital subject matter both as a crucial experience in its own right and as a metaphor of so many other human liberation struggles, both personal and collective. I wanted to dream, to vision; I wanted to be in a setting where I could freely, openly invite my students to active participation in these struggles for a new humanity.

I had already taken an important step in that direction before Iliff's invitation; between 1979 and 1981, Rosemarie and I were on the staff of the Quaker-based adult student center called Pendle Hill, near Swarthmore College in Pennsylvania. It was a far cry from the colleges and universities I had known before. So when the Iliff invitation came it found fertile ground.

What's more, the invitation was a very encouraging one. Essentially the institution opened itself to me and said that I was free to establish my presence in any way I chose and could teach whatever was important to me, with no limitations. What I had found over the years was that there were very few places in American higher education where one could speak unabashedly of education for service and humanity. What was also clear was the fact that the theological schools, the seminaries, the schools of religion—whatever they called themselves—were among these relatively few places. At their best, they were seeking to develop religious leadership for the creating of a more humane society. That kind of setting was important to me.

Of course, some of my friends ask me the question that is likely on your mind: why this particular setting, in the midst of an overwhelmingly white institution way out in the Rockies? Perhaps I should first say that when the Iliff invitation came, I immediately contacted some of my friends at the Black seminary in Atlanta, the Interdenominational Theological Center. I had decided with Rosemarie that if we were going to take the Iliff invitation seriously, if we were really going to consider a theological school, then we wanted to be sure to make ourselves available to deal with anything that ITC might want to say to us. Unfortunately, ITC said nothing.

It was also very important to me to be able to be offered a situation in which I had the responsibility for naming and defining my own professorship, where I did not have to fit into any preexisting slot, and where there was a welcome for a new professorship of religion and social transformation. (Under that rubric I teach a series of courses on the religious foundation of the Black struggle for freedom in the United States, another series—with Rosemarie—on the relationship between personal spirituality and social responsibility, and several dealing with alternative visions of a new society.)

So the freedom, the opportunity to create my own situation, the chance to teach with Rosemarie, the chance to bring in visitors of my choice—all these were very important to me. But there was more. One of the basic convictions we had developed at IBW over the years was the need for Black men and women to assume roles of critical leadership in any movement for the revolutionary transformation of this society. In the light of that conviction, I had a sense that most of us who might assume such leadership were very limited in our experience with the vast middle expanses of the U.S. and its people. Except for a few weeks of summer school teaching out there, I knew nothing about that part of the country. Somehow, I thought it would be important to learn to explore the area. Rose and I were especially intrigued and drawn by the Native American and Chicano communities in these parts. As a matter of fact, we're convinced there can be no fundamental transformation in our nation that does not take the experiences of these ancient peoples as seriously as it takes our Black experience. So we have come to listen, to learn, to find new bases for solidarity and hope. Slowly, surely this is happening.

I suppose I should also say that I am personally very drawn to the mountains. Sometimes I feel that in another life I might have lived right in the midst of them. I feel something very strong and very deep in their presence. That, too, was part of the appeal of Denver.

Having said all that, friends, it would be important for me to repeat that Rosemarie and I are convinced we are still on pilgrimage, still seekers, that neither Denver nor any other place that we know of now is our final destination. Our children sense this, too. We are all here as part of our search. For now it is good to be here. There is a lot of light, a lot of space, a lot of openness. Let's see where they lead.

Notes

1. Staughton Lynd was one of the foremost anti-war spokespersons and organizers in the 1960s. As a result of his early courageous stands, he was unable to continue his career as a professional historian. Taking this as an opportunity to deepen his commitment to grass-roots organizing, Lynd went to law school and became a lawyer specializing in work with insurgent labor unions (see page 155).
2. The 1954 Supreme Court decision in *Brown* v. *Topeka Board of Education* reversed the 1896 *Plessy* v. *Ferguson* decision that had approved segregation of public accommodations. The 1954 decision ordered the integration of public education. Just over a year later Mrs. Rosa Parks refused to give up her seat on a Montgomery, Alabama, city bus to a white man and was arrested. Within two days the Black people of Montgomery had organized a massive boycott of the city bus system and had called a young pastor, Martin Luther King, Jr., to leadership.
3. Paul Robeson (1898–1976), socialist actor and singer, was told by the State Department in 1952 that if he left the United States, he would be subject to five years' imprisonment. In 1956 he was summoned before the House Un-American Activities Committee and told them, "You are the Un-Americans." Robeson lived in semi-exile between 1958 and 1963 and continued his activism in behalf of civil rights. W. E. B. Du Bois (1868–1963), a founder of the NAACP in 1909, founder and editor of *The Crisis*, 1910–34, socialist, historian, and pan-Africanist, was indicted, tried, and acquitted of the charge of being an unregistered foreign agent because of his leadership of the Peace Information Center. He ran for the United States Senate from New York as a candidate of the Progressive party in 1950. He joined the American Communist party in 1961. In the same year he became a resident of Ghana at the

invitation of President Nkrumah. He became a Ghanaian citizen in 1963 and is buried in Accra.

4. Marcus Garvey (1887–1940), born in Jamaica, founded the UNIA (Universal Negro Improvement Association) in 1914. He came to the United States in 1916. By 1919 the UNIA had branches throughout the world, a newspaper that was the most widely read news weekly in the world, and the Black Star Steamship Company. It was the first Black organization in the United States to attract a mass membership, totaling over two million at its peak. Charges of fraud led to his imprisonment in 1925. This sentence was commuted in 1927, and he was deported as an undesirable alien. He died in London.

5. Martin Luther King and others organized the Southern Christian Leadership Conference in 1957. It was a base for economic boycotts, desegregation, voter registration campaigns, and other non-violent action throughout the South.

6. The spring of 1967 saw the biggest demonstrations against the Vietnam War up to that time in New York City. King's Riverside Church statement was his attempt to present the religious grounding for his principled opposition to the war and for his active participation in the anti-war movement.

7. See John Hope Franklin, *From Slavery to Freedom* (New York: Knopf, 1947); Benjamin Quarles, *Black Abolitionists* (London and New York: Oxford University Press, 1969); Helen G. Edmonds, *The Negro and Fusion Politics in North Carolina, 1894–1901* (Chapel Hill: University of North Carolina Press, 1951); Rayford Logan, *The Negro in American Life and Thought: The Nadir, 1887–1901* (New York: Dial Press, 1954).

8. Ralph Ellison, *Invisible Man* (New York: Random House, 1952); *Shadow and Act* (New York: Random House, 1964).

9. See Lerone Bennett, *Before the Mayflower* (Chicago: Johnson Publishing Co., 1962 revised ed. 1966), *The Shaping of Black America* (Chicago: Johnson Publishing Co., 1975); Joyce Ladner, *Tomorrow's Tomorrow: The Black Woman* (Garden City: Doubleday, 1971); William Strickland, "Black Intellectuals and the American Scene," *Black World* 7 (October 1975), pp. 4–10, and "Whatever Happened to the Politics of Liberation," *Black Scholar* 7 (October 1975), pp. 20–26; Stephen Henderson and M. Cook, *The Militant Black Writer in Africa and the United States* (Madison: University of Wisconsin Press, 1969) and Stephen Henderson, *Understanding the New Black Poetry* (New York: Morrow, 1973). Robert Hill is the editor of the Marcus Garvey Papers at the University of California at Los Angeles.

Walter Rodney, historian and Africanist, was expelled from Jamaica in 1968 for his political militancy and returned to his native Guyana where he helped found and lead the Working People's Alliance. Challenging the regime of President Forbes Burnham he was murdered by a car bomb in June 1980. Margaret Walker is the author of the novel *Jubilee* (New York: Houghton, 1965) and several books of poetry. See St. Clair Drake, *Our Urban Poor: Promises to Keep and Miles to Go* (New York: A. Philip Randolph Educational Foundation, 1967) and *The Redemption of Africa and Black Religion* (Chicago: Third World Press, 1970); St. Clair Drake and Horace Cayton, *Black Metropolis* (New York: Harcourt, Brace and World, 1945); Edward

Kamau Braithwaithe, "The African Presence in Caribbean Literature," *Daedalus* 103, no. 2, 1974, and "Introduction" to Melville Herskovits, *Life in a Haitian Valley* (Garden City: Doubleday, 1971).

10. Sylvia Wynter has taught at the University of the West Indies and is the author of *The Hills of Hebron* (London: Jonathan Cape, 1962). George Lamming is one of the best-known West Indian novelists and critics. He is the author of *In the Castle of My Skin, Natives of My Person,* and many other works of fiction and social and literary criticism. Gerald McWorter, a well-known Marxist scholar-activist, is a professor of Black studies at the Urbana campus of the University of Illinois.

11. James and Grace Boggs are political activists and writers living in Detroit. For twenty-seven years a worker in auto plants (1941–1968), James Boggs quit his job at the age of forty-eight "to project a vision of what we must do in this country to develop another way for man to live." He is the author of *The American Revolution: Pages from a Negro Worker's Notebook* (New York: Monthly Review Press, 1963) and *Racism and the Class Struggle,* (New York: Monthly Review Press, 1970). The Boggses co-authored *Revolution and Evolution in the Twentieth Century* (New York: Monthly Review Press, 1974).

12. Lerone Bennett is senior editor of *Ebony* and author of many books on the Black experience including *Before the Mayflower* (Chicago: Johnson Publishing Company, 1962) and *The Making of Black America* (Chicago: Johnson Publishing Company, 1966).

13. Howard Thurman became a living legend in the Black community in the decades just preceding and after World War II. He was one of the master preachers of the twentieth century and published more than a dozen books. One of his earliest and best known was *Jesus and the Disinherited* (Nashville, Tennessee: Abingdon Press, 1949). His last book was his autobiography, *With Head and Heart* (New York: Harcourt, Brace, Jovanovich, 1980).

14. George Washington Williams, *History of the Negro Race in America from 1619 to 1880* (New York: G. P. Putnam and Sons, 1883, Vol. II, p. iii).

15. Eugene Genovese is a Marxist historian of American slavery and author of *Roll, Jordan, Roll: The World the Slaves Made* (New York: Pantheon Books, 1974) and *From Rebellion to Revolution: Afro-American Slave Revolts in the Making of the New World* (Baton Rouge: Louisiana State University Press, 1979).

16. The conference was held August 16–21, 1982, in Boston and was sponsored by the Kushi Institute and the East West Foundation. It explored "the origins and dynamics of human consciousness and behavior."

SELECT BIBLIOGRAPHY

Books
Black Chaos: Black History and the Search for a New Land. Atlanta: Institute of the Black World, 1970; and in *Amistad, I,* edited by J. Williams and C. Harris. New York: Vintage, 1970.

The Other American Revolution. Los Angeles: Center for Afro-American Studies, University of California, and Atlanta: Institute of the Black World, 1980.
There Is a River: The Black Struggle for Freedom in America. New York: Harcourt, Brace, Jovanovich, 1981; New York: Vintage, 1982.

Articles
"Amazing Grace." *East/West Journal,* November 1982.
"Black Radicalism: The Road from Montgomery." In *Dissent: Explorations in the History of American Radicalism,* edited by Alfred F. Young, 319–54. Dekalb: Northern Illinois University Press, 1968.
"Black Students and the Impossible Revolution." *Journal of Black Studies,* 1 (1970):1.
"The Black Wedge in America: Struggle, Crisis and Hope, 1955–75." *Black Scholar,* 4 (1975).
"The Land Beyond." *Sojourners,* January 1983.
"King and Revolution." *The Progressive,* April 1983.
"Long Hard Winter to Endure: Reflections on the Meaning of the 1970s." *Black Collegian* 10 (January 1979).
"Never Too Desperate to be Human." *Sojourners,* February 1983.
"Out of the Cauldron of Struggle: Black Religion and the Search for a New America." *Soundings,* 3 (1978): 61.
"W. E. B. Du Bois and the Black Messianic Vision." *Freedomways,* 1969, 9.

JOHN WOMACK

AFTER F. VILLA
+ E. ZAPATA

JOHN WOMACK

J

OHN WOMACK IS THE AUTHOR
of *Zapata and the Mexican Revolution,* a book respected by historians and
critics for its scholarship and loved by its readers for its depiction of the
loyalties that compelled Mexican peasants to fight for their way of life. This
major contribution has been translated and published in Mexico, Cuba,
France, Italy, the German Federal Republic, and Japan, giving it one of the
widest audiences of any work on Latin America. Born in Norman, Oklahoma,
in 1937, Womack has taught Latin American history at Harvard University
since 1965. He is currently the chair of the Harvard University history department. A frequent contributor to the *New York Review of Books* and former
editor of *Marxist Perspectives,* he is now working on a history of the working
class and economic development in the southern Mexican state of Veracruz.

*This interview was conducted by Judith Evans, who has worked in Latin
American history for fifteen years and who is now an economic analyst for* Business Latin America.

Q. How did you decide to become a historian?

WOMACK I was probably twenty-four years old before I realized it was something you could become. I thought the historians there already were the only
ones there were ever going to be. The people I knew worked for a living and
that meant you had to dig ditches or drive a truck or get some, to me
evidently, unattainable job such as working for the railroad or in a store or
office.

A profession that I figured took no more training than I had, with a college
degree, was journalism. I had a very romantic idea of what journalists did. I
thought they made a living by telling the truth on crooks and tyrants. And
I thought that was what I wanted to do. I discovered very quickly that I

couldn't write as fast as journalists had to. I couldn't just write that ten cars had been stolen off a certain street last week. I'd have to find out what color they were, if they were all blue, if ten blue cars had been stolen off other streets of the same length, what the pattern was. Pretty soon I'd have an outline for a treatise on car theft while the newspaper just wanted last night's police report.

Becoming a historian was accidental. I was in England studying politics in the hope that I could learn to write at least about power. A friend of mine had heard about a fellowship at Harvard and that struck me as yet another chance to make myself a better journalist. I applied for the fellowship, which meant having to get recommendations. I wrote to the professor who'd known me best in college, and he wrote back, "Well, if you're interested in going to graduate school, why don't you apply for one of our fellowships in Latin American history?" That was something out of the blue. It had never occurred to me to study Latin America, but it was interesting at the time, particularly from a journalistic point of view, because of the Cuban Revolution and the Bay of Pigs. So I thought: I'll do that and see about getting a Ph.D. in Latin American history as a way to write in the papers about that stuff. Then when I got the degree, they paid me to do this, teach history at Harvard. It was a lot of work, but it was indoors and there was no heavy lifting, and it was exciting, too. It was 1965, and there were all kinds of things going on. You could run around thinking that you were being very political, although all you did was go to meetings and read the paper with great intensity. So that's how I stumbled into it.

Q. What drew you to work on Mexico?

WOMACK I was also very docile as a student. When I came to graduate school to do Latin American history on this fellowship, I thought I would do a thesis on Colombia; one of the faculty people around here then told me that Mexico had already been *done,* and why didn't I do something that hadn't been *done,* like Colombia. So I took a train to Mexico, and a bus to Costa Rica, and a rattletrap airplane to Bogotá, and spent about a month in Colombia sliding more and more helplessly into despair and confusion. I realized I didn't understand anything about the country. I read everything I could get, like a sort of dummy, a foreign kid going into bookstores and buying the history of this, the history of that. But I couldn't understand it. I thought I would write a thesis about *La Violencia.*[1] This was like some French kid coming to the United States in 1862 and saying, "See here, I'd like to do a thesis on your Civil War, so give me a pass to roam around the Shenandoah Valley." So I spent a lot of time trying to figure out how to study *La Violencia,* and then one day realized it was out of the question. I was going to go south of Bogotá, down to Cali, but just before I left the rebels took people off a bus on that road and cut their throats. I was married then and had an expectant spouse. I thought, I'll go in the other direction. So I went back north, on the train, to Santa Marta. In a book of political speeches I had read about a banana strike there in 1928. I went to the local office of the Banana Growers Association and asked about the strike, thinking that maybe I would write a thesis about it. And they said, "There was never a strike here. We have excellent relations with our employees and always have had. Never been any problem." That befuddled me again. I thought, I've made a serious mistake about all of this. Finally I got back here, and I thought, I've got to write a thesis if I'm going to do this Ph.D., and if I don't write about something that feels important, I'm never going to do it. If I'm not going to do it, I might as well not waste any more time and money and go off and do something else for a living. The country I felt I really wanted to write about was Mexico, still. I thought, what about the Mexican Revolution? What about that?

In England I had read a book by Richard Cobb on the French revolutionary armies,[2] and that's what I decided I would do—something about the Mexican revolutionary armies, in particular the Zapatista army. It did not occur to me, in 1963 at age twenty-six, that guerrilla armies in those days didn't do a periodic census of their members or keep close records on them. But when I got to Mexico to do research, historians and other people were very helpful. I went stumbling around libraries and archives, talking with people and falling in with this person and that, eventually got into some archives that had been only slightly used, put them together with my reading, and wrote a thesis. And what started out to be about the Zapatista army turned out to be about the movement and how you couldn't separate the movement from the villages.

I think what interested me in Mexico, what made it feel important to me, what made it feel like something I would understand, was the interest I already had in the history of agrarian movements in the United States, especially tenant farmers in Oklahoma, on which I wrote my undergraduate thesis. Those sorts of agrarian movements have been central in Mexican history; they are repeatedly defeated, but reemerge over and over. That was something I felt I could get a grip on. Of course, every Latin American country has similar movements in its history. If it had been ten years later, I might well have studied Peru. But then it was easier to get a hold on Mexico.

The title of the thesis was "Emiliano Zapata and the Revolution in Morelos, 1910–1920." The title of the book was *Zapata and the Mexican Revolution*, which is better but still not quite right. I wrote in the introduction that Zapata was there not because I was interested in him, but because those people made him their leader, and what I most wanted to understand was where this kind of movement came from and how it operated, where it got its strengths, and where its weaknesses were.

What I did in the thesis and in the book was go back to the kinds of stuff I had been interested in earlier, movements and organization and how you change things. In both the Mexican and the southwestern agrarian movements, the Zapatistas and the guys in Oklahoma didn't change anything fundamental except their own lives, and most of them wound up in jail. These movements were failures. That's possible to say only in retrospect, and it's not their fault they were failures: they were movements of protest and resistance that were, I think, bound and right to happen and, under the circumstances, also bound to get crushed. But in Mexico, what couldn't be crushed were the villages themselves—the basis of reproducing labor power. Since the landlords didn't purchase them and keep them as slaves, the people were left to themselves to do things, as much as they could, the way they were used to, and they maintained the grounds of their survival in their villages. The movements of resistance couldn't be stopped from cropping up. They could be dismantled once they got to political proportions—the landlords would get the government to break the movement, kill the leaders, run the heroes out of the villages—but sooner or later the movement was bound to happen again.

Q. You are one of the few historians in this collection of leftist historians who has actually written about a revolution per se, and I was wondering what your idea of revolution was before you started *Zapata* and whether and how it changed in the course of writing.

WOMACK   Oh, yeah, it changed. My idea of revolution in 1962–63 was typical of a romantically populist, socialist, but politically inexperienced American school kid. I thought a revolution was the abolition of power. I had spent a long time in school. Being a student, where are you going to learn about power? Especially if you are a grindy and bookish student, you don't learn very much about power. But in this research, in archives, in old newspapers, in talking with old people, in writing my thesis and working it into a book, I learned some of the things my experience had kept me from knowing. I learned that it took organization and strategically concentrated force to get the things people wanted. They could get what they wanted only by being useful to somebody else so that it was given to them out of reciprocity; or by money, buying it somewhere; or by force, taking it away from somebody for themselves. I saw how those Mexican peasants had done it, what logistics means, and that impressed me. I saw that power mattered to the peasants and the guerrillas. First, I had thought it's a question of popularity, how much the people are behind the guerrillas. And then I thought, yeah, well, that's important, for a lot of reasons, but until the people are organized so the guerrillas can count on them and not have to organize their base every day, they are not going to get what they want. And it's clear they knew that. So I think I learned something about organization and the importance of organized power and concentrated force in revolutions.

Also, I started out thinking of revolutions as events. I mean, if they were successful, they were immediately successful: one day the old guys, the next day the new guys. I was like other bookish, politically interested but ignorant young people. All the stuff in Africa in the 1950s, especially in North Africa, in Algeria, we tried to understand, but misunderstood. Somebody surrendered and somebody else took over. Ha. The image we had of the Cuban

Revolution was the same: you come out of the hills, take power, and set about dealing with complete victory.

When I started studying the history of the Mexican Revolution I looked for surrenders and victories, and I couldn't find them. It's more than confusing in Mexico. The Mexican government spends much money propagating the idea that the revolution has never ended. For sixty years its legitimization is that the revolution continues; the government is the revolution. It's ridiculous: since you know they are as smart as we are, they don't believe it themselves. But a kind of conflict does continue there, which, in shorthand, we would call class struggle. It is the conflict that goes on necessarily in any bourgeois society. It's not a revolution in that it's not a question of taking power: one side has already taken power, and over the last sixty years it's managed its power very well. Nevertheless the struggle goes on.

My work on the years from 1910 to 1920 got me to thinking—well, did the peasants win? Well, no, they certainly didn't win—a bunch of them were killed and some others were eventually bought off—but they didn't lose, either. This was no simple case of surrendering, getting wiped out, sent off to a concentration camp, decertified, or displaced. It didn't happen the way it does with states at war or with one class making its interests juridically protected and another class having its interests abolished. That didn't happen. The Zapatista movement was a class war, a continuation of the peasant struggle by armed and violent means for a good ten years. The people in Morelos were obliged to fight, obliged to their ancestors and to their families. Once it didn't make sense to keep fighting, they had to do their duty otherwise. But the struggle went on.

Trying to figure out who won worried me for a long time. When did the damn thing end? What changed? I think what I learned was what many smarter people already knew: all that happens in some revolutions is that the terms and the conditions of the class struggle change. I saw there was no revolution accomplished in Mexico in 1910–20: a new class did not take power and begin to reorganize society on new bases; the fighting did not issue in a new epoch. And yet the fighting made a difference—I think a good difference, not a definitive, epochal difference, but at least a shift to ground more favorable to peasants and workers in the struggle.

Q. You are continuing to explore these questions in your new book. What is this new work about?

WOMACK It's a social history of industrial workers in Veracruz from 1880 to 1940. In part it's a history of the development of modern industry there, but largely, centrally, it's a history of the formation and evolution of some industrial contingents of the Mexican working class over those years. It's about origins and movements of the working class, unions, parties, and the state. But essentially, it's about class struggle over a long run, neither of the modern forces definitely winning or losing. It takes at least two classes for a class struggle, and neither can get rid of the other—each in many ways needs the other—until there's a revolution, and then both start to disappear, change into other kinds of groups. In Mexico, I think, the bourgeoisie made a revolution in the 1850s and 1860s, consolidated their power with a lot of foreign money behind them in the 1880s, and have more or less successfully managed their affairs ever since. They've had to take important and interesting reforms, for example, in the 1910s, again in the 1930s, and again very recently, but nothing fundamental. During this long development there emerged the industrial contingents of the working class, which, because they're concentrated, have a peculiar and crucial importance in the country's reforms.

Q.   What made you decide to work on Veracruz?

WOMACK   Ignorance. Ignorance of all the work it was going to take. But also arrogance—I mean unbelievable arrogance. I was not yet thirty when I wrote the book about the Zapatistas. I thought, Jesus, it takes only a couple or three years to write a book. My arrogance was this: since I've done peasants, next I'm going to write a book about workers in the revolution, then another about cowboys in the revolution, and then bankers—and then my synthesis. I thought I'd crack one off every two or three years. So I started hunting subjects. In 1906–1907, Veracruz had had a famous strike. The reason it was famous was that some wildcat strikers were massacred. It was one of those mythologically terrible events that really happened. I went off to Veracruz to study it. I realized immediately I didn't understand it at all. I ought to be grateful that I didn't think, "Oh, boy, I've got it," and sit down and whip off a book about it that I would now be unbearably ashamed of. Something, despite my arrogance, got to me, so that I knew I didn't understand what I was doing. I could see those workers were not like peasants and, moreover, I could tell that nobody else knew anything about them either. A lot of anthropology and sociology, as well as a considerable amount of history, on Mexican Indians and peasants, is available, especially in the colonial period. But start trying to find out about Mexican workers; it was really hard. Anthropologists? Might as well ask them to study Martians as workers. And mainstream sociologists couldn't make any sense of workers even in the United States or Europe. And there weren't any reliable histories, just these mythologies, celebrations, memorials. You couldn't find out anything about who they were, what they did. And the industrial towns were very different from the villages. You couldn't just sit down and find some old veterans. People were very suspicious talking to you about their struggles, about unions and strikes and such. I spent a long time in those towns, trying to understand them.

Then I thought I had to find out something about the companies. And there are a lot of them. At first I thought I would write only about the workers who got massacred, who were textile workers. Then I thought, it's not only those guys, there's a brewery here, a big brewery, and there are these railroad shops, and sugar mills all around. So I started reading about them and more about other industries and towns, and finally I decided I should write about the whole state. The only blessing, grace, or dispensation I have had so far is that there is very little mining in the state.

Veracruz comes up from the gulf, and there are several railroads across it. So a number of modern industries located there, and capitalist agriculture was developed relatively early. The state had an economic complexity that no other state in the country had. The only comparison is Mexico City and its environs. But the contrast between Veracruz and the District—the Federal District, where Mexico City is—is very important. Mexico City had an ancient artisan tradition, a world of artisan industries and artisan associations and organizations and traditions that didn't exist in Veracruz. There was no considerable artisan past in Veracruz. What they had there were several modern industries with different markets drawing on different kinds of labor power and people coming, most of them, from other states to work. Studying the whole state isn't like studying a mining camp or a railroad town. You've got something like a microcosm of a country, with a modern working class arrayed in commercially and technically different industries. You have railroad workers, port workers, textile workers, electrical workers, brewery workers, cigar workers, sugar workers, oil workers, and the sailors in the port. That's a microcosm that you wouldn't find anywhere else in Mexico. It is complex. I hope it doesn't take me longer to figure it out and write this history than it took to happen.

Q. People who will be reading this interview really won't know that much about Latin American history as a field, and it is a curious field in the sense that it has been formed, it seems to me, by two kinds of people. One are the eccentrics—I think that is the category you might fall into—and the other are people who are interested because this has been a government-sponsored field, sponsored largely for security reasons. In point of fact, there was no Latin American field before World War II. And the field has responded to the ups and downs of our concern as a country about how Latin America threatened us. In that sense, it's a field that has almost no sustained intellectual tradition in the United States, and also a field in which there haven't been major questions laid out as there have been for U.S. history. There are some outstanding pieces of individual scholarship, but does it add up to a coherent body of work?

WOMACK   You're right. I think the reason is that in comparison with Europe or Asia or Africa, Latin America has not been very important to Americans, to the development of American power, to the curiosity of the American mind. Relatively few got excited about it until the Second World War, and then, I think, because they started worrying about the Nazis there. Before that, there was not much serious American scholarship on Latin American subjects. There was a small but rich tradition of historical work, mostly amateur, on the colonial period. But on the national period there was almost nothing serious, much less professional. You couldn't do much professionally. Miron Burgin,[3] for instance, did one of the very few good books on the national period, about the economics of Argentine federalism; but he had to work out of the Commerce Department. Those people didn't have academic jobs or sabbaticals or grants. Ph.D.s appeared in America in the 1880s, and who in the hell was going to get a doctorate in Latin American history? How would you start, with whom, why? It wasn't until after the Second World War that much serious scholarship on the area became possible. And then most of the money for it—from Ford, the State Department, the Fulbrights —was nothing compared to the money for Russian, African, or Middle Eastern studies. The first suggestion I got to study something outside my own country was to learn Arabic and study the Middle East. Not until the Cuban Revolution did the money start running high into Latin American studies. And then people getting Ph.D.s were also getting academic jobs. But that lasted only about ten to fifteen years. And it created weird cohorts. It's very difficult to find coherent schools of analysis or interpretation.

Q. Why has colonial history in Latin America been, in some ways, the most advanced field in terms of the theoretical issues that it has grappled with— the transition from feudalism to capitalism, imperialism, and mercantile capitalism?

WOMACK   There were sources to study: there were a few good books, and there were archives. You could go to Seville. But if you wanted to study modern or national Latin American history, what would you do? Say Mexico. You'd go to the Archivo General de la Nación, and what would you find? You want to study a topic in the nineteenth century, which is essentially the history of finances and the army. Try to find that in the Archivo General. It is there, but until five or six years ago it was practically buried. There was a pretty thorough organization of much colonial stuff, but if you wanted to study national history, you couldn't do it. The archives for that period were nightmares. I have to say, however, that in the last few years there's been a tremendous improvement in the archives for the colonial and the national periods.

American historians don't understand how political doing history is in Latin America. The politics comes from two directions. First, from the outside, as you say, from the United States, from our scholarly establishments, which define subjects and sponsor and cultivate research on them. Second, from the inside, from the past and the present of the country itself, which accounts for the difference in the condition of the archives of different periods. For the colonial period, they had Spain as the enemy, and the organization of colonial archives is in the interest of the national states, to provide records of the empire's oppression. But for the national period, the archives are to a highly significant and embarrassing extent a collection of records of collaboration, first with the British, later with Americans, so the organization of these records and the convenience of scholarly access to them aren't attractive propositions to families who are still powerful, and the records go to the dogs.

Q.   Which is probably also one of the reasons there have been so many archive burnings in other Latin American countries: practical, strategic cleaning of archives. What do you see as the possible effects of the present conservative trend in the United States in funding institutions and universities as well as in American foreign policy? Might that have some effect on the field of Latin American history in the future, or what other things might affect it?

WOMACK   Well, God only knows what the effect will be if the Righties now ruling us hold on to power for some time. If they are able to entrench their stooges culturally, so that they can declare certain sorts of research as not scholarly, then you'll see doctoral dissertations that will take a mindreader to understand and there won't be any mindreaders. This is all the more likely to happen because the doing of Latin American history is political in yet another way. I believe that most of the people who've gone to Latin America to study its history—I don't mean sociologists, because they do that in clean, air-conditioned offices, I mean the people who go to study history—come back reds of one kind or another. Maybe not smart reds, but they come back on fire. It's like American priests and nuns who come from protected American backgrounds where they are taught to be conscientious about their values and principles, to live by them. They go in all innocence to Latin America and are turned inside out by the overpowering, laughing, snotty, rampant, and rank injustice around them there. American graduate students too: you're trying to do well in school, and believe in truth and honesty and no favorites in class and so on. But then you go and spend time there in the archives. It's not like being an economist studying the central bank or a sociologist or an anthropologist with AID [Agency for International Development]. It's much more like the ordinary, everyday work of the lowest bureaucrats, the hired help in the archives tramping up and down the stairs, breathing all that dust, holding documents valued more highly than themselves, year in, year out. You very quickly get something of the same sense of the world as poor white-collar workers there. And you get furious. I suppose some people come back Fascists, but most of them, I believe, come back flaming red, with all the indignation of a poor clerk in their hearts. It seems to me that unless you can invent a way to do Latin American history without going to live in Latin America and working in a Latin American archive, you are going to create many people intensely critical of U.S. foreign policy and Latin American social structures and governments. So *caveat emptor* [buyer beware]. But the emperor knows all this already. And I suppose he watches us as well as we deserve.

Q.   What do you see as the differences between the writing of history in Latin America and the writing of history in the United States, between being a historian in Latin America and being a historian in the United States?

WOMACK   My experience is that historians there, with few exceptions, are intellectually very old-fashioned. In the regular departments of history they still do *historia patria*, the history of the fatherland. History for them is what it was to the Romans. It's civics. Here, historians of Latin America are like historians of anywhere else: it's from progressivism, I think, that we almost all get our sense of our work and our social role, which is both provocative and responsible. There, it's the tradition of an established Catholic church that orients intellectuals, in praise or in defiance. And as the church used to function, so the universities do now. They don't offer very reliable protection to historians who go provocatively, even critically, into controversial questions. So it's the traditional and cautious people who last. They justify their caution on the grounds that as scholars they shouldn't take political positions. For them, scholarship is the preservation of the established and officially preferred consensus. So they write extremely conservative histories in the illusion or at least on the claim that this is objective work.

There are exceptions. Usually they're not in the national universities, not in the regular departments. Usually they're people who got a bundle of money from a friend momentarily in the government, set up an independent research institute or center for studies in such and such history, and then held on to it. In the way that here in the 1960s people set up poverty programs, scholars there have been able from time to time to set up academic programs for independent research and writing. Spawn them and spin them off, and try to keep going. Some of the best and most interesting research has appeared in these places, and some of them have started to establish themselves. There's an example at the National Institute of Anthropology and History, the Dirección de Estudios Históricos.

Q.   My experience in Argentina, and to some extent Chile before the coup was that there are many historians who are not established historians in Latin America and operate totally outside the institutional frameworks we have in this country. We think of historians in the United States as people who always work in universities and who inevitably earn their living from history—either teaching or writing it—whereas there are at least as many historians in Argentina who have no hope of ever gaining any income from it.

WOMACK   True. Here you typically have a neat academic package of work. It comes in a nine-month teaching service every year, with three months for research and writing. There, people have to make strange arrangements to make a living. They are used to working at three universities at once. That would get us fired. But, for them, it is a matter of course to be teaching at different universities, plus working at a bank, or for the government, or God knows where, being unemployed for stretches of time, writing newspaper and encyclopedia articles, hack writing, all that Bohemian kind of work. It's a very different life.

Q.   Is there much exchange between Latin American historians and U.S. historians of Latin America?

WOMACK   Well, the only exchange is personal. I don't think that's how it should be, but that is what in fact happens—and usually when Americans go to Latin America to do their work in the archives. The Social Science Research Council is the main bridge for historians going south or north. But it can't support institutions. Most older American historians of Latin America don't go back very often. It's mainly people working on their first or second book, young people, who are the Americans in direct touch with Latin American historians.

An example of the difficulties in institutionalizing exchange is the Congress of United States and Mexican Historians of Mexico, which holds meetings every four to seven years, alternating back and forth from Mexico to the United States. It's useful: people meet one another, deliver and hear papers, carry on discussions, public and private. And it doesn't happen so often that it's boring, like the AHA [Association of American Historians] meetings. But somebody has to pay the bills. It takes a chunk of money to get a hundred people on both sides to Mexico or up here for the better part of a week. For a meeting on this side, it takes a university, and there aren't many American universities with Latin American centers concentrating on Mexico able to provide the infrastructure necessary for a three- or four-day conference. If we figure that in the coming years the U.S. government, whatever the party, is going to be politically more conservative, then you can figure there's going to be less support than ever for these meetings. We'll have fewer friends high up. Why should the Righties sink money into our activities? Our universities won't pay for them. So institutionally there's not much chance of expanding exchanges, much less institutionalizing them. The connections between North Americans and Latin Americans are going to be more and more personal, and take place almost only when some of us go to Latin America.

At least Americans who've had the good luck to deal with the Latin Americans in independent institutes and centers have learned from them. Americans —there's no way to get out of it—are damnably innocent. They go with questions they have ever so tidily contrived, that may be properly isolated and tractable in American or European history, but turn into nitroglycerine in Latin America. They learn there two kinds of lessons. One is the intellectual concerns of modern French historians, which the Latin Americans have already learned in Paris or in translation. The other is that the tidy problem they carry has an indelible political significance, that they must think questions further than they had ever imagined they could; that Latin Americans like them, who seriously pursue also evidently innocent questions, become politically suspect; that doing any kind of history honestly and intensely in Latin America can get you killed; that history is real, not only in having happened, but also in that people care mortally about what happened, because they think it still bears on them, is catching up with them. They learn that, and some of them are affected by it and come back moved, changed, not Latin-Americanized but certainly more aware of history's power.

Q. Do you consider yourself a radical historian?

WOMACK   Well, I think radical is an adverb. I would want to know, radical what? I think I am in many ways radically conservative, fundamentally conservative. But that doesn't mean anything when you get to politics, except determination.

So far I belong to no party, but I consider my political principles as those of a communist. When it comes to politics, I try to associate myself as much as I can with socialist activities. But since this is America, where people are crazy about freedom, you cannot get people to commit themselves politically in the same way for long. So you call them radical, which may mean anything, and let them roam around however they please. And since these movements became academic in the 1960s, they are also departmentalized. So you have radical sociologists, radical anthropologists, radical economists, radical everything elses. Among these are radical historians, and since my profession is in history, I come under this rubric.

My interest in Marxism came from my interest in history and my preoccupations as a historian. When I was in college in the 1950s, Marxism had about as much respect from teachers and students as astrology. I look at books I had then and the things I wrote in the margins of them: it's shameful. The notes I see in those margins are what I was thinking then, very Jacksonian populism, social democracy, reforms, the people yes. I really believed that. But then I spent two years in England, 1959–61, mainly reading Hegel and Marx with teachers who took them seriously. And then the sixties happened. Vietnam above all: death to many people, mutilation to many others, derangement and misery to countless more, and for a privileged few, among them me, a long and grim reeducation. Nobody in our generation has a right not to have learned something radical from that war—I don't necessarily mean socialist, but something radical—about life, business, power, the state. Trying to deal with my own vague populism and socialism, trying to fathom America, trying to understand what I was learning in Mexico, I could make sense of it best from reading Marx. Not the only sense. There were other things I read. Simone Weil illuminated problems that I ran into.[4] I can't find anyone else like her. I learned good things from her. And if I wanted to find out about bureaucracy, I read Max Weber.[5] But on the questions that seemed to me fundamental in modern history and our condition, I read Marx, because that is where I felt I found out the most about the world.

Q.   What do you do teaching at Harvard? For all that it may have changed, it is still a place where people go who want to be secretary of state.

WOMACK   That's a hard question to answer. I often worry about it; not about teaching here, but about teaching at all. I am very interested in politics: I mean the politics about life, death, and control of the means of production. But these are not items on the agenda of the Harvard history department. Indeed I trust they're not on the agenda of any history department. It'd be ridiculous if they were.

Here I'm simply an "officer of instruction," which is what Harvard calls teachers. I give instruction in Latin American history, and I teach what I think these kids have bought in the market for $10,000–$12,000 a year. I think what's important for them to know in my field, whether they're going to become secretary of state, chief liar for the State Department, chief in charge of bombing, chief in charge of the reserve army of labor, chief in charge of the rules for contracting, or some kind of red, is the way into the deepest reality of Latin American history from 1750 to the present. I can't take more than a year to teach it, and I have to do it very generally. But what I try to teach them is that they can best understand modern Latin American history by understanding its periods of economic and social development, each defined by particular movements of capital and particular readjustments in the terms of class conflict. I don't put it theoretically. I try to keep it very concrete so they can follow what I'm talking about. I think there's too much theoretical language in historical presentations by the Left, which are supposed to be open. What the theory does is dull the point and reduce the impact of what you're saying. Ordinary people, including students, don't know what you mean. Theoretical language is jargon for professionals trying to figure out in shorthand a problem among themselves. They shouldn't use it when they're trying to express their answers or their discoveries to other people. So what I try to do in concretely worded lectures is talk about the history of classes in Latin America over the last 230 years. This seems to me worthwhile for anybody to know. I can't determine what the students do with it. It seems vain in all senses of the word to try to reform students that come through here. It seems to me that the most radical thing there is, is the truth about something. In a world of many kinds of lies, coerced, compulsive, and deliberate —I remember reading in Gramsci—it's not only a communist but a revolutionary act just to tell the truth. And the most important truth about Latin American history, so far as I know, is the history of classes there, which means the struggles between them. And so I teach the most important thing I can think of in my field.

Q. What do you think are the costs of being a historian?

WOMACK The overwhelming fact in the life of most people in the United States and other capitalist countries is that they're doomed to daily dealing in the market. The exceptions are remarkably privileged: people in the armed forces, people in the church, trust-fund babies, and, among a few other types, professors who have tenure. But the privilege means that like soldiers and priests or nuns, professors don't know directly how other people live—in the security they have, it's easy to forget the risks other people have to take. Myself, I hate going into the marketplace. I hate buying and selling things. I don't even like to go to the grocery store. And it's not laziness: I work my butt off otherwise. But I hate going into the market at all levels and in all ways. Here, I go from my apartment to the office or to the library, where there is no market. So I seldom have to buy or sell anything. Only once a week I go buy groceries. The price I pay for being a professor, therefore, is my isolation from the anxieties and concerns that most other people have, what it feels like not to know from month to month if you'll be able to make the mortgage payment or pay the rent or buy meat or settle the heating or phone bill. It's a price that never occurs to some academics that they're paying, but this only shows how isolated they are. To me, the isolation means I have to work extra to remember what life is like for most people.

There are other prices to pay in this particular profession. I think academic life is a lot like monastic life, for men or women. You can see that in the vices the university breeds, which are precisely the vices Luther rants about monks having: this petty bitchiness and trivializing malice, ducking responsibilities, padding accounts.

Q. What I think is so difficult about history is that it has the sense of being everything. And, of course, the better the history, the more it has that sense. Or it has a narrow set of questions presented or addressed in such a deep way that it is the kind of work where you never know if you finished it.

WOMACK Yes. I think history is everything that ever happened and the infinity of questions about it. There is always bound to be something else that happened that we don't know yet. But the world of production resolves for us how much we can discover and understand and tell. No socialist or capitalist economy is going to support anybody to find out everything about anything. So forget universal wisdom. Better figure that we are no better than other people who have come along and written history books. There is no point in my writing, say, five thousand pages on workers in Veracruz; a thousand will be plenty. I know how much I will have left out, a world of things and people. All I can do is finish each day, have a drink, go to bed, and think, I put in all I could. I'm sure sorry I have to leave that particular episode out. God, I wanted to tell about that, but I just couldn't. It would throw everything else in the chapter out of balance and open questions I can't enter. But you're right. Intellectually, history is unending and incessant. It's more than we can bear.

But it's good. Since it's already happened, nobody is going to make much money out of it. And it can make people more careful. History can show that everybody hurts. I think it's hard to believe in other people's pain. The sight of someone else suffering seems to trigger a virtually instinctive reaction of flight. I doubt we have innate sympathy with someone suffering. I remember a friend telling me that in Bolivia the manager of a mine swore to him that the acid they used in the mines didn't hurt the miners when it ran into their shoes. "They're Indians, just brutes." All the same my friend saw how a man with acid in his shoes would jump and cry, hurting. I think it takes more than education, I think it takes instruction to persuade people in safety that people in danger and pain are truly suffering. I think it takes instruction to instill sympathy, not to mention solidarity. It seems to me that teaching about pain is the most important thing history can do. Literature does it, too, but literature is deliberately an imagination. History is deliberately about reality, what really happened. It's a way of instructing the reader that people who really lived went through certain pain, which would have hurt the reader as badly as it hurt them. And this is a highly important lesson for the reader to understand and learn because it blocks the instinct to flee and leads to sympathy.

Q. Especially in Latin America, stereotypes have been culturally developed to make that empathy hard. You could think a lot about the way racism has influenced the field of Latin American history, the way we have written about Latin America, the way we think about it.

WOMACK And the way we read about it. They lock Lech Walesa up and that's the whole front page. They kill a union leader in Chile and it's five lines on page twelve. Geopolitically, strategically, Poland does matter more than Chile, but there's still something significant in difference of attention to white pain and colored pain. "Niggers and Indians don't hurt like white people," is what white people believe. But it's more than race. "Poor people don't hurt like rich people," is what the rich believe. And what they believe counts most. This is why historians telling the truth are subversive.

NOTES

1. The term *"La Violencia"* is used to describe the period between 1946 and 1958 in Colombia during which struggles that began between the Liberal and Conservative parties spread, engulfing all levels of society and leaving over 200,000 dead.
2. Richard Cobb, *Armées Revolutionaires,* 2 Vol. (Paris: Le Haye, 1961).
3. Miron Burgin, *Economic Aspects of Argentine Federalism* (1st edition, 1946; New York: Russell Publishing Co., 1971).
4. Simone Weil (1909–43) was a French social philosopher and activist in the Resistance during World War II. See Simone Weil, *First and Last Notebooks,* Richard Rees, translator (New York: Oxford University Press, 1970) and *The Simone Weil Reader,* George A. Panichas, editor (New York: McKay, 1977).
5. Max Weber (1864–1920) was a German sociologist and political scientist best known for *The Protestant Ethic and the Spirit of Capitalism,* Talcott Parsons, translator (New York: Scribners, 1958). His writings on bureaucracy appear in Max Weber, *Theory of Social and Economic Organization,* A. M. Henderson and Talcott Parsons, translators (New York: Oxford University Press, 1947).

SELECT BIBLIOGRAPHY

Books
Zapata and the Mexican Revolution. New York: Alfred A. Knopf, 1969.

Articles
"An American in Cuba." *The New York Review of Books,* August 4, 1977, 25–29.
"An American Marxist Visits Cuba." *The New Republic,* May 31, 1980, 19–23.

"The Bolivian Guerrilla." *The New York Review of Books,* February 11, 1971, 8–12.

"The Chicanos." *The New York Review of Books,* August 31, 1972, 12–18. Reprinted in *Many Pasts: Readings in American Social History, 1600–The Present* (2 vols.), edited by Herbert G. Gutman and Gregory S. Kealey, II, 443–65. Englewood Cliffs, N.J.: Prentice-Hall, 1973.

" 'El Che' Guevara." *The New York Review of Books,* January 28, 1971, 3–8.

"The Historiography of Mexican Labor." In *Labor and Laborers through Mexican History, Proceedings of the Fifth Congress of Mexican and American Historians of Mexico,* 739–56. Mexico and Tucson: El Colegio de Mexico and University of Arizona, 1979.

"The Mexican Economy during the Revolution, 1910–1920: Historiography and Analysis." *Marxist Perspectives* 1, no. 4 (Winter 1978):80–123.

"Mexican Political Historiography, 1959–1969." In *Investigaciones contemporaneas sobre historia de Mexico, Proceedings of the Third Congress of Mexican and American Historians of Mexico,* 478–92. Mexico and Austin: El Colegio de Mexico, Universidad Nacional Autonoma de Mexico and University of Texas, 1971.

"The Mexican Revolution, 1910–40: Genesis of a Modern State." In *Latin American History: Select Problems,* edited by Frederick B. Pike, 293–338. New York: Harcourt, Brace and World, 1969.

"The Mexican Revolution, 1910–1920." In *The Cambridge Modern History of Latin America.* Cambridge: Cambridge University Press, forthcoming.

"Recent Studies of Camilo Torres." *The New York Review of Books,* October 23, 1969, 13–16.

"The Spoils of the Mexican Revolution." *Foreign Affairs,* July 1970, 677–87.

"Unfreedom in Mexico." *The New Republic,* October 12, 1968, 27–31.

C. L. R. JAMES

B
AFTER E. CARAVIA

C. L. R. JAMES

Cyril Lionel Robert James is a writer and activist. He was born in Trinidad in 1901 and educated there. Early in the 1930s he served as one of the leaders of the Trinidadian struggle for complete self-government. In 1932 he moved to England, worked as a cricket correspondent for the *Manchester Guardian,* and wrote a novel, a play, and a powerful history of the Santo Domingo revolution, *The Black Jacobins,* which some readers regard as his masterpiece. He also became a Marxist of the Trotskyist school and served as editor of a periodical published by an England-based organization called the International African Service Bureau, which aimed at independence for all the colonial states of Africa. Associated with him at the Bureau were Jomo Kenyatta and George Padmore, who after the achievement of Ghanaian independence was to become an important adviser to President Kwame Nkrumah.

James visited Trotsky in Mexico and discussed with him colonialism and Black liberation, worked in the Trotskyist movement in the United States, and completed most of the work for *Notes on Dialectics,* perhaps his chief contribution to Marxist theory. In 1938, James moved to the United States and lived here until 1952, when he was expelled.

Since 1952 he has lived mostly in Trinidad and England and lately has been permitted to return to the United States. While in Trinidad he served as secretary of the Federal West Indian Labour party and as editor of the West Indian newspaper, *The Nation.* In both capacities he played a crucial role in the achievement of Trinidadian independence from Great Britain in 1962. A year later he published *Beyond a Boundary,* a delightful and moving essay on cricket and anti-colonialist struggle. In 1980 he brought out a new edition of *The Black Jacobins* with an appendix titled "From Toussaint L'Ouverture to Fidel Castro." He now lives in London and is at work on his autobiography.

The text that follows is a conflation of two separate interviews—one conducted by Alan Mackenzie in 1975, the other by Paul Gilroy in 1982.

Q. What are you most conscious of as a revolutionary writing history?

JAMES   History begins with the great mass of the population because they have tremendous importance. Yet the average writer, the average newspaper, the average television news program doesn't bother with them at all. So the historian has a great necessity to deal with them. First because other people don't, and second because they have the impact on history that is decisive. That's what I think and what I've always done. Without that commitment I wouldn't be able to do any history at all.

Q. How do you characterize the relationship between the kind of history you write and your understanding of Marxist philosophy?

JAMES   My philosophy about history is in my opinion the Marxist philosophy. The understanding of the struggle of classes is what Marx insists upon. Now, when you are studying classes, you must, at critical moments, see what the great mass of people are doing. That is Marxism. Marx says that repeatedly. So there is no conflict between my saying that and Marxism. If the work I have done has any significance and people are still reading it, it is because this method, which is primarily concerned with the great mass of the population, has had results which after all these years people are beginning to accept.

My purpose is to understand fundamentally the different social movements that are taking place. In those social movements, the emotions, activities, and experiences of the great mass of the population must be the most important aspect. I have written in *The Black Jacobins* that the French Revolution is impossible to explain unless you look at the vast mass of the population, not just in France, but internationally.

Q. Is there any change between your position in that book and the stance adopted in your later work? *Notes on Dialectics,* for example?

JAMES   In 1938 I wrote that "the writing of history becomes ever more difficult. The power of God or weakness of man, Christianity or the divine right of Kings to govern wrong, can easily be made responsible for the downfall of states and the birth of new societies. Such elementary conceptions lend themselves willingly to narrative treatment and from Tacitus to Macaulay, from Thucydides to Green, the traditionally famous historians have been more artist than scientist: they wrote so well because they saw so little. Today, by a natural reaction, we tend to a personification of the social forces, great men being merely or nearly instruments in the hands of economic destiny. As so often, the truth does not lie in between. Great men make history, but only such history as is possible for them to make. Their freedom of achievement is limited by the necessities of environment. To portray the limits of these necessities and the realisation, complete or partial, of all possibilities, that is the true business of the historian."[1] I didn't write off the power of the individual. But he faces a situation and he can do something with it or he can oppose it, but what he can do is strictly limited. I wrote that then, and I have never deviated from it.

Q. Some of the people on the British Left regretted that you didn't spend more time working on the African struggle in the early days. Reginald Reynolds,[2] for instance, later commented that it was unfortunate you turned your back "on the problems of your own people . . . to follow the barren cult of Trotskyism." Do you think now that working within the narrow confines of the British Trotskyist movement was a political loss for you?

JAMES   It was not narrow confines. *The Black Jacobins* was not conceived within narrow confines, and neither was the next book I wrote, *The History of Negro Revolt*, which was not limited to a Trotskyist position.

Q. But it is true that the Trotskyists in Britain, including your own organization, the Revolutionary Socialist League, were hardly influential, and in any case did not give the majority of their attention to the issues of colonialism or Black nationalism.

JAMES   That's true, and it was only when I went to the United States in 1938 that I really became active in those issues. By that time I had written *The Black Jacobins*, which created quite a stir. When it was published in Britain, in 1938, it received a very critical review in *The New Statesman*. The reviewer was very hostile to my claim that what I was doing was in anticipation of the upheaval that was sooner or later going to take place. But the book made political people aware of the problem.

Q. *The Black Jacobins* marked an opening in the debate over imperialism in which the racial question received as much attention as purely political questions. I would like to know what your motivation was for writing the book at that particular period in the 1930s?

JAMES   I was in the colonies and reading everything I could. I read one or two books about the Haitian revolution that had been written by British authors around 1850. Then there was another man, Percy Waxman, who wrote a very bad book called *The Black Napoleon*. I said, "What the goddam hell is this? They are always talking about the West Indians as backward, as slaves, and continually oppressed and exploited by British domination and so forth." So I decided that I would write a book that showed the West Indians as something else. I came to this conclusion in the Caribbean, before I came to London, before I joined the Trotskyists, and before I became a Marxist. I imported from France the books that became the basis of that work. But by the time I settled down to write, I had reached the conclusion that the center of the Black revolution was Africa, not the Caribbean. If you read *The Black Jacobins* carefully you will see that time and time again it is Africa to which I am referring, and the political purpose of the book had little to do with the Caribbean. That is why that book was written and that is how it got its reputation. Nkrumah[3] and others who read it were very much concerned because it placed the revolutionary struggle squarely in the hands of the Africans.

Q. What lasting impact has the nature of the British and French colonial systems had upon post-colonial politics in the Caribbean?

JAMES   To this day the Black colonials in ex-British Caribbean countries are dominated by the British sense of parliamentarianism. They think narrowly in those terms. In the French-speaking islands the metropolitan influence is very different, since the working class in France thinks not only in terms of parliamentarianism but much more in terms of parties. In my appendix in *The Black Jacobins* I point out that, if you read the writings and observe the activities of Blacks in Martinique, Guadeloupe, and French Guiana, you will find that their politics are in the tradition of the French revolutionary movement. The ex-British colonials have got to break away from parliamentarianism. I did it through becoming a Marxist. But even the French ex-colonials who are not Marxists are by instinct revolutionary, what with the background of French history and language they have absorbed.

Q. Before you came to London, had you been influenced by the ideas of the Communists or other revolutionary groups?

JAMES   Communist sailors were taking copies of the Comintern's paper *Negro Worker* to the Caribbean, but there must not have been large consignments, otherwise I would have seen some. By the time I arrived in London I knew some West Indians who were taking all the literature that they could. They were reading Lenin and they were taking George Padmore's[4] newspaper, but I don't think the International Trade Union Committee of Negro Workers [an affiliate of the Soviet-based Red International of Labour Unions] was doing anything in an official way there. Marcus Garvey's[5] paper, *Negro World*, circulated among the Black intellectuals. We also read Du Bois[6] and were stimulated by him, but I hadn't really the faintest idea about Black politics then, nor was there any talk about any African or Black revolt.

Q. By the time you met George Padmore in London he was on the point of breaking with the Comintern. He had accumulated a vast amount of political experience by then. Was he instrumental in moving you in a different direction?

JAMES   No, when I met him I was already a Trotskyist, but we never let that affect us, since in those days the Communist party, of which he was still a member, was for the Black revolution, so we were able to collaborate on that basis.

Q. In the early thirties the Communists paid special attention to the Negro question and succeeded in attracting a number of Blacks into the League Against Imperialism [LAI] and its subsidiary, the Negro Welfare Association. However, with the demise of the LAI and of anti-imperialist work by the Communists in general during the Popular Front period, the Black members turned from communism to a militant Black nationalism. I believe that two of the more prominent, the Barbadians Chris Jones and Arnold Ward, moved away from the British CP at this time.[7]

JAMES   Yes, they both became strong members of the International African Service Bureau [IASB][8] and followed Padmore's political lead. The Communists were able to disgrace and demoralize others who broke with them, but they weren't able to do that to Padmore, whose reputation by then was too secure. Chris Jones was very militant and had been previously in the Party, so when it turned to the Popular Front policy he was very bitter about it. Often he would attend CP meetings with myself and Padmore to criticize their policy. While I would ask a question, and Padmore might say a word or two, it was Chris Jones who made a hell of a row. The IASB was a tremendous organization—the basis of the African anti-colonial revolt that came after the war. Padmore and I spoke a great deal in Hyde Park. We held numerous small meetings. By such activity we kept the question alive (I cannot remember the Labour party ever holding one meeting on the colonial question). When Padmore started the paper, the *International African Opinion*, he asked me to be the editor; so at one time I was responsible both for that and the Trotskyist paper, *Fight*, which I had helped to found.

Q.   Padmore remained a Marxist even though he opposed the CP's line on the colonial question in the later 1930s. Did he ever move closer to the Trotskyists?

JAMES   No, the group to which he was closest was the Independent Labour party [ILP],[9] although he always retained his own organization. If you refer to the ILP's paper, the *New Leader*, you will find a great deal written by Padmore. He would collaborate with the Labour Left also, though they were not Marxist. Many liberals were sympathetic to the idea of the progress of the colored peoples, but got nervous when Communists actively began advocating it. Most of the liberals and humanitarians were much more willing to support the work of groups like Harold Moody's League of Coloured Peoples [LCP],[10] whose meetings Padmore and I would attend chiefly with the idea of asking them inconvenient questions. Nevertheless, it attracted some support from liberals and church people—an archbishop or reverend here and there. But it had no political perspective; nor did it carry out any serious work, since it had no real contact with the peoples of Africa or the Caribbean.

Slowly revolutionaries are beginning to realize that the great movement for African emancipation, particularly in that great continent, was started, nursed, and developed by George Padmore. That alone makes him one of the greatest revolutionaries of the twentieth century, and it is of extreme importance that historians of the revolutionary movement begin to say this and illustrate it.

Q.   Did you know any of the French-speaking Black African nationalists of the 1930s?

JAMES   I knew one man who was very friendly with Padmore—that was Garan Kouyauté.[11] When I went to Paris, Padmore insisted I see him. I discussed the Trotskyist movement with him and he commented that he could agree with me about everything except that one thing would be needed. I asked what that was. "That Trotsky was a Black man, that's all." Apart from Kouyauté I had few other contacts and seldom attended any of the nationalist conferences in Paris. As an active Trotskyist I went to Paris periodically, but only to take part in Trotskyist business and to make investigations for *The Black Jacobins* in the Archives Nationale. I did not do much with the Black movement there.

Q. This was the time in Paris when Aimé Césaire[12] was beginning to develop the theories of *négritude*. How did you feel about that?

JAMES I have written about that in the appendix to *The Black Jacobins*. My opinion about *négritude* is twofold. Number one, that in essence it was a poetical idea, and number two, that Césaire wrote about this to make it clear that Black people should not subordinate themselves to the feeling that they had to aspire to what white civilization had done. *Négritude* was not of African origin at all. It was West Indian and could only have come from the West Indies. It was not only a revolt against assimilation, but an assertion of an African civilization. Many Africans today are hostile to *négritude* because they argue that bourgeois and petty-bourgeois intellectuals have taken it up rather than taking part in concrete struggles against the imperialists. But I would not criticize *négritude*. There is nothing negative about it, and the particular point I always make is that when Césaire wrote about it he was also a member of the Communist party of France [PCF]. In other words, he didn't say that *négritude* could take the place of a political program.

Q. *Négritude* seems to have been a transitional stage in the political development of many West Indian radicals. A number of Black intellectuals, such as Franz Fanon,[13] seem to have evolved through that pattern: either followers of Marcus Garvey or *négritude* first, but arriving finally at a Marxist viewpoint.

JAMES That is quite correct, but in my case it had nothing to do with *négritude*. When my autobiography is published you will understand how I became a Marxist. I became a Marxist through the influence of two books I read. One was Trotsky's *History of the Russian Revolution* and the other was *The Decline of the West* by Oswald Spengler. What Spengler did for me was to illustrate pattern and development in different types of society. It took me away from the individual and the battles and the concern with the kind of things that I had learned in conventional history. Trotsky did that also by his reference to historical development in the *History of the Russian Revolution*. *Négritude* had nothing to do with it.

Q. What is distinctive about the histories of Black people?

JAMES The European workers had their own experiences, and the Caribbean workers have had theirs. What I have had to emphasize is that the Caribbean experience is an important one, and that when you are dealing with history you must be aware of it. Let me give you an example that occurred to me the other day. British capitalism went to Africa and bought slaves chiefly to work on sugar plantations. Then, after many years, the British economy needed some labor to do special work in Britain. So British capitalism went to the Caribbean and brought workers to Britain. Capitalism creates its own grave diggers. Now there are two or three millions of them in Britain, and the recent upheaval in this country shows that they are a tremendous force in the struggles against this society. The method by which I work emphasizes those connections.

Q. *Notes on Dialectics* is deeply concerned with the dialectic of spontaneity and organization in the process of struggle. How do you explain why this has not been taken up by other historians?

JAMES   People can call themselves Marxists, but they are dominated by Moscow. The Moscow tradition ruins Marxism. These people are not Marxists; they are economic materialists. Marx insists that it is not economic relations that produce social movement. Economic relations produce certain types of people, and it is the class struggle of those people that makes history move. In my work previous to *Notes* I didn't make that clear enough, although I was always working on that basis—the class struggle. Many American historians working in American history examine economic relations, but stop there. They don't go back to look at the relations between classes. Otherwise, they would have to confront, for example, the domination of organs of expression in their country by American capitalism.

Marx was able to do what he did because he studied previous examples. He studied slavery, he studied the Middle Ages, he studied commercial capitalism, and eventually he came to the capitalism of his own day. With all that in the past he was able to look forward to what was going to take place during the next generation. The most marvelous piece of writing that I know is the chapter before the last in *Capital,* volume I—"The Historical Tendency of Capitalist Accumulation." It's a masterpiece of summing up and pointing out the implications for the future. I have tried to do the same. What was important about my work in the United States was this: I insisted on analyzing the capitalist society of the age in which we live. In *Facing Reality* I said, "Here it is, it's state capitalism, that's what it is." On the basis of the careful examination of what was taking place at the time, I was able to project the future. The most important thing that I have done so far was to say that the party of the future is not going to be like that of social democracy. That was the first political party. Lenin said that the future is the soviets, which had developed out of the commune, and Marx had shown the importance of that. We learned that when something new takes place, if you want to understand it, you must begin from the highest peak of the previous form. Lenin, working on that premise, had seen what the soviet was and said, in *The State and Revolution*, "The way we are going to judge in future is to what extent they approximate to the soviet." When I was writing I said, "The kind of capital we have now is not the same capital that the second international knew and saw. Where you have state capitalism, everything in the country deals with the state. The eventual result is that you have no party, you have the great mass of the population." I was saying that in '51 and '52. My circle were very much taken with that, and I said, "In the future, the party is not going to be like anything we've seen so far, it won't be only a million or two people. The nature of capital is such that the party will have to correspond to the nature of capitalist society." That was before the Hungarian Revolution of 1956. Poland makes this clearer than ever, so we look forward to the future on the basis of the method that has helped us to reach where we are. We examine the objective situation and say we are using the method Marx and Lenin used, but we must apply it to new conditions.

Q. Is there a general argument in your work that can relate the social movement we have seen recently in Poland with, for example, what happened in England during July 1981?[14]

JAMES They are aspects of the same process. The Blacks are here. It's not an accident. That is part of the movement of capital. I would like to point out that Richard Wright wrote a book called *Native Son*.[15] He said that the Black boy in it was suffering from the problems of Blacks. But don't be misled by the fact that he was a Black. The kind of struggle he put up was not because he was a Black man, it was because he was an American. I am pointing out that after these West Indians came here and lived in England for twenty years, particularly given their Caribbean past, their attack on bourgeois society is inherent in the circumstances. That can be examined and tested.

Q. In Wright's introduction to George Padmore's *Pan Africanism or Communism* he speaks of the oppression of Blacks becoming a tradition and a culture. How do you respond to these remarks?

JAMES They are very important but not decisive. Last July the British workers did what they did because they were in Britain and they were trained in Britain. No doubt simply because they are Black people they have an extraordinary sense of persecution and the need to resist. But they are Black people living in a particular society—a society that has trained them to act in the most advanced possible way. That's why they did what they did. Look at this statement by Lord Scarman. He wrote a report about last summer's events. He said that the answer is to develop the police. He was criticized but stuck by his report. He said that he had not learned anything subsequently that would lead him to believe that any of his recommendations were wrong or his analysis faulty. In other words, Scarman was in trouble and he was defending himself: "The need to strengthen and support the police was imperative. There was an occasion in Brixton on the Saturday when a few unreinforced police, many of them young, under local and courageous leadership, had stood between the inner city of London and total collapse." This "total collapse" was the Houses of Parliament, 10 Downing Street, and the Queen—and he goes on to say that a thin line of police was all that prevented it. "If that thin blue line had been overrun, and it nearly was on that Saturday night, there would be no way to deal with it save the awful requirement of summoning the army. To turn the military towards the British people is not something which our tolerant and free society can possibly accept."[16] He goes on. He is in effect saying that the Black people here succeeded in posing the question of the revolution.

Q. What is your view of the labor movement today?

JAMES Let's take what is happening in the labor movement in the Western world. In my opinion the problem that exists today is due to fundamental difficulties arising from the last hundred years. The war of 1914–18 killed ten million people. Any society that kills ten million people is a disaster. When the war was over, within ten or eleven years came the economic crisis, and the society that had exploded in the war went to pieces. All over the Western world there were millions of unemployed people and breakdown. Capitalism managed to patch its way out of that and then it was into another war from '39 to '45. Now, in the name of God, if that's the way you are carrying on from 1914 to 1945, it's obvious that there are problems. Then came the cold war. The Communist party in the Western states corrupted the labor movement, but even the Communists realized that there was a desire to strike among the mass of the population. Fascism could not suppress labor; there is no place among the advanced countries today where fascism could be attempted. Instead, capitalism uses the democratic system to pass laws to suppress the working class. The working class is in difficulty primarily because, as a result of state capitalism, a state labor bureaucracy develops which says what the Labour party is saying. Labor bureaucrats are scared of the revolutionary upheaval of the mass.

The labor movement in The Second International[17] supported capitalist society. When that failed, the movement turned to Moscow's working class. The movement became the Cominform, that too failed, so what do they do? Today that labor movement calls itself Euro-Communist. Euro means that it supports Europe, that is to say the United States, but Communist means Moscow. It doesn't know which, so it is Euro-Communist.

The Soviet regime today is electrification with no soviets. The result of this, I have insisted, is that the revolution will explode there. I came to England in July 1980 and the *Manchester Guardian* interviewed me. I told them I am looking for the revolution in Moscow. It came in Poland, but it's the revolution in Moscow that matters, for were it not for the military might of the Moscow regime, the Polish government would have been swept away. The Russian regime is the most reactionary force in the world at large and the revolution depends on the revolution in Russia. The crisis is certain, nothing can stop it except the Moscow people. In 1968, France exploded. The government was powerless. What prevented revolution in France was the French Communist party. In that same year, the movement broke out in Czechoslovakia. The Stalinists were the ones who choked it in both places. The Stalinists have no use for the working class, that's the situation we are in today.

273

Without the labor bureaucracy, capitalism couldn't function at all. It is the bureaucracy that keeps down the working-class movement in Britain. What you have here is a bureaucracy that is prepared to share power with the capitalists. The Labour party doesn't intend to overthrow anything, but it wins the election, goes in, tinkers around, and then Labour loses and the others come in. The Labour party won't change the system but it will administer the system. Karl Marx is very clear about this. We have to create new structures that suit our purpose. When people asked him, "What will the working class do?" Marx was very snappy. He said, "They will do what they have to do. Do you expect me to tell them?" In Poland today you have the finest example you could wish for of the creative capacity of the mass of the population.

Q. I understand you, but how do you apply these insights when trying to reconstruct the past? The problems of Poland today present different problems of method than does the era that commenced with the voyage of Christopher Columbus.

JAMES   You have raised the question of Christopher Columbus. I'll tell you what I as a historian believe of him. Most of the American writers on that period are not handling the thing properly. Columbus discovered America, that by itself is nothing. What is important is this: Columbus went across the Atlantic to what became the United States; Magellan went south at the same time and went around South America to the Far East; Vasco da Gama went around Africa. They established the world market. So Columbus is an abstraction, but these three within twenty years of one another means that you have to see that capitalism had reached a stage where this was necessary. That's how I see it, and if you don't see it that way you risk writing all sorts of romanticism. Or take the historiography of slave systems. Herbert Aptheker[18] is very bad. When two workers get together in a tree he says, "You see, the Blacks are revolutionary." What is important is that slavery was a regular part of a certain economic and social system. The French Revolution wrecked that system, and the role that the Haitian Revolution played in the destruction of mercantilism was decisive. The capitalist system felt that it was time to finish up with slavery. It had been useful in the mercantilist days, but with the development of the Industrial Revolution it was time for slavery to go. And for slavery to go, monarch and all that had to go, too. The Blacks played a part in it, they played a tremendous role in the breaking up of that order and in the establishment of a modern capitalist system. They played that role in France, and they played it indirectly elsewhere, too. Here is Fortescue writing the history of the British army: "The secret of England's impotence for the first six years of the [Napoleonic] war may be said to lie in the two fatal words *San Domingo*."[19]

Q. What about the importance of history to the struggle of Black people?

JAMES   When the Blacks began to feel the need for history, in 1936, Du Bois wrote *The Black Reconstruction* in which he showed the role that Blacks had played in the creation of modern America. In 1938 I wrote *The Black Jacobins* in which I showed the role the Blacks played in the creation of modern Europe. I don't think that's an accident. The Blacks reached a stage where they felt the need for some historical understanding of what had taken place. I was writing in 1936, but I had no idea what Du Bois was doing.

Q. Do you yet feel that the time has come to write a volume on the role of Blacks in the destruction of capitalism?

JAMES Capitalism is coming to an end because Poland and Hungary are showing the way. It must be tackled by the population as a whole. That's what is happening in Ghana, too. I will write about this in my autobiography. That's what it is about, among other things.

I know that an autobiography is the best way for me to sum up and to draw some conclusions. It isn't going to be purely what I have already said.

Notes

1. *The Black Jacobins*, rev. ed. (New York: Random House, 1963), p. x.
2. Reginald Reynolds is a British socialist and pacifist and author of *My Life and Crimes* (London: Jarrolds, 1956).
3. Kwame Nkrumah (1906–72) was the first prime minister of Ghana and president of the republic. He headed the country from independence in 1957 to 1966.
4. Born Malcolm Nurse, George Padmore (1903–59) was a childhood companion of James in Trinidad. In the twenties, he went to the United States and joined the Communist party and eventually became head of the Negro department of the Profintern, the Communist Trade Union International. Padmore broke with the Party in 1933 over the first hints of the emerging Popular Front policy. He moved to London in 1935 and worked mostly for the liberation of Africa through the International African Service Bureau. In Ghana from 1956, he served as an important assistant to Nkrumah. Padmore is widely regarded as the founding father of African independence.
5. Marcus Garvey (1887–1840) founded the Universal Negro Improvement Association in 1914, which some scholars believe to have been the largest mass movement of Blacks in American history.
6. W. E. B. Du Bois (1868–1963) was an American Black scholar, civil rights activist, pan-Africanist and Communist.
7. Chris Jones (c.1880–1944) was born in Barbados, but worked mostly in England. He was president of the Colonial Seamen's Association in the thirties and broke with the Communist party of Great Britain in 1933. Arnold Ward, who was also born in Barbados, was a contributor to the Comintern journal, *Negro Worker*. He broke with the British Communist party in 1935.
8. The International African Service Bureau is an England-based organization devoted to anti-colonialist struggles in Africa. Founded in 1937, it was especially active in the 1940s.

9. The Independent Labor party, founded in 1893, was a nonrevolutionary socialist political party active in the trade union movement and in local community struggles.

10. The League of Coloured Peoples was founded in 1931 by the Jamaican Harold Moody. A social welfare organization for Blacks, it was especially active in Jamaica and England.

11. Garan Kouyauté was a Black nationalist and member of the Communist party until 1933 when he was expelled from the Party.

12. Aimé Césaire is a writer and politician who was born in Martinique. In his poem "Cahier d'un Retour au pays natal" (1939) he wrote of négritude in a way that has been widely understood as an appeal to Blacks everywhere to root themselves in African civilization and culture.

13. Franz Fanon (1925–61) was a psychoanalyst, social philosopher, and revolutionary in the African, and especially Algerian, liberation movements. His books include *Wretched of the Earth*, Constance Farrington, translator (New York: Grove Press, 1963) and *Toward the African Revolution: Political Essays*, Haakon Chevalier, translator (New York: Monthly Review Press, 1967).

14. During the spring and summer of 1981, Blacks in Brixton—a section of London—rioted in protest against Margaret Thatcher's economic policies, police racism, and unemployment.

15. Richard Wright (1908–1960) was an Afro-American novelist whose books include *Native Son* (New York: Harper, 1940) and the autobiographical *American Hunger* (New York: Harper and Row, 1977). Wright became a member of the American Communist party in 1932 and left the Party in 1944.

16. James quotes from an investigative report on the Brixton militance commissioned by the British government and written by Lord Scarman, *The Scarman Report: The Brixton Disorders.*

17. The Second International—founded in 1889, dissolved in 1914—was an international organization of socialist parties and trade unions that advocated parliamentary democracy, the prevention of war, and promotion of social revolution.

18. Herbert Aptheker is an American historian whose works include *American Slave Revolts* (New York: International Publishers, rev. ed., 1969) and *Essays in the History of the American Negro* (New York: International Publishers, 1964).

19. Sir John Fortescue, *A History of the British Army* (London: Macmillan and Company, 1899–1930), IV, Part I, p. 565. Quoted in *The Black Jacobins*, p. 214.

Select Bibliography

Books
Beyond a Boundary. New York: Pantheon Books, 1984; London: Hutchinson, 1963.
The Black Jacobins. London: Secker and Warburg, 1938; rev. ed., New York: Random House, 1963.
The Case for West Indian Self-Government. London: Leonard and Virginia Woolf, 1933.

Facing Reality. Detroit: Bewick Editions, 1974.

The Future in the Present: Selected Writings. Westport, Conn.: Lawrence Hill, 1977.

A History of Pan African Revolt. 2nd rev. ed., Washington: Drum and Spear Press, 1969.

Mariners, Renegades, and Castaways: The Story of Herman Melville and the World We Live In. Detroit: Bewick Editions, 1978 c. 1953.

Minty Alley. London: Secker and Warburg, 1936.

Nkrumah and the Ghana Revolution. Westport, Conn.: Lawrence Hill, 1977.

Notes on Dialectics. Westport, Conn.: Lawrence Hill, 1981.

Spheres of Existence. Westport, Conn.: Lawrence Hill, 1981.

World Revolution: The Rise and Fall of the Communist International. London: Secker and Warburg, 1937.

M O S H E   L E W I N

MOSHE LEWIN

BORN IN 1921, MOSHE LEWIN spent his youth in Poland, the Soviet Union, and France before emigrating to Israel in 1951. He studied Russian history in Israel and France. His first significant work was published in 1966. This was *Russian Peasants and Soviet Power*, the first empirical study of collectivization by a Western historian, and one of the first approaches to the social history of the USSR. Lewin is one of a handful of Western Marxist historians working on the Soviet Union and is now engaged in a major effort to write the social history of the period 1920–41. He has taught in France and Great Britain and is now professor of history at the University of Pennsylvania.

Paul Buskovitch, who conducted this interview on October 30, 1982, teaches Russian history at Yale University.

Q. To start with, please tell us about your early life, why you decided to go to Israel, your attitudes then toward socialism and toward Zionism.

LEWIN   First, my Zionism came to me almost in my childhood and, I would say, quite naturally. I was born in a city remarkable for many of its traits and historical destiny. Wilno, Polish at that time, was an important center of Jewish culture. It was inhabited by Poles, some Lithuanians, White Russians, Russians, and Germans. Jews constituted probably a third of the population. The city changed hands often because several countries coveted it. Lithuanians claimed it as their historical capital city; the Poles claimed it (and clearly the whole of Lithuania); and the Russians considered it an old Russian city. So this was a place where cultures clashed and coexisted, where Jewish culture flourished, and where Jews were prominent but discriminated against because of anti-Semitism. The Polish period—1920–39—was tough for us. We called their brand of anti-Semitism "zoological" because of the frequent applications of physical violence against Jews, not only fists but also knives and stones. The Lithuanian brand of anti-Semitism in the interwar period was not that virulent—and it made quite a difference, if you want my personal opinion. I have on my body enough marks to illustrate this difference. Walking to school, going anywhere—alone, with friends, with a girl—could always end up in an attack, a bloody nose, humiliation. The attackers—it was not usually just a single stone—acted in packs, rarely one-to-one, which would have given you a chance to defend yourself. But we trained ourselves in school, especially in the youth movement, to cope with such situations whenever possible. Self-defense was even more important for morale, for preserving self-confidence.

The role of a youth movement in this situation was crucial. Mine, which I joined probably at the age of twelve, was a left-wing Zionist group, Marxist, Socialist, quite pro-Soviet in those years, Freudian, and initially strongly influenced by the *Frei-Deutsche Jugend-Bewegung.*[1] In other words, it was pretty eclectic. It also followed Ber Borokhov,[2] the Jewish-Russian theoretician of the Zionist labor movement. Borokhov offered a Marxist blueprint for deducing a Zionist solution for the unhealthy socioeconomic structure of East-European Jewry, which lacked a peasantry and proletariat but had an abundance of small traders, artisans, and *luft-menschen*—economically marginal people living off the air, i.e., without profession or definable position in the economy. Now, out of all these threads came a *Weltanschauung*—world view—and a movement of great cultural intensity, one deeply interested in social sciences, literature, and politics and well versed in what was going on in Polish politics and culture and strongly opposed to any type of nationalism.

"No accident," as some like to quip. Life in this area meant discrimination, an environment where one was treated with incredible hatred and contempt for being Jewish. The Polish word for Jew, *Zyd*—officially banned in Russia as derogatory—was so effectively imbued with hateful connotations that it was not at all easy to raise one's head and call oneself *Zyd.* Many Poles, trying to be friendly, would use a diminutive form, to soften the sound of it to Jewish ears. It was all deeply disturbing. So Zionism offered a dignified and honorable way out of the predicament, a way to save one's sanity as well as one's physical and cultural identity, and to say loudly "no" to a virulent national and human discrimination.

But my movement (the Young Guard or *Hashomer Hatsair* in Hebrew) was interested in other, broader problems. Zionism, through a normalization of the Jewish national existence and by getting rid of Jewishness as a kind of hump on your back, was supposed to allow those who wanted it to get involved in socialist ideas and actions and offer a contribution, on this score. In the diaspora it was a problem to contact workers, peasants, and others and join them in political battles when you knew that they had a problem with you because of your Jewishness. There was a barrier there that did not allow you—in Eastern Europe at least, but often elsewhere too—to talk class or to share seriously a humanistic ideology because other people could not get rid of their deep-seated sense of your peculiarity. The answer to this handicap was supposed to be some kind of Jewish statehood that would allow us to become a nation among nations.

There was one more specific trait in this organization: it knew that there were Arabs in Palestine. Therefore, to remain true to its internationalist brand of Zionism, the movement did not favor a purely national Jewish state. Till the creation of Israel, it remained committed to an idea of a binational state, offering full equality of rights to Jews and Arabs—on the condition that the Arab partners accepted that there was a Jewish problem and Jewish persecutions and agreed that any number of Jews who wanted to come could do so. The constitution was supposed to assure equality in power independently of numbers of each ethnic component. Belgium was probably the inspiration for such an idea. This idea was not shared by the majority of Zionists and was forgotten soon after Israel was proclaimed. So much for the theme of my Zionism.

The other elements of biography stemmed from the catastrophies for which this region was destined: the First World War, the Russian Revolution, the Russo-Polish war, and only nineteen years later, the Second World War, Germany attacking first Poland, next the USSR. As the Polish state collapsed, the Hitler-Stalin pact gave us the entry of the Soviet army (then still "the red army")—a quite unusual sight, as armies go, with its huge tanks, simple if not primitive uniforms, plenty of Mongol faces, and simplicity of relations between officers and men; it was an army which would be revised heavily in later years. For the time being, the red army was giving us a sanctuary from war. Moreover, Wilno, now becoming Vilnius, was turned over by the USSR to Lithuania—and so we were back, after a short spell of Soviet-style socialism, in a small capitalist country. With the Lithuanian army came yet another set of national and nationalist myths: loving only this side of the river and disliking the fields on the other side, presenting themselves, worldwide, as some kind of center of things. One saw enough of it in Poland, later in the Soviet Union. It is the repetition of syndromes of nationalism on a smaller scale, in miniature, as it were, that makes the whole phenomenon more understandable, but also more ridiculous—in addition to being pernicious. It was the beginning of a lesson I was learning that occupied much of my life, a lesson in comparative nationalisms. I have had many more experiences of this and other types of nationalism and I have come to understand the power of nationalism without acquiring any taste for it. Later years that I spent in the Soviet Union (during the war), in postwar Poland, in France, in Israel, again in Gaullist France, in Great Britain, visits to the US, and finally with emigration to the US, suggested to me—actually thrust upon me—a comparative perspective in my thinking on most problems that has never left me. The main problem, as far as scholarship is concerned, is how to practice comparison, what the methodology should be. This is another story. But I would like to repeat that it was the making of imperial and nationalist myths—the ideological and psychological mechanisms of mythmaking and their power—that impressed me as one of the moving forces of our times, though all too often a deadly force.

The principles and mechanisms of mythmaking are quite similar in both mighty and tiny countries though, of course, it makes a difference whether the country is booming and expanding, or shrinking, losing out, in crisis.

Q. How did you become interested in Russia?

LEWIN It was the Second World War that brought me into Russia, as a refugee fleeing the Germans in June 1941. My city was conquered by the Germans coming from East Prussia only a few days after the beginning of the German attack. I, along with three friends, managed to get far away, unlike many others who were caught by German troops, especially by their motorcyclists. Those who were not shot on the spot were returned to their homes; Jews, to ghettos. My success and that of my friends was due to retreating Russian soldiers who allowed us to climb onto their trucks. I remember this scene vividly, it was a crucial moment in my life. I was about twenty at the time. The officer forbade the soldiers to take civilians on the trucks, but the peasant-soldiers, sitting there, terribly tired, waited till the officer went back to the driver's cabin, winked to us, and called us in: "The young guys don't understand much of life." (They meant the officers.) "To-morrow you will be our soldiers too." And so, thanks to their disobedience, we were taken into pre-1939 Russia. Next came a long period of wandering, ever deeper into Russia, because the thrust of the Germans seemed almost unstoppable. I traveled through enormous chunks of territory, saw numerous *kolkhozy*—collective farms—and stayed for some time in one of them in the Tambov region, observing its functioning firsthand, before and during the crucial period of harvesting. This kolkhoz made a favorable impression on me because it clearly was a success. It made me think, then and later, that there was nothing wrong with the idea of a kolkhoz. But I also saw other kolkhozy, huge ones ("mine" was small and did not use the services of the Machine-Tractor Station), that were real wrecks and were laughed at by "my" kolkhoz-niki. Toward the end of harvesting, or soon thereafter, the Germans came too near again, and the authorities evacuated the youth of the district deeper into Russia. We marched a whole month from Tambov to Penza where a train was waiting to take us to an induction center in the Urals. My friends from Wilno were taken into the army but I was not. This was because my documents showed Vilnius as my birthplace, and I didn't know at that time that there was an instruction not to take "westerners" (from the recently incorporated western provinces). The officials knew where Vilnius was, but the names of the villages near it, in which my friends were born, were White Russian and carried White Russian names. So they went to the army and were sent to the front. I soon began a career as a member of the Soviet working class: first, briefly, as an iron ore miner not far from Serov; but primarily as a blast furnace operator, doing pig iron in a metallurgy plant in Serov (previously called

Nadezhdinsk). Today it is a powerful industrial center, but it was much less impressive in those years, probably a good example of the pre-revolutionary Ural industry. Soviet industrialization hadn't yet had enough time to modernize this metallurgy plant. The war came before reconstruction had begun and the engineers managed to adapt the old furnaces to produce ferrochrome, which was necessary for tanks. Thus, for two years, I was a Soviet worker in a plant with 25,000 others. I had chosen one of the toughest jobs, working on the blast furnace, out of pride, I would say, to show that one is not abusing one's education, that could easily lead to the more "lucrative" and certainly warmer premises of accounting or supply. I remember we used to get half a liter of milk every day because the job was considered "hot" (goriachii) and dangerous. And hot it was, though this was not the whole story. I was getting so much hot air and gases in my face that my brows burned down—as you can see. Worse—we would faint sometimes, mainly toward the end of the day (or night). I also saw how once, after the furnaces were loaded and closed to begin the melting process, the sturdy cover gave in to the pressure of the gas and heat from inside, and the glowing and melted metal and coal erupted like a volcano. There were quite a number of casualties. Another problem was that there was so much heat before you, blowing into your face (sometimes 800°C, if my memory doesn't fail me), and your back was exposed to some 45–50°C of Siberian cold. No wonder lethal pneumonia—if that is what it was —plagued our barracks and cut down people suddenly and quickly during the night.

In 1942—a bad year in every possible way—I became severely swollen. Lack of protein, the doctor said. I was barely able to drag my feet for several months. There was not enough food to recover. But some relief was nevertheless forthcoming—egg powder and other American canned stuff, and better: I was sent to help peasants with the harvest in the summer of 1943. A thousand kilometers away from Serov! I never returned to the factory. After the harvest, I traveled another thousand kilometers to join a friend in Vereshchagino, near Perm, and from there applied, yet again, to be enrolled into the army. This time I was accepted. I learned later that the previous ban had been repealed. I served in a military unit in Balakhna, on the Volga, and later was sent to officer's school in Shuia (Ivanovo region). I was promoted the very day the war was over. A year later, after having served in my city of Vilnius, I proved that I was a Polish citizen and I was allowed to emigrate to Poland. I had other plans and expectations; I didn't feel I belonged in Russia and the year in Vilnius, where everything I was attached to was destroyed by the Germans, gave additional impetus to get away. But there was no animosity of any kind toward Russians or other people of the Soviet mosaic. On the contrary, for five full years I was hobnobbing with these people, sharing their misery and hopes, learning about their uglier sides sometimes, but very often enchanted by their generosity and—I would like to underline this—their grandeur. I wasn't up there in the higher spheres of power, with the elite, not even in the middle layers. A mobilized worker, a kolkhoznik, a soldier, and a lieutenant—all this is "the people," cogs in the state machine, but also part of the huge "gray mass," mainly peasants or still barely "deruralized" people. It was their bodies that had won the war. So it was a time both of woe and suffering, but it was also an epic—their epic, Stalin or no Stalin. The idealized version of a Russian peasant-soldier, Vasilii Terkin, from Tvardovsky's poem,[3] really meant something for every Russian—and for me too. I knew, therefore, that if I ever had the chance to write history, it would be the history of those popular layers. I thought then, and continue to think now, that concentrating mainly on the politically more visible leaders and institutions of Russia is not only insufficient, but misleading. The great gray mass, the popular classes, do count, weigh, and inflect—to say the least.

Q. What were the circumstances that influenced you to become a historian?

LEWIN   The answer can be found by just continuing the story. The first part of my biography explains why I couldn't become a historian up to this time and for quite a long time thereafter. But the idea that this is what I would like to be was some kind of predestination. I knew this already in high school and never thought of any other profession. My biography kept educating me in this direction and strengthening my feeling that history was my vocation. But the key events that led me to take up history occurred when I was in Israel. I came to Israel in the beginning of 1951, pursuing my ideological commitments. Israel was the place where I was supposed to be. But very soon, as an idealistic Zionist of the "old school," I found myself confronted with a heap of problems. The country was changing rapidly, with an influx of new people who were "normal" human beings, pursuing their own ends, not members of avant-gardes of any kind. The transition to what I would later call, jokingly, the post-revolutionary period, was very swift. At that time I didn't realize that, at least to some extent, outcomes of romantic movements always deceive the tenets of original creeds. And new realities bring new people to the fore and demand adaptations.

But there were also more worrying signs. The party to which I belonged, "Mapam,"[4] was shedding, sometimes imperceptibly, sometimes openly, quite a lot of its older beliefs, and adapting too much. In 1955 it joined Ben-Gurion's government whom they fiercely criticized before—and quite rightly so—and the country lost its most important opposition force on the Left. This was not smart, but it did express "new realities" that pushed people to accept evermore nationalism, expansionism, and other trappings of a young and self-confident statehood. Mapam entered into a period of decline (which they probably hoped to slow down by joining the governmental fold) and I reacted by participating in the making of a splinter party led by the brilliant persuader Dr. Sneh.[5] About two years later, after many debates, Sneh persuaded this party to join the Communists—an idea that did not enchant me very much. I thought that this party did not have, at least in Israel, any bright future. I felt it was a spent force, but I joined it. It was for me a kind of protest vote against tendencies around me that worried me.

The really crucial moment for me was participating in the 1956 Sinai campaign, which brought me to the shore of the Sinai estuary.[6] We remained there in the desert a couple of days before going back home, and I remember having used those days to reflect about this campaign, and about how more of the same in the future now seemed inevitable, and about my life and politics in Israel. (I had spent three years on a kibbutz, too, another highly interesting chapter.) I felt that Israel was now in the grip of a dynamism that was taking it in new directions that I had no influence on and didn't want to follow. Before, the motivations of most of us and the whole little country stemmed from a response to anti-Jewish persecutions and discrimination, especially in Eastern Europe, partly also in some countries of Northern Africa. For many this response still counted, but the new politics, vistas, strategies, and hopes were shaped by the new statehood, armies, international relations, changes and ambitions belonging to a different power game. New ideas and mentalities emerged, notably militarism; all kinds of assessments of the world and of the Arabs, with "real-political" overtones that smacked of something not too realistic in the long run. Brilliant military victories were just clouding the future evermore.

The realities for Jews in other countries and the whole character of Zionism was changing too. This resulted from a confluence of three experiences in Jewish life: the destruction of the East-European Jews by the Nazis and whoever helped them, the emergence of the state of Israel, and the power and well-being of American Jews. A peculiar and highly significant interplay of these factors opened up a host of results and outcomes. It is impossible to improvise an analysis on all those fascinating facets in this interview, but some things can be touched upon.

Take Zionism. In one of its classic formulations, for example the Ben-Gurion formula, Jews in the diaspora were endangered, either physically or, equally menacingly, by assimilation. According to this formula, staying in a prosperous and tolerant country constituted an act of national self-destruction and an act of treason. This formula was not acceptable to American Jews, but it allowed the mobilization of energies and cadres that made Israel possible. Once the state was created, and American Jews couldn't accept this kind of ideology, Zionism actually died, notably because the state lived. What is now often called Zionism is therefore quite a different formula, accepted in Israel too, that consists in supporting Israeli policies without giving it the Jewish kids. Out of this came the later chain of events, an American-Israeli alliance, a strengthening of the ethnic identity of American Jews, and the peculiar role of the symbolism of the holocaust in this process. Such symbolism, though a cement of sorts, doesn't block in any effective way the cultural assimilation of American Jews; neither does it have much of an impact on the phenomena of profound crisis that affects Israeli society.

But these things were not yet very clear to me in the Sinai in 1956. What I saw then was a situation that was going to produce more Sinais unless deep changes in policy were undertaken to help Israel become a part of the region in different ways, not just by the sword, or by the continuous though not guaranteed support of a superpower. I didn't see any serious forces ready to act effectively to change policy. There was a rout of such forces. So I could now decide that chapters whose roots were in my East-European past were now closing, or had already been closed, and I said to myself: "On to this other vocation of mine."

I registered at Tel-Aviv University and took a B.A. there. Then I left for Paris University, which offered me a modest fellowship to do a Ph.D. at the Sorbonne. When I finished this, two years and three months later—no need now to doubt that the subject was picked up from the social history of Russia —I got a job in the École Pratique des Hautes Études. A few months later Fernand Braudel offered me a post that was temporary but of professorial rank and salary—and I could reflect about my profession and begin paying off debts that had accumulated because the fellowship was extremely meager.

I was attracted to social history almost spontaneously (I told you about the circumstances in my life that favored just this) but the problem was to work out methods, to understand what was involved. There was not much written on Russian-Soviet society and its development. Previous work was primarily on the regime and its leaders, with the eerie implication that it is possible to deal with a regime without its social body. Lenin, Trotsky, Stalin, the Polit-bureau, ideology, terror—they were obviously topics as legitimate and as natural as any. So it wasn't a criticism or a grudge I had, but just a sense of some horizons still to discover, an important area looming ahead and promis-ing many surprises. The Lenins and the parties, regimes in general, emerge in a historical milieu, are formed by social and cultural influences, and these, somehow, were not as yet known and were not therefore incorporated in our thinking. Moreover, all too often those who studied tsarist periods and those who studied Soviet periods just coexisted without talking to each other, as if there really were two disconnected chunks of history. I didn't feel comforta-ble with this state of affairs, and I decided to plan my professional life better, to plan what I was going to do in the years ahead. Of course, I was now in my forties and so it was high time.

Q. In your political and scholarly activities before, when you were in Israel and after, when you got into the historical profession, how were you affected by the cold war personally?

LEWIN   The cold war had a deep effect on the young Israeli state and on the Zionist movement to which I belonged, and it introduced enormous tensions, deeply and very personally felt by those who were thinking politically in those years. It was in 1949 that Ben-Gurion, in a kind of a coup d'etat against the opposition, Mapam, which counted in its ranks some of the most prestigi-ous military and political leaders of the war of independence, put an end to friendly relations with Russia and took Israel straight into the action and rhetoric of the cold war. Till that moment Russia was quite popular in Israel, despite its highly unpalatable Stalinism, because of the role the USSR played in helping establish the state. Gromyko was the great name in Israel at that time.[7] Now, according to the new outlook, Israel was supposed to serve as a Western springboard—I remember the term sometimes used—against the Arab-Communist world. So this was what was going on in Israel, cutting through all the parties and involving many in interminable debates—because a lot was at stake. Somewhat later we got the trials, notably in Hungary and Prague, that were part of the cold war strategy from the East-European and Soviet side. Acts of brutality and of defiance of common sense, those trials finally split my party and had a deeply anti-socialist effect. I remember my reasoning during the Prague trial[8] against Slansky in which a Mapam representative was also entrapped; the debate around this event moved many people to the Right. It was very worrying. I didn't believe one word of what the prosecutor was saying because it was illogical and phony. But I still thought for some time that there may have been some political reason behind the staging of those trials. Maybe the fact that the Western side was in the process of a cold war and ready for a hot one succeeded in creating some defeatist moods in Party circles and the response consisted in a spectacular tightening up of the internal front. It was difficult to believe that all this was just pure degeneration, a decaying system in love with its bloody theatrics. After all, irrational acts could be reflections of some real menaces. I even believed for a short moment that the victims of McCarthyism in the US were also, or might have been, really dangerous. In fact, inventing dangers and acting upon the invention was essential to this kind of phenomenon. Without the ideology of mythical "enemies of the people" Stalinism wouldn't have been what it was. If it didn't look for a tool for devouring people, it would have been different.

By 1956 these things became clearer to me. First I realized that I simply was talking without really knowing what I was talking about. Many were in this situation and many still are. Politics is deceptively easy to talk about. In any case, it was naive to judge politics, politicians, and regimes by their programmatic statements. The political world has underpinnings; systems don't operate according to proclaimed aims. They are penetrated by trends and interests and demand knowing and digging. The more friendly you are toward systems or movements, the more vigilance you should exercise. This is not, of course, the normal reaction of a fan or militant. But analysis by a politician or a scholar cannot operate without the principle of "methodical doubt" that is expressed by the saying *de omnbus dubitandum esse*—all is doubt. (At the beginning of my academic life I still thought that this was just a nice slogan, also showing that you knew some Latin.) You say this and people answer, how come? How can you live and act when you are going to doubt all the time? This was a profound misunderstanding. Methodical doubt is a way of probing, checking, asking questions—the right ones—avoiding taking appearances for realities and pretenses for essences. I lived in a political world and devoted a lot of time to debating and arguing about politics, sometimes thinking that we were learning something. Often it was just juggling with formulae instead of gathering all the right data and being careful about the conclusions drawn.

The phenomena of the cold war and its rhetoric sobered me up, I think, although the thrust on all sides was to indoctrinate. The powerful presence of propaganda and its immense capacity to mislead became a theme of reflection for me. It was clear to me, before I went to study, that I really didn't know enough about how to think about systems, although I thought I had so much to say about them—capitalism, socialism, imperialism. By 1956 I was quite aware of numerous errors of judgment I was making about Russia, and it was the ease of imagining that I knew when I didn't that suddenly struck me. Having read volume one of *Capital* at age fifteen, I felt unbeatable. Knowing became expanding, contracting, reformulating formulae. The complexity of problems could then escape one forever. The intense, creative thinking in the fifty-odd volumes of Marx and Engels demand hard work to be assimilated. It does not come alone, it is a battle. But so many young adepts tend to "get it" as a revelation, like suddenly getting the stigmata when joining a movement. And once in such a movement, especially when it does really espouse a great, worthy cause, a whole ideological construct tends to be accepted on faith, helped and protected by the good cause, and you may not realize for a lifetime, or until it is too late, that you never really checked, rarely studied, and never understood your ideological sources.

The need for simplicity and certitude is deep-seated in people—hence the craving for a few formulae without acknowledging that they may have only a weak relation to the historical process. And though it may soon become obvious, one sticks to the soporific formula. I remember that such thoughts were occurring to me at the end of 1956 when I was thinking about next steps in my life. It was clear that my Marxist political past was unfolding without my understanding Marx.

Q. What do you think historians can learn from studying Marx?

LEWIN Some decades after the reflections I was just talking about, your question is even more difficult to answer. Many people are meeting these days to think about just these types of problems on the occasion of the Marx centenary. Marxists are more cautious and more skeptical these days and such meetings often raise the problem of "a crisis of Marxism" and a long list of important social phenomena that Marxists failed to account for and interpret. Or the problem that maybe Marxism does not have the wherewithal to deal with them.

Maybe the "crisis of Marxism," which also has important political aspects, that are well known, is part of a larger problem: a crisis of broad theories of social and historical development. First, technological development and enormous changes and complexity of societies these days discourage any effort to grasp "totalities" in broad theories. It is easier to do useful, even impressive, work in the framework of the proliferating specialized fields and branches of social sciences. And this is in itself the second problem. Is it possible to unite the findings of those disciplines in one interpretative theoretical construction? Many say that this is a utopia and that such efforts no longer have any chance of succeeding.

But what is the purpose of all those specialized efforts if they do not lead, at least at some time, to explaining what happens to social systems? If this question emerges—and it does and will constantly—a return to Marx, even if just to rethink what social theory may mean, is a must. His was a study of a social system, an effort to offer a method for defining the character of an epoch a society is living in, or entering into, or leaving. Anyone who feels he needs answers to this kind of question will turn to Marx for inspiration. Marx proposed a way of understanding change. He demanded that such study begin from the process of social production; his economics were actually also a sociology, and this is crucial. The "forces of production" do not exist alone in this conception; they are always wrapped up in "production relations," and there are always tensions between these facets. This is why Marx, when he talks about economics, naturally raises the problem of social classes.

This is very important, but there is much more in Marx. His alienation, of which he offered different versions, also contains a methodology for social theory. After all, systems socialize, shape, and indoctrinate classes and individuals, and scholars have minds that are not immune to being conditioned like everybody else. But when thinking about a system one is living in, one cannot just adopt the prevailing self-images and ideologies that are an emanation of "interests" of all kinds. An independent point of departure, and a torchlight that helps to pierce the crust and penetrate into the deeper "essences" and trends, is indispensable. Marx proposed some: one is precisely the mechanism of change that brings one to see, in any reality, a stage, and in any defense of a status quo, a passing ideology. He next proposed to adopt the view of the underdog in society, "the proletariat," that might then help to question and demask whatever needs demasking, and gain a new, deeply penetrating point of view. Marx's solution is controversial, but not the methodological approach. Combining a concept of the dynamic socioeconomic nexus with another concept of the main social divisions of the time in order to find out what the system is and where it is moving, is a good way of doing these things. Of course, Marx's choice of the "carrier" of progress, the proletariat—a tribute to the thinking of his time and of his search for a force that would actually carry through the important changes he hoped for—were partly mythical, and produced important miscalculations, such as his theory on the growing pauperization of the proletariat, or his reliance on a basically two-class model as the main moving force. But there was also the excellent anticipation of a growing concentration of capital and the concomitant phenomenon of socialization of capital, and the contradiction between the obvious social or public character of capital and the private form of appropriation. Marx's anticipation was correct and its implications are still hanging over our heads. But it is not the working class alone that is going to correct the anomalies. The working class is perhaps the one class that, at least in some important countries, is not in any hurry to do so.

But classes are with us—more of them than were usefully studied in Marx's time. Also there are more social groups that receive salaries and don't own the means of production than there were peasants and artisans a hundred years ago. Where Marx erred, one should correct him, if one knows how. Yet classes remain with us. He concentrated on class struggle; we are also aware of class cooperation. He assigned to industrial workers a Promethean role. We may deny it, or find that a similar role is played by other groups or alliances of groups, or none at all, but the inspiration is from Marxism. I think that Marx did have a theory that was of importance for an earlier stage, but that today there is no Marxist theory. The concept of theory needs redefining— happily you didn't ask me about this—but whatever the definition, the ideas of Marx can still be called a construction having the vocation of a theory. Any theory, Marxist or not, has to use many of his approaches and proposals or it won't succeed at all. This is already the case de facto, because he initiated so many lines of inquiry that helped to develop most of our modern social sciences. Many use his ideas, at the same time wasting quite a lot of energy on petty criticism of his work. I think that the study of the great Max Weber[9] could illustrate the influence of Marx on the making of an important social thinker. He gave us new methodologies, the impressive foray into sociology of religion, state, law, and political domination, but always returned to economics and classes albeit with his own definitions. How else? Weber also "discovered" modern bureaucracy and anticipated its role (and might) in socialism, which Marx might have done on the basis of his prediction on concentration of capital—had he not been riveted to the working-class–bourgeoisie dichotomy. Attention: Marx knew Prussia and bureaucracy—but he didn't anticipate the bureaucratization of the world, which Weber already saw.

Mythmaking is one of the troubles with Marxism, and maybe Marx didn't warn enough against making theory itself into a myth. Marxists wanted too much from a social theory. It became for them a tool of analysis of societies, but also of the universe—a way of understanding but also emancipating the masses, a social science and also a political program; a way of raising problems and a source of ready answers. All this leads to having a theology instead of a tool of inquiry—and it drove many Marxists into a bog. Attention, again! Many others didn't buy these myths and lies. But Marxists didn't always understand what a social theory should and can do. A theoretical tool is a way of asking questions and conducting an inquiry, not of producing preconceptions that tend to become also answers that discard the need of inquiry. You ask the right questions and see what the material brings you. You tread cautiously when formulating your hypothesis and check to see whether the material bears it out. The theory behind it all is an inspiration for asking those questions—not a universal grand theory for all history. I do not know whether Marx should or should not be charged with this sin. After all, in his historical studies he flexibly discerned classes and groups, knew that each working class is different in each country—likewise the bourgeoisie and higher-ups—that bureaucracies, leaders, and states play a complex role for or between the classes and so forth. He produced thoughts around important central methodological assumptions and kept developing and changing ideas as he reacted to the unfolding historical scene.

A hundred years after Marx, one can still learn from him about theory making, knowing that there will be no universal grand theory for all history; there are and will be more than one theory of Marxist inspiration, just as there are and should be different socialist parties and currents. And theories of non-Marxist inspiration too. The idea of a monopoly for one school of thinking about society and the historical process is dead.

Q. What was your reaction, when you first became a historian and also what is it now, to American and West-European scholarly writing about the Russian Revolution and the Soviet period of Russian history?

LEWIN   When I began reading things in a more systematic way, in the early 1960s, there were still sequels of the cold war lingering around. There were many authors and researchers of quality doing good or impressive work, but conceptually there were basically two schools: the one represented by Isaac Deutscher;[10] the other, the more influential and popular "totalitarian" school.[11] I was impressed by many things Deutscher had to say. He was a good thinker and a talented biographer, but the central concept that guided him was an idea, derived from Trotsky, that Russia is a kind of a double-edged social revolution and system that would sooner or later return to its Octobrist origins. This approach colored many of his assessments and expectations. The working class was to come and reclaim its due one day.

There was also E. H. Carr[12] whom I read after Deutscher—only one part of his history was out then. He too was, and remains, an important factor— not a school maybe, and quite different from Deutscher, but they had many ideas in common. Carr handled mainly the early stages of the Soviet regime —basically till mid-1929—and he saw the installment of Lenin in power and the unfolding of his regime as a legitimate product of Russian history, not some kind of accident. It was an argument to which many authors at that time reacted with a vehemence that does not always become them. He produced a broad and impressive canvas dealing with most of the problems and classes; it remains a study of the making of the regime—no sin in itself—but seen mainly from the state's point of view, a study of the victors, with little to say about the vanquished. This somehow, I feel, narrowed down his sensitivity to the character of what was coming. His picture was one of an unfolding

Leninism that Stalin continued, and it seemed, in the earlier books and articles, as if he did not see in Stalinism anything particular. I think Carr never really studied the later stages, and he simply projected his assessments based on the 1920s onto the 1930s. I did discern an important switch in this attitude in his later work when Stalin is suddenly seen as eventually a "counterrevolutionary," but by then Carr was perhaps too old to draw deeper conclusions.

I felt all this was missing something important. If Stalin continued Lenin and that was it, 1917 was either the positive inspiration for Stalin too, or, as in the eyes of the totalitarians, it was the sinister springboard for both Lenin and Stalin. I had the impression that such attitudes—either with the plus or minus sign—closed the discussion instead of enlarging and deepening it. First of all, there was no unfolding of Leninism in Stalinism, but a transformation of Leninism and then its destruction as well as the destruction of bolshevism —the movement that adopted Leninism, but not without debating its tenets sometimes quite fiercely. Second, the country's past, its social realities, its in-depth historical processes that did not depend on either Lenin or Stalin— not on them alone at any rate—was in fact the kettle in which all of them— Lenin and Leninism, Stalin and Stalinism—were boiling or brewing. This is why, to my mind, these kinds of interpretations were missing much of the essence of events.

The totalitarian school saw in the whole business "a permanent purge," but otherwise not much of a past or much of a future. There is only some kind of eternal present (unless something, probably from outside, topples it) in which a state is basically a controlling and indoctrinating mechanism and society barely exists, or whatever there is of it is no more than an appendage to the state. There is no mechanism for change in this very flat concept and the appearance of Khrushchev and his de-Stalinization, however modest, dealt the concept a severe blow.[13] It wasn't difficult to see that the totalitarian construction was itself a tool for the ideological battle produced by the cold war. It was quite inadequate, not because Stalinism wasn't the murderous thing it was, but because the whole system was getting evermore complex, whereas the concepts were getting evermore shallow. It was even worse than the older style of history that dealt with kings, heroes, and battles. They, at least, told a much more interesting story.

The study has actually to begin in tsarist Russia, then explore what happens to society, the state, and the Party during the civil war and the NEP [New Economic Policy, 1921–28]; then it must follow the social classes and social groups, the old ones and the emerging or reemerging ones, also paying close attention to such things as culture and mentality. Then many of the rules of the game, by which I mean the process of the making of this system, would appear in a different light. I do not mean better or more palatable or beautiful —who talks about this?—but less simple, less predictable, and at any rate, more frustrating for those supposedly almighty rulers. If you take the 1930s, for example (and it was so earlier and is going on even stronger in our own day), the workers were not just your simple recipients of orders and of increased norms. They had ways of doing things or not doing them, and they often forced on the administrations of factories a degree of connivance that the leadership didn't want. Massive breaches of discipline or of turnover that amounted almost to widespread strikes induced the regime to conduct real pitched battles against the workers, but also imposed on its leaders retreats and concessions.

Now, take the peasants. They couldn't avert collectivization, but they too imposed concessions and redesigned many of the features of the system that the state intended to create in 1929–30; they imposed on the regime quite a battle through a massive destruction of cattle as well as by other means. Or the bureaucracy itself: supposedly just a tool to do what the leadership wished, it was becoming a maze, forcing the leaders to adapt themselves—although not without a fight, notably those notorious purges and dismissals. We can quote Ordzhonikidze[14] complaining bitterly that you can never get any data from the bureaucracy if the bureaucracy does not wish to give it to you. Here is this totalitarian member of the Politbureau that is supposed to give order to the "atomized society" that is then supposed to do as ordered, and he is openly exhibiting his despair.

It was often so. The first five-year plan, in itself a kind of "battle order," actually ushered in a mess and a deep crisis because too many people just couldn't or didn't want to do as they were told. Obviously, many did things nonetheless. Let us remember that the idea of industrialization was acceptable to many people, otherwise there wouldn't have been any industrialization at all. But in addition, they also reacted in many ways, as people and social groups normally do, whatever the circumstances. They produced perceptions of their own of the reality around them; thought about their interests; developed ideologies of their own, however rudimentary; and so on.

It was clear to me from conversations with workers, peasants, officials, and soldiers—when I lived there—that people reacted to the world in their own way, with their own words. Studies will show this convincingly. You couldn't come to a worker and tell him in private that he was a member of a ruling class. When I worked in the Urals, workers knew who they were and that it was the *nachalstvo*, the bosses, who had the power and the privileges. How many times did I hear from fellow workers that the *nachalstvo* take care of themselves but very little of "our kind"? The engineers and administrators had their own restaurant in the factory, and they came out from it clearly having eaten quite enough. Even their waitresses were fatter than the ones that served us. Or, at least, this is what workers were saying. And they really were hungry then.

Again, it is not just a problem of workers or of reacting to bad conditions. The whole growing social maze was producing feedback, input into the system, wanted or unwanted, as well as opinions, widespread moods and ideological constructs that the regime was aware of and had, finally, to adapt to. I would risk saying that there was never really an end to "civil society," even at the height of oppression, except in the sense of a flux that was created by abrupt social change, when people in transition from place to place and from one social position to another were temporarily put out of gear. Otherwise, as industrialization unfolded and matured, a social structure emerged, got complex and firm and began to impose its moods, aims, ideologies, and mentalities upon the system. I do not doubt that today the fifteen million party members are not just Janissaries—an elite corps. Party members are part of Soviet society, and they carry influences both ways, sometimes more in one direction than in the other. The popular French term *mentalité* is useful here. I define it as a cross between culture and social psychology, those parts of culture colored by group psychology that are operative, that actually guide everyday reactions of people in their everyday life. A party cannot really shape such mental structure, except maybe more in some of its functionaries. I think that the party shares more than shapes these structures.

It was different in Stalin's day, but only to some extent. The state was then a real driving force in a peasant nation, but it had to make changes too. The idea that here was a system that imposed on people one mold—Marxism-Leninism—and that everyone just shared it and explained the world and life to themselves in such terms, was a myth. Some did, but many didn't because the official terms didn't fit the reality of their lives and the regime knew it. Marxism-Leninism didn't fit its needs either. The system was evolving into a superstate, uniting a splintered national diversity into a unified empire, reproducing, in a new garb, an old-style autocracy and forms of control and oppression that were not there in the earlier stage. The Marxist-Leninist framework could express what was going on, but it couldn't account for it. So, it was embalmed, so to say, in the "short course of the CPSU"—a catechism to learn by heart—but also flanked by other official ideologies, quite incompatible with each other but fitting better the different facets of what was going on. Even the dictatorial, despotic Stalinism couldn't cope, couldn't usefully impose just one ideology. With one it didn't master the minds—and the regime knew this.

Q. What should be the intellectual and political role of the study of Soviet Russian history in the West? Do you think that the intellectual, political, and academic climates have helped or hindered the kind of work that should be done?

LEWIN The first thing to say is that the study of Soviet history is not in very good shape, in my opinion. In certain countries, say in France where they do talk a lot about Russia, there barely exists such a field (except for a few individuals, who are really first rate). In this country such work is done, it does exist, but it shares, in part, the same general fate of Russian studies and in part suffers from a lack of strong tradition. Russian studies had a better time in the late fifties and sixties, and then interest and funds declined. Yes, the political climate in the last years, the primacy of propaganda over study and knowledge, the weight of the media compared to the input of academic work in the public eye and public debate and, finally, the pliability and vulnerability of academic opinion to political moods of the moment, all contributed to a considerable drop in the attraction of this field for talented youth, to the trivialization of the subject, and to the weak influence of serious scholarship on public opinion and political circles.

Enough about Russian studies in general. Soviet history suffers quite a lot from this general state of affairs. The tsarist period, I feel, is better developed in the US. It has more and better-trained people. But the knowledge of the Soviet period is so inadequate that people often take virtual gossip for history. The problem here is not of positive or negative opinions of Russia; the problem is ignorance. Sometimes you think: how can people, who may be competent in other fields, allow themselves impossibly naive and shallow statements on Russia and, let us say, its foreign policy? If you don't like, or actually hate, this country, does it mean that every piece of nonsense goes? Russia is cheating so it cannot be trusted—you hear it from coast to coast. But few people are saying that Russia doesn't cheat, that it conducts politics in a complicated world, and its foreign policy is composed and shaped by a variety of factors that demand study, not emotional rhetoric. Some of the people who claim they know Russian politics talk about it as if it existed without a China, a Europe, a Japan, and a US, as if it acted in a world of its own definition and making. Approaches of this kind—though I read, of course, some excellent, serious studies too and hope such authors do agree with me—show that there is too little influence of good scholarly work and of academic culture in this area.

Considering that so much of importance to the West and of potentially terrifying consequence turns around Russia, I ask: what is more important to understand and to know well? Good knowledge and an active academic participation in debates certainly could and should help. At least some current clichés, which are operated by the media and influence academics too, could have been dissipated or corrected. We need critical studies—and good studies always are critical—but distortions are plainly dangerous. Take a big subject of international discussion and propaganda battles such as human rights. This is an incorrect term. Incorrect terms, or false or exaggerated ones, are good for one's emotional or mobilizational needs, but they distort the reality of the other side and therefore may misfire. If the statement says that Russians do not have human rights (or even that they are the worst transgressors in this respect) you are painting a picture of a country of serfs, of rightless and mute victims, a concentration camp, a Gulag, and whatnot—you make it all too easy for yourself. The truth is that the USSR offers the people many important human rights, economic, educational, juridical, and cultural; and I know that to say this sounds to some indoctrinated people like some kind of heresy. If the Russians didn't have many of the rights they fought for and achieved, they wouldn't be able to function at all, to send people abroad to serve their country, to have military secrets, to attract talent to serve them, to have able leaders. They would just run away en masse. If you really think they work like slaves, you do not understand how the country really functions, you do not grasp the type of crisis the Russians are facing. People these days take statements like mine to be compliments to Russia, or worse—some sort of KGB propaganda. These are just facts, but not all the facts. What the Russians do not offer is political rights for their citizens, and there is no compliment to them for this. I frankly do not bother very much with the reproaches on this score that I hear sometimes from people who do not mind allying themselves with all kinds of bloody regimes, or who suddenly praise China and do not yell at the Chinese for not allowing free emigration or giving human rights. Why are the rights of a billion human beings not as important as the rights of 270 million Soviets? It's a great bafflement. Something is rotten in this logic. The USSR is an authoritarian state that has changed considerably, from the point of view of the different rights Russians have, compared to where they were thirty years ago. But the USSR is now an industrial country —though rather recently developed—and the lack of political freedom is a reason why the Russians no longer have any influence in Western countries, why almost all socialist and many Communist movements deny them their socialist claims and reject their claims to any kind of leadership. In fact, the Western Left and many elsewhere are hostile to Russia today. But what does an arms race have to do with political rights for Russians? Or with stories that "you cannot sign any treaty with them?"

An ill-conceived and overstated campaign on human rights in Russia is not a campaign for a better and freer life for Russians. It is an excuse for not signing treaties in which the world is deeply interested. The fact that Russia does not offer the liberties other countries do (not many countries have them, incidentally, and many have much less than Russia) has nothing to do with needing more arms. It is only when these things are shown to be fraudulently connected that the problems can be seen for what they really are. The most important thing is to sign good treaties, lower the tensions, stop the arms race, help the Third World—and let the Russians liberate themselves exactly as the Chinese are allowed to do. If tensions are heightened and all kind of destabilizations attempted, human rights will suffer everywhere.

Q. How do you evaluate the New Left's attitude toward the Soviet Union in general? Is it another programmatic statement or do you think the New Left had or potentially has anything to offer on the problems you have been discussing?

LEWIN I am not sure which New Left you see, because it's different in America, different in Europe. There are many New Lefts. After 1956 we had a great variety of different left wing movements, most of them very critical of the Soviet Union. The Left is not pro-Soviet anymore so far as I know. And that doesn't bother me. I consider that any movement that wants to be socialist has to state that it doesn't condone the Soviet model for socialism.

When you state this, you purify the atmosphere. You are not going to listen to them as your comrades-in-arms, you are not going to treat them as the men of your camp. And you are not going to go to Moscow for some common ideological conference or God knows what. Once you have made this statement, you don't have the backlog anymore. You can come up and quietly study what the USSR actually is and actually isn't, and you can be angry at them for certain things, and accept certain things as positive. You don't have to ascribe to them policies and actions that they are not taking. It's enough to ascribe to them only what they are doing. Once you have liberated yourself from the commitment that characterized the previous Communist movements, the time comes to take a good critical view of them.

Now in certain socialist circles, especially in France, instead of the previous, very often fetishistic, subservience, there is an almost anti-Russian racism. That is, they accept almost any slander, almost any rubbish, almost any sort of gossip, mistaking it for knowledge or analysis. Well-known left wing writers will quote anything provided it's negative. This is losing the sense of reality. It's not your camp anymore, it's not your ideological ally anymore. You should take it coolly. Russia is an enormously complicated country. But it's not going to conquer the whole world; it doesn't have the strength to do it. It's a society that has problems, and it has some sort of a crisis that is interesting to define. When some people see a crisis there, they think it's terminal, they hope it's terminal. Why? It's a chunk of humanity that has to live. There's no reason to transform them into enemy number one. And this tendency has reached some socialist circles to my great amazement. I am suspicious of it; if you concentrate all your efforts on Russia and you're worried so much about it, what about capitalism? We didn't get from the New Left much on Russia that enriches us theoretically. As a scholar this is one of my main criticisms.

Q. Do you think the recent emigration from the Soviet Union and the dissident movement has contributed anything profound to our understanding of Soviet society and culture and the state?

LEWIN If anything, it contributed to misinterpretations. There are some people who came and gave us something we didn't know. But they were very few. Mostly emigrés have wanted to justify their leaving and they hoped that by being fiercely anti-Russian they would make a better impact here. In fact, this whole emigration did not enrich our knowledge. What on earth is new about people getting sent to a camp for politics? We know this. There is, however, a difference between the camps of the 1930s and those of today. The very fact that people come out alive, some in normal health, shows there is a difference. Prior to going to a camp, you now go through some sort of a trial; before there was no trial. Before you would just disappear entirely. Emigrés come here and tell us that there is a secret police. What are they saying that we didn't know word for word? But the distortion is that they take the atrocious reality of the Stalinist era and want us to think that is how

Russia operates today. Gulag is the image that is accepted. Gulag contained millions of people who never did anything wrong. They were put into conditions in which they were starving to death. Is this what goes on in Russia today? The Russia of Khrushchev eliminated Gulag. The fact that there are labor camps in the USSR today, well it's not such a bad idea that you have a labor camp instead of a prison where people sit behind bars. This is their prison system and I do not believe that it contains millions of innocent people. There are political prisoners in Russia and no one is complimenting them or their leadership for it. But we know that, today, they survive. Before they would have been tortured, they would have been destroyed, there wouldn't have been any trace of them. Now this is the kind of progress that doesn't warm the heart because the real progress would be to permit political differences and to let people discuss politics. This doesn't exist. But the emigrés who came here and darkened the picture didn't help us very much. They helped the hawks who pushed for armaments. They blocked interest in studying in-depth; they furthered the decline of Russian studies, I think. Except for a few people—the literary figures who came and added to our knowledge of literature and some political critics who contributed something—we were not enriched. And again the concentration of the Western media blew the problem out of proportion. For a time you couldn't produce a good critical study of Russia and get a hearing in the media. There was an almost total concentration on dissidents and critics. Russia is a big complicated country, with very many dissidents, of course, for it is a multi-ideological society now. How could one imagine that a country like that could not have many critics of different types? But it is characteristic that the sort of people to whom America listened didn't produce anything new because they were giving us what a few influential Americans wanted to hear. America was getting its own advertisement back, so to speak, and thought that it was getting some revelation.

Q. I would like to ask you about your work on the Russian peasantry. When you were writing your book, *Russian Peasants and Soviet Power*, were you already influenced by the work of Chayanov[15]? And, in any case, what is your reaction to the revival of Chayanov's writings in the West?

LEWIN Chayanov didn't play a role in my thinking at that time because I worked on primary sources. I read Chayanov while writing the book and found that he had some valuable ideas that fit the situation of a Russian-type peasantry running small private farms, but it's interesting that Chayanov has nothing to say about the *obshchina*.[16] He produces a concept that is abstract, probably because he thought that the *obshchina* was disappearing. Chayanov doesn't have a place for social differentiation of a serious kind, although such a phenomenon exists in peasant life. And he doesn't show the dynamism. Nor does he doesn't have a place in his theory for the disappearance of the peasantry. He gives a mechanism that just automatically adapts hands to land, but can also contribute to lowering the peasantry's standard of living. Well, they couldn't always adapt hands to land, and they didn't want to tighten the belt anymore. If they could, there wouldn't have been an agrarian crisis in Russia that toppled the regime. Now there are interesting ideas in this thinking: for example, the very idea of trying to find the mechanism of the resilience of the private farm, of a small-scale parcellary peasantry. But the scheme *in toto* is insufficient, from my point of view. So I try to stick to what the material dictates to me and the real historical variety that I observe. I learned much more from Chayanov's 1927 book on cooperation than from his big theory.

In my own thinking about the peasantry, I moved from the one-sided attitude that peasantry is mainly about agricultural production. Of course most groups are engaged in production and feeding themselves and exporting, but the peasantry is a society. It's a sociocultural system. But we didn't try to crack it from the village. There is a village and a set of villages in interrelation; there are elements of culture or a definite culture, and elements of religions, not just one religion. You have the orthodox religion adapted to rural life as with every other peasantry, and you have the rural sects, the concept of *naroduoe pravo*, customary law. This is very complicated because peasantry means local. We are not going to find over the immensity of Russia the same habits of inheritance, for example. We are talking about more than one Russian peasantry, and yet you have to crack the village, so to speak, in scholarly terms. It forms people, it forms a certain unity, it formed the *obshchina* as long as that existed. The village was a socializer through neighborhood networks, family networks, seniority and the status system, the relations of richer peasants to the others, plus all the beliefs and mythologies that flourished there. Very often all the components were still tightly knit: this is why the peasantry was very often something like a nation within a nation, a complete entity with almost everything necessary for them to survive in times of trouble or crisis. We have to see all those elements, including the folklore and art, and try to describe them, both art and institutions, in much more detail than has been done previously. How to deal with peasant society is, for me, still very complicated.

Then the big question remains: what is the real impact in the twentieth century of this peasantry and its mentality on Russia as a country and as a culture? I don't recollect any book that shows the impact and influence of Russian peasantry on Russian culture. In the thirties there was a ruralization of the cities on an unprecedented scale. What did this do to the mentality of the Soviet people and the character of the regime? I think peasants did a lot even without doing anything, just by being themselves and trying to cope with a very complicated world. But they also did things, actively. All this has to be studied.

I would mention another problem you didn't ask me about: the Party. We have histories of the Party, but I think this is a real example of what going for the social, going for the reemerging civil society, means. The histories of the Party are histories of its politics, policies, and leaders. We don't have a history of the Party, or for that matter of Soviet bureaucracy at all, in the sense of historical sociology. When you think about it, how did this begin? We all clamor: bureaucracy, bureaucracy, especially on the Left. But there are very few studies, some just repeating "the revolution betrayed" thesis and other very general statements. We need a history of the Party as an organization, a system of social relations, a system of promotions, a system of tops and bottoms, of rank and file. What is the real position and role of the rank and file, of a variety of layers in the bureaucracy? What happens to their concepts of status, their self-image and ideology? This is the sort of thing that should be studied and we are dragging our tails. The task, it is true, is staggering, but now is the time to continue to attack very great subjects, all the social classes, and the bureaucracy, and the combination of the social, economic, and cultural. Such is the road to define this regime theoretically. Writers keep on using "state capitalism" or "state socialism" or "totalitarianism"—terms that don't say too much but leave us with the illusion that we are saying something really revealing, and that we are reasoning. We could have profited more from certain superb pages in Weber's "On Domination," in his work on the sociology of law, and many pages and chapters in *Wirtschaft and Gesellschaft*. Very deep insights about the Soviets can be gotten from a general examination of the bureaucracy. We hope to understand the system without knowing its bureaucracy and without any sort of social history of the Party. This is inadequate and simplistic to say the least.

Q.   Do you think that the same sort of social history that ought to be done for the peasantry could be done for the Soviet working class?

LEWIN   On the Soviet period we don't have much as yet. We have a group of scholars dealing with the Russian working class. They are moving from 1905 to 1917 into the twenties and things are looking up. There is no doubt that this work can be done and up to our own time. The amount of material keeps growing. Today, Russia produces a lot of material about itself. It even has its own sociology, for instance, dealing, say, with the shortage of labor and the problems of education and promotion. The working class is now the biggest social class in Russia. So questions about what it is, how it's thinking, how it's reacting to the system around it, what it's carrying with it, what kind of potential it has, are fascinating, important for them and for us. But we don't yet know enough.

Direct contacts are not easy. But they can be handled sometimes. I had an American student in Birmingham who went to Russia and who was very successful there. They let him into factories to discuss things with the engineers and workers. It's unpredictable. If one is persistent, this kind of direct contact can be achieved. But the problems I am raising can also be studied on the basis of a growing amount of published evidence, old and new. There are books by sociologists on criminality, there are books on women. These are books by Western sociologists, some of them Americans. All of these scholars might have thought at the outset that there would be no material. In fact, there is a lot of material on a great variety of subjects.

But you have to train people to work better. It's time-consuming; it demands a good mastery of statistical analysis and other techniques; but especially it demands a good knowledge of the great variety of sources because, for broad subjects, variety of angles means abundance of evidence. You have to be able to handle law, statistics, belles-lettres, literature, biographies, and autobiographies; and if you know all of those, you have to learn to synthesize them. But I don't know, and let somebody correct me if I'm wrong, whether the normal academic training produces these skills adequately. I'm teaching now myself; I see what kind of training a graduate or undergraduate gets, and I am not sure that in this field a student doesn't finally depend too much on himself, on his own definition and dialogue, without getting enough guidance. If we want to accelerate the advance of the discipline, ways have to be found to train historians, especially social historians, more intensely. And when we have this training, including the problem of finding sources, then we can handle important subjects "from a distance," exactly as historians handle any past. You don't visit ancient Rome: it doesn't exist. So even if you don't get to Russia, or do not get all the sources you want, you can handle it. But in addition to skills and conceptual mastery, the cultural mastery, the mastery of Russian language and culture must also go up in level.

Q. I would like you to expand on some of the things you said about the massive ignorance that exists in the West, even among academics, about Soviet society and the forms in which it has changed since the revolution, and the difficulty in forming a theory about what is going on there.

LEWIN   This may be a hard judgment, but examples are numerous—and I feel the inadequacy not simply of others' work but of my own. Let us take the idea that Russia is not known, not really deciphered. Well, maybe it's become a new social system. If you take 1930, it's still a peasant country. But if you take the 1960s and 1970s, it's an industrial society. The whole social system has changed. You have a maze of classes. You have a maze of social groups. You have a scientific establishment, a bureaucracy of various types, popular classes. Some people keep talking about Russia as if all this had not occurred. And when someone goes there, although it's obvious, he doesn't notice it. He thinks that what he sees is old, already on the decline. He thinks the queues are something new. In fact, taken historically—which is more serious—much of what he sees is really brand new and not yet fully grasped, whereas the queues are old. The novelty of this state of affairs is also a novelty for the political institutions, which are under enormous pressure to adapt. This is one of the elements of the sense of malaise and of crisis, and some scholars and political scientists have already talked about it. We are looking at a social system that wasn't there thirty-five or forty years ago. The success of this social change is so swift that the political institutions pay a price, they have to change; there's a strain on them, their propaganda doesn't work in the new circumstances. I call it the reemergence of a civil society. But we do not put these things together. All we see or think we see is malaise. We do not see the new forms, possibilities, and potentials.

People continue to use the term *totalitarian,* as if it explained something. Such a simplified notion doesn't cover the whole mosaic. Without a more adequate, deeper conceptual framework, you cannot really anticipate where the system is going. The broad spectrum of these systems presents a variety of types and should make our approaches more flexible. You have Hungary of '56 and Hungary of today; you have the Yugoslavian state in economic crisis, yet legitimate in its society; you have Poland in crisis, yet illegitimate; you have the Russians, the Chinese. They don't all have the same fate, in spite of the fact that they have the same regime. Look how much more we need to know about these systems in order to make sense out of them. One way not to solve our problems is to keep talking as if they are just all one thing, totalitarian. So there is a theoretical effort to be carried out. I understand that this is difficult because there is not enough empirical knowledge on a variety of subjects, not enough historical knowledge.

Theoretical thinking both in the West and outside the West remains on the level of the 1920s. We haven't added very much compared to those years. You take state capitalism. It's already in Arthur Rosenberg's book, *The History of Bolshevism,* [17] in 1930. Or you take one or another version of bureaucratization theory: you have it in Rizzi in 1939.[18] I don't remember what he called it— bureaucratic collectivism, or something like that. The ruling class composed of intellectuals comes from Bogdanov in 1919,[19] as a sort of continuation of Makhaiskii.[20] What is it that we added? Totalitarianism? Trotsky already used it in the 1930s. And, of course, there is nothing wrong with the term itself, but the efforts of theoretical elaboration on the ground of a system of "total control" got us nowhere. The interplay of economics, politics, culture, and social psychology in the framework of a highly differentiated social system is only partly affected by an appetite to control, by a mono-party system, especially at the stage of development Russia finds itself today. The leadership does rule, does control, and does plan. But the historical process is not planned, society is not an appendix to the Politbureau. History, there as everywhere, is moving "elsewhere" all the time, creating changing social structures, crises, stagnations, and renewals. We are after this process and its forms whoever the general secretary or president.

I believe that the few colleagues who do good historical research in this or similar directions agree with the contention that the historical profession— and Russian studies in general—is seriously lagging behind the unfolding intricate social system. We live through some kind of crisis in the West, accumulating instabilities in the Third World, growing signs of stagnation in the USSR. These phenomena everywhere are connected in many ways, but the US-USSR axis has an additional dimension with apocalyptic overtones that doesn't need specifying. This is, literally, the most explosive history in the making of all time, or at least since the supposed great biblical catastrophies. Good knowledge is not in itself a guarantee of better outcomes—much more is involved than that—but the price of ignorance is fatal. This has already been proven all too often.

―――――――――

NOTES

1. The *Frei-Deutsche Jugend* was a Left youth movement composed of a variety of streams, among them the *Wander Vogel.* The Wander Vogel movement, which emerged near Berlin in 1896 and spread throughout German-speaking Europe, reacted to the deficiencies of bourgeois adult culture and sought to create an alternative youth culture through wandering and camping. The ideas of the *Wander Vogel* influenced the Vienna founders of *Hashomer Hatsair.*

2. Ber Borokhov (1881–1917) was the founder and leading Marxist theoretician of the *Poale Zion* (Workers of Zion) party, the first mass socialist Zionist movement. Borokhov advocated political independence for Jews in Palestine and the creation of a socialist society there through class struggle.

3. Alexander Tvardovsky (1910–71) was a Soviet poet whose popular poem "Vassily Tyorkin" celebrated the comic and tragic adventures of an "ordinary fellow" who saw war as a dire necessity waged "not for glory but for life on earth." Written in a vernacular style, the poem drew on peasant folklore and humor while at the same time fulfilling the tenets of socialist realism.

4. Mapam (United Workers party) was a Marxist Israeli party formed in 1948. Its program called for a classless society under kibbutz leadership, equality for Israel's Arabs, an end to military rule in Arab areas, and nonalignment in foreign policy. Though it was Israel's second largest party in 1949, by 1955 it had declined in popularity because of schisms over relations with the Soviet Union.

5. Moshe (Kleinbaum) Sneh (1909–72) was a Polish socialist Zionist leader who, in 1940, emigrated to Palestine, where he led clandestine immigration and self-defense operations. In 1953, he left the Mapam party to form an independent Left faction that merged, in 1954, with the Israeli Communist party. When the Communist party divided along Arab-Jewish lines in 1965, Sneh led the Jewish wing and adopted a policy of independence from Moscow.

6. In October 1956 Israeli defense minister David Ben-Gurion orchestrated the Sinai military campaign to eliminate Egyptian commando bases on the Gaza Strip and to thwart Egyptian plans for an attack on Israel. The 1956 war brought Israel into full possession of Palestine.

7. In a special session of the United Nations in May 1947 Soviet delegate Andrei Gromyko announced his government's support for the formation of a Jewish state through the partition of Palestine, if necessary.

8. In a series of trials from 1948 to 1952, the Soviet regime purged party leaders and members in Eastern European bloc countries. In the 1952 Prague trials, party secretary Rudolf Slansky, along with thirteen others (ten of whom were Jewish), was

tried for treason, espionage, and activities as a "Zionist agent." In 1963 the Party posthumously absolved Slansky and the others.

9. Max Weber (1864–1920) was a German sociologist and political economist. His work on bureaucracy and law can be found in *Max Weber on Law in Economy and Society*, Max Rheinstein, ed. (Cambridge, Mass.: Harvard University Press, 1954) and in *The Theory of Social and Economic Organizations*, Talcott Parsons, ed. (Glencoe, Ill.: Free Press, 1947). The latter is a translation of Part I of Weber's *Wirtschaft and Gesellschaft*.

10. Isaac Deutscher (1907–67) wrote a trilogy on the life of Leon Trotsky: *The Prophet Armed: Trotsky 1879–1921* (New York: Oxford University Press, 1954), *The Prophet Unarmed: Trotsky 1921–29* (N.Y.: O. U. P., 1959), *The Prophet Outcast: Trotsky 1929–40* (N.Y.: O. U. P., 1963). Other books by Deutscher include *Stalin: A Political Biography* (New York: Oxford University Press, 1949; 2nd ed., 1967) and *The Unfinished Revolution: Russia 1917–1967* (New York: Oxford University Press, 1967).

11. Influential historians in the "totalitarian school" include Zbigniev Brzezinski, who wrote *The Permanent Purge: Politics in Soviet Totalitarianism* (Cambridge, Mass: Harvard, 1956) and *Ideology and Power in Soviet Politics* (New York: Praeger, 1962; rev. ed., 1967); Leonard Schapiro, who wrote *The Communist Party of the Soviet Union* (New York: Random House, 1960; rev. ed., 1971) and *The Origins of the Communist Autocracy* (Cambridge, Mass: Harvard, 1977); and the late Merle Fainsod, *How Russia Is Ruled* (Cambridge, Mass.: Harvard, 1963).

12. E. H. Carr (1892–1982), at one time a British foreign officer, later a historian, wrote a seven-volume history of Russia: *History of Soviet Russia: The Bolshevik Revolution*, 3 volumes (London: Macmillan, 1951–53); *The Interregnum 1923–24* (London: Macmillan, 1954); *Socialism in One Country*, 3 volumes (London: Macmillan, 1958–61). Other works by Carr include *The Russian Revolution from Lenin to Stalin* (New York: Free Press, 1979) and *Twilight of the Comintern, 1930–35* (New York: Pantheon, 1982).

13. At the Twentieth Congress of the Communist Party in 1956, Nikita Khrushchev, first secretary of the Central Committee, repudiated Stalin's "cult of personality" and repressive regime. De-Stalinization refers to reforms under Khrushchev that included an end to Stalinist terror, restoration of the Party to political primacy, greater economic and political autonomy for Eastern European Communist states, and cultural thaw.

14. G. K. (Sergo) Ordzhonikidze (1886–1937) was a Bolshevik military and administrative leader who became a member of the Politbureau and commissar of heavy industry in 1930. Disagreement with Stalin over the terror in 1937 led to his alleged suicide.

15. Aleksandr V. Chayanov (1888–1939) was the leading Soviet theoretician on the organization of peasant economies and head of the Agricultural Economy Institute. His theoretical work can be found in *The Theory of Peasant Economy*, Daniel Thorner, Basile Kerblay, and R. E. F. Smith, eds. (Homewood, Ill.: American Economic Association, 1966). His book on agricultural cooperation has not been translated: *Osnovnye idei i formy organizatsii sel'sko-khozyaistvennoi kooperatsii* (Moscow, 1927).

16. The *obshchina* refers to village communes found in the central regions of Russia that

periodically redivided communal land among members to maintain equilibrium between the population and the land available.

17. Arthur Rosenberg, *History of Bolshevism from Marx to the First Five-Year Plan* (London: Oxford University Press, 1934).

18. Bruno Rizzi, *Le Bureaucratisation du monde: Le collectivisme bureaucratique* (Paris, 1939).

19. A. Bogdanov (A. A. Malinovskii) (1873–1928) was a medical doctor, philosopher, economist, sociologist, and early Bolshevik leader who parted company with Lenin in 1909. In the first year of the Soviet regime, Bogdanov produced a theory of proletariat culture ("*Proletkul't*") that inspired a movement of the same name. Bogdanov saw the Soviet revolution as a power take-over of intellectuals who became the new ruling class. Lenin attacked the anti-party implications of Bogdanov's theories in his 1908 essay, "Materialism and Empirio-criticism" (Peking: Foreign Language Press, 1971).

20. Jan Wactaw Makhaiskii (pseudonym: A. Volskii) (d. 1928), a Russian revolutionary and anarchosyndicalist of Polish origin, developed a critique of socialism as an ideology that endorsed a social order in which intellectuals (managers, technicians, bureaucrats, and Party leaders) would be substituted for the capitalists as a new privileged class of exploiters. Under the Stalin regime, any critique of educated specialists was attacked as "*Makhaevshdine*." Makhaiskii's main work was *Umstvenngi rabochii* (The intellectual worker) (Geneva, 1904).

Selected Bibliography

Books

Lenin's Last Struggle. Translated by A. M. Sheridan Smith. New York and London: Monthly Review Press, 1968.

Political Undercurrents in Soviet Economic Debates: From Bukharin to the Modern Reformers. Princeton, N.J.: Princeton University Press, 1974.

Russian Peasants and Soviet Power: A Study of Collectivization. Translated by Irene Nove. New York: W. W. Norton & Co., Inc., 1966.

Articles

"The Disappearance of Planning in the Plan." *Slavic Review* 32 (1973): 271–87.

"Grappling with Stalinism." In *Storia di Marxism*, vol. III. Torino, Italy: 1982.

"The Immediate Background of Soviet Collectivization." *Soviet Studies* 17 (1965): 162–97.

"An Open Depiction of Soviet Society." *Soviet Studies* 31 (1979):118–24.

"The Social Background of Stalinism." In *Stalinism: Essays in Historical Interpretation*, edited by R. C. Tucker. New York: W. W. Norton & Co., Inc., 1977.

"Society and the Stalinist State in the Period of the Five-Year Plans." *Social History* 1 (1976):139–75.

"Society, State and Ideology During the First Five-Year Plan." In *Cultural Revolu-*

tion in Russia, 1928–31, edited by Sheila Fitzpatrick. Bloomington: Indiana University Press, 1977.

"Stalin and the Fall of Bolshevism." *Journal of Interdisciplinary History* 7 (1976): 105–17.

"Stalinism—Appraised and Reappraised." *History* 60 (1975):71–77.

" 'Taking Grain': Soviet Policies of Agricultural Procurements Before the War." In *Essays in Honor of E. H. Carr,* edited by C. Abramsky. Hamden, Conn.: Archon Books, 1974

"Who Was the Soviet Kulak?" *Soviet Studies* 18 (1966):189–212.

INDEX

MARHO: The Radical Historians Organization was founded in 1973 to provide a forum for discussing new perspectives on the study and teaching of history. It grew out of a shared commitment among younger scholars, teachers and students to resist the narrowing of the boundaries of professional history and the separation of the academy from social and political concerns. MARHO seeks to develop a critical history that contributes to an understanding of capitalism as a mode of production and as a complex of changing social relations. MARHO organizes forums, does radio programs, and publishes the *Radical History Review.*

Henry Abelove, associate professor of history at Wesleyan University, received his B.A. from Harvard College and his Ph.D. from Yale University. He is now finishing a psychohistorical study of early English Methodism.

Betsy Blackmar, who received her Ph.D. from Harvard University in 1981, has taught in the American studies program at Yale University, and is now teaching in the history department at Columbia University. She is writing a book on the history of housing and property relations in antebellum New York City.

Peter Dimock received his B.A. from Harvard College in 1975. He is an instructor at Yale University, and is writing a Ph.D. dissertation on early nineteenth-century American historians.

Jonathan Schneer, assistant professor of modern British history at Yale University, received his B.A. and M.A. from McGill University, and his M. Phil. and Ph.D. from Columbia University. Co-editor of *Social Conflict and the Political Order in Modern Britain* and author of *Ben Tillett: Portrait of a Labor Leader,* he is now writing a book about the British Labour Left during 1945–1960.

Josh Brown, an artist/historian, is a member of the editorial board of *Radical History Review* and director of visual research and graphic art for the American Working-Class History Project. He is a doctoral candidate in American history at Columbia University.

Subscriptions to the Radical History Review ($15 employed; $12 unemployed, students, and senior citizens) and back issues on microfilm are available from MARHO, 445 West 59th Street, New York, NY 10017.